A BIRDER'S GUIDE TO FLORIDA

by
Bill Pranty

American Birding Association

Library of Congress Catalog Number: 96-83564

ISBN Number: 1-878788-04-3

Fourth Edition

  2   3   4   5   6   7   8   9

Printed in the United States of America

Publisher
   American Birding Association, Inc.
   George G. Daniels, Chair, ABA Publications Committee

Series Editor
   Paul J. Baicich

Associate Editors
   Cindy Lippincott and Bob Berman

Copy Editor
   Hugh Willoughby

Layout, Typography, and Maps
   Cindy Lippincott and Bob Berman
      using CorelVENTURA, ver. 5.0 and CorelDRAW ver. 5.0

Photography
   front cover: Ned Harris *Swallow-tailed Kite*
   back cover: Kevin T. Karlson *Sooty Tern*
   author photo: Dawn Berry

Illustrations
   Georges Dremeaux, Shawneen E. Finnegan, Diane Pierce,
   Gail Diane Yovanovich, and Louise Zemaitis

Distributed by
      American Birding Association Sales
      PO Box 6599, Colorado Springs, Colorado 80934   USA
         tel: (800) 634-7736 • fax: (800) 590-2473
         tel: (719) 578-0607 • fax: (719) 578-9705

European and UK Distribution
      Subbuteo Natural History Books, Ltd.
      Pistyll Farm, Nercwys, Nr Mold, Flintshire CH7 4EW UK
         tel: +1352-756551 • fax: +1352-756004

For Mom and Dad.

AMERICAN BIRDING ASSOCIATION

PRINCIPLES OF BIRDING ETHICS

Everyone who enjoys birds and birding must always respect wildlife, its environment, and the rights of others. In any conflict of interest between birds and birders, the welfare of the birds and their environment comes first.

CODE OF BIRDING ETHICS

1. Promote the welfare of birds and their environment.

1(a) Support the protection of important bird habitat.

1(b) To avoid stressing birds or exposing them to danger, exercise restraint and caution during observation, photography, sound recording, or filming.

Limit the use of recordings and other methods of attracting birds, and never use such methods in heavily birded areas or for attracting any species that is Threatened, Endangered, or of Special Concern, or is rare in your local area.

Keep well back from nests and nesting colonies, roosts, display areas, and important feeding sites. In such sensitive areas, if there is a need for extended observation, photography, filming, or recording, try to use a blind or hide, and take advantage of natural cover.

Use artificial light sparingly for filming or photography, especially for close-ups.

1(c) Before advertising the presence of a rare bird, evaluate the potential for disturbance to the bird, its surroundings, and other people in the area, and proceed only if access can be controlled, disturbance can be minimized, and permission has been obtained from private land-owners. The sites of rare nesting birds should be divulged only to the proper conservation authorities.

1(d) Stay on roads, trails, and paths where they exist; otherwise keep habitat disturbance to a minimum.

2. Respect the law and the rights of others.

2(a) Do not enter private property without the owner's explicit permission.

2(b) Follow all laws, rules, and regulations governing use of roads and public areas, both at home and abroad.

2(c) Practice common courtesy in contacts with other people. Your exemplary behavior will generate goodwill with birders and non-birders alike.

3. Ensure that feeders, nest structures, and other artificial bird environments are safe.

3(a) Keep dispensers, water, and food clean and free of decay or disease. It is important to feed birds continually during harsh weather.

3(b) Maintain and clean nest structures regularly.

3(c) If you are attracting birds to an area, ensure the birds are not exposed to predation from cats and other domestic animals, or dangers posed by artificial hazards.

4. Group birding, whether organized or impromptu, requires special care.

Each individual in the group, in addition to the obligations spelled out in Items #1 and #2, has responsibilities as a Group Member.

4(a) Respect the interests, rights, and skills of fellow birders, as well as those of people participating in other legitimate outdoor activities. Freely share your knowledge and experience, except where code 1(c) applies. Be especially helpful to beginning birders.

4(b) If you witness unethical birding behavior, assess the situation and intervene if you think it prudent. When interceding, inform the person(s) of the inappropriate action and attempt, within reason, to have it stopped. If the behavior continues, document it and notify appropriate individuals or organizations.

Group Leader Responsibilities [amateur and professional trips and tours].

4(c) Be an exemplary ethical role model for the group. Teach through word and example.

4(d) Keep groups to a size that limits impact on the environment and does not interfere with others using the same area.

4(e) Ensure everyone in the group knows of and practices this code.

4(f) Learn and inform the group of any special circumstances applicable to the areas being visited (e.g., no tape recorders allowed).

4(g) Acknowledge that professional tour companies bear a special responsibility to place the welfare of birds and the benefits of public knowledge ahead of the company's commercial interests. Ideally, leaders should keep track of tour sightings, document unusual occurrences, and submit records to appropriate organizations.

PLEASE FOLLOW THIS CODE—
DISTRIBUTE IT AND TEACH IT TO OTHERS.

Additional copies of the Code of Birding Ethics can be obtained from: ABA, PO Box 6599, Colorado Springs, CO 80934-6599, (800) 850-2473 or (719) 578-1614; fax: (800) 247-3329 or (719) 578-1480; e-mail: member@aba.org

7/1/96

TABLE OF CONTENTS

PREFACE

After my first trip to Florida . . . I knew that I had to return and write a guide to this fascinating land. Since 1972, my annual visits have lasted from a few weeks to six months. I have had the great pleasure of traveling the highways and byways of every nook and cranny of the state, and of meeting hundreds of helpful birders, without whose help the book would never have been written.

The above passage was written in 1980 by the late James A. Lane (1926-1987), a pioneer of regional birdfinding guides. Beginning in 1965, Jim Lane published a number of books in his innovative *A Birder's Guide to . . .* series. For this, he was honored by the American Birding Association in 1986 with the Ludlow Griscom Award for outstanding contributions to the birding world.

A Birder's Guide to Florida was written in the 1970s by Jim Lane with the assistance of many of the state's birders. It was first published in 1981 by L & P Press. A second edition published in 1984 was nearly identical to the first edition; mainly, the English names of a few species were changed to conform with the 6th edition of the American Ornithologists' Union Check-list, published in 1983. The third edition of the guide was produced in 1989, two years after Jim Lane's death, with modifications and additions made by Lane's friend and long-time collaborator, Harold Holt. (The collaboration between Lane and Holt went back to their joint authorship of *A Birder's Guide to Eastern Colorado* in 1973, and had continued through a number of books.)

This fourth edition of *A Birder's Guide to Florida* has been completely rewritten. It is an up-to-date birdfinding guide that supplements the original with much new information.

This guide will be revised in the future. Corrections and additions are welcomed for future editions. Send all comments to: Florida ABA/Lane Guide, c/o American Birding Association, P.O. Box 6599, Colorado Springs, CO 80934.

Paul J. Baicich, Series Editor
ABA/Lane Birdfinding Guides

ACKNOWLEDGEMENTS

The rewriting of this book was a major endeavor that took nearly two years and required the assistance of many of the state's top birders and ornithologists. The following individuals wrote or rewrote the text for their local areas and/or checked directions to birding sites. They have my deepest appreciation for their efforts. In alphabetical order, they are: Beverly Anderson, Jon Andrew, Sybil Arbery, Steve Backes, Jocie Baker, Paul Bithorn, Maggie Bowman, Greg Braun, Greg Bretz, Jane Brooks, Ron Christen, Ruth Clark, Buck and Linda Cooper, Mort Cooper, Jim Cox, John and Linda Douglas, Jack Dozier, Bob Duncan, Will Duncan, Todd Engstrom, Steve Fickett, Keith Fisher, Saul Frank, Dot Freeman, Greg Gilbert, Dave Goodwin, Jon Greenlaw, Wendy Hale, Al and Bev Hansen, Dale Henderson, Ollie Hewitt, Paul Hinchcliff, Wayne Hoffman, Gloria Hunter, Su Jewell, Dave and Stephanie Johnson, Mike Kemmerer, Jerry Krummrich, Howard Langridge, Dave Leonard, Thom Lewis, David Lysinger, Lorne Malo, Larry Manfredi, Jim McGinity, Doug McNair, Jeannie Melvin, Tony Menart, Gail Menk, Peter Merritt, Jane Monahan, Jeff Palmer, Rich Paul, Becky Payne, Peggy Powell, William B. Robertson, Jr., Don Robinson, Harry Robinson, Rex Rowan, Kevin Sarsfield, Joe Schwagerl, Susan Sigsbee, David Simpson, Parks Small, P. William Smith, Betty Smyth, Ken Spilios, Stephen Stedman, Gene Stoccardo, Jean St. John, Jack Taylor, Juan Villamil, Billi Wagner, Noel Wamer, Don Ware, Jeff Webber, Chuck Weber, Ira Weigley, Mickey Wheeler, Margie Wilkinson, Don Woodard, Meric Woodward, and Robbie Wooster.

Portions of the Introduction, the specialties section, and the bargraphs were reviewed for accuracy by Wes Biggs, Bob Duncan, Fred Lohrer, Dave Goodwin, Wayne Hoffman, Howard Langridge, Doug McNair, Peggy Powell, William B. Robertson, Jr., and P. William Smith.

Fritz Davis, Artie Fleischer, Nathalie Hamel, Sami Hoag, Heather Lake, Dave Leonard, Mike McMillian, Ann Venables, Lee Walton, and Becky Yahr helped me to check some sites. Fritz Davis also prepared the lists of dragonflies and butterflies, and Walter Meshaka revised the lists of amphibians and reptiles. Buck and Linda Cooper assisted with the butterfly list.

For sending to ABA corrections to and comments on the 3rd edition of the guide, I thank Page Brown, Jochen Dierschke, Paul DuMont, Harold Holt, Steve Kistler, Everett Knapp, Alan Littau, Terry McEneaney,

Joel Rhymer, Alice Smith, Michael Stoneman, Mike Street, and Hal Wiedemann. This book was written during "off" hours at Archbold Biological Station in Venus, Florida, which includes excellent computer resources, a superbly equipped library . . . and Lake Annie. For their help in various ways, I thank Dawn Berry, Liz Borst, Reed Bowman, John Fitzpatrick, Vikki Holt, Fred Lohrer, Roberta Pickert, Doug Stotz, and Glen Woolfenden.

I also acknowledge the artists whose attractive work is found in the book: Georges Dremeaux, Shawneen E. Finnegan, Diane Pierce, Gail Diane Yovanovich, and Louise Zemaitis. The cover photographs were taken by Ned Harris (Swallow-tailed Kite) and Kevin T. Karlson (Sooty Tern).

The staff at the American Birding Association has been responsible for the production of this book. Cindy Lippincott produced the maps that are an important feature of this guide. Bob Berman designed the bar-graphs and helped with the layout. Hugh Willoughby assisted by doing the copy-editing. Bringing the myriad elements of the project together was the series editor, Paul J. Baicich.

Finally, I thank Dan Canterbury, who suggested that I take on this project, and Dr. William Shriner and his staff for their extreme kindness.

I hope that this book helps the reader to find many of Florida's spectacular birds and to experience the state's unique scenery. I also hope that the book's conservation theme will be recognized, encouraging the preservation of Florida's natural flora and fauna.

Bill Pranty
Venus, Florida
March 1996

For updating information and/or correcting errors to the first printing of this edition, I thank Jocie Baker, Al and Bev Hansen, Bruce Neville, Rich Paul, and Su Jewell. I am most grateful to Cindy Lippincott for her cooperation with the editing of this reprinted edition.

Bill Pranty
Avon Park, Florida
November 1997

Barred Owl
Shawneen E. Finnegan

INTRODUCTION

Florida Before Human Arrival

The beginnings of what today is known as Florida can be traced back about 600 million years, when the state was a submerged part of Africa, itself a part of the supercontinent of Gondwanaland. It was not until about 25 million years ago that a combination of sea-level rise and uplifting of the land allowed Florida to become exposed. During its lengthy inundation, the area had accumulated a thick layer of limestone deposits, which are the fossil remains of coral reefs and of the shells and skeletons of other marine creatures which absorb calcium carbonate from sea water. Eventually, a vast, dry, arid ecosystem of woodland savannahs and grassy plains covered Florida. (This expansive zone extended west to the Pacific Ocean and south through much of South America.) Animals that inhabited the state during this period included mastodons, bison, horses, camels, llamas, jaguars, sabertooth cats, giant ground sloths, capybaras, porcupines, peccaries, vampire bats, and giant tortoises. Prehistoric birds of Florida included *Titanus walleri*, a 10-foot-tall ancestor of the Ostrich, Merriam's Teratorn, an early vulture with a 12-foot wingspan, and the California Condor.

One of the most abundant ecosystems in Florida up to about 11,000 years ago was scrub; it thrived on the area's extensive well-drained sandy soils. During the Ice Age, sea levels were as much as 300 feet lower than they are currently, and the Florida peninsula was at times twice its present width. As sea levels increased while the glaciers melted, much of Florida became flooded, and scrub became restricted to the well-drained sandy soils that remained: the tops of coastal and inland ridge systems that represent earlier shorelines. The plants and animals that survived on these ridge systems would eventually evolve into species distinct from their western and southern relatives, now isolated by many hundreds or thousands of miles.

By about 11,000 years ago, extensive Longleaf Pine forests and Longleaf Pine/Turkey Oak sandhills had become established in the northern and central peninsula. These two most extensive upland habitats in Florida would remain unchanged until their widespread destruction by humans beginning in the late 19th century. The lower-lying Everglades region was not formed until about 5,000 years ago, and vegetation on the Keys is even more recent.

1

Human History

Unlike Florida's long 25-million-year floral and faunal history, human settlement of the state did not occur until about 12,000 years ago (perhaps somewhat earlier), when a few "Paleo-Indians" migrated south from what is today Georgia. They were nomadic people, hunting mastodons, bison, horses, deer, and smaller animals. As the Florida peninsula shrank in size because of sea-level rise, Florida's first human inhabitants began to form more-permanent settlements, and many began cultivating crops. Eventually, six major Indian tribes with a total population of about 25,000 members inhabited Florida: the Apalachee (6,800 members) in the Panhandle, the Timucuan (13,000) in the northern peninsula, the Tocobago (1,300) around Tampa Bay, the Ais (800) along the central Atlantic coast, the Calusa (2,375) of the southwest coast, and the Tequesta (800) along the southeast coast. By the late 1700s, they were all gone from Florida. Most Indians had died of diseases brought by European explorers or had been captured and put into slavery; the few survivors had fled to Cuba and other West Indian islands.

Florida was the first mainland area in the present U.S. to be discovered and occupied by European explorers. In 1513, Juan Ponce de Leon of Spain landed near present-day St. Augustine, searching for the Fountain of Youth. Of course he didn't find it, but de Leon's "discovery" of Florida fueled later explorations by the Spanish, French, and British. By the late 1600s, Spain had established many colonies in Florida, including forts at Pensacola, near St. Marks, and at St. Augustine, and had built over 30 missions to convert the Indians to Christianity. The late 1600s and early 1700s marked a period of warfare among Spain, England, and France, as all three countries battled for control of North America (and other possessions around the world). In the mid-1700s, Lower Creek Indians moved southward and eastward into Florida. Eventually, they would split into two distinct tribes: the Miccosukees and the Seminoles. The Seminole tribe was the larger of the two and became involved in extensive warfare with the European countries and later with the U.S.

In 1763, with the end of the Seven Years' War (called the French and Indian War on this side of the Atlantic), the Treaty of Paris gave England control of Florida. (England traded land with Spain, receiving Florida while Spain got Cuba.) In October of that year, England divided Florida into two provinces, East Florida and West Florida, separated by the Apalachicola River. St. Augustine became the capital of East Florida, and Pensacola the capital of West Florida, which extended west to the Mississippi River. The economies of both territories were small and relied heavily on agriculture, including the production of cotton, tobacco, and sugar. East Florida was more successful than West Florida because settlements were established more securely at St. Augustine than at Pensacola. Possession of Florida was returned to Spain by the 1783 Treaty of Paris, but Spain was unable to govern the land. Furthermore, the land was coveted by the newly formed government of the United States. The sale of the Louisiana Territory (which included parts of West Florida) to the U.S. in 1803 signaled the beginning of the end of Spanish rule in North America. In 1818, U.S. General Andrew Jackson invaded Florida to recapture fugitive slaves, to pacify the Indians who controlled the cattle trade, and to trade cattle. This invasion was called the First Seminole War. On 22 February 1822, Florida was ceded from Spain to the United States. The population of the territory was about 4,300.

The Second Seminole War began in 1835, lasted seven years, and cost the U.S. government $20 million and the lives of 1,466 soldiers. Over 3,800 of the surviving Indians were removed from the state and sent to reservations in the West. The 300 Indians who resisted fled into the Everglades, where they waged war with the U.S. until the end of the Third Seminole War in 1858. (Today, the Miccosukee tribe numbers about 400 Indians who live mostly in the Everglades. The Seminoles, numbering almost 2,000, live on five reservations from Tampa southward.)

Florida officially became a state in 1845, with a population of about 65,500. In 1861, before the Civil War began, Florida was the third state to secede from the Union and join the Confederacy. The state contained many Union sympathizers, and portions of Florida (e.g., Fort Pickens) were under Union control at the beginning of the war. Although there were many skirmishes in the state, Florida did not witness any major battle during the Civil War (still called The War Between the States by many Southerners). The state supplied men, cattle, and salt to the Confederate Army. After the war ended in 1865, Florida was placed under military rule for three years.

In 1881, Hamilton Disston, an industrialist from Philadelphia, purchased 4 million acres of the Everglades for $1 million (25 cents per acre!) with the promise of draining it for human settlement. However, Disston's drainage and development plans ultimately failed, and he committed suicide.

Prior to the 20th century, production of cattle was king in Florida (and it remains a major industry today). Early Spanish excursions into Florida left about 400 to 500 cattle that are descended from the same breed as Texas Longhorns. These Florida Longhorns became acclimated to the natural range-grasses of the state. Originally, the Spanish and Indians controlled the cattle trade, and Indians controlled it in the 1700s and early 1800s. By the latter half of the 19th century, whites controlled the trade, and new "cow towns" such as Kissimmee and Arcadia had sprung up. (About 600 pure-bred Florida Longhorns remain, and an association was formed in 1989 to perpetuate the breed.)

In 1884, Henry Plant began building a railroad south along the Gulf coast. Henry Flagler began a similar line down the Atlantic coast two years later, and the great Florida land boom was on. By 1896, Flagler had reached Miami, and in 1904 he began building a line to Key West. After eight years and 43 bridges, Flagler finally reached Key West. (In 1935, Flagler's "Overseas Railroad" line was destroyed by a hurricane and was abandoned. The railroad bed soon was converted to a roadway named the Overseas Highway, which opened in 1938.)

In 1905 the Everglades Drainage District was created to drain 7,500 square miles of the Everglades for agriculture and cattle-ranching. Eventually, most of the southern peninsula would be criss-crossed by canals draining the Everglades. These canals continue to disrupt the entire Everglades ecosystem, which is in turn threatening the drinking-water supply of the 4½ million residents who live along the coast from West Palm Beach to Homestead.

In 1940 Florida's population was 1.9 million residents, in 1950 it was 2.7 million, and in 1960 it was 4.9 million. By 1970 the state's population had grown to 6.7 million, then to 9.7 million (a 40% increase) by 1980. In 1990 the population reached 12.9 million (a 34% increase), and rose to 14.1 million by 1996. The population is expected to reach 16 million by 2000 and 20 million by 2020.

Currently, about 900 people move into the state *each day*. To accommodate the millions of new residents, an appalling amount of habitat destruction has taken place in the past 50 years, which has caused many of Florida's native inhabitants to decline. In 1994, 803 races or species of native plants and animals were listed by Don Wood as "endangered, threatened, or otherwise categorized as vulnerable or of concern." Five birds (Passenger Pigeon, Carolina Parakeet, Ivory-billed Woodpecker, Bachman's Warbler, and Dusky Seaside Sparrow) that occurred in Florida within the past century are now extinct or are probably extinct.

Fortunately, the government and citizens of Florida have realized that the only way to prevent the continued destruction of vital environmental and ecological sites was to purchase them outright. From 1963 to 1994, Florida spent over $1.1 billion to purchase over 1 million acres of land. In 1990, the Florida Legislature created the state's (and country's) most ambitious land-acquisition project to date: Preservation 2000, designed to raise $300 million per year for 10 years under the Conservation and Recreation Lands (CARL) and Save Our Rivers (SOR) programs. *Florida now spends more state money on land acquisition within its boundaries than the Federal government spends on acquisition in all 50 states combined!* Many county governments are also acquiring land for preservation. Palm Beach and Hillsborough counties have each raised $100 million to purchase environmentally sensitive lands in their counties, Dade County has raised $90 million, and many other county governments are raising lesser amounts. It is to the credit of the government and citizens of Florida that such steps are being taken, but there is really no alternative; our natural heritage is at stake. Our actions within the next two decades will determine whether we succeed or fail in saving vital portions of Florida's native ecosystems and their inhabitants.

According to Jim Cox et al., the amount of land protected in Florida currently totals about 7 million acres, or about 20% of the total land in the state. Another 4.8 million acres are currently under consideration for state purchase (at a projected cost of $5.7 billion), but authorized monies under Preservation 2000 total "only" $3.2 billion. Considering the volume of people who are moving into the state, it is likely that in 20 to 30 years land in Florida will be either protected or developed (i.e., destroyed); there will be little privately owned undeveloped land remaining in the state. About 8 million acres of Florida (24% of the state's total land) have already been destroyed for human development, mostly within the past 50 years.

FLORIDA BIRDS

An extensive history of ornithology in Florida is beyond the scope of this birdfinding guide, but a summary of events important to Florida ornithology follows. The first recorded observation of birds in Florida was made by Jean Ribault, a French explorer. Ribault (*in* Howell) reported seeing "herons, corleux, bitters, mallardes, egertes, woodkockes", and "other kinds of small birds" in what is now Jacksonville, on 1 May 1562. The first serious attempt to catalog some of the area's abundant birdlife was made by William Bartram during a series of explorations in the 1770s. Among dozens of discoveries, Bartram reported seeing King Vultures, a South American species, along the St. Johns River in 1774 or 1775. To this day, ornithologists debate whether Bartram's identification was correct or a misidentification of Crested

Royal Terns
Louise Zemaitis

Caracaras. (Except for two recent reports of birds that escaped from captivity, there have been no subsequent reports of King Vultures in Florida or anywhere else in North America.)

John James Audubon visited Florida from November 1831 to May 1832, exploring northeast Florida and the Keys. About 30 Florida birds were included in his monumental *The Birds of America*, published in sections between 1826 and 1838. The validity of three of the birds that Audubon painted while in Florida (Common Greenshank, Blue-headed Quail-Dove, and Black-throated Mango) has been questioned recently.

Ornithological interest in Florida began in earnest after statehood was attained in 1845. The state was visited by many well-known ornithologists, numerous lesser-known ones, and countless "sportsmen," all of whom brought along guns and shot virtually every bird that they encountered. (Such was the state of ornithology in the 1800s, before the use of binoculars and field guides.)

The first state Audubon Societies were formed in 1896 to protest the slaughter of birds for their use in apparel. (In the mid-19th century, it became fashionable for women in America and Europe to adorn their hats and dresses with feathers. The range of species killed to supply this millinery trade was quite varied; Snowy Egrets, Herring Gulls, Pileated Woodpeckers, and Wilson's Warblers were among the birds observed decorating hats in shops in Manhattan, New York, in 1896.) The Florida Audubon Society was formed in March of 1900, just months after the formation of the National Audubon Society (then called the National

Association of Audubon Societies). Florida was at the forefront of the American conservation movement because of the great numbers of wading-birds that were being killed at their rookeries for the millinery trade. Wading-birds, especially Great and Snowy Egrets, were desired by milliners more than other birds because of the fine plumes (aigrettes) produced by the birds for courtship displays. As a result, adult birds were killed while at their breeding colonies, which also caused the deaths of their orphaned nestlings.

To protect the wading-bird colonies, the American Ornithologists' Union and the National Audubon Society hired wardens to patrol the rookeries. (Although there were laws protecting wading-birds and other species, they were often ignored.) In 1902, Guy Bradley was hired (for $35 per month) to patrol wading-bird rookeries from present-day Naples through Flamingo to Key West—a huge area. On 8 July 1905, Bradley was killed by plume-hunters at Flamingo. Two other wardens (Columbus MacLeod in Florida and L. P. Reeves in South Carolina) were killed in 1908. These murders, coupled with stricter laws and a change in the public's attitudes about the killing of wild birds, led to the end of the millinery trade in 1913. (A plaque honoring Bradley was placed at Cape Sable, now a part of Everglades National Park.)

In response to the killing of plume birds, President Theodore Roosevelt set aside Pelican Island (north of present-day Vero Beach), as a preserve and breeding-ground for native birds. Pelican Island became the first National Wildlife Refuge established in the U.S. Roosevelt established

52 other refuges before he left office; there are now over 500 National Wildlife Refuges in the country.

Despite all the ornithological attention which Florida received in the late 19th and early 20th centuries, the first state bird book was not published until 1925. In that year, Harold H. Bailey published *The Birds of Florida*. The book includes accounts for 370 species (including 3 exotics) but contains unfortunately little specific information on bird distribution and occurrence in the state. It also contains numerous questionable statements and a few errors (e.g., Black-billed Cuckoos breeding in the state), but the color plates by George Miksch Sutton are great. Long out of print, the book is difficult to locate and costs $150 or more for a good copy.

In 1932, *Florida Bird Life* was published. Written by Arthur H. Howell, it was instantly a classic, and its importance remains undiminished to this day. The book includes accounts for 361 species, including 2 exotics. Although long out of print, it can still be obtained rather easily from rare book dealers for about $75. In 1954, *Florida Bird Life* was updated somewhat by Alexander Sprunt, Jr., who published an Addendum in 1963. The bird list had increased to 411 species, including 3 extinct and 5 exotics.

Vertebrates of Florida, written by Henry M. Stevenson and published in 1976, updated the state's avifauna in a brief but comprehensive manner. The book included 463 species, including 10 exotics. Nonetheless, *"Vertebrates"* was not a state bird book; a year before it was published, Stevenson officially began working on an update of Howell, which would not be published until 1994.

In 1978 the Florida Committee on Rare and Endangered Plants and Animals (FCREPA) published the *Birds* volume, edited by Herbert W. Kale II. It included 68 species and races of Florida birds classified as Endangered, Threatened, Rare, or Species of Special Concern. A revision was published in 1996.

The Florida Ornithological Society, which was formed in 1972, publishes a quarterly journal, the *Florida Field Naturalist*. Occasionally, FOS publishes larger manuscripts as Special Publications. Two early Special Publications (numbers 2 and 3, respectively) may be of interest to birders: *The Carolina Parakeet in Florida* by Daniel McKinley and *Status and Distribution of the Florida Scrub Jay* by Jeffrey Cox. McKinley's book details the complete history of human involvement in the extinction of Florida's only native parrot. It is as sobering as it is informative. To quote McKinley: "It would be unfair to call the 1890s the decade when bird-lovers of the world lined up for a chance to shoot the last Carolina

Parakeet . . . however, it would be easy to do so." Cox mapped the specific location of every Florida Scrub-Jay known to exist in the state at the time. Although it is very incomplete and now almost completely out of date, Cox's book provides important baseline data on the precarious status of Florida's only endemic bird species.

Florida's Birds: A Handbook and Reference, published in 1990, was written by Herbert W. Kale II and David S. Maehr "for the average citizen or visitor to Florida who wants to identify the birds he or she is likely to see in the course of a day." It includes information for 326 species.

In 1992, *Florida Bird Species: An Annotated List* was published by the Florida Ornithological Society as Special Publication Number 6. Written by William B. Robertson, Jr., and Glen E. Woolfenden, the state's two foremost living ornithologists, the book was instantly hailed as the first comprehensive treatment of Florida birds since Howell, published 60 years earlier. The book contains accounts for **681** species, including 461 "verified" species (including 4 recently extinct and 11 established exotics), 75 "unverified stragglers," and 145 unestablished exotics. Costing under $20, this book is an essential reference for all Florida birders and is also recommended to visitors to the state.

In fall 1994 the long-awaited *The Birdlife of Florida* by Henry M. Stevenson and Bruce H. Anderson was at last published. Taking almost 20 years to write, the book offers up-to-date, comprehensive information on all aspects of birds in Florida. In many ways, it is the 1990s equivalent of Howell. Sadly, Dr. Stevenson died in November 1991, so he did not live to see the book published. *Birdlife* ... contains accounts for about 666 species, with 481 "accredited" species (including 4 recently extinct and 22 established exotics) and about 185 non-accredited species (hypothetical species and unestablished exotics combined). In addition to about 9,000 bibliographic references, the 907-page book includes 450 range maps giving seasonal distribution for each of Florida's 67 counties. Because *The Birdlife of Florida* sells for $120, it is of interest largely to only the most serious students of Florida ornithology.

Two other Florida bird books may be of interest to birders. The updated FCREPA volume on birds, edited by James A. Rodgers, Jr., Herbert W. Kale II, and Henry T. Smith, was published in 1996. *The Atlas of the Breeding Birds of Florida,* by Herbert W. Kale II, Bill Pranty, Bradley M. Stith, and C. Wesley Biggs, is based on data gathered by hundreds of volunteers during 1986 to 1991 as part of the Florida Breeding Bird Atlas project. A publication date of fall 1998 has recently been set.

Florida avifauna—As of 15 March 1996, the birdlife of Florida numbered a few more than 700 species. About 470 of these, consisting of about 460 native species and 11 established exotics, comprise the accepted state list using the criteria established by Robertson and Woolfenden. Added to this total are about 70 unverifiable (i.e., hypothetical) native species and 162 unestablished exotic species. The breakdown of species is shown in the table below.

Native species	533
Verifiable	461
Year-round (breeding) residents	117
Summer (breeding) residents	35
Migrants	49
Winter residents	154
Non-breeding visitors	12
Occasional visitors (< 25 reports)	94
Non-verifiable	73
Exotic species	173
Established	11
Unestablished	162
Total	707

(Note that the largest category of native species is that consisting of winter residents. Florida is perhaps unique among the states in this regard.)

Bird collections—With the recent dissolutions of the collections at the University of South Florida (USF, Tampa) and the University of Miami, there are only 5 significant bird collections remaining in Florida. Listed according to the number of specimens in each, they are: **Florida Museum of Natural History** (University of Florida, Gainesville, FL 32611; 352/392-1721), **Archbold Biological Station** (P.O. Box 2057, Lake Placid, FL 33862-2057; 941/465-2571), **Tall Timbers Research Station** (Route 1, Box 678, Tallahassee, FL 32311; 850/893-4153), **University of Central Florida** (Department of Biological Sciences, University of Central Florida, Orlando, FL 32816-3268; 407/823-2917); and **Everglades National Park** (4001 SR-9336, Homestead, FL 33034; 305/221-8776). These collections exist for a number of scientific purposes and may be examined by interested parties (not necessarily scientists) by prior arrangement with the curators. As Robertson and Woolfenden point out, if these collections are not used and appreciated, university officials may eliminate them to free for other uses the office space that they occupy (as happened with the USF and Miami collections).

Nomenclature—The official names of birds and the order in which they appear are determined by the Check-list Committee of the American Ornithologists' Union. The nomenclature used in this guide matches that of the 6th edition of the *AOU Check-list of North American Birds* published in 1983 and supplements through July 1997. Five of the recent changes are substantial. They are the splitting of Marbled Murrelet into Marbled and Long-billed Murrelets, Canary-winged Parakeet into Canary-winged (or "White-winged") and Yellow-chevroned Parakeets, Gray-cheeked Thrush into Gray-cheeked and Bicknell's Thrushes, Solitary Vireo into Blue-headed, Cassin's, and Plumbeous Vireos, and Sharp-tailed Sparrow into Nelson's Sharp-tailed and Saltmarsh Sharp-tailed Sparrows. A relatively minor change enacted recently was the removal of the word "American" from the Swallow-tailed Kite's name.

Marbled Murrelet *(Brachyramphus marmoratus)* is restricted to the Pacific coast of North America, and Long-billed Murrelet *(B. perdix)* is found in Siberia, but has strayed to North America on numerous occasions. All 4 Florida records of this complex are of Long-billed Murrelet.

Yellow-chevroned Parakeet *(Brotogeris chiriri)* seems restricted to Dade County currently, but Canary-winged ("White-winged") Parakeet *(B. versicolurus)* may also occur in the Fort Lauderdale and West Palm Beach areas. Although both species are fairly common within their ranges, and appear to be equally established, breeding in the wild by the Yellow-chevroned Parakeet has not been documented in Florida. (The Florida Breeding Bird Atlas unfortunately did not distinguish between the two species.) The ABA Checklist Committee requires proof that a species is reproducing in the wild before its establishment can be considered. The Committee will reassess the placement of one or both of these taxa on the *ABA Checklist* and evaluate their status in both Florida and California. Birders are encouraged to send their observations (especially those which document possible breeding for either species) to Bill Pranty, Compiler of Field Observations, *Florida Field Naturalist*, 8515 Village Mill Row, Bayonet Point, FL 34667. Your reports may also be sent to the Florida Ornithological Society (see pp. 39-40) and the Regional Editor of *Field Notes*. Smith and Smith (1993) give additional information for both species. It should be noted that the AOU has not yet specified a common name for *Brotogeris versicolurus*; this guide uses Canary-winged ("White-winged") Parakeet to cover the most likely possibilities.

Gray-cheeked Thrush is a rare-to-uncommon migrant throughout Florida, but the status of Bicknell's Thrush is uncertain due to the difficulty in separating it from Gray-cheeked Thrush. See McLaren (1995) and Smith (1996) for more information.

Blue-headed Vireo is the only species of the Solitary Vireo complex that has been verified in Florida, but Plumbeous Vireo has been reported a few times in South Florida. See Heindel (1997) for more information on the Solitary Vireo complex.

The distribution of the two sharp-tailed sparrows is somewhat confusing, but Nelson's Sharp-tailed Sparrow should dominate on the Gulf coast, and Saltmarsh Sharp-tailed Sparrow should be more common on the Atlantic coast. See Greenlaw (1995) and Sibley (1996) for more information. Until we have better information about their distribution, all forms of this pair of species in the birdfinding portion of this book are treated with quotation marks: "Sharp-tailed Sparrow."

FLORIDA HABITATS AND "COMMON" BIRDS

Over 300 species of trees are native to Florida, which accounts for almost half of all species native to the United States. Historically, the state was nearly 90% forested, but human development has reduced this amount by about half and has caused severe fragmentation of many habitats. The highest point in Florida is only 345 feet above sea level, but, nevertheless, elevation is important in determining plant communities. These elevational differences are frequently measured in *inches* or a few feet. The state's abundant rainfall, high humidity, varied drainage patterns, extensive coastline, and subtropical climate also affect the distribution of plant life, which in turn affects the distribution of birds and other animals. For more information, consult the excellent *Ecosystems of Florida* edited by Ron Myers and John Ewel, from which much habitat information for this summary was taken.

In Florida, there are birds that are widespread in one or more habitats in the state. To save space, most of these "common" species are listed together here by habitat, but are *not* listed in the birdfinding section of this guide, which instead emphasizes "good" birds to look for. You should have little trouble finding most of the species listed below, provided that you visit the proper habitat during the proper season, and, for some species, the proper region of Florida. In this section, "northern Florida" refers to the Panhandle and North Florida, and "southern Florida" refers to South Florida and the Keys.

PINEWOODS were formerly the most widespread terrestrial plant community in Florida, covering about half the state's uplands. In Central Florida, these forests are called "flatwoods" because of the terrain, which stretches for miles with little or no elevational change. Frequent low-intensity, growing-season lightning fires maintained pinewoods as open forests with an understory dominated by Saw Palmetto and Wiregrass. Three dominant species of pines make up Florida's pinewoods: Longleaf Pine, Slash Pine, and Pond Pine. Longleaf Pine was the most widely distributed pine in North and Central Florida up to the late 1800s, but was logged extensively. Most of these cutover lands were then replanted with the faster-growing Slash Pine, now the most widely distributed pine in the state. Many writers of the late 1800s and early 1900s commented on the extent of Florida's open pinewoods. Below is a typical example, written in 1923 by Charles Torrey Simpson, as quoted in Bent:

"The northern tourist, seeking a winter sojourn in Florida, rides in the southbound train for hour after hour with nothing to see from the car window but apparently endless miles of uninteresting flat pine barrens, until he wearies of the monotony. He does not appreciate the intriguing vastness of these almost boundless flatwoods . . . One may wander for many miles through these park like woods, along the winding, grass-grown cart roads, but he never seems to get anywhere, as the trees seem to lead him on indefinitely."

Today, timber practices, habitat fragmentation, and widespread fire-exclusion have turned most of Florida's open pinewoods into monoculture pinelands or pine forests with dense understories of oaks and other woody invaders. Eventually, the shaded understory prevents young pines from sprouting, and the pines succeed to an oak forest. Because some other habitats are strongly protected from development, Florida's pinewoods, under little or no environmental protection, are being destroyed at an alarming rate. Unless laws protecting pinewoods are enacted soon, one of Florida's most abundant plant communities will continue to be one of its most threatened.

Permanent residents: Black Vulture, Turkey Vulture, Red-shouldered Hawk, Red-tailed Hawk, Northern Bobwhite, Mourning Dove, Common Ground-Dove, Eastern Screech-Owl, Great Horned Owl, Red-headed Woodpecker, Red-bellied Woodpecker, Downy Woodpecker, Northern Flicker, Pileated Woodpecker, Blue Jay, American Crow, Fish Crow, Carolina Chickadee (not in southern Florida), Tufted Titmouse (rare in southern Florida), Brown-headed Nuthatch (rare in southern Florida), Carolina Wren, Blue-gray Gnatcatcher, Eastern Bluebird, Brown Thrasher, White-eyed Vireo, Yellow-throated Warbler, Pine Warbler, Common Yellowthroat, Northern Cardinal, Eastern Towhee, Bachman's Sparrow, Common Grackle, and Brown-headed Cowbird (rare to uncommon in summer in Central and southern Florida). **Summer residents:** Mississippi Kite (northern Florida), Broad-winged Hawk (northern Florida), Yellow-billed Cuckoo, Common Nighthawk, Chuck-will's-widow,

Great Crested Flycatcher, Eastern Kingbird, Purple Martin (mostly around human habitation), Northern Parula, and Summer Tanager (rare in southern Florida). **Winter residents:** Sharp-shinned Hawk, American Kestrel (local permanent resident), American Woodcock (uncommon), Yellow-bellied Sapsucker, Eastern Phoebe, House Wren, Sedge Wren, Ruby-crowned Kinglet, American Robin, Gray Catbird, Cedar Waxwing, Blue-headed Vireo, Orange-crowned Warbler (uncommon), Yellow-rumped Warbler, Palm Warbler, Black-and-white Warbler, and American Goldfinch.

OAK FORESTS of different varieties comprise another widespread habitat in Florida, especially on interior peninsular ridge systems that have gently rolling reliefs. In these areas, Longleaf or Slash Pines were mixed with Turkey Oaks and other species to form a habitat known as sandhills. (In the Panhandle, these areas may be called clayhills.) When the pines were logged, the habitat changed to one dominated by oaks. Other mixed forests also occur widely in the state. Along the coast especially, but inland as well, oak forests and oak hammocks are popular birding sites during migration. (Most migrant landbirds strongly prefer oak habitats to pines, apparently because of a greater amount of food and cover.) Widespread in Florida, and one of its most characteristic species, is the Live Oak, which grows very large (but rarely tall), with limbs that hug the ground. A few of these trees have lived for over 1,000 years. The tree is named because it is nearly or entirely evergreen, rare in an oak, shedding and replacing its leaves in a short period in spring. Still a familiar sight in Florida's less-developed areas are huge solitary Live Oaks growing in fields and pastures.

On old dune systems, the vegetation is often dominated by endemic oaks classified as xeric oak scrub; see the paragraph on scrub below.

Permanent residents: Black Vulture, Turkey Vulture, Red-shouldered Hawk, Red-tailed Hawk, Northern Bobwhite, Wild Turkey, Mourning Dove, Common Ground-Dove, Eastern Screech-Owl, Barred Owl, Red-headed Woodpecker, Red-bellied Woodpecker, Downy Woodpecker, Northern Flicker, Pileated Woodpecker, Blue Jay, American Crow, Fish Crow, Carolina Chickadee (not in southern Florida), Tufted Titmouse (rare in southern Florida), Carolina Wren, Blue-gray Gnatcatcher, Brown Thrasher, White-eyed Vireo, Northern Cardinal, Eastern Towhee, and Common Grackle. **Summer residents:** Swallow-tailed Kite, Mississippi Kite (northern Florida), Broad-winged Hawk (northern Florida), Yellow-billed Cuckoo, Common Nighthawk, Chuck-will's-widow, Great Crested Flycatcher, Purple Martin (mostly around human habitation), Red-eyed Vireo (rare in South Florida), Northern Parula, and Summer Tanager (rare in southern Florida). **Winter residents:** Sharp-shinned Hawk, American

Kestrel (local permanent resident), American Woodcock (uncommon; breeds in northern Florida), Yellow-bellied Sapsucker, Eastern Phoebe, House Wren, Ruby-crowned Kinglet, Hermit Thrush, American Robin, Gray Catbird (local breeder in the Panhandle), Cedar Waxwing, Blue-headed Vireo, Orange-crowned Warbler (uncommon), Yellow-rumped Warbler, Yellow-throated Warbler, Palm Warbler, Black-and-white Warbler, and American Goldfinch.

SCRUB is a plant community dominated by stunted oaks and woody shrubs that grow in sandy soils along both coasts and on ancient coastal dunes that now comprise interior peninsular ridges. The largest of the central ridges, the Lake Wales Ridge, was formed 2 to 3 million years ago when sea levels were much higher than they are today and the rest of Florida was under water. Because of their long isolation from the rest of the continent, many scrub plants and animals have evolved into distinct species. The Lake Wales Ridge contains more endemic plant species than any other region of Florida and is one of the most diverse areas in the country. About half of Florida's scrub plants are endemic (i.e., found nowhere else).

Because its soil is pure sand dozens of feet deep, rainwater filters quickly through scrub, creating a nutrient-poor, well-drained environment not unlike a true desert. As a result, scrub vegetation is frequently sparse and stunted, dominated by endemic evergreen oaks, palmettos, shrubs, cactuses, and flowering plants. Fairly frequent (5 to 15 years) intense fires maintained the scrub in a low, open habitat. In a long (40-year) absence of fire, many scrubs succeed into forests of Sand Pine, a scrub endemic tree. Under these conditions, many of the scrub's other specialized species decrease in abundance or die out entirely. Ocala National Forest, where fire is excluded specifically for the production of pulpwood, is an example of a Sand Pine forest. Other forests of Sand Pine occur in a narrow band along some of the Panhandle coast and elsewhere in the peninsula.

Examples of oak scrub remain as a narrow strip along much of the Atlantic Coast (now fragmented heavily by human development), including Canaveral National Seashore, Merritt Island National Wildlife Refuge, and Jonathan Dickinson State Park, in Oscar Scherer State Park (near Sarasota), and along the Lake Wales Ridge in Polk and Highlands Counties, where the country's first national wildlife refuge specifically set aside for the protection of endangered plants is being established. Because most interior scrubs have been destroyed by the citrus industry and those along the coast have been lost mostly to residential and commercial development, scrub is the most endangered of Florida's ecosystems.

Birds typical of oak scrub include Northern Bobwhite, Common Nighthawk (spring and summer), Florida Scrub-Jay (endemic), Gray Catbird (winter), Northern Mockingbird, White-eyed Vireo, and Eastern Towhee. Sand Pine forests contain an almost completely different set of species, such as Cooper's Hawk, Eastern Screech-Owl, Hairy Woodpecker, Great Crested Flycatcher, Blue Jay, Pine Warbler, and Summer Tanager (spring and summer). Many other species listed in the pinewoods and oak forests habitats will also occur, depending partially on the extent of pine overstory, if any.

HAMMOCKS are island-like stands of palms, Red-cedars, or deciduous trees surrounded by pine flatwoods, marshes, or prairies. Cabbage Palm hammocks are a conspicuous part of coastal marshes and of the extensive prairie region west and north of Lake Okeechobee. The tropical hardwood hammocks dotting the Everglades are unique in the U.S. because the vegetation is largely of West Indian origin, containing species such as Mahogany, Gumbo Limbo, Jamaican Dogwood, Royal Palm, and various figs.

Breeding birds vary with the type of hammock and the location within Florida, but include Red-shouldered Hawk, Wild Turkey, White-crowned Pigeon, Yellow-billed Cuckoo, Barred Owl, Great Crested Flycatcher, and White-eyed Vireo. Upland hammocks will have most species listed under oak forests, while hydric (wet) hammocks will contain many birds listed under swamps. During winter and in migration, hammocks are excellent birding sites for landbirds.

SWAMPS are poorly drained and frequently flooded areas grown mostly to hardwoods and other non-coniferous trees. Many different species of trees are found in swamps, depending on water levels, geographic location within Florida, and other factors, but the Bald Cypress is probably Florida's best-known swamp tree. Others include Grand Magnolia, Tupelo, Swamp Bay, Sweet Gum, Red Maple, and various oaks and willows. Swamps vary in size from small depressions to vast areas, such as Big Cypress Swamp in South Florida and the extensive riparian swamps of the Panhandle.

Permanent residents: Anhinga, Great Blue Heron, Great Egret, Snowy Egret, Little Blue Heron, Tricolored Heron, Green Heron, Black-crowned Night-Heron, White Ibis, Wood Stork, Wood Duck, Osprey, Bald Eagle, Red-shouldered Hawk, Wild Turkey, Limpkin, Eastern Screech-Owl, Barred Owl, Red-bellied Woodpecker, Downy Woodpecker, Pileated Woodpecker, American Crow, Fish Crow, Carolina Chickadee (not in southern Florida), Tufted Titmouse (rare in South Florida), Carolina Wren, Blue-gray Gnatcatcher, White-eyed Vireo, Northern Cardinal, Red-winged Blackbird, and Common Grackle. **Summer residents:** Swallow-tailed Kite, Mississippi

Kite (northern Florida), Broad-winged Hawk (northern Florida), Yellow-billed Cuckoo, Acadian Flycatcher (northern Florida), Great Crested Flycatcher (year round in southern Florida), Red-eyed Vireo, Northern Parula, and Prothonotary Warbler (rare in South Florida). **Winter residents:** Sharp-shinned Hawk, American Woodcock (uncommon), Belted Kingfisher, Red-headed Woodpecker (irruptive), Yellow-bellied Sapsucker, Ruby-crowned Kinglet, Hermit Thrush, Gray Catbird, Cedar Waxwing, Blue-headed Vireo, Orange-crowned Warbler (uncommon), Yellow-rumped Warbler, Yellow-throated Warbler, Black-and-white Warbler, Ovenbird (mostly southern Florida), Chipping Sparrow, Rusty Blackbird (mostly northern Florida), and American Goldfinch.

Widespread Neotropical migrant landbirds (of any of the above habitats, especially oak hammocks and swamps, plus mangroves, marshes, etc.): Many of these species are widespread breeders in parts of Florida (and a few winter widely), but all move through the state in spring and/or fall. Migratory periods are limited mostly to March to May and August to October. They include Yellow-billed Cuckoo, Ruby-throated Hummingbird, Eastern Wood-Pewee, Acadian Flycatcher, Great Crested Flycatcher, Eastern Kingbird, Bank Swallow (uncommon), Northern Rough-winged Swallow, Barn Swallow, Blue-gray Gnatcatcher, Veery, Gray-cheeked Thrush (including Bicknell's Thrush; uncommon), Swainson's Thrush, Wood Thrush (uncommon), Gray Catbird, White-eyed Vireo, Yellow-throated Vireo (uncommon), Red-eyed Vireo, Blue-winged Warbler (uncommon), Golden-winged Warbler (uncommon), Tennessee Warbler, Northern Parula, Yellow Warbler, Chestnut-sided Warbler, Magnolia Warbler, Cape May Warbler, Black-throated Blue Warbler, Black-throated Green Warbler, Blackburnian Warbler, Yellow-throated Warbler, Prairie Warbler, Bay-breasted Warbler, Blackpoll Warbler, Cerulean Warbler (uncommon), Black-and-white Warbler, American Redstart, Prothonotary Warbler (near water), Worm-eating Warbler (uncommon), Ovenbird, Northern Waterthrush (near water), Louisiana Waterthrush (near water), Kentucky Warbler (uncommon), Hooded Warbler, Summer Tanager, Scarlet Tanager, Rose-breasted Grosbeak, Blue Grosbeak, Indigo Bunting, Painted Bunting, Bobolink, Orchard Oriole, and Baltimore Oriole.

In Florida, the observation of migrant cuckoos, swallows, thrushes, vireos, warblers, grosbeaks, buntings, tanagers, orioles, and other species is dependent upon three variables: season, location, and weather. Most spring migrants occur from April through mid-May, but the first Purple Martins return in mid-**January**, while a few other species (e.g., Yellow-billed Cuckoo, Barn Swallow, and American Redstart) are still moving north in early June. "Fall" migration is similarly drawn out; Purple Martins and Louisiana Waterthrushes begin southward migration by late **June**, and many species are still moving through in early November, but most species are most common from late August through October. Although you will find migrants virtually every day during the migratory periods, observations of hundreds (occasionally thousands) of birds, called a "fall-out," occur typically one or two days after a storm has moved through an area (but fall-outs sometimes occur the day of a storm). Because birds are reluctant to fly into a strong weather-system, they will land ahead of the storm and "wait it out" before continuing to migrate. Birds caught in the storm will fly until they see land, then will "put down" and wait until the storm passes. These fall-outs are great for birders but bad for the birds; many hundreds or thousands must drown at sea. During a big fall-out it is often possible to see over 20 species of warblers in a small area, along with many other colorful species. (But note that major fall-outs are extremely rare occurrences.)

Because migrants winter in different areas south of Florida, their distribution in the state varies geographically and seasonally. Caribbean-wintering species, such as Bicknell's Thrush, Black-throated Blue Warbler, and American Redstart, are much more common in spring on the Atlantic coast, while species that winter in tropical America, such as Cerulean and Hooded Warblers and Orchard Oriole, occur more frequently along the Gulf coast.

All spring migrants must cross hundreds of miles of water before arriving in Florida. For this reason, they typically land immediately (i.e., on the coast), unless weather conditions are favorable, in which case they continue flying until they are many miles north of the state. (This is the reason why far more migrants are found along the coasts in spring than at inland sites in Florida.) Although certain sites attract migrants regularly, *any coastal site can be good during spring, especially oak hammocks and oak woodlands.* By contrast, fall migrants fly south over land to reach Florida, and the birds fan out throughout the state before most depart to spend the winter in Central or South America or the West Indies. Because of this, many fall migrant traps are located inland.

An excellent source for weather effects on migrating landbirds is *Bird Migration, Weather, and Fallout: Including the Migrant Traps of Alabama and Northwest Florida* by Bob Duncan. In addition to listing important migrant traps along the Panhandle coast, the book uses a series of weather maps to teach the reader how to predict good birding days by studying weather patterns.

Reddish Egret
Georges Dremeaux

MANGROVES comprise three species (and genera) of salt-tolerant trees that form extensive forests in coastal areas. Red Mangroves are identified easily by their complex network of curved "prop roots" that rise above the water. The other two species in Florida are Black Mangrove and White Mangrove. (Buttonwood is often considered Florida's fourth mangrove, but it is not technically a mangrove.) Because they are tropical trees, mangroves cannot tolerate areas with very cold temperatures and are limited to the central and southern peninsula and the Keys, except for scattered areas farther north. The Black Mangrove is the most cold-tolerant and therefore occurs farther north than the other two species. Mangrove forests reach their greatest extent along the extreme southern peninsula and in the Keys.

Many large birds nest in mangroves in Florida, including Magnificent Frigatebird, Brown Pelican, Double-crested Cormorant, all wading-birds, and even Osprey and Bald Eagle, but six landbirds are especially associated with mangrove forests. These six are White-crowned Pigeon, Mangrove Cuckoo, Gray Kingbird, Black-whiskered Vireo, Florida Prairie Warbler, and the Cuban race of Yellow Warbler.

SALT MARSHES are found in coastal areas where wave action is insufficient to create beaches and dunes. In Florida, the greatest extent of salt marshes occurs along the Gulf coast from Apalachicola to Tarpon Springs. Other salt marshes form behind barrier islands and at the mouths of rivers. Many species of sedges and grasses are found in Florida's salt marshes, but Needle-rush (*Juncus*) and Cordgrass (*Spartina*) are two principal plants. Because these wetlands are now protected from development, extensive areas of salt marshes remain in Florida.

The following list includes species found in habitats associated with salt marshes (e.g., birds roosting or foraging on oyster bars and mudflats exposed at low tide) in addition to species found in the marsh itself. **Permanent residents:** Brown Pelican, Double-crested Cormorant, Great Blue Heron, Great Egret, Snowy Egret, Little Blue Heron, Tricolored Heron, Reddish Egret, Green Heron, Yellow-crowned Night-Heron, White Ibis, Wood Stork, Clapper Rail, Killdeer, American Oystercatcher, Willet, Laughing Gull, Royal Tern, Black Skimmer, Marsh Wren, Seaside Sparrow (not in southern Florida), Red-winged Blackbird, and Boat-tailed Grackle (rare in the western Panhandle). **Summer residents:** Magnificent Frigatebird (mostly peninsula; resident in the Keys), Least Tern, and Gray Kingbird. **Migrants:** Semipalmated Sandpiper, Common Tern, and Black Tern. **Winter residents:** Northern Harrier, Virginia Rail (uncommon), Sora, Black-bellied Plover, Semipalmated Plover, Greater Yellowlegs, Lesser Yellowlegs, Spotted Sandpiper, Marbled Godwit (local), Ruddy Turnstone, Western Sandpiper, Least Sandpiper, Dunlin, Short-billed Dowitcher, Ring-billed Gull, Herring Gull, Great Black-backed Gull (mostly Atlantic coast), Caspian Tern, Sandwich Tern, Forster's Tern, Belted Kingfisher, Sedge Wren, Common Yellowthroat, Saltmarsh Sharp-tailed Sparrow, Nelson's Sharp-tailed Sparrow, and Swamp Sparrow.

COASTAL SHORELINE includes beaches and adjacent waters offshore. **BEACHES** represent one of the best-known of Florida landscapes and are singularly responsible for attracting millions of tourists to the state annually. Beaches extend along the entire Atlantic coast and along the Gulf coast in the western Panhandle and from Tarpon Springs southward to Naples. They account for over 750 miles of coastal frontage, mostly along a series of barrier islands located a few miles off the mainland. Today, beachfront development has obliterated extensive areas of the beach/dune habitats in the Clearwater/St. Petersburg area, along the Atlantic coast from West Palm Beach to Miami, and elsewhere. **BAYS AND OTHER INSHORE WATERS** are salt or brackish water areas just offshore or between the mainland coast and barrier islands. These waters are calmer and much shallower than those far offshore.

Permanent residents: Brown Pelican, Double-crested Cormorant, Great Blue Heron, Great White Heron (southern Florida), Great Egret, Snowy Egret, Little Blue Heron, Tricolored Heron, Reddish Egret, Green Heron, Yellow-crowned Night-Heron, White Ibis, American Oystercatcher, Willet, Laughing Gull, Royal Tern, and Black Skimmer. **Summer resident:** Least Tern. **Migrants:** Semipalmated Sandpiper, Common Tern, and Black Tern. **Winter residents:** Common Loon, Pied-billed Grebe, Horned Grebe, Blue-winged Teal, Northern Shoveler, American Wigeon, Canvasback (not in southern Florida), Redhead (not in southern Florida), Lesser Scaup, Bufflehead (not in southern Florida), Hooded Merganser, Red-breasted Merganser, Ruddy Duck (local), Black-bellied Plover, Semipalmated Plover, Greater Yellowlegs, Lesser Yellowlegs, Spotted Sandpiper, Marbled Godwit (local), Ruddy Turnstone, Red Knot, Sanderling, Western Sandpiper, Least Sandpiper, Dunlin, Short-billed Dowitcher, Ring-billed Gull, Herring Gull, Great Black-backed Gull (mostly Atlantic coast), Caspian Tern, Sandwich Tern, and Forster's Tern.

OPEN SALT WATER includes the Atlantic Ocean, Gulf of Mexico, Straits of Florida, and Caribbean Sea. Birds that occur here regularly are seabirds and other pelagic species. Except for days with strong winds blowing toward shore, special pelagic boat trips are usually required to observe these species. Note that during spring and (to a much smaller extent) fall migrations, numerous landbirds may be observed over open water. When birds are heavily stressed from strong winds or other factors, many may land on the boat.

Year-round visitors: Audubon's Shearwater (less common in winter), Masked Booby (uncommon), and Brown Booby (uncommon). **Summer visitors:** Greater Shearwater, Cory's Shearwater, Wilson's Storm-Petrel, Bridled Tern, and Sooty Tern. **Migrant visitors:** Common Tern and Black Tern. **Winter visitors:** Northern Gannet (often seen from shore), Red-necked Phalarope (uncommon), Red Phalarope (uncommon), Pomarine Jaeger, and Parasitic Jaeger (uncommon).

FRESH WATER HABITATS include wet prairies, marshes, lakes, and rivers. **WET PRAIRIES** and **FRESH WATER MARSHES** are areas flooded seasonally or permanently by a few inches to a few feet of water. These wetlands are most abundant in the southern half of the peninsula, where the land is extremely flat and poorly drained. The Everglades, which originally occupied over 7,500 square miles, is a fresh water marsh system unique in the world. Today, only about 50% of the Everglades remain in a semi-natural state, although an ambitious, costly, controversial, but essential restoration plan is being implemented gradually. Other marshland is created when agricultural fields are flooded after crops are harvested. Two areas in particular, Zellwood (northwest of Orlando) and Belle Glade (southeast of Lake Okeechobee), are well-known birding sites in late summer and early fall. **LAKES** are numerous in Florida, especially in the northern two-thirds of the peninsula. There are over

7,800 lakes in the state that are at least one acre in size. The largest is Lake Okeechobee (448,000 acres or 700 square miles), after Lake Michigan, the largest fresh water lake wholly within the United States. Florida's abundance of lakes is partially the result of the limestone base that underlies the state. Rainfall, which is slightly acidic, percolates down to the limestone and eventually dissolves portions of it, forming a cavity. When the cavity collapses, a sinkhole lake is formed. **RIVERS** are also numerous in Florida, with over 1,700 in the state, including creeks, sloughs (pronounced *slews*), and streams. Rivers in the Panhandle originate in the foothills of the Appalachian Mountains in Georgia or Alabama. Many rivers in the state are spring-fed. About 320 springs are found in Florida, which exceeds the number found in any other state—or even country! Twenty-seven of these are classified as "first magnitude," which means that they each discharge a minimum of 64 million gallons of water per day. Total daily discharge by Florida's springs is estimated to be 8 billion gallons of water. Spring Creek near St. Marks releases 1.3 billion gallons per day and is the largest spring in Florida.

Permanent residents: Pied-billed Grebe (more common in winter), Anhinga, Least Bittern (withdraws from the north in winter), Great Blue Heron, Great Egret, Snowy Egret, Little Blue Heron, Tricolored Heron, Green Heron, Black-crowned Night-Heron, White Ibis, Glossy Ibis (peninsula), Wood Stork, Fulvous Whistling-Duck (local; central and southern peninsula), Muscovy Duck (areas of human habitation), Wood Duck, Mottled Duck (rare or absent in northern Florida), Mallard (areas of human habitation), Osprey, Bald Eagle, King Rail, Purple Gallinule (withdraws from northern Florida in winter), Common Moorhen, Limpkin (local in eastern Panhandle, absent farther west), Sandhill Crane, Killdeer, Black-necked Stilt (local in the Panhandle and usually only in spring and summer), Common Yellowthroat, Red-winged Blackbird, and Boat-tailed Grackle. **Summer resident:** Least Tern (local). **Migrants:** Solitary Sandpiper (mostly spring), Spotted Sandpiper (uncommon), Semipalmated Sandpiper, White-rumped Sandpiper (uncommon), Pectoral Sandpiper (local), Stilt Sandpiper (local), Wilson's Phalarope (local), and Black Tern. **Winter residents:** American Bittern (uncommon), Green-winged Teal, Northern Pintail (local), Blue-winged Teal, Northern Shoveler, American Wigeon, Ring-necked Duck, Hooded Merganser, Northern Harrier, Virginia Rail (uncommon), Sora, American Coot, Greater Yellowlegs, Lesser Yellowlegs, Western Sandpiper, Least Sandpiper, Long-billed Dowitcher (uncommon), Common Snipe, Laughing Gull (local), Ring-billed Gull, Forster's Tern, Belted Kingfisher, Sedge Wren, Marsh Wren, American Pipit (muddy shorelines), Swamp Sparrow, and Common Grackle.

DRY PRAIRIES in Florida are quite different from the rolling grasslands of the West. In Florida, dry prairies are flat lands found mostly west and north of Lake Okeechobee and consist of sandy soils covered with Saw Palmettos and grasses, an understory very similar to that of pine flatwoods. Lightning fires burn dry prairies almost annually, maintaining the low, open cover of grasses and preventing invasion of woody shrubs and trees.

Birds characteristic of prairies include three "relic" species that are virtually or entirely limited to Florida east of the Mississippi River, but that occur widely in the western plains or southwestern grasslands: Crested Caracara, Sandhill Crane, and Burrowing Owl. The Florida Grasshopper Sparrow, an Endangered endemic race, is limited to dry prairies in the Lake Okeechobee region. Although over 80% of Florida's native dry prairies has been converted to human uses, much artificial "dry prairie" habitat has been created as forests have been cleared for cattle grazing. Burrowing Owls, taking advantage of this newly available habitat, have greatly expanded their range in the state during this century.

The following list includes species that are also widespread in pastures, fields, golf courses, and other artificial open grassy habitats. Other species not listed here (e.g., Swallow-tailed Kite) may forage over fields and pastures. **Permanent residents:** Cattle Egret (withdraws from the north in winter), Black Vulture, Turkey Vulture, Red-shouldered Hawk, Red-tailed Hawk, Crested Caracara (Central Florida only), Wild Turkey, Sandhill Crane, Killdeer, Rock Dove, Eurasian Collared-Dove, Mourning Dove, Common Ground-Dove, Burrowing Owl (local), American Crow, Fish Crow, Eastern Bluebird, Northern Mockingbird, Loggerhead Shrike, European Starling, Eastern Meadowlark, and Brown-headed Cowbird (less common in summer). **Summer residents:** Common Nighthawk and Eastern Kingbird. **Migrant:** Upland Sandpiper (local). **Winter residents:** Northern Harrier, American Kestrel (local permanent resident), American Woodcock (uncommon), Barn Owl (less common in summer), Eastern Phoebe, Tree Swallow, Sedge Wren, American Pipit, Palm Warbler, Chipping Sparrow, Vesper Sparrow (rare in South Florida), Savannah Sparrow, Grasshopper Sparrow, and Swamp Sparrow.

URBAN and SUBURBAN HABITATS are unfortunately increasing in Florida as human residents continue to invade the state in large numbers. Nonetheless, if discretion is used when in residential neighborhoods, birding can be interesting and often rather good. Well-stocked bird feeders have made backyards excellent winter birding sites in northern Florida for Purple Finches and Pine Siskins. House Finches are most common in suburban areas, predominately from Gainesville north. Wintering hummingbirds are also easiest to find in backyards with well-stocked feeders, especially in the Panhandle. At least 7 species were found in the Panhandle in the winter of 1995-1996!

With a few possible exceptions, all exotic species that occur in Florida are limited to suburban and urban areas. Of the 10 officially countable exotics in the state, 4 are found nearly throughout the U.S., the Eurasian Collared-Dove is nearly confined to Florida but is expanding its range outside the state, and 5 species are restricted to Florida. Of these 5, Budgerigar is confined to a few coastal sites in the northern Tampa Bay area, Red-whiskered Bulbul is restricted to one district in Greater Miami, Monk Parakeet is found in several suburban areas, notably Tampa Bay and the southeast coast, and Canary-winged ("White-winged") Parakeet and Spot-breasted Oriole are restricted to the southeast coast. The remaining non-countable exotics occur in numerous suburban areas from St. Augustine to the Keys, but most of them are most numerous in the Miami area.

EXOTIC BIRDS

An "exotic" species is one that occurs in an area to which it is not native, through either deliberate or accidental introduction by humans. A few exotic birds are familiar to all American birders: Rock Dove, European Starling, House Sparrow, and a few game birds imported deliberately for hunting purposes (e.g., Ring-necked Pheasant). The usual "policy" regarding most exotic birds has been to ignore them. For many decades, for instance, the National Audubon Society deleted from its publications most exotics reported on Christmas Bird Counts, thereby preventing the later use of these valuable data by researchers. Fortunately, the attitude of ignoring exotics is beginning to change, although many birders and some ornithologists still scoff at the idea of including exotics on lists. However, *ignoring exotics does not make them go away; it only prevents accurate determination of their status.*

In most states, the presence of a parakeet "in the wild" means simply that a pet owner left a cage door open. Most escaped cage birds last usually only a few days or weeks before succumbing to cold temperatures, predators, or starvation. In a few southern states, however, numerous species of escaped cage birds have bred successfully, and some of these have attained sizable populations. Three states in particular have many exotic species reproducing in the wild: Florida, California, and Hawaii. While the variety of exotics is surprisingly large, most are parakeets, parrots, macaws, and the like, collectively called psittacids (pronounced *sit-TASS-ids*).

The most (only?) sought-after exotics in Florida are the very few considered established in the wild (i.e., maintaining or increasing in range and numbers without direct assistance from humans), but these few only scratch the surface of the state's exotic avifauna. Florida leads the country in the recognition of exotics, due in part to two state bird books published recently, a third book to be published in the next 1 to 2 years, and a state ornithological society with many members who recognize the importance of monitoring exotic birds. Robertson and Woolfenden compiled the first thorough list of exotics reported in Florida. The list which they published includes the startling total of 146 species, which they regard as "undoubtedly . . . very incomplete."

As of March 1996, the current number of exotic birds reported in Florida is **173** species, which includes 13 species reported since the publication of Robertson and Woolfenden only three years earlier. Of these 173 species, 61 have been reported to breed in the wild in the state, but only 10 of these (Rock Dove, Eurasian Collared-Dove, Budgerigar, Monk Parakeet, Canary-winged ("White-winged") Parakeet, Red-whiskered Bulbul, European Starling, Spot-breasted Oriole, House Finch, and House Sparrow) are considered "established" by the checklist committees of the AOU and the ABA. Following Robertson and Woolfenden and Kale et al., this guide also considers the Muscovy Duck to be established in Florida, although the AOU and the ABA have not yet acted on this decision.

In an attempt to increase awareness of the multitude of exotic birds found in the state, this edition of A Birder's Guide to Florida includes exotic species, even those considered not established by the AOU and ABA. It is hoped that by including these non-countable species here, statewide interest in exotics will be spurred so that we may better understand more about them and about any effects that they may have on native birds and habitats. As Robertson and Woolfenden point out, "It seems that the exotic avifaunal element is in Florida to stay, and we need to know much more about it." Smith and Smith agree by adding, "If birders really care about birds and the environment, then they should care about the identity and impact of exotics, too."

Exotic gamebirds and doves have been reported from many areas of the state, but most psittacids and exotic finches are limited to the Greater Miami area. As listed by the Smiths, seven factors make southeast Florida ideal for the presence of so many exotic birds:

1) a subtropical environment conducive to the survival of most birds out-of-doors;

2) a vegetative environment as exotic as the birds;

3) a high demand for cage birds by the local public;

4) a transient human population that often releases caged pets rather than move them;

5) a major port-of-entry for legally imported birds and a region attractive for smuggling contraband birds;

6) a thriving and unregulated backyard avicultural industry;

7) an occasional hurricane that destroys bird cages but usually not their occupants;

to which I add four others:

8) many zoos and "tourist traps" with extensive collections of exotic birds;

9) an extensive suburban area offering almost limitless food in the form of at least hundreds of bird feeders;

10) a human population very protective of "their" free-flying exotics; and

11) a lack of eradication programs by governmental agencies, unlike those in some states that have exterminated all feral individuals of selected exotics (e.g., Monk Parakeets in New York).

A complete list of all 173 species of exotic birds reported in Florida begins on page 313.

CALENDAR OF BIRD ACTIVITY

To help you learn what birds you are likely to find when you visit Florida, this monthly calendar has been prepared. It is modeled after a similar feature in *Birds of Pennsylvania* by Merrill Wood and briefly summarizes events that usually occur in a given month. Keep in mind that this is only a general guide and that regional (e.g., coastal vs. inland) differences exist in the distribution of many birds. For more precise information, consult the bar-graphs on pages 318-344.

January—The beginning of the new year marks the middle of the breeding season for Bald Eagles, Barn Owls, and Great Horned Owls. Other species (e.g., most colonial breeders, Crested Caracaras, Rock Doves, Eurasian Collared-Doves, and Mourning Doves) may nest in Florida in nearly any month of the year. Many Sandhill Cranes begin egg-laying in January, and Masked Boobies are nesting in Dry Tortugas National Park.

January marks the beginning of "spring" migration for Purple Martins. The first male scouts searching for nesting sites typically arrive from Central and South American wintering grounds around the middle of the month.

Breeders and migrants aside, January is a mid-winter month and a good time to look for loons, grebes, waterfowl, shorebirds, larids (i.e., gulls, terns, and Black Skimmers—Family Laridae), and sparrows. Wintering landbirds such as Ruby-crowned Kinglets, Palm Warblers, and Savannah Sparrows are widespread, while the occurrence of winter "irruptive" species (such as Red-breasted Nuthatch, American Robin, Cedar Waxwing, Purple Finch, and Pine Siskin) is highly variable.

February—The final winter month is a relatively quiet one. Waterfowl generally depart in February, but most other winter residents remain through the month. The first individuals of a few more spring and summer residents (e.g., Swallow-tailed Kites and Northern Parulas) appear, usually around mid-month. Many permanent residents begin to sing, especially in years with mild winter temperatures. American Woodcocks begin nesting activities.

March—Most winter residents are still present at the beginning of March, but many have returned to northern breeding grounds by the end of the month. Many permanent residents begin nesting, and more spring and summer residents (e.g., Great Crested Flycatchers, Eastern Kingbirds, Red-eyed Vireos, and Orchard Orioles) begin arriving in late March. Warbler migration is dominated by understory species like waterthrushes and Kentucky and Hooded Warblers. This is also a month when West Indian strays may show up along the southeast coast or in the Keys. Mid-March gives Florida birders an opportunity to hear Chuck-will's-widows and Whip-poor-wills singing side by side.

April—The height of spring landbird migration occurs in April, usually between the 10th and the 20th. Most Florida birders head to Gulf coastal areas like Fort Pickens and Fort De Soto County Park to witness the migration. At times, 20+ species of warblers are seen, along with Summer and Scarlet Tanagers, Rose-breasted and Blue Grosbeaks, Indigo and Painted Buntings, Orchard and Baltimore Orioles, and many other species. April is *the* month when birders head also to Dry Tortugas National Park via boat trips from Key West. On the mainland, West Indian vagrants may be found in April, usually along the coast. Shorebird migration is also at its peak. The vast majority of winter residents that did not depart in March will do so this month. Permanent residents and most summer residents are beginning to nest, and a few early nesters (e.g., Florida Scrub-Jays and Pine Warblers) are fledging young by the end of April.

May—Most species are nesting, and singing is at its peak. Purple Martins have completed their breeding cycle in Central and South Florida, and colonies may be deserted in late May; it is not known whether the birds move north and breed again or head south for the "winter". Bald Eagles also have completed nesting, and many adults move north for the summer. Shorebird migration is still under way, but landbird migration ends largely in early to mid-May. A few migrants (e.g., White-rumped Sandpipers and Connecticut Warblers) are seen more frequently in early May than in April. West Indian strays continue to be found this month along the southeastern coast and in the Keys.

June—Most breeding species have fledged young, and many are laying second broods, but the breeding season is beginning to end. Some species (e.g., Barn Swallows and American Redstarts) are still moving north in the first part of June, while many non-breeding birds (e.g., shorebirds and gulls) appear to remain through the summer. "Fall" migration begins by mid-June with the appearance of a few Purple Martins and Louisiana Waterthrushes outside their breeding ranges.

Most Breeding Bird Survey (BBS) routes are run from mid-May to early June. These surveys are 24½-mile-long transects located along public roadways that consist of 50 stops, one every half mile. BBS route-runners spend 3 minutes at each stop and record all birds seen or heard during that time within a ¼-mile radius. BBS data, which have been recorded since 1966, are a great aid in monitoring the late spring/early summer abundance and distribution of breeding birds throughout North America. For more information on Florida BBS routes, contact Jim Cox, the state coordinator, at the Florida Game and Fresh Water Fish Commission, 620 South Meridian Street, Tallahassee, FL 32399-1600; 850/488-6661.

June marks the beginning of hurricane season in Florida. Tropical storms and hurricanes often bring many pelagic birds from the tropics, especially Magnificent Frigatebirds and Bridled and Sooty Terns.

July—Although a few species (e.g., Blue Jays) are still nesting, the breeding season is generally over by the beginning of July. Fledglings of most species are present and often conspicuous. Fall migration of landbirds is obvious by the end of July with the appearance of the first warblers (e.g., Yellow, Yellow-throated, Prairie, Prothonotary, Black-and-white, and Hooded Warblers and American Redstarts). Some Ruby-throated Hummingbirds seen in late July may also be migrants. Fall migration of shorebirds is well under way by the end of the month. Roseate Spoonbills appear inland after dispersing from coastal breeding sites, and the first Belted Kingfishers arrive in Central and southern Florida to spend the winter.

August—Shorebird migration is conspicuous, and many birders head to flooded vegetable fields at Zellwood and Belle Glade. More migrant landbirds appear (e.g., Barn Swallows are common) and Osprey migration is evident in the Keys. Early-returning ducks like Blue-winged Teal begin to appear, while Swallow-tailed Kites depart for Central and South America. Migration of some larids (e.g., Black Terns) begins in earnest, and pelagic species increase offshore.

September—The height of warbler migration occurs in September, and other landbirds are moving through in numbers as well. Shorebird migration is also at its peak, and pelagic species continue offshore. Raptor migration begins with Mississippi Kites and Broad-winged Hawks moving through the western Panhandle, and the first Merlins and Peregrine Falcons appear throughout the state.

October—Raptor migration peaks in the first half of the month. The annual Boot Key hawk watch is conducted during this period and has recorded single-day totals of 993 Sharp-shinned Hawks, 415 Broad-winged Hawks, and 190 Peregrine Falcons. Along the Panhandle coast, look for western-breeding species that have moved eastward to winter in the Florida peninsula, such as White-winged Dove, Vermilion Flycatcher, Ash-throated Flycatcher, Western Kingbird, and Scissor-tailed Flycatcher. Other winter residents begin to appear by the end of October. Migration of pelagic species offshore increases (especially in the Atlantic), and large numbers of Pomarine and Parasitic Jaegers have been observed recently from Turtle Mound in Canaveral National Seashore.

November—Fall migration of birds *through* the state ends generally early in the month, although a few migrants may be found later. Southward movements of birds *into* Florida continue for waterfowl, Yellow-rumped Warblers, and irruptive species such as American Robin and Cedar Waxwing. Many Turkey Vultures move into the state, and a small movement of Red-tailed Hawks is obvious in the Panhandle. Numerous jaegers moving off the Atlantic coast are joined later in the month by Northern Gannets and Black Scoters. Toward the end of November, loons, grebes, and waterfowl are becoming common along the coast and inland. Most winter residents are present in numbers by the end of the month. In the western Panhandle, look for western vagrants such as Golden Eagle, Franklin's Gull, Varied Thrush, and Harris's Sparrow. Nesting season begins for Bald Eagles, Barn Owls, and Great Horned Owls.

December—The final month of the year marks the beginning of winter. Nearly all winter residents are present by the beginning of the month, but a few species (e.g., Bonaparte's Gull and Cedar Waxwing) may not appear until late December or even later. Loons, grebes, and waterfowl are common in the Gulf and Atlantic and on bays, lagoons, and many interior lakes and impoundments. Pelagic birds are still moving offshore early in the month. About 50 Christmas Bird Counts are conducted annually in Florida. To participate in one or more, contact the National Audubon Society, 700 Broadway, New York, NY 10003; 212/979-3000 or obtain a copy of the CBC issue of *National Audubon Society Field Notes*, which contains the names and addresses of all CBC compilers.

BIRDING "HAZARDS"

Animal pests—Because of its subtropical climate and extensive wetlands, Florida has an abundance of mosquitoes, totaling over 70 species. Visitors are frequently stunned at the abundance and ferocity of these pests, which are at times overwhelming. Although mosquitoes are worse in spring and summer, they can be bad year round, especially during rainy years. Many of Florida's most widespread mosquitoes occur in salt water habitats. Two areas famous for their salt marsh mosquitoes are Everglades National Park and the Florida Keys. In urban areas, mosquitoes are far less of a problem, because of eradication programs that cost millions of dollars annually. The only defense against mosquitoes is to use a good insect repellent. Apply the repellent carefully because some contain chemicals that melt the rubber coating on binoculars.

Mosquitoes are not the only pests in Florida; others which you may encounter include the following. Fire ants are small (2mm) reddish ants native to Brazil but released accidentally into the U.S. early this century. They now occupy most of the Southeast. Their sandy mounds, which may be up to a foot tall and contain 500,000 ants, are the easiest means of locating them. They are most common in dry, upland areas (but mounds are conspicuous in wet pastures) and are usually associated with areas of disturbance (e.g., pastures, road edges, etc.). The ants sting viciously when they are disturbed.

Deer Flies are annoying half-inch-long flies with yellow, orange, or gray bodies. Their bite is painful, but they are not known to carry diseases. They occur commonly in spring and summer. Fortunately, Deer Flies have the habit of circling repeatedly (and noisily) before they land on you, giving you the opportunity to squash them before they bite. Horse Flies (about an inch in length) are larger than Deer Flies and have black bodies. Their bite is much more painful than that of Deer Flies, but fortunately these large flies are not nearly as numerous as Deer Flies.

Biting midges are more popularly known as "no-see-ums" because of their size—so tiny that they pass through window screens. Their bite is annoying, but relatively painless. Midges are most common at dawn and dusk. They transmit malaria and other diseases in birds and some other animals, but are harmless to humans.

Ticks are common in areas with a dense cover of grass or brush. Lyme Disease is very rare in Florida, but a few cases have been reported. Check yourself and your clothing after walking through grassy or brushy woodlands. Chiggers are extremely tiny red larval mites that feed by burrowing under the skin, causing severe itching that may persist for many days. Chiggers may be common in grassy areas, but they are encountered infrequently by Florida birders.

Spiders are a conspicuous part of Florida's oak hammocks and other forested habitats. Four species (Black Widow, Red Widow, Brown Widow, and Brown Recluse) are poisonous to humans, but the chance of encountering any of them is remote. Two groups of spiders (Golden Orb-weavers and Banded Garden Spiders) are common in fall, when they build webs that may be 5 feet or more in diameter. Females of both species have body lengths of over an inch, excluding the legs. These spiders are harmless to humans, but many birders have walked face-first into a web, which is very annoying. The webs are so strong that small birds have been caught in them on occasion.

Of course, mites, chiggers, ticks, and spiders are not insects, but one more true insect needs to be mentioned, although it neither bites nor stings. "Love-bugs" are flies that swarm mostly in late April, early May, and September. Males and females remain mated for a few days (hence their name), until the male dies. In some areas, love-bugs form large, dense clouds over open areas. Driving though a swarm causes thousands of the insects to become smeared on the windshield, grille, and hood of vehicles. Screens are available to fit over the grille of your vehicle to lessen the damage caused by the insects; if not removed quickly, chemicals in the flies' bodies can dissolve the paint from vehicles.

Scorpions are widespread in Florida but are seldom seen because of their secretive habits (e.g., living under leaf litter). Nonetheless, one may still encounter scorpions anywhere in the state (even in the campground on Garden Key in Dry Tortugas National Park). Florida scorpions are small (1½-2 inches) and are not dangerous to humans; although their sting is painful, the pain lasts only a few minutes.

Florida is home to six species of poisonous snakes. Except for the Cottonmouth, all are extremely unlikely to be encountered while birding. Should you be lucky enough to find a snake, use common sense and leave it alone; *do not kill it.* The **Coral Snake** is found throughout the state and is inconspicuous and docile (but can be dangerous if handled). This beautiful animal is easily distinguished from the harmless Scarlet Kingsnake and the Scarlet Snake by its black snout and wide red bands surrounded on both sides by narrow yellow bands. (Remember the rhyme, "Red touch yellow kills a fellow; red touch black won't hurt Jack.") The two harmless species have red snouts and red bands bordered by black. The **Copperhead** is restricted to the Panhandle and is most common in wooded areas near water. It is nocturnal and not aggressive. The **Cottonmouth**, also called the Water Moccasin, is common in fresh water habits throughout the state, even on barrier islands (e.g., St. George Island). These dangerous snakes are often confused with water snakes, which are non-poisonous. When provoked, Cottonmouths gape, exposing their fangs and the white interior of their mouths (whence their name). The **Eastern Diamondback Rattlesnake** is among the largest snakes in North America, reaching a length of 8 feet. Formerly widespread in Florida's pinewoods, this magnificent but potentially dangerous animal is declining rapidly due to habitat destruction and needless persecution. The **Timber Rattlesnake**, also called the Canebrake Rattlesnake, is limited to north-central Florida. Formerly considered two species, the timber form is found in uplands, while the canebrake form occupies wet flatwoods, hammocks, and riparian forests. The species is not aggressive. The **Dusky Pygmy Rattlesnake** is a small species, averaging 15" to 20" in length. It is widespread in the state but is most common in wet areas. Although it can be aggressive, its small size lessens the severity of its bite.

The American Alligator, once hunted relentlessly in Florida, now numbers over 1 million individuals, and limited hunting is again legal. Alligators have attained lengths of over 12 feet in Florida, but most average 6 to 8 feet. Although they appear slow-moving and docile, alligators are capable of surprising speed for short distances. It is illegal to feed alligators, because this practice causes them to lose their fear of humans. "Nuisance" alligators are usually killed rather than relocated to other areas. When near alligators, keep your distance and do not provoke them. (The American Crocodile is an Endangered species restricted to the extreme southern peninsula and Upper Keys. It avoids humans and is extremely unlikely to be seen.)

Poisonous plants—Poison Ivy is common and widespread in moist wooded areas (e.g., oak hammocks) in Florida, as it is in most of the U.S. Poison Sumac is found south to south-central Florida, but it is not common. In South Florida, two poisonous tropical plants are widespread, especially in the Keys, and both have sap that causes a rash upon contact. Poisonwood is fairly common in most forested habitats; its fruit is a staple of the White-crowned Pigeon's diet. Its sap causes a rash similar to that of Poison Ivy. The sap of Manchineel causes severe itching, and its fruits may be lethal if ingested in quantities. Because of this property, the tree is removed from most areas of human habitation. The best way to avoid contact with both species is to stay on trails when walking through tropical hardwood hammocks.

Crime—In the past few years, Florida has made international headlines due to a few well-publicized murders, including some that targeted tourists. As is the case in all other areas in the world, there exists in Florida a criminal element. Adding to this is a state visited annually by millions of tourists, major drug-smuggling and drug-trafficking areas, a state with an extensive elderly population (who are also frequent crime victims), and an ever-growing resident population plagued occasionally by racial problems. Because tourists are usually unfamiliar with the area they are visiting, they are often targeted by criminals. Florida rental companies no longer identify rental vehicles with special license plates or bumper stickers, and this policy has helped to decrease tourist-related crimes.

Lightning—Along with central Africa and the Amazon River basin, Florida is the lightning capital of the world, receiving more ground strikes than any other area in North America. Most lightning occurs during spring and summer, when frequent (i.e., almost daily) afternoon thunderstorms form over the state. In Central Florida, about 25 cloud-to-ground strikes *per square mile* are recorded annually! In 1994, a record number of 128 people were struck by lightning in the state, 8 of these fatally. You should be safe if you take the usual reasonable precautions.

Roads—Many county and forest roads in Florida are unpaved and may be hazardous for those driving passenger vehicles. It is easy to get stuck in muddy and clay roads when they are wet, and some can be extremely slippery. Likewise, it is easy to get stuck in sand roads when they are dry. Use good judgment when driving on unpaved roads.

BIRDING ETHICS

Trespassing—There are three words to be said about trespassing on private property in Florida: *Don't do it.* Florida is very similar to many western states in that landowners believe very strongly in their rights, and they rigidly enforce trespass laws. Nearly every birding site in this guide is on public property, and those sites that are privately owned are clearly marked as such. When birding on private property with the landowner's permission, always be on your best behavior. Keep in mind that privately owned land is not under protection and may change ownership or be developed, resulting in loss of access or loss of all habitat.

The use of tapes—It is well known that small to medium-sized landbirds respond well to a recording of an Eastern Screech-Owl's calls. (Birds often mob the tape just as they would harass the real predator.)

The use of such a tape to attract fall migrants or wintering landbirds on Christmas Bird Counts is a widespread and accepted event. However, the use of recorded songs to attract individuals of the same species during the breeding season can create problems. It is true that some species are unlikely to be seen without the use of a tape, especially if only a few minutes or hours are allocated to finding it. (The Mangrove Cuckoo is probably the best example of this problem in Florida.) However, this disturbance during the most critical and stressful time in an adult bird's life is difficult to justify. This fact is especially true for rare species with restricted ranges (again, the Mangrove Cuckoo is the best Florida example). On Sugarloaf Key, for instance, one or more birding groups artificially attract the same few cuckoos virtually every day for weeks at the height of the nesting season. This disturbance must have some negative impact on the nesting success of the birds. Unfortunately, few birders will avoid using tapes when life birds are at stake, but it is important that the use of these tapes during the breeding season be used only sparingly. In fact, *excessive use of tapes by birders is the reason why many areas now prohibit the use of all "mechanical devices" to attract birds,* an unfortunate (and in many ways unnecessary) decision. Birding sites that prohibit the use of all tapes, even the use of Eastern Screech-Owl calls, include Everglades National Park, Key Deer National Wildlife Refuge, Corkscrew Swamp Sanctuary, and J. N. "Ding" Darling National Wildlife Refuge.

Please follow the *ABA Code of Birding Ethics,* printed on pages *iv* and *v* of this guide.

WHERE TO STAY

Florida probably has more motel rooms than any other state. (There are over 8,000 rooms on Walt Disney World property alone.) In fact, it is hard to find a spot without one. However, during peak tourist season, all may be full. Reservations made weeks (or months) in advance are recommended, especially in major tourist areas. Rooms are usually much more expensive on barrier islands than on the mainland, although many convention-type hotels in large cities are also quite expensive.

Campgrounds are likewise found throughout the state, available in many national, state, county, and city parks, and there are also numerous private trailer parks and campgrounds. Birders planning to camp out should purchase a copy of *Florida Parks: A Guide to Camping in Nature* by Gerald Grow, an excellent guide to camping facilities in about 250 publicly owned parks in the state. Information on facilities, prices, and directions to the sites is provided. The guide, which costs about $15, is published by Longleaf Publications, P.O. Box 4282, Tallahassee, FL 32315. Tourism and Florida are synonymous, and Orlando is now the top tourist destination in the world. Over *40 million* visitors spend over $25 billion in Florida annually, and the number of tourists visiting the state continues to increase. Nearly everything in the state is geared to tourism, and motels, restaurants, novelty shops, roadside attractions, and theme parks are widespread, not to mention the thousands of unsightly billboards advertising these attractions. US-192 in Kissimmee is probably the best example of how horribly tacky Florida can become when it caters to tourist dollars; drive the road at night for the best (i.e., worst) effect. Consider also that much of the area was home to Bachman's Sparrows and probably Red-cockaded Woodpeckers less than 30 years ago.

WEATHER

Florida's high humidity (often over 70% during spring and summer) makes 90-degree temperatures seem at least 15 degrees higher. Those not used to such stifling conditions should avoid prolonged exposure to the sun and should drink plenty of fluids. Fortunately, most if not all rental vehicles in Florida are equipped with air-conditioning, which helps greatly. In summer, birding is mostly limited to 7 to 10 am and 4 to 8 pm. Florida's hot and humid climate requires that comfortable clothing be worn out of doors. Tennis shoes and loose-fitting clothing such as T-shirts and pants are typical. ("Natural fiber" clothing works best.) Shorts may feel great in summer, but long pants should be worn to protect your legs from the sun, biting insects, and thorny vegetation. Long-sleeved shirts may be worn by those especially sensitive to the sun, and in areas infested heavily with mosquitoes or biting flies. Many birders wear a hat to keep the sun out of their eyes—and, of course, don't forget to apply sunscreen.

Winters in Florida are usually unpredictable: hot and dry one day, cold and wet the next. Cold fronts frequently cause temperatures to drop briefly into the 20°s in North Florida, and 30°s in the central peninsula, but these cold fronts usually last only a day or two. Only South Florida and the Keys are truly subtropical (i.e., free from freezing temperatures).

Florida receives almost 60 inches of rain a year, mostly from May to September, when brief afternoon thundershowers occur almost daily, boosting the humidity to 100%. These storms usually contain lightning, discussed in the "Hazards" section. Another effect of Florida's high humidity is fog, which can occur year round but is most common from late fall to early spring. Fog is most prevalent at night and early in the morning. Use caution when driving through dense fog banks, and turn on your vehicle's headlights.

Hurricanes are high-intensity storms that form over water. In Florida the hurricane season lasts from June to November. Besides delivering large amounts of rainfall, hurricanes spawn frequent tornadoes. The hurricane itself creates extremely high winds. A storm is not officially a hurricane until sustained winds exceed 74 miles per hour. Until then the storm is first a tropical depression and then a tropical storm. Hurricanes are grouped into 5 categories according to their intensity. Category 1 hurricanes are the weakest, while Category 5 hurricanes are the most intense.

The most destructive hurricane to hit the U.S. recently was Hurricane *Andrew*, a Category 4 hurricane that struck the Homestead/Florida City area in the early hours of 24 August 1992. The highest recorded gust (before the anemometers blew away) was 217 miles per hour! *Andrew* caused $30 billion in damages, killed 85 people, caused 180,000 residents to become homeless temporarily, and left almost 3 million people without power for two months or longer. (Imagine living in South Florida in late summer without air conditioning.)

In Homestead, which was hit hardest by *Andrew*, effects of the storm are barely apparent today, as most of the houses have been rebuilt (and the demolished trailer parks have been replaced with more trailer parks). Although *Andrew* caused considerable damage to human-modified parts of Florida, the damage would have been far more substantial if the storm had made landfall only 20 miles farther north and made a direct hit on Miami.

In October 1995, Hurricane *Opal* caused nearly $2 billion in damages to the western Panhandle.

HOW TO USE THIS GUIDE

The main purpose of this book is to help you learn about Florida's birds, and it includes many spots in which to find them. This guide divides Florida into five fairly standard regions. From north to south and west to east, they are: the Panhandle, North Florida, Central Florida, South Florida, and the Florida Keys. The Panhandle is subdivided into eastern and western sections; the three peninsular regions are subdivided into Gulf coastal, inland, and Atlantic coastal thirds; and the Keys are subdivided into upper, middle, and lower thirds.

Good birding spots are given for most areas of the state, even those that are probably never visited by tourists. However, no attempt is made to list all birding sites (which is impossible), nor even all publicly owned sites. Rather, this guide concentrates on those sites considered by local birders to be most worth visiting. These sites are usually easily accessible to the public during daylight hours and typically contain "special" birds sought by visiting birders. Not included in this guide are most areas with only common, widespread species, and sites located in areas not covered by local birders. Many state parks and other similar areas are therefore excluded from this guide, although they may be worthwhile to visit. Most of the sites in this guide are clustered around a particular area or along a particular circuit, and most are publicly owned.

An attempt has been made to **bold-face** the names of the best birding sites. As you travel around the state, you may wish to visit only these sites, as they offer some of the best birding opportunities in Florida. Sites accessible only on foot (e.g., most water management district lands) are not bold-faced, nor are sites that allow hunting (e.g., wildlife management areas). A few areas that are bold-faced (e.g., Ocala National Forest, Corkscrew Swamp Sanctuary, and Big Cypress National Preserve) are so treated more for their scenic beauty or ecological importance than for their birding possibilities. These sites allow the visitor to gain a better understanding of how Florida's natural communities once functioned and how the rest of the state once looked.

All birding sites in this guide include specific directions from landmarks or intersections located easily on maps. Most points of interest and road junctions are followed by a number in parentheses (6.2). This indicates the mileage from the last point so marked. Keep in mind that vehicle odometers vary somewhat, so mileages listed in this guide may differ slightly from what you find in the field.

The various types of roads in Florida are given standard abbreviations in this book followed by a hyphen and the road number: Interstate Highway (e.g., I-75); Federal Highway (e.g., US-19); State Road (e.g., SR-52); County Road (e.g., CR-1), and Forest Road (e.g., FR-9). Many of these roads also have a name (e.g., Little Road). This guide lists the road number first, followed by the road name in parentheses. Major roads in urban areas are frequently given a second number by the city; in these cases, the local number follows the road name in parentheses. Additionally, roads that are oriented north-south are odd-numbered (e.g., I-75, US-19), while those oriented east-west are even-numbered (e.g., I-10, SR-70).

A map is included for nearly every site in this guide. Some maps even show the location of parks and other public areas that are not mentioned in the text. This method points out additional areas to explore, but they are usually not great birding areas, or access to them is limited.

Many birding sites in this guide are state parks or state recreation areas. Almost all these have a "standard" entrance fee of $3.25 per vehicle (up to 8 people). Many federal parks and wildlife refuges charge similar fees, which are also listed. All state parks open at 8 am and close at sunset. Most other natural areas with facilities follow a similar schedule. Undeveloped sites are often accessible anytime.

Nearly all parks, refuges, recreation areas, and wildlife management areas have published a list of the birds seen in the area. These can be picked up at the entrance booth or requested by mail. This guide rarely refers to these bird lists, however, because many are out-dated, some are compiled poorly, and there is a large degree of inconsistency between them (e.g., abundance categories and seasons).

Unlike other ABA/Lane guides to "big" birding areas (e.g., southeastern Arizona, southern California, and two Texas guides), the original Florida guide by Jim Lane encompassed the entire state rather than only one or more portions. For the sake of continuity, this guide continues to list sites statewide. However, most birding tourists would likely not notice if every birding site north of the Tampa Bay and Orlando regions were omitted from this guide. One could easily write a birdfinding guide limited to the southern half of the peninsula and the Keys that would be larger than this present edition.

Because this book covers all regions of Florida, information contained in each of the 250+ sites listed herein must be brief. In particular, common, widespread species found throughout the state are omitted intentionally from the birding sites and are instead listed on pages 12-24.

In recent years, local birdfinding guides have been published for the western Panhandle, Bay County (Panama City area), Gainesville, Hernando County (Brooksville/Weeki Wachee areas), Manatee and Sarasota Counties (Bradenton and Sarasota areas), and the Keys. The quality of these regional guides varies, but they typically contain many small, local birding sites that are not included in this statewide guide. These local guides are a welcome addition to birding in Florida, and similar guides to other areas are needed.

Although *A Birder's Guide to Florida* is written predominantly for the visiting birder, Florida residents and "semi-permanent" (seasonal) visitors should also find the guide useful. Those with much more time to spend in the state need to keep in mind that birds are found literally everywhere, even in urban areas. Sites included in this book are among the best accessible birding sites in Florida, but hardly do they represent the only worthwhile birding spots in the state. *Explore the state on your own and you are sure to discover excellent birding sites not included in this guide.*

"Route for those in a hurry"—The most difficult part of planning a birding trip is picking the route that allows you to see the maximum number of "wanted" species in the minimum amount of time. It is worthwhile to look over the specialties section (pages 266-312) and the bar-graphs (pages 318-344) to better plot the locations for the species you are seeking. *If you are planning your first birding trip to the state, plan to spend 7 to 10 days in late April or early May in Central Florida and South Florida, including a boat trip to Dry Tortugas National Park.*

Birders who come to the state in spring seeking "Florida specialties" have little or no reason to go farther north than the Tampa Bay and Orlando regions. Although northern Florida contains numerous excellent birding sites, they can all be skipped without missing any birds restricted to the state as long as one visits appropriate habitats in Central and southern Florida.

Birders visiting Florida in the winter months will find excellent birding throughout the state. Because all but one of the South Florida specialties depart the state to winter in the Caribbean or Neotropics, a trip to the Keys is not a necessity. (The one South Florida specialty present also in winter is the Mangrove Cuckoo, which is secretive and difficult to locate in that season.) In fact, the farther north one goes in Florida in winter, the more abundant waterfowl and many other species become. The Panhandle in particular has many fairly common wintering species that are rare or absent elsewhere in the state. In Central Florida, Honeymoon Island State Recreation Area and Merritt Island National Wildlife Refuge are excellent sites for shorebirds and ducks, respectively, as are numerous other sites. Miami is still a "must" for the multitude of exotics in that area, and Short-tailed Hawks are fairly common in Everglades National Park.

ORGANIZATIONS

The **Florida Ornithological Society**, with about 400 members, is *the* statewide birding and ornithological society in Florida. FOS publishes a quarterly journal, *Florida Field Naturalist*, the state's primary outlet for publications about Florida birds, and the *FOS Newsletter*, which contains notices and announcements about upcoming events, requests for information, and assistance in research projects. FOS holds two conventions each year (in spring and fall) in cities within the state, and occasionally in neighboring states. Each fall, FOS publishes a list of all Florida Christmas Bird Counts and their compilers. Membership in FOS is essential for all serious birders in Florida. Subscription rates are $15 per year. For more information, write to Linda Douglas, Treasurer, 3675 1st Avenue NW, Naples, FL 33964.

The **American Birding Association** is the national equivalent of FOS, and has over 20,000 members. ABA publishes *Winging It*, a monthly newsletter, *Birding*, a bi-monthly magazine, *Field Notes*, a quarterly journal, and *A Bird's-Eye View*, a bi-monthly youth newsletter. ABA also publishes the ABA/Lane series of birdfinding guides and operates ABA Sales, a mail-order bird book and birding equipment source. Membership rates are $36 per year U.S. and $45 international. See pages 369-370 for more information about the American Birding Association.

The **Florida Audubon Society** has over 30,000 members in 46 chapters throughout the state. Some local Audubon chapters have excellent, well-organized birding programs, while others exist largely as social clubs for their members. For the locations of all local chapters and their current officers, contact the Florida Audubon Society, 1331 Palmetto Avenue, Suite 110, Winter Park, FL 32789; 407/539-5700. FAS also exists as its own organization and publishes *Florida Naturalist* every quarter. Subscription rates are $25 per year. For information on FAS's Adopt-A-Bird program, see page 145.

The **Nature Conservancy** has 800,000 members nationwide and 42,000 members in Florida. Its primary function is to purchase environmentally sensitive lands that are in danger of being destroyed. TNC has helped to protect over 710,000 acres in Florida. Subscription rates are $25 per year and include memberships in both the national and state organizations. For information, contact TNC's Florida Chapter at 222 S. Westmonte Drive, Suite 300, Altamonte Springs, FL 32714; 407/682-3663.

Water Management Districts (WMD) were created by the Florida Legislature to regulate water resources in the state. Through the Save Our Rivers portion of the CARL program, WMDs have purchased vast amounts of riparian and other wetlands habitats and many upland habitats important as water-recharge areas. Because most WMD properties lack facilities, are accessible only to those on foot or horseback, and allow hunting in season, they are not listed in this guide. For information on WMD land holdings, contact the districts: **Northwest Florida WMD**, Route 1, Box 3100, Havana, FL 32333; 850/487-1770; **Suwannee River WMD**, Route 3, Box 64, Live Oak, FL 32060; 904/362-1001; **St. Johns River WMD**, P.O. Box 1429, Palatka, FL 32178-1429; 904/329-4500; **Southwest Florida WMD**, 2379 Broad Street, Brooksville, FL 34609-6899; 800/423-1476; and **South Florida WMD**, P.O. Box 24680, 3301 Gun Club Road, West Palm Beach, FL 33416-4680; 800/432-2045.

FINAL NOTES

Although maps are included in this guide, it is recommended that visitors purchase a state map of Florida. Visitors who plan to travel extensively in Florida may consider purchasing a copy of DeLorme Publishing's *Florida Atlas and Gazetteer.* Although it is becoming out-of-date, this excellent atlas contains 100 large-scale maps covering the entire state and identifies many parks, historical sites, and other points of interest. The Atlas costs about $17 and is available at most Florida bookstores, ABA Sales, or it can be ordered from DeLorme Mapping, P.O. Box 298, Freeport, ME 04032.

This edition of *A Birder's Guide to Florida* was written between May 1994 and March 1996. All information was current at the time of writing. However, *things quickly become out of date in Florida, especially concerning the status and location of exotic birds.* Therefore, use this book as a site guide only. New roads are constantly being built, and some roads in service in the next few years may not be present on maps in this guide. Also, the state's land-acquisition programs are constantly adding new public lands that may become excellent birding sites in the future. It is important to note that many publicly owned sites are off-limits to the public to protect fragile habitats or rare species. *If a site is posted, stay out.* It is always best to contact local birders in areas you wish to visit.

This edition was reprinted in November 1997 and corrects all significant errors in the original printing that were brought to our attention. Also, we have deleted from the book two unproductive sites, revised directions to other sites, changed telephone area codes as needed, and included taxonomic changes as previously outlined in this Introduction.

Telephone birding reports—Many states rely on "rare bird alert" telephone numbers updated regularly to inform birders of recent rarities. In Florida, however, an informal loop "hotline" system composed of birders around the state calling each other has been in place for many years. Only recently has a statewide phone number been established to update bird sightings from around Florida. Begun by Dan Canterbury, the "Florida Birding Report" (561/340-0079) is now updated by Dotty and Hank Hull. Not limited to rare birds, it often gives general birding information, reports of recent sightings, and specific directions to rarities, when they are present. Three other telephone numbers are available for local birding reports. In Tallahassee, call 912/244-9190 (a Georgia phone number), in Miami, call 305/667-7337, and in the Lower Keys, call 305/294-3438.

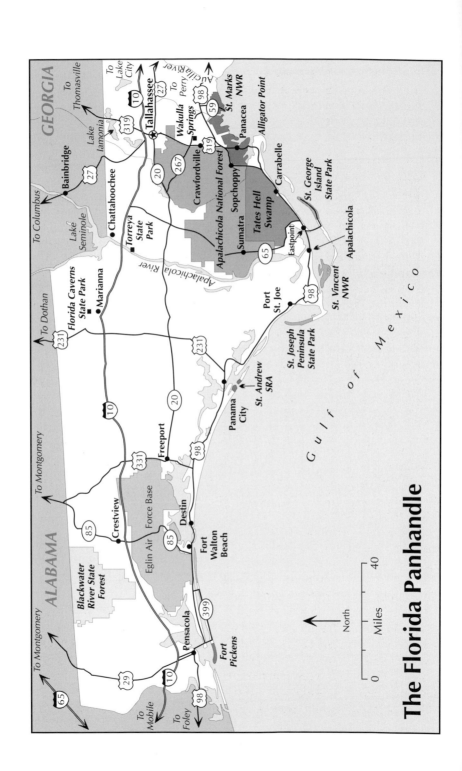

The Florida Panhandle

PANHANDLE

In this book the Panhandle is considered to be the part of Florida west of the Aucilla River. The area is divided into western and eastern portions by the Apalachicola River. The Panhandle is also divided by the central and eastern time zones. Although many Floridians are unaware of it, the western Panhandle is in the central time zone, so times in the west are one hour "earlier" than elsewhere in the state.

In many ways, the Panhandle is more closely related to Alabama and Georgia, Florida's neighbors to the north, than to the rest of the state. The Panhandle's hilly terrain is a result of erosion of the Appalachian Mountains. The highest point in Florida (345 feet) is located near Lakewood, on the Alabama border. The reddish clay soils of the northern portion of the Panhandle, covered with a mixture of hardwoods and pines, are an extension of those to the north.

The Panhandle is the least-populated region of Florida, and much of it remains forested. Timber production is one of the most important industries in the area. Another "industry" for which the region is famous is the harvesting of the rich oyster beds in Apalachicola Bay, a highly productive estuary and a recognized International Biosphere Reserve. There are many large publicly owned areas in the Panhandle, including Blackwater River State Forest, Eglin Air Force Base, Tyndall Air Force Base, and Apalachicola National Forest. All but Tyndall are vital refuges for the Red-cockaded Woodpecker—in fact, Apalachicola National Forest contains the world's largest population of this Endangered species. Other popular birding sites in the Panhandle include the Fort Pickens area of Gulf Islands National Seashore, the Fort Walton Beach sewage treatment facility, St. Joseph Peninsula, St. George Island, Florida Caverns State Park, Torreya State Park, the Panacea area, St. Marks National Wildlife Refuge, and Wakulla Springs State Park. Many of the coastal sites can be excellent for migrant landbirds in spring.

The Apalachicola River, with bluffs up to 150 feet above the river, is unique in Florida. Ravines amid the bluffs contain many endemic species and many other plants common in the Appalachian Mountains, but found nowhere else in Florida. In fact, the Apalachicola River watershed is believed to contain more plant and animal species (per unit area) than any other region in temperate North America. Fortunately, the river is little-developed, and the State of Florida and conservation organizations

43

have purchased most of the lands along the river for preservation. The vast Tates Hell Swamp area on the east side of the river (and adjacent to Apalachicola National Forest to the north) contains over 215,000 acres, currently being purchased largely by the state at a cost of about $68 million (a bargain price compared to that of other areas in Florida).

The Apalachicola area is regionally significant from a birding perspective, also. The area marks the normal westward breeding range in Florida for Bald Eagle, American Oystercatcher, Gray Kingbird, Marsh Wren, and Boat-tailed Grackle. (A few individuals of some of these species breed also in the Pensacola area, and eagles are increasing rapidly in the western Panhandle.) The *peninsulae* race of the Seaside Sparrow also reaches its western limit in the Apalachicola area (at St. Vincent National Wildlife Refuge), but other races breed farther west.

The relatively few birders in the Panhandle are clustered around the larger cities, mostly Pensacola and Tallahassee. Birders in the Pensacola area are allied much more closely to Alabama than to the rest of Florida because of the distances to other sites in the state. Excellent birding sites in Alabama (e.g., Fort Morgan and Dauphin Island) are within an hour's drive from Pensacola, whereas Tallahassee is three hours away, Orlando is seven, and Miami requires a drive of about twelve hours.

Because it is so far from the major tourist destinations, the Panhandle is birded rarely by the state's visitors. Although the region offers excellent birding opportunities, the species to be found here are those that occur largely throughout eastern North America, with a few western breeding species straying east in fall and winter. Few "Florida specialties" are found as far north and west as the Panhandle. Sought-after breeding species that occur in the region include Swallow-tailed Kite, Purple Gallinule, Snowy Plover, Wilson's Plover, Eurasian Collared-Dove, Red-cockaded Woodpecker, Gray Kingbird, Brown-headed Nuthatch, and Bachman's Sparrow, but all these species also occur in nearly every other region of Florida, also.

Birders from the rest of the state come here mostly to search for wintering species that are rare or absent in the peninsula. These include many waterfowl, including Tundra Swan (irregular), Snow Goose, American Black Duck, Mallard, Greater Scaup, all three scoters, Common Goldeneye, Golden Eagle (rare), Groove-billed Ani (rare), western-breeding hummingbirds (mostly Black-chinned and Rufous Hummingbirds, but others have included Buff-bellied, Anna's, and Calliope Hummingbirds), Red-breasted Nuthatch (irruptive), Brown Creeper, Winter Wren, Golden-crowned Kinglet, Sprague's Pipit (extremely local), sparrows (nearly all species are much more common in the Panhandle than elsewhere, but Le Conte's and Fox Sparrows and Dark-eyed Junco are almost restricted to the Panhandle), Rusty Blackbird, Purple Finch (irruptive), and Pine Siskin (irruptive). Breeding species more-or-less restricted to the Panhandle and generally difficult to find at other seasons elsewhere in the state include Canada Goose (exotic; resident), Mississippi Kite, Broad-winged Hawk, White-breasted Nuthatch (resident), Swainson's Warbler, Kentucky Warbler, Yellow-breasted Chat, and House Finch (exotic; resident).

Panhandle sites are listed west to east, and most sites in this guide are coastal locations.

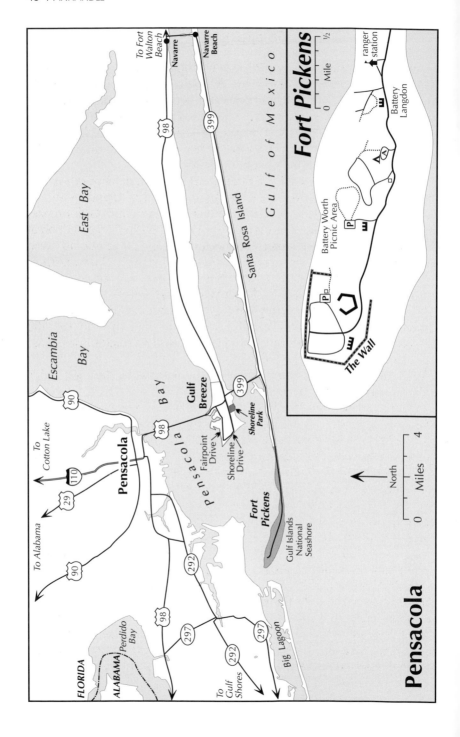

Pensacola

PENSACOLA

A good spot for migrants is Shoreline Park in Gulf Breeze. In spring it is good for migrant landbirds, and in fall for migrating raptors, mostly Broad-winged Hawks. Mississippi Kites are regular from August to mid-September. To reach the park from Pensacola, take US-98 over the Pensacola Bay Bridge to Gulf Breeze. At Shoreline Drive (the second traffic light) (1.4 miles), turn right to the park on the left (0.8). Walk the east-west nature trail at the bottom of the hill.

The favorite location of local birders seeking migrant landbirds is **Fort Pickens Park** (1,742 acres; $4/vehicle), a part of **Gulf Islands National Seashore** (28,976 acres in Florida). To reach the park from Gulf Breeze, go east on US-98 to SR-399 (0.4) and turn right. At the T intersection at the beach, turn right to the park entrance (3.2). From November to April, numbers of Northern Gannets may be seen from the beach road. Continue to the ranger's station (the building with the red roof) (4.0). The area's first two Shiny Cowbird sightings were made here.

Turn right into **Battery Langdon** (0.3). From the parking lot, note the large oak near the northeast corner of the battery. Known locally as "the oak on the east side," this tree should be searched for migrants from late March into April. Walk the shell bicycle path to the left and turn left onto a sand trail just past the maintenance building road on the right. This trail returns you to the battery.

After exploring the battery, continue west to Campground Loop A (0.6). Drive around to the parking area for non-campers. Walk north past the restrooms to Blackbird Nature Trail and go either right or left at the fork. Although this area is not usually as productive as others in the park, it should be searched.

Return to the main road and continue west to **Battery Worth Picnic Area** (0.6), considered the premier birding hotspot of the park and possibly of the western Panhandle. Begin birding around the picnic tables; then from the east side of the parking area, walk east on a loop trail about 1,000 feet long. This trail goes through individual campsites, so take care not to disturb those camping. The trail makes a loop around a marshy area, which should be checked for Swainson's Warblers and other species. The only Caribbean Elaenia reported in North America was found here 28 April 1984. At the small bridge, check both sides of the ditch for waterthrushes. The oaks past the bridge can be excellent for numerous migrants. As the trail heads west toward an amphitheater, search the large oaks. After this, the trail returns you to the parking lot.

Continue west on the main park road to the west end of the island (0.9). At the "Fort Information" sign, turn right onto a narrow road that leads to a small white building. Park here and walk east down the shell bicycle trail. The concrete wall on your left is known locally as "**The Wall**," which can be good for migrant landbirds in spring and for migrating raptors in fall. On the grassy area behind the fort, watch for Bobolinks in spring and sparrows in spring and fall. Continue along the path to the wooden bridge. From here to the parking area, check the brushy edges for Groove-billed Anis in October and November. Although they are rare here (as elsewhere in the state), they have been observed in this area almost regularly.

Two species of local significance breed in the park: Least Bittern (mid-March to mid-October) and Gray Kingbird (May to September). The bitterns nest in the canals behind the fort (walk the Wall trail) and between Battery Langdon and the main campground. At least two pairs nested near the Wall trail in 1993. Gray Kingbirds are uncommon but regular breeders in the area. In 1993, pairs bred near the Museum, Campground A, and west of Battery Langdon.

Contact: Gulf Islands National Seashore, 1801 Gulf Breeze Parkway, Gulf Breeze, FL 32561; 850/934-2600.

To reach **Cotton Lake** (not shown on map), a hardwood swamp along the Escambia River, go north on US-98 across Pensacola Bay and through Pensacola. After curving left, turn right onto I-110, which ends at I-10. Go west and turn right onto US-29 (2.0), heading north. Cross over Pine Barren Creek (20.0) and turn right onto the first dirt road (0.3). From here to the river (1.8), look for breeding species such as Barred Owl, Acadian Flycatcher, and Swainson's, Kentucky, and Hooded Warblers. In winter, watch for American Woodcock, Winter Wren, Brown Creeper, and sparrows. In summer, parts of the road may be inundated, so drive with caution.

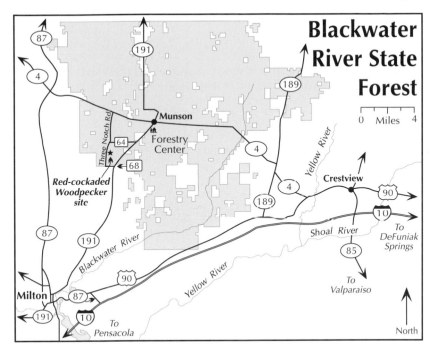

Blackwater River State Forest

0 Miles 4

Munson

Forestry Center

Red-cockaded Woodpecker site

Milton

To Pensacola

Crestview

Shoal River

To DeFuniak Springs

To Valparaiso

North

CRESTVIEW

Blackwater River State Forest (183,381 acres; no fee) is composed mostly of pinewoods, but extensive hardwood forests grow along the streams, and oak woodlands cover the hillsides. To reach the forest from the west, exit I-10 at SR-87 and head toward Milton on US-90/SR-87. Just past the Blackwater River, turn right onto SR-191 to Munson (the junction with SR-4). From the east, exit I-10 onto SR-85 and go into Crestview. Go west on US-90 to SR-4 and then northwest to the forest. The following 8-mile birding route is recommended by Susan Cerulean and Ann Morrow. From SR-4, turn south onto SR-191 in Munson and stop at the Forestry Center on the left (0.2). At FR-64 (Spanish Trail) (2.6), turn right to a Pitcher Plant bog on the left (0.8). The peak bloom is in April and May. Continue on FR-64 to unmarked Three Notch Road (2.2) and turn left. An active Red-cockaded Woodpecker cluster is along this road (0.7). At FR-68 (1.7), turn left to return to SR-191 (0.5). Birding in the forest is best in spring and summer, when you can find breeding species such as Mississippi Kite, Acadian Flycatcher, Wood Thrush, Prothonotary, Hooded, and Swainson's Warblers, Louisiana Waterthrush, Yellow-breasted Chat, Blue Grosbeak, and Indigo Bunting. Winter rarities that have been reported here include Red-breasted Nuthatch, Winter Wren, Golden-crowned Kinglet, Le Conte's Sparrow, Dark-eyed Junco, and Rusty Blackbird. Many stands of Longleaf Pine contain Red-cockaded Woodpecker clusters; cavity trees are marked with white paint. Brown-headed Nuthatches and Bachman's Sparrows are fairly common throughout the forest.

Contact: Blackwater River State Forest, 11650 Munson Highway, Milton, FL 32570; 850/957-4201 or 957-4590.

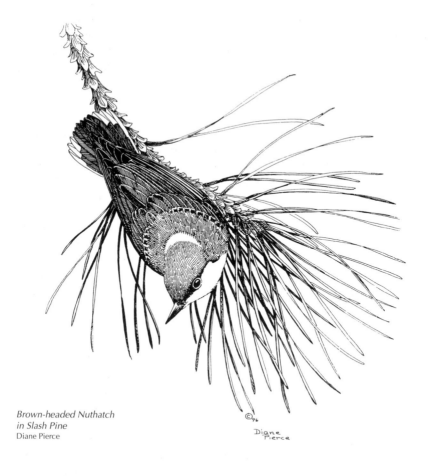

Brown-headed Nuthatch in Slash Pine
Diane Pierce

FORT WALTON BEACH/ DESTIN AREA

Waste-water spray fields and holding-ponds in Fort Walton Beach provide habitat for many waterbirds and wintering sparrows. To reach the **Fort Walton Beach Spray Field** (no fee, open 24 hours every day) from US-98, go north on Mary Esther Boulevard to SR-189 (Beal Parkway) (1.8) and continue north. At the first road north of Green Acres Road (2.5), turn left and continue north on Beal Street Extension to the end (1.0). The spray fields are on the right. Park across from the office and check in. At the office on the left, ask for permission to drive the perimeter road.

During wet summers, the spray field attracts many wading-birds, ducks, and shorebirds. In October 1994, a White-faced Ibis was found here, the first one reported in Florida since 1966. Black-necked Stilts have begun to breed in the area and forage in the holding-pond, as do other shorebirds during migration. Eared Grebes are found regularly in fall. Glossy Ibises are seen on occasion, and a variety of ducks winter on the pond, including Hooded Merganser. Also during this season, sparrows of many species frequent the weedy fields. Besides common species, look for Grasshopper, Le Conte's, "Sharp-tailed," White-crowned, and, occasionally, Lark Sparrows. Mississippi Kites are regular in spring and summer, and Swallow-tailed Kites appear occasionally.

Just northwest of the spray-field facility is a landfill pond that is always worth a look when the landfill is open (Monday to Saturday).

Located along the eastern edge of the spray field are the **Okaloosa County holding-ponds** (usually open Monday to Friday 8 am to 5 pm; no fee). To reach the county holding-ponds from the spray field, go back to SR-189 (Lewis Turner Boulevard) and turn left. Proceed to Roberts Boulevard (0.8) and turn left (just past Mama Rosa's Pizza). The ponds are ahead (0.5). The perimeters of the ponds on the right may be walked, but *do not enter the spray field here*. Be careful to avoid getting locked inside. Sixteen species of ducks have been reported here, and one or two Eared Grebes usually are present from October to December. Baird's Sandpipers are present occasionally in April and September.

Five miles east of Fort Walton Beach, the Destin Bridge (US-98) has parking lots at both ends on the south side of the road. The lake on the west side should have ducks in winter. Clapper Rails and wintering "Sharp-tailed" Sparrows are found in the surrounding grasses. A walk along the beach to the jetty may produce shorebirds, including Snowy Plovers. In winter, Northern Gannets and sea ducks may be observed

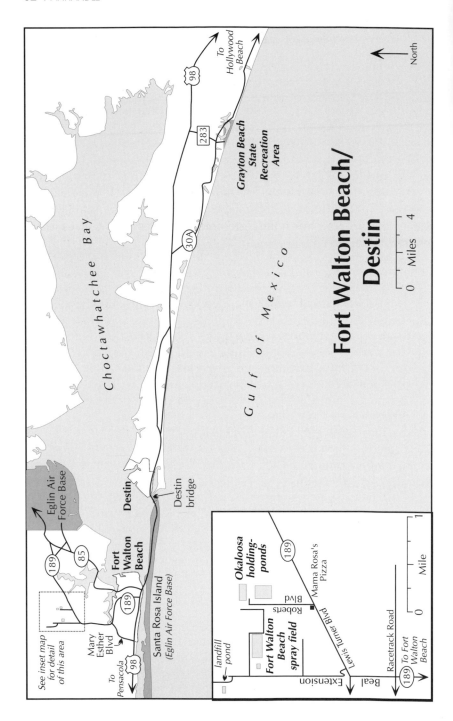

Fort Walton Beach/
Destin

from shore. In summer, Least Terns and Black Skimmers nest near the east end of the bridge.

The area west of the bridge is part of Eglin Air Force Base, which contains 464,000 acres (725 square miles), of which more than half is accessible to the public. Most of this acreage is composed of sandhills that contain numerous Red-cockaded Woodpecker clusters and other pinewoods species. Other habitats on the base include 810 miles of rivers and streams, 57 miles of estuarine shoreline, 20 miles of frontage on the Gulf of Mexico, 32 lakes, and 26,000 acres of other wetlands. The bird list for the entire base contains 335 species.

All visitors to the base must have a permit ($3/year), obtained Monday to Friday until 3:15 pm at the Natural Resources Branch on SR-85 in Niceville. The exception is the easternmost 14 miles of Santa Rosa Island (ending at the Destin bridge), which may be visited without a permit.

Contact: Eglin Air Force Base, Natural Resources Branch, 3200 SPTW/DEMN, Eglin Air Force Base, FL 32542-5000; 850/882-4164.

Farther east, the sand dunes, beaches, and fresh water ponds of Grayton Beach State Recreation Area (276 acres; standard fee) on SR-30A south of US-98 may be worth a visit. The grassy marshes harbor resident Clapper Rails and Seaside Sparrows, which are joined in winter by Soras, Virginia Rails, and "Sharp-tailed" Sparrows.

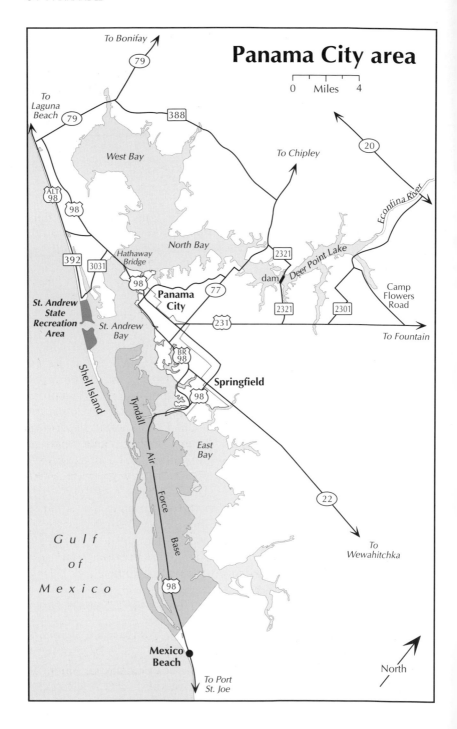

Panama City area

0   Miles   4

To Bonifay
79
To Laguna Beach
79
388
To Chipley
20
West Bay
ALT 98
98
Econfina River
North Bay
2321
Deer Point Lake
392
3031
Hathaway Bridge
98
dam
Camp Flowers Road
Panama City
77
2321
2301
St. Andrew State Recreation Area
St. Andrew Bay
231
To Fountain
BR 98
Shell Island
Springfield
98
Tyndall
East Bay
Air
Gulf
Force
of
Base
22
To Wewahitchka
Mexico
98
Mexico Beach
North
To Port St. Joe

PANAMA CITY AREA

St. Andrew State Recreation Area (1,063 acres; standard fee) contains sand dunes, beaches, bays, marshes, and pinewoods. Birding is best in winter but may also be good for migrant landbirds. To reach the area from US-98 just west of the Hathaway Bridge, go south on CR-3031 (Thomas Drive). At CR-392 (3.7), turn left to the entrance ahead (0.6). Proceed to the boardwalk over Buttonbush Marsh on the right (0.6) to look for wading-birds, rails, and shorebirds in season. Continue east to the camp store and turn left to the boat ramp on Grand Lagoon. Look for sea ducks and other waterbirds here in winter. As you head back to the store, turn right to Lagoon Campground. The oaks here can produce numerous migrants in spring and fall. Return to the store and go south. Alligator Lake on the left may be worth a stop for wading-birds and migrants. Turn left to reach the jetties into the Gulf. From here, look for Northern Gannets (a scope may be necessary), sea ducks, and other wintering species.

From spring through fall, a ferry from St. Andrew carries visitors to Shell Island, located east of the boat channel. Shell Island is an undeveloped island accessible only by boat. The western portion of the island is part of the recreation area and is composed of Sand Pine scrub and dunes. The remainder of the island, of which the eastern portion is part of Tyndall Air Force Base and the middle is private property, is composed of extensive salt marshes. These marshes support wintering populations of Sedge and Marsh Wrens and "Sharp-tailed" and Seaside Sparrows. "Sharp-tails" are especially common. Some 120 were counted here on the Christmas Bird Count in 1977. Also in winter, the beaches are used by numerous shorebirds, including Snowy (resident), Wilson's (numerous at the east end), and Piping Plovers. Larids (gulls and terns) are also present; look for Caspian and Sandwich Terns among the common species, and wading-birds are found year round. Offshore, watch for Red-throated Loons (rare) and sea ducks in winter. Rarities reported in the park include Eared Grebe, Masked Booby, Brown Booby, Harlequin Duck, Purple Sandpiper, Black-legged Kittiwake, Horned Lark, Black-whiskered Vireo, and Shiny Cowbird.

Contact: St. Andrew State Recreation Area, 4415 Thomas Drive, Panama City, FL 32408; 850/233-5140.

Deer Point Lake to the northeast can be a good spot for waterbirds, especially in winter. To reach it from US-98 in Panama City, go north on SR-77 to the bridge over North Bay (4.8). Scan the bay for American White Pelicans, wintering ducks, and other waterbirds. At CR-2321 (1.9),

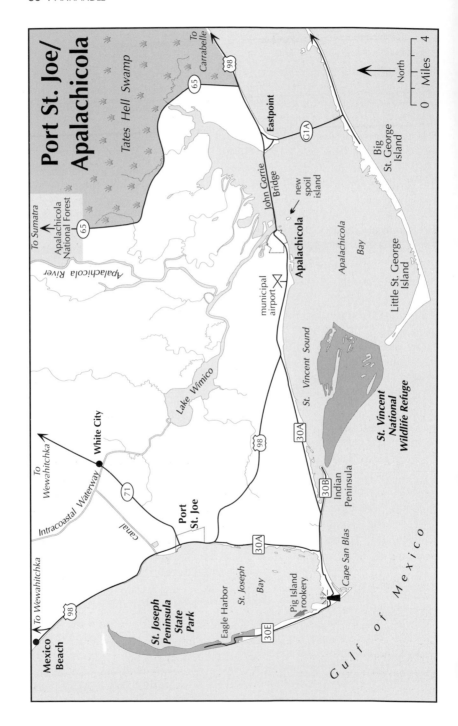

Port St. Joe/ Apalachicola

turn right to the dam ahead. Deer Point Lake was formed when the Econfina River was dammed. The lake is fresh water, but the bay on the south side of CR-2321 is brackish. Many ducks winter on the lake. Continue on CR-2321 to its end at US-231 and turn left. At CR-2301 (2.9), turn left to the bridge (5.2). Search this area for wading-birds, wintering waterfowl, Purple Gallinules, and other species. From here, you can return to US-231 via CR-2301 or Camp Flowers Road, or continue north to SR-20 to bird the upland forests. Breeding species in the area include Mississippi Kite, Yellow-breasted Chat, Blue Grosbeak, Indigo Bunting, and others.

Birds of Bay County, revised by Richard Ingram, was published by the Bay County Audubon Society in 1995. It is an excellent guidebook to the Panama City area and includes a list of the 334 birds reported from Bay County. It also contains information to birding sites in neighboring counties. It may be ordered ($7 by mail) from Bay County Audubon Society, P.O. Box 1182, Panama City, FL 32402.

PORT ST. JOE

Port St. Joe was the site of Florida's first constitutional convention in1838. It is also the gateway to some fine birding. About 2 miles south of Port St. Joe on US-98, bear right onto CR-30A, which follows the shoreline of St. Joseph Bay. At CR-30E (6.6), turn right onto St. Joseph Peninsula. (To reach this area from Apalachicola, go west on US-98, bear left onto CR-30A, and continue to CR-30E [12.0]). The peninsula is less than a mile wide, nearly 15 miles long, and 3 to 7 miles off the mainland, making it an excellent place for observing landbird migration in spring and raptor migration in fall. The first birding site to check is **Cape San Blas** on the left (2.6 from CR-30A). The cape has a lighthouse and an installation of Eglin Air Force Base. The woodlands and brushy edges along the road should be checked for migrants. In fall, watch exposed perches for Vermilion Flycatcher, Western Kingbird, and Scissor-tailed Flycatcher. A Northern Wheatear was once observed here. The cape is also a good spot for migrant raptors. The beach to the left, which leads to Cape San Blas, requires a walk of about ½ mile each way. *Do not drive on the beach.* The pool at the cape is good for wading-birds, including Reddish Egrets. In winter, look for American Bittern, Marsh and Sedge Wrens, and "Sharp-tailed" and Seaside (rare) Sparrows. Other rarities that have been seen here include American Golden-Plover, Long-billed Curlew, and Buff-breasted Sandpiper. Northern Gannets (winter), wading-birds, sea ducks (winter), shorebirds (including a few breeding Wilson's Plovers), and a variety of gulls and terns are also found here.

Return to CR-30E and go north to **T. H. Stone Memorial St. Joseph Peninsula State Park** (2,516 acres; standard fee) (5.9). A map and bird list are available at the entrance station. Wading-birds and larids are common, and Snowy and Wilson's Plovers nest in the dunes along the Gulf. In spring, wooded areas should be checked for migrants; impressive fallouts have occurred here in the past. In fall, landbirds may be common, but the big attraction is the raptor migration. The species observed most commonly are Sharp-shinned and Broad-winged Hawks and American Kestrels. On some days, 1,500 Sharp-shins and 200 American Kestrels have been seen, but daily totals of 200 to 300 birds are considered good. Eagle Harbor, where the peninsula is most narrow, is the best place to observe raptors, but any place with an unobstructed view of the peninsula from Gulf to bay is good. An interesting feature of the fall raptor migration here is dictated by the shape of the land. Raptors fly *north* up the peninsula to St. Joseph Point and then cross the few miles of water before continuing west along the mainland.

Eagle Harbor is also good for sea ducks in winter. Harlequin Duck, scoters, Oldsquaw, and Common Merganser have all been reported here. Productive spots for migrant landbirds are around the campgrounds and the picnic area. Brown-headed Nuthatches and Yellow-throated Warblers may be found in the taller pines throughout the park. The paved park road ends about 2 miles from the entrance, but park property continues for another 7 miles to St. Joseph Point. Hiking in that area is permitted.

Contact: T. H. Stone Memorial St. Joseph Peninsula State Park, Star Route 1, Box 200, Port St. Joe, FL 32456; 850/227-1327.

APALACHICOLA

This historic town, center of Florida's oyster industry and a locale of regional importance, is situated at the mouth of the Apalachicola River. The area boasts a diversity of habitats. A spoil island created in early 1995 one mile offshore from the mouth of the river hosted nesting seabirds within months (e.g., American Oystercatchers, Gull-billed Terns, Least Terns, and Black Skimmers). The island is also used as a roosting site year round by a variety of migrant and resident seabirds, primarily pelicans, cormorants, and larids. Specialties here include American White Pelican and Caspian, Sandwich, and Common Terns. An increasing number of shorebirds also use the island as a roosting site.

As is the case for a few other good birding sites in this area, a private boat is required to reach the island.

Specialties of the Apalachicola area include Least Bittern, Bald Eagle, Marsh Wren, and Boat-tailed Grackle. Eurasian Collared-Doves have recently begun to breed in town and are joined in fall by a few White-winged Doves moving east. Several pairs of Gray Kingbirds and a single pair of Painted Buntings (unique in the Panhandle) are other local breeding specialties. A large flock of Vaux's Swifts roosted in the chimney of the town hall in the winter of 1994-1995, and a few were present in the winter of 1995-1996.

The point of land near the boat basin at the mouth of the river and the causeway of the John Gorrie Bridge (US-98) are good sites from which to observe vagrant birds blown onshore during tropical storms or hurricanes, especially if the causeway to St. George Island is closed because of the storm. The most common vagrant is Magnificent Frigatebird, but other species that may be seen include shearwaters, storm-petrels, jaegers, and terns. These storms also blow local birds onshore in large numbers, including White-rumped Sandpipers and Sandwich, Common, and Black Terns.

Apalachicola Municipal Airport is located about 3 miles west of town. Drive north from US-98 to the terminal's parking area (0.7). This is probably the best accessible site in the state for Sprague's Pipit, which has wintered here (1 to 3 birds) for the past several years, including 2 birds in 1995-1996. The proprietor is very understanding of birders; *request permission* to walk the short grassy margins of the runways.

To reach **Indian Peninsula**, go west from Apalachicola on US-98, bear left onto CR-30A, then turn left sharply onto CR-30B. Marshes near the bridge on CR-30B are good in winter for Marsh Wrens and Seaside Sparrows. Follow this road to the boat ramp at the end. The peninsula is a good, easily accessible spot for wading-birds, shorebirds, larids, and other species. Walk north from the boat ramp several hundred yards to scope the western part of St. Vincent Sound. Black-crowned Night-Herons and American Oystercatchers (up to 50 may be present, but only 3 or 4 pairs breed) are regular here. Rarities have included Eared Grebe, Greater White-fronted Goose, and American Avocet.

Southwest of Apalachicola is St. Vincent National Wildlife Refuge (12,358 acres; no fee), accessible only by boat. Group tours led by U.S. Fish and Wildlife Service personnel may be arranged in Apalachicola. Call the refuge for information. Birders with their own boat may reach the island from Apalachicola, which requires a trip of 7 to 9 miles across Apalachicola Bay to reach the eastern side of the island, or from Indian

Peninsula, only ¼ mile to reach the western tip of the island. Motorized vehicles are prohibited on the island, so access is limited to those on foot. Except during hunting season, all public use must be during daylight hours. St. Vincent Island currently is an Island Propagation Site for the critically Endangered Red Wolf.

The refuge contains a variety of habitats, including salt water and fresh water marshes, pinewoods, scrub oak dunes, oak and hardwood hammocks, and 9 miles of Gulf beaches. Nearly 250 species of birds have been reported from the island. Among the breeding species are Bald Eagle (4 nests), American Oystercatcher, Least Tern, Boat-tailed Grackle, and possibly Black Rail. (During surveys in April 1989, 10 Black Rails were counted at four sites on the island, but the birds were not located subsequently, so they may have been just migrants or winter residents.) During winter, numerous waterfowl are present on ponds and offshore, including Redheads, Common Goldeneyes, and scoters. Wading-birds (including Wood Storks), shorebirds, and larids are common on the beaches. Migrant landbirds may be found in the oak-clad ridges and dunes, and raptors may be common in September and October.

Contact: St. Vincent National Wildlife Refuge, P.O. Box 447, Apalachicola, FL 32329; 850/653-8808.

St. George Island is a barrier island nearly 30 miles long. To reach it from Apalachicola, go east on US-98 across the John Gorrie bridge to Eastpoint and turn right onto SR-G1A (6.2). Once on the causeway, pull off the road and walk the grassy shoulders in winter, when you should flush American Pipits and sparrows. The most sought-after bird here is Sprague's Pipit, which occurs here almost frequently, but not annually. In spring and summer, Wilson's Plovers, American Oystercatchers, Laughing Gulls, and Least Terns nest on the causeway, very close to the road. (In the past few years, Laughing Gulls have been reducing the numbers of the other species, and Black Skimmers no longer nest here.) To protect the birds, *observe the birds only from your vehicle.* Beyond the second bridge, shorebirds can be numerous on both sides of the road as you reach the island; American Oystercatchers breed here.

Much of St. George Island is privately owned and is being developed. Virtually any remnant patch of woodland can be good for migrant and wintering landbirds, but most birders proceed to the state park that occupies the eastern end of the island. Rarities reported on St. George include Mangrove Cuckoo (the only Panhandle report), Lesser Nighthawk, Western Kingbird (regular), Scissor-tailed Flycatcher (regular), Rock Wren (the only Florida record), Black-whiskered Vireo, Yellow-headed Blackbird, Curve-billed Thrasher, Northern Wheatear, and West-

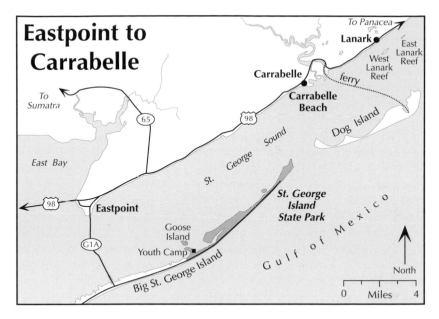

Eastpoint to Carrabelle

To Panacea
Lanark
East Lanark Reef
West Lanark Reef
Carrabelle
ferry
Carrabelle Beach
To Sumatra
65
98
St. George Sound
Dog Island
East Bay
St. George
Eastpoint
St. George Island State Park
Gulf of Mexico
Goose Island
Youth Camp
G1A
98
Big St. George Island
North
0   Miles   4

ern Tanager. In fall 1995, a *Myiodynastes* species believed to be a Streaked Flycatcher was found in the park. Breeding specialties include Snowy Plover, Wilson's Plover, American Oystercatcher, Gull-billed Tern (irregular; on the causeway), Least Tern, and Gray Kingbird. Be aware that the island contains a large population of Cottonmouths, so it is best to stay on the trails.

To reach **Dr. Julian D. Bruce St. George Island State Park** (1,962 acres; standard fee), turn left onto Gulf Beach Drive to the entrance (4.0). (Another option is to turn left onto the first dirt road upon reaching the island and to take this little-traveled road eastward.) Once inside the park, the road continues for about 8 miles. The best place for migrant landbirds is the **Youth Camp** area on the left (0.7). At the boat ramp at the end of the road, scan for sea ducks in winter and wading-birds and American Oystercatchers year round. Several pairs of oystercatchers nest on oyster bars just off Goose Island to the north. Return to the main road and turn left to the first of two boardwalks on the left. Check the beaches here (and elsewhere on the island) for Northern Gannets (often seen from shore in winter), wading-birds, sea ducks including Common Goldeneyes and scoters (winter), shorebirds, and larids. The boardwalks lead to St. George Sound, which has sea ducks and other waterbirds in winter and wading-birds year round. At the campground between the two board-walks, check for migrant and wintering landbirds in the trees and brushy areas, which may have sparrows and finches in winter. Gray Kingbirds breed here. Toward the end of the road and beyond, the beach is less crowded. A few (3 to 4 pairs) Snowy Plovers nest in the dunes and may be observed along the shore year round. Other wading-birds, shorebirds, and larids will also be present here.

Contact: Dr. Julian D. Bruce St. George Island State Park, P.O. Box 62, Eastpoint, FL 32328; 850/927-2111.

Apalachicola National Forest (558,380 acres; no fee), the largest of the three national forests in Florida, extends from the Apalachicola River east to the Ochlockonee River, a distance of about 35 miles. The four resident specialties of Florida's pinewoods, Red-cockaded Woodpecker (often just shortened to "RCW" by researchers), Brown-headed Nuthatch, Pine Warbler, and Bachman's Sparrow, occur widely in the forest. As noted earlier, Apalachicola National Forest contains the largest population of RCWs in the world. In spring 1993, the forest had 685 clusters (i.e., families) of RCWs, representing about 1,500 birds. Other birds of interest are such breeding species as Swallow-tailed and Mississippi Kites, Broad-winged Hawk, Red-headed Woodpecker, Eastern Wood-Pewee, Acadian Flycatcher, Wood Thrush, and Swainson's, Kentucky, Prothonotary, and Hooded Warblers. Another feature of the forest is Henslow's Sparrow, which is a fairly common to common migrant and winter resident from mid-October to mid-April in pinewoods with a grassy ground cover, and in open savannahs. (A savannah is a prairie or bog in pine flatwoods.) These savannahs may also contain other grassland species, including Yellow Rail and Grasshopper and Le Conte's Sparrows.

The forest is divided into the Apalachicola and the Wakulla ranger districts. Overall, habitats in the Apalachicola ranger district are more diverse and less disturbed, but the largest sandhills tract is located in the Wakulla ranger district. The forest service currently burns about 30,000 acres of the forest annually to maintain the fire-adapted plant communities. An emphasis on uneven-aged pine forests also furthers the goal of integrated ecosystem management. Detailed publications and maps are available from either district office or from the supervisor's office in Tallahassee. Particularly useful publications and maps are Recreation Guide R8-RG16 for National Forests in Florida, Recreation Area Directory (free), and the Apalachicola National Forest map ($3), which is essential.

The following section includes a birding route in the western part of the forest. (A shorter, less-scenic birding route close to Tallahassee is on page 72.) The village of Sumatra is an excellent starting point to reach prime habitats within the Apalachicola ranger district. From Eastpoint, go east on US-98 to SR-65 (3.0) and turn left. Drive to the Sumatra

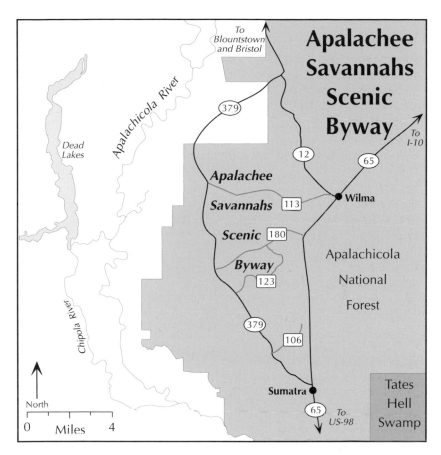

Grocery Store at SR-379 (26.9) and turn left onto **Apalachee Savannahs Scenic Byway**. An 8-mile section of the byway from here to FR-180 offers a variety of habitats and is the heart of the naturally open savannahs dominated by grasses, sedges, and herbs. Other pristine habitats located along or adjacent to the route are mature Longleaf Pine/Wiregrass woods and titi swamp, cypress stringers, and bayheads, picturesquely inter-woven with the pinewoods and savannahs. Red-cockaded Wood-peckers, Brown-headed Nuthatches, and Bachman's Sparrows are all common in this area. In winter, Sedge Wrens and Henslow's Sparrows are also common in savannahs here. A particularly good location for Henslow's Sparrows is the two savannahs and adjacent forest at the junction of SR-379 and FR-123 northwest of Sumatra (6.2). Two forest roads also provide a loop of 6.2 miles around one large semi-continuous savannah. Follow FR-123 east from CR-379 to FR-180, turn left, and loop back to SR-379. (FR-106, closer to SR-65, is another short 1.7-miles road through typical savannah habitat.)

Contact: Supervisor's Office, National Forests in Florida, Woodcrest Office Park, 325 John Knox Road, Suite F-100, Tallahassee, FL 32303; 850/942-9300, Apalachicola Ranger District Office, Florida Highway 20, P.O. Box 579, Bristol, FL 32321; 850/643-2282, Wakulla Ranger District Office, U.S. Highway 319, Route 6, Box 7860, Crawfordville, FL 32327; 850/926-3561.

Two mainland beaches west of Carrabelle off US-98 have modest numbers of shorebirds depending on the tide and the time of year. From Carrabelle, drive west to Cafe Snapper's near Carrabelle Beach (2.1), turn left, and park near the beach. Walk east to the tip, where most of the shorebirds congregate (0.7). At low tide, American Oystercatchers usually feed on the exposed oyster bars, and other species (e.g., Piping Plover) are possible as well.

Yent Bayou is currently an undeveloped subdivision that allows access to the beach. From the public parking area at Carrabelle Beach, drive west on US-98 to the conspicuous sign *Hidden Beaches at Yent Bayou* (4.8) and turn left. Bear right and drive to the end of the dirt road (0.7).

Dog Island, about 3 miles off the coast at Carrabelle, is excellent for migrants in spring and fall and for shorebirds and larids in winter. About 1,300 acres (75 percent) of the island is owned by The Nature Conservancy. The island is accessible only by boat. During the peak season, a ferry ($14/Florida residents, $18/non-residents) in Carrabelle runs twice a day on weekends (morning and evening). The ferry departs from the Carrabelle River several blocks south of "downtown" Carrabelle at 11 am and returns at 4 pm. From US-98, head south on CR-30A to where it turns left (0.5). The dock is opposite this intersection. Dog Island is a breeding site for Snowy and Wilson's Plovers, American Oystercatchers, Least Terns, and Black Skimmers. During spring and fall migration, large numbers of migrant landbirds may be found. A banding station set up a few years ago has recorded many significant migrants. A Sage Thrasher was banded here in November 1995.

East from Carrabelle on US-98 is Lanark Village (5.5). About a mile offshore is Lanark Reef, the premier site in the Big Bend region for nesting seabirds and migrant and wintering shorebirds. The reef, which can be reached only by private boat, is a single system at least 3 miles long during extreme low tide, but is transformed at high tide into two small islands separated by about 1½ miles of water. To reach the island, launch your boat at the Fina gas station on the south side of US-98 ($4), which is directly north of the reef, or use a vacant lot opposite the golf course (0.3) to put your canoe into the water.

Brown Pelicans (100 to 250 pairs), four species of wading-birds, American Oystercatchers, Wilson's Plovers, Willets, Laughing Gulls, and Royal and Least Terns all nest here. *During the breeding season, nesting colonies should be avoided to protect the birds.* Numerous shorebirds are found on the island in fall and winter, including Piping Plovers (up to 90 birds, but 30 to 50 are more typical), Marbled Godwits (common), and Red Knots. Reddish Egrets are usually present year round. Lanark Reef is a favorite roosting site for larids year round, especially terns during migration and in winter. Featured species are Sandwich, Common, and Black Terns, although Forster's Tern is most numerous. (In winter 1994-1995, over 3,000 terns roosted here.)

Directions for coastal areas to the east continue on page 73.

MARIANNA AREA

One of the unique natural areas in the state is **Florida Caverns State Park** (1,284 acres; standard fee). To reach it from I-10 westbound, exit (#21) at SR-71 and go north to its end at US-90. Turn left and proceed to another section of SR-71 (1.4; second traffic light) and turn right. At CR-166 (Caverns Road), turn left to the park entrance on the right (2.9). From I-10 eastbound, exit (# 20) at CR-267 and go northeast to its end at SR-73 (Jefferson Street). Turn left (the road becomes CR-167) to the park entrance on the left (2.9). Brown-headed Nuthatches, Pine Warblers, and Bachman's Sparrows are common in the pinewoods. In spring and summer, Swallow-tailed and Mississippi Kites, Broad-winged Hawk, Eastern Wood-Pewee, Acadian Flycatcher, Wood Thrush, Swainson's, Kentucky, and Hooded Warblers, and Summer Tanager are species which breed in the park. In winter, look for Red-breasted Nuthatch (irruptive), Winter Wren, Golden-crowned Kinglet, Fox and White-throated Sparrows, Dark-eyed Junco, and Rusty Blackbird. Winter Wrens are often found near the spot where the Chipola River disappears underground, and elsewhere along the river.

Contact: Florida Caverns State Park, 3345 Caverns Road, Marianna, FL 32446; 850/482-9598.

From Marianna, go east on US-90 about 12 miles to SR-69 and turn right. At Old Spanish Trail (0.7), turn right to some ponds on the left (1.0). A Vermilion Flycatcher has wintered here the past few years, and the ponds can be good for waterfowl and shorebirds in winter.

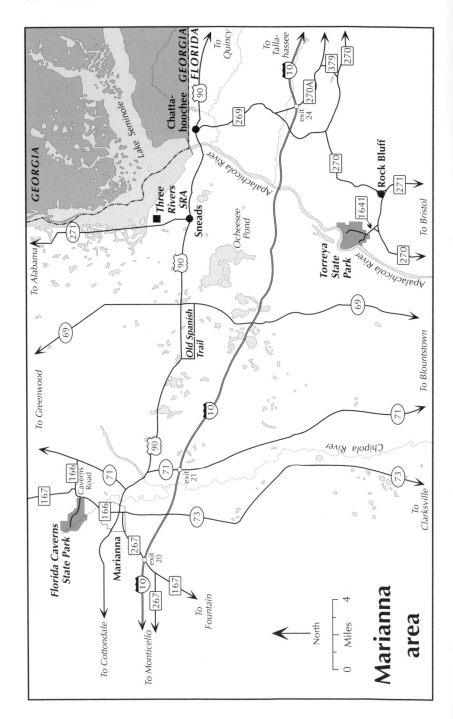

Marianna area

Return to US-90 and continue east to Sneads. At SR-271, turn left onto Rivers Road (2.0), and turn right to Three Rivers State Recreation Area (683 acres; $2/vehicle). In winter, a good assortment of waterfowl may be found on the lake, including Tundra Swans on occasion.

Contact: Three Rivers State Recreation Area, Route 1, Box 15A, Sneads, FL 32460; 850/482-9006.

About 10 miles south of Sneads on the east side of the Apalachicola River is picturesque **Torreya State Park** (1,063 acres; $2/vehicle). To reach it from I-10, exit (#24) onto CR-270-A and go south. At CR-379 (2.9), turn right to CR-270 and turn right again. Proceed west to Rock Bluff (9.0) and continue west. At CR-1641, turn right to the park ahead (2.5). To reach the park from SR-71 in Blountstown, go east on SR-20 to SR-12 in Bristol (4.5) and turn left. At CR-1641 (6.4), turn left to the park (5.9). From the coast west of Apalachicola, take SR-71 north to Blountstown. From Eastpoint or Carrabelle, take SR-65 north to SR-20, then west to Bristol.

Two endangered trees, the Torreya Tree and Florida Yew, are main attractions of the park. From the Gregory House, a majestic pre-Civil-War house on the bluffs of the Apalachicola River, Swallow-tailed and Mississippi Kites can be seen in spring and summer. Pines at the campground contain Brown-headed Nuthatches and Pine Warblers, which may be joined in winter by Brown Creepers, Golden-crowned Kinglets, and Purple Finches. Bachman's Sparrows prefer the grassy areas near the entrance. The nature trail from the Gregory House down the bluff to just above the river is good for Winter Wrens in winter, and in spring and summer for many breeding species, including Louisiana Waterthrush. From the Gregory House parking area, drive the main park road back to the picnic area, where there are other trails. Bald Eagles have nested here for the past few years.

Contact: Torreya State Park, Route 2, Box 70, Bristol, FL 32321; 850/643-2674.

TALLAHASSEE

The state capital of Florida, Tallahassee, is located in the "Red Hills" at the eastern edge of the Panhandle. This physiographic region, named for its red clay soil, was used for agriculture by Indians and later by early settlers. After the Civil War, many plantations were purchased by wealthy industrialists for "quail" (Northern Bobwhite) hunting. Many of these plantations remain intact today and contain some of the finest Longleaf Pine forests remaining in the state. The big pines in the Red Hills are the last stronghold in Florida for White-breasted Nuthatch, which formerly occurred widely in the state. House Finches first bred in Florida in Tallahassee in 1989 and are now fairly common in parts of the city. Tallahassee has a small but active birding community, served by a southern Georgia/northern Florida birding hotline at 912/244-9190.

For birders in Tallahassee on business, two small city parks offer fair birding possibilities within a short distance of downtown. Myers Park (16 acres; no fee) is less than five blocks from the Capitol. It attracts the usual spring and fall migrants and supports breeding pairs of Broad-winged Hawks, Barred Owls, and Yellow-throated Vireos. To reach the park, take Apalachee Parkway (US-90/27) east from the Capitol to Myers Park Drive (0.6) and turn right. The park is one block ahead.

A park in the Indianhead neighborhood is also visited frequently by local birders. In fall this park can have numerous migrants. Notable breeding birds include Mississippi Kites, Broad-winged Hawks, White-breasted Nuthatches (resident), and occasionally Louisiana Water-thrushes and Kentucky Warblers. To reach the park, take Apalachee Parkway (US-90/27) east from the Capitol to CR-265 (Magnolia Drive, the first major intersection) and turn right. At Hokolin Nene (0.9) turn left and proceed two blocks to where the road crosses a creek. A foot-path on the left parallels the creek on both sides and runs through the center of the park. It is acceptable to park on the street. Be sure to depart the area the same way you entered; it is easy to get lost amid the circuitous streets with strange names.

Two sewage treatment facilities on the south side of Tallahassee can be good for migrant shorebirds. From SR-61 (Monroe Street) just south of the Capitol, go west on CR-362 (Gaines Street) to CR-371 (Lake Bradford Road) (1.5) and turn left. Bear left onto CR-373A (1.1), which soon becomes CR-373. **Springhill Road Sewage Treatment Facility** (no fee) is on the left just past CR-263 (Capitol Circle Southwest) (0.1). Obtain permission from the plant office (open 8 am to 4 pm Monday through Friday and sporadically on weekends) to walk around the holding-ponds.

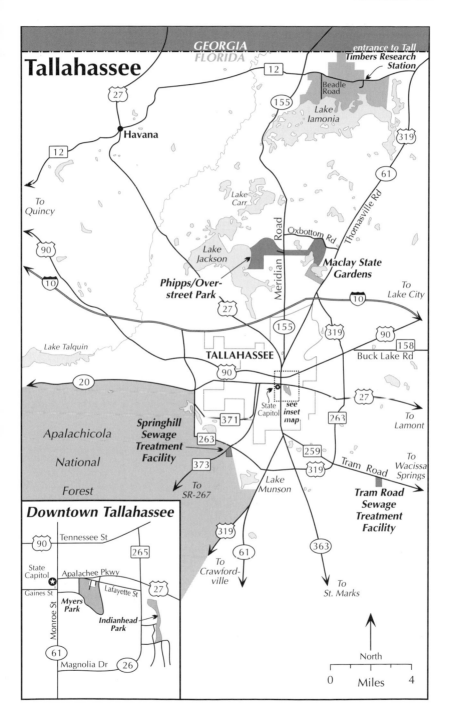

Tallahassee

GEORGIA
FLORIDA

entrance to Tall
Timbers Research
Station

Beadle
Road

Lake
Iamonia

Havana

To
Quincy

Lake
Carr

Oxbottom Rd

Lake
Jackson

Phipps/Over-
street Park

Maclay State
Gardens

To
Lake City

Lake Talquin

TALLAHASSEE

Buck Lake Rd

Apalachicola

State
Capitol

see
inset
map

To
Lamont

National

Springhill
Sewage
Treatment
Facility

To
Wacissa
Springs

Tram Road

Forest

To
SR-267

Lake
Munson

Tram Road
Sewage
Treatment
Facility

Downtown Tallahassee

Tennessee St

State
Capitol

Apalachee Pkwy

Lafayette St

Gaines St

Myers
Park

Indianhead
Park

To
Crawford-
ville

To
St. Marks

Monroe St

Magnolia Dr

North

0   Miles   4

Do not drive on the dikes separating the ponds. During weekends and holidays, permission to enter the plant may be obtained by calling 850/891-1011 in advance.

For a brief stop at Lake Munson, which usually has wintering waterfowl, go east on CR-263 (Capitol Circle Southwest) to US-319 (Crawfordville Road) (2.2) and turn right. At Munson Boat Landing Road (0.6), turn right to the lake (0.2).

To reach **Tram Road Sewage Treatment Facility** (no fee), return to CR-263 (Capitol Circle Southeast) and turn right to CR-259 (Tram Road) (3.5). Turn right to the facility on the right (2.8); look for the corn silos. Check in at the office, usually open only on weekdays (8 am to 4 pm). To obtain permission to enter on weekends and holidays, call 850/898-1295 in advance. You are allowed to drive south on the paved road to the sprayfields, but *do not drive on the gravel side roads.* The holding-ponds near the office usually contain hundreds of wintering ducks (mostly Bufflehead and Lesser Scaup). Three of Florida's four Ross's Goose sightings were made here: 1987, 1991, and 1995. Shorebirds can be common at the ponds in winter or migration. Fields south of the ponds contain many sparrows in winter. Other rarities reported at Tram Road have included Brant, American Golden-Plover, American Avocet, Franklin's Gull, Short-eared Owl, and Horned Lark.

To reach Alfred B. Maclay State Gardens (251 acres; $3.50/vehicle) from the Capitol, go north on SR-61 (Monroe Street). Bear right onto SR-61 (now called Thomasville Road) (1.0) and continue to the entrance on the left (5.6, or 0.6 past the junction of US-319). From I-10 take the Thomasville Road exit, go north, and proceed as above. The gardens are good for breeding species such as Mississippi Kite, Purple Gallinule, and White-breasted Nuthatch, but are rarely birded, perhaps because of the entrance fee.

Adjacent to Maclay Gardens on the north and west is Phipps/Overstreet Park (1,450 acres; no fee) acquired in 1994. The park includes frontage along Lake Jackson, a large beech/magnolia forest, and sandhills. To reach the park from Maclay Gardens, continue north on US-319/SR-61 (Thomasville Road) to Oxbottom Road (1.2) and turn left. At the T intersection at SR-155 (Meridian Road) (4.0), turn left. The park is on the right; look for the soccer fields (1.3). Trails and other amenities were under construction at the time of writing, so obtain directions at the information booth near the soccer fields. A bird list is being compiled, but a few of the breeding species are White-breasted Nuthatch, Kentucky Warbler, Yellow-breasted Chat, and Field Sparrow.

North of town is **Tall Timbers Research Station** (4,000 acres; no fee), an ecological research institute located just south of the Georgia/Florida state line. The station is working actively to preserve Red Hills habitats by purchasing conservation easements on local plantations, which removes development rights to the properties while allowing hunting and selective timber harvesting to continue. To date, over 30,000 acres have been protected in this manner. To reach Tall Timbers from I-10, go north on US-319/SR-61 (Thomasville Road) to CR-12 (13.3), and turn left. The station is on the left, just before the WCTV tower (2.7). (Prior to being lowered to 300 feet in 1989, the WCTV tower was a significant source of tower-kill data used to study nocturnal migration of numerous species. The most amazing bird recorded from here occurred the night of 10-11 September 1964, during Hurricane *Dora*, when a Black-capped Petrel hit the tower.)

Bear left at the end of a straight dirt road and look for the white wooden building on the left (0.4). The station contains a variety of habitats, including hardwood forest, fields, and prescribed-burned mixed pine forests. A 1.3-mile nature trail traverses these habitats and offers the chance to observe one of Florida's most restricted permanent residents: White-breasted Nuthatch. Other permanent residents that may be seen on the trail are Cooper's Hawk, Wild Turkey, Hairy Woodpecker, Brown-headed Nuthatch, and Bachman's Sparrow. Spring and summer residents include Broad-winged Hawk, Acadian Flycatcher, Eastern Wood-Pewee, Wood Thrush, Prothonotary, Kentucky, and Hooded Warblers, and Yellow-breasted Chat. In winter, look for Sedge Wren and sparrows in the field.

The nature trail begins behind and ends to the left of the building. The trail is open to the public from 8:30 am to 4:30 pm Monday through Friday and at other times by prior arrangement. *All visitors must check in at the main building.* A bird window overlooking a pond is also open to the public by appointment. The station is an archive for photographs of rare Florida birds and maintains an excellent regional bird specimen collection. These collections and the research buildings are available to the public by appointment only.

To reach another portion of the station, return to CR-12 and turn left to Beadle Road (2.4), and turn left. The road goes through a mature beech/magnolia forest with typical breeding species such as Wood Thrush, Louisiana Waterthrush, and Kentucky Warbler before ending at Lake Iamonia. A small boat launch here provides a good view of the lake. Look for Anhinga, wading-birds, Bald Eagle, and Purple Gallinule.

Do not cross the fence. The road is public property, but the surrounding land, owned by Tall Timbers, is off-limits to the public.

Contact: Tall Timbers Research Station, Inc., Route 1, Box 678, Tallahassee, FL 32312; 850/893-4153.

Canada Geese were formerly abundant winter residents in the Tallahassee/St. Marks area, but the geese now winter north of Florida. (Land-use changes farther north now allow the geese to forage in agricultural fields rather than having to migrate farther south to Gulf coastal marshes.) In order for Florida sportsmen to continue to hunt the species, the Florida Game and Fish Commission released many geese of the non-migratory race *Branta canadensis maxima*, the Giant Canada Goose, into the Tallahassee area in the late 1960s. The species is now established in many areas east of the city. To reach the best area from downtown, go northeast on US-90 (Mahan Drive). After crossing US-319 (Capitol Circle), continue to CR-158 (Buck Lake Road) (0.7) and turn right. For the next 3 to 5 miles, you should see Canada Geese and other waterbirds (including Wood Storks) in the many lakes and ponds.

Apalachicola National Forest is detailed on pages 62-64, but a section close to Tallahassee may be visited to search for Red-cockaded Woodpeckers and other species. A good loop trip into the Wakulla ranger district begins between Tallahassee and Crawfordville. From US-319, turn west onto SR-267. You are now in the forest. Drive about 5 miles to the "Entering Leon County" sign. Turn left onto FR-309 (opposite

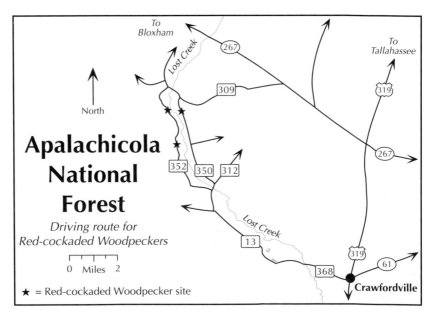

To Bloxham

Lost Creek

267

To Tallahassee

309

319

North

Apalachicola National Forest

352 350 312

267

Driving route for Red-cockaded Woodpeckers

Lost Creek

13

319

0   Miles   2

368   61

★ = Red-cockaded Woodpecker site

Crawfordville

CR-267A, Helen Guard Station Road). At FR-350 (4.8), turn left. Look for Brown-headed Nuthatches and Bachman's Sparrows here. The first woodpecker cluster is about ¼ mile south; cavity trees are painted with white bands. At the junction with FR-312 (5.5), turn right. After the bridge over Lost Creek (0.2), turn right onto FR-352 (0.2). This area is good for Swainson's Warblers in spring and summer. Two additional RCW clusters are located about 3 and 4½ miles from FR-350. (Again, look for the white bands.) After about 6 miles from FR-350, turn right onto FR-309. Past another bridge over Lost Creek (0.6), bear left to return to SR-267.

PANACEA AREA

To reach the Gulf coast from Tallahassee, go south on US-319, bear right onto US-98, and continue south. Just north of Panacea, turn right onto CR-372A (Bottoms Road), which passes through salt marshes before ending at a boat ramp overlooking Dickerson Bay. The area is good for wading-birds, shorebirds, larids, and "Sharp-tailed" (winter) and Seaside Sparrows. Good concentrations of Wood Storks may be found here in fall.

To reach Mashes Sands County Park (50¢/vehicle), return to US-98, go south to CR-372 (Mashes Sands Road) just north of the bridge over Ochlockonee Bay, and turn left. Marsh Wrens and "Sharp-tailed" (winter) and Seaside Sparrows are found in the marshes, and Gray Kingbirds often perch on wires along the road in spring and summer. At the end of the road (3.0), the mudflats can be great at low tide for wading-birds (including Roseate Spoonbills) and shorebirds (including Piping Plovers and Red Knots). Black Terns may be seen during fall migration.

Return to US-98 and continue south. After crossing Ochlockonee Bay, turn left onto SR-370 (1.3). At the T intersection, turn right to **Alligator Point**. *Almost the entire peninsula is private property, so bird only from the road.* Alligator Point is one of the few spots along Florida's Gulf coast where scoters winter annually. All three species (Black, Surf, and White-winged) occur here, along with flocks of Lesser and Greater Scaups and other ducks and waterbirds. As you drive along the beach, scan the offshore waters for Red-throated Loon (rare), Northern Gannet, Common Goldeneye, Bufflehead, and even jaegers. Be sure to scan Alligator Harbor (north of the road) frequently, because scoters and other sea ducks are also seen here regularly, and larids frequently perch on docks in the bay. American Oystercatchers breed at Peninsula Point and along the eastern half of Alligator Harbor. On powerlines along the road,

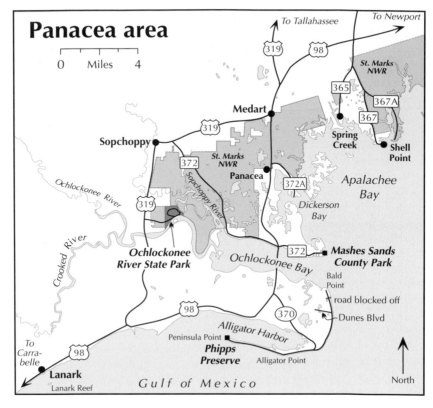

Panacea area

0   Miles   4

To Tallahassee

To Newport

319   98

St. Marks NWR

365

367A

Medart

367

Sopchoppy

Spring Creek

Shell Point

St. Marks NWR

372

Panacea

372A

Apalachee Bay

Ochlockonee River

319

Dickerson Bay

Crooked River

Ochlockonee River State Park

Ochlockonee Bay

372   Mashes Sands County Park

Bald Point

road blocked off

98

Alligator Harbor

370   Dunes Blvd

To Carra-belle

98

Peninsula Point

Phipps Preserve   Alligator Point

Lanark

Lanark Reef

Gulf of Mexico

North

watch for Eurasian Collared-Doves (now resident) and Gray Kingbirds (spring and summer). The latter species is a specialty of the area, with about 15 breeding pairs.

Directly across from the KOA campground is the southernmost tip of land on the peninsula. It is a good place to set up a scope and scan the Gulf.

At the very end of the peninsula is Phipps Preserve, owned by The Nature Conservancy. Shorebirds (including Snowy and Piping Plovers), gulls, and terns will roost here. However, access to the preserve is by scheduled field trip only; *do not cross the fence on your own.* Call TNC for information at 850/222-0199. Check the pines in this area for wintering Red-breasted Nuthatches (irruptive) and other wintering and migrant landbirds.

Turn around and backtrack to the T intersection. Continue north along the shoreline toward **Bald Point**. Dunes Boulevard on the left (2.0) is a small road through an unsuccessful subdivision. The oaks in this area can be excellent for migrant landbirds, especially in spring.

The final 0.6 mile of SR-370 is gated off pending future disposition of the property. Park before the gate, walk to the beach, then continue to the northern tip. (If the gate is down, you may drive to the end.) Bald Point is a productive site to scan in winter for sea ducks and other waterbirds, wading-birds, shorebirds, and larids. Marsh Wrens and "Sharp-tailed" (winter) and Seaside Sparrows occur in the salt marshes. In fall, watch powerlines along the road for White-winged Doves, Western Kingbirds, and Scissor-tailed Flycatchers. Check the oak hammocks along the road for migrants.

Northwest of Alligator Point is **Ochlockonee River State Park** (392 acres; standard fee). To reach it, return to US-98 and turn left to US-319 (9.0). Turn right to the park on the right (7.0). From US-98 at Medart, go west on US-319 to Sopchoppy, then continue south on US-319 to the park on the left (4.8). Pinewoods in the park should yield Red-cockaded Woodpeckers, Eastern Wood-Pewees (spring and summer), Brown-headed Nuthatches, Pine Warblers, and Bachman's Sparrows. RCW-cavity trees are marked with white paint. Henslow's Sparrows are often found in winter in fairly wet, short grassy areas of recently burned pinewoods and under the powerlines across the main road.

Contact: Ochlockonee River State Park, P.O. Box 5, Sopchoppy, FL 32358; 850/962-2771.

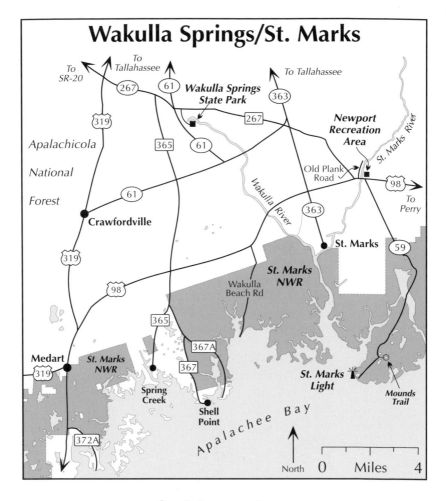

Wakulla Springs/St. Marks

ST. MARKS AREA

One of the best birding sites in the area is **Edward Ball Wakulla Springs State Park** (2,860 acres; standard fee). The entrance is located just east of the junction of SR-61 and CR-267 between Tallahassee and Crawfordville. At over 250 feet deep, Wakulla Springs is the deepest spring in the world and releases about 850 million gallons of water every day. The park contains extensive hardwood forests, but the main attractions are the waterbirds. The best way to see them is to take the 30-minute "Jungle Cruise" glass-bottom-boat ride ($4.50/person) from the Wakulla Springs Lodge. Besides the many ducks that winter at the springs (especially

American Wigeon), you should see Anhinga, wading-birds, Purple Gallinule (rare in winter), and Limpkin. In summer, Yellow-crowned Night-Heron nests are easily visible. Because the birds have no fear of the boat, the cruise provides excellent photographic opportunities. (Birders on the right side of the boat have a view of the shore, while those on the left view the water.) A short woodland path next to the entrance booth can be good for migrant and wintering landbirds. Watch for American Woodcocks along the park road before dawn.

Contact: Wakulla Springs State Park, 1 Spring Drive, Wakulla Springs, FL 32305; 850/922-3633. Lodge: 850/224-5950.

After leaving Wakulla Springs, turn right onto CR-267 to its end at US-98, then turn left. Just before the bridge over the St. Marks River (0.4), turn left onto unpaved Old Plank Road. All the land here is privately owned, so *bird only from the road.* In spring and summer, look for breeding Swainson's and Kentucky Warblers and Yellow-breasted Chats in brushy areas for the next mile. (Stop at the point where you can smell the sulphur springs.) Swallow-tailed and Mississippi Kites also breed here.

Return to US-98, cross the St. Marks River, and turn left to Newport Recreation Area. In fall the area can be good for migrants, and Winter Wrens may be present along the river in winter.

Cross US-98 and go south on SR-59. Wet brushy areas underneath the first set of powerlines across the road have been a good spot for

Limpkin
Louise Zemaitis

Henslow's Sparrows in winter, but the birds seem harder to find in recent years. Continue south on SR-59 to **St. Marks National Wildlife Refuge** (65,248 upland and 32,000 submerged acres; $3/vehicle), one of the best birding areas in Florida. In winter, a large variety of waterfowl is found here. The woodlands around the visitor center on the right (open 10 am to 5 pm but *closed on weekends*) can be good for migrant and wintering landbirds.

For the next 5 miles, the main refuge road (SR-59) offers access to many birding sites. The numerous impoundments offer excellent birding in winter for ducks and other waterbirds, and the woodlands can be good for wintering and migrant landbirds.

Mounds Pool Nature Trail on the left is worth hiking. Shorebirds (including Long-billed Dowitchers and Stilt Sandpipers) can be common along the dikes, and this is one of the most reliable spots in Florida for wintering Snow Geese. Black Rails have been heard in the pools but probably occur here only irregularly. A few (1 to 5) Vermilion Flycatchers have wintered along the back dike of Stoney Bayou #2 since the early 1990s. In winter, many shorebirds roost near the tower on Mounds Pool. Wintering and migrant landbirds can be common in the oaks near the restrooms.

At the end of SR-59, scan the bay for Brant (rare), Common Goldeneye, Redhead, Greater Scaup, Bufflehead, scoters, and other species. A Western Grebe was found here in November 1990. Walk the dike to the right to look for more ducks and shorebirds. Take the path down the beach (*sometimes posted off-limits, in which case stay out*) to the left past the lighthouse for about 0.1 mile to the palms and cut through to a dry section of the salt marsh. Marsh Wrens and "Sharp-tailed" (winter) and Seaside Sparrows are found here. Check the mudflats for Wilson's Plover, Whimbrel, and Gull-billed Tern in season. The oaks around the lighthouse and the saltbushes and myrtles around Lighthouse Pond are good for migrant and wintering landbirds. On 3 July 1983, Florida's first Yellow-nosed Albatross was photographed gliding around the lighthouse!

The Wakulla Beach section of the refuge has shorebirds and other waterbirds at low tide. Marsh Wrens and "Sharp-tailed" (winter) and Seaside Sparrows are found in the marshes. To reach this area from Newport, go west on US-98, cross SR-363 and the Wakulla River (2.4), and turn left onto the first dirt road (1.2). The beach is at the end of the road (4.0). Check the woodlands along the road for landbirds.

Contact: St. Marks National Wildlife Refuge, P.O. Box 68, St. Marks, FL 32355; 850/925-6121.

Black Rail
Georges Dremeaux

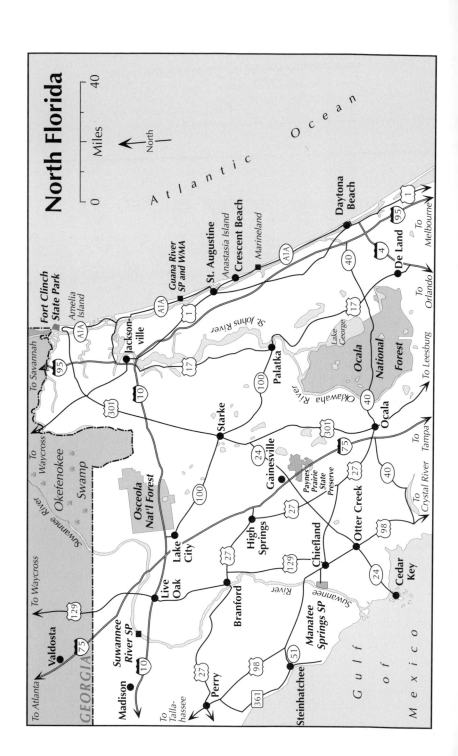

NORTH FLORIDA

As might be expected, this part of the state is similar in many ways to neighboring Georgia. Uplands are covered with mixed forests of Longleaf Pine, Turkey Oak, Live Oak, and other hardwoods. The many tree farms are planted with Slash Pines, and the river bottoms are lined with Tupelo swamps. Along the Atlantic Coast a sandy ridge representing a former shoreline extends south all the way to Miami. This ridge, formerly covered with scrub vegetation and supporting a large population of Florida Scrub-Jays, is now largely destroyed and fragmented by oceanside developments. This development, combined with widespread fire exclusion, has caused the range of the jays to decline severely in North Florida. Except for scattered small groups near Cedar Key and along the Atlantic coast, Florida Scrub-Jays are now limited in North Florida to the extensive scrub region centered around Ocala National Forest.

Most of the breeding species of the Panhandle occur also in North Florida (White-breasted Nuthatch is a notable exception), and many of these reach their southern breeding limits in the state in the North Florida region. Some of these species include Mississippi Kite, Broad-winged Hawk, Eastern Wood-Pewee, Wood Thrush, Gray Catbird, Prairie Warbler (eastern race), Hooded Warbler, Louisiana Waterthrush, Field Sparrow, and Orchard Oriole. A few House Finches are now breeding in Gainesville and elsewhere, but the species is still extremely local in North Florida. Although present in small numbers south to Merritt Island, Painted Bunting is easier to find in spring and summer in the Jacksonville and St. Augustine areas. Breeding species of the Florida peninsula that reach their northern breeding ranges in the region include Glossy Ibis, Mottled Duck, Sandhill Crane, Burrowing Owl (except a small isolated colony in the western Panhandle), and Florida Scrub-Jay.

The three largest cities in North Florida are Jacksonville and St. Augustine on the Atlantic coast and Gainesville inland. The Gulf coast contains extensive salt marshes rather than sand beaches, so the area is still relatively undeveloped. The interior of North Florida is composed of extensive areas of planted Slash Pines. Except for Gainesville and Ocala, human development is rather sparse and is contained in many small towns. The Atlantic coast of North Florida, with its wide sandy beaches, is developed extensively, like the rest of Florida's east coast.

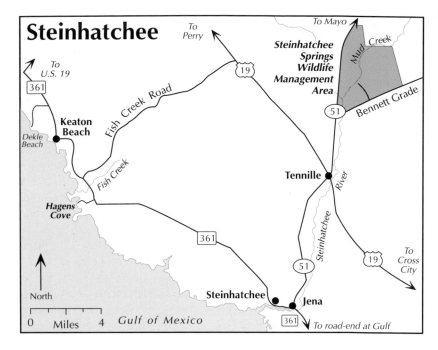

North Florida – Gulf Coast

BIG BEND REGION

The northern peninsular Gulf coast is part of the Big Bend region of Florida that extends west to the Alligator Point area in the eastern Panhandle. Because of the shallowness of the water offshore, wave action is insufficient to create sand beaches. Rather, coastal areas are covered extensively by *Juncus* (needle-rush) and *Spartina* (cordgrass) salt marshes that contain populations of Clapper Rails, Marsh Wrens, Seaside Sparrows, and in a few areas, Black Rails. Just above high-tide line are extensive hammocks of Cabbage Palms, Florida's state tree (even though palms technically are not trees). A die-off of hammocks in some coastal areas appears to be due to increased soil salinity caused by rising sea levels.

Most of the Big Bend is sparsely inhabited and relatively unexplored. The few towns are small fishing and shellfishing villages on the Gulf and old logging towns inland. The state has been purchasing large portions of the coastal hardwood hammocks in the Big Bend, but much of these areas is inaccessible to birders in passenger vehicles. The few birding sites listed below are all small and lack most facilities.

Hagens Cove, a part of Big Bend Wildlife Management Area (58,177 acres; no fee), features a natural sand beach, rare in the region. To reach this area from US-19 south of Perry (4.5 miles from US-98), go southwest on CR-361 and turn right to Hagens Cove Road about 5 miles south of Keaton Beach. To reach Hagens Cove from the south, go west from US-19 on SR-51 in Tennille to CR-361 in Steinhatchee and go north about 12 miles. An observation tower at the end of the road offers an impressive view of the surrounding marshes and mudflats. In winter, numerous ducks (including an Oldsquaw once), shorebirds, and larids are present, especially at low tide. In spring and summer, look for Gray Kingbirds. The area east of CR-361 is the Jena unit of the wildlife management area, a large intact area that has been little-birded. On the Fish Creek CBC in 1989, 16 Fox Sparrows were found here. The hammocks should be great for fall migrants, but the area is accessible only during hunting season.

A well-known site for Black Rail is located south of Steinhatchee in the Jena unit of the Big Bend Wildlife Management Area. From Steinhatchee, follow CR-361 to its end after about 12 miles. The 13 March 1993 "Storm of the Century" damaged parts of the road, but it can still be driven if you use caution. One site along CR-361 recommended by Noel Wamer is the trail that leads east (left) from the end of the road.

Steinhatchee Springs Wildlife Management Area (5,262 acres; no fee) contains cypress swamps and flooded hardwood forests reached from old logging trams (roads). To reach it from US-19/98 in Tennille, go north on SR-51 to the Water Management District sign at Bennett Grade (3.7), and turn right to a tram road (2.1). Turn left and proceed into the swamp. In 1993 and 1994 Swainson's Warblers were suspected of breeding near Mud Creek and the Steinhatchee River, and breeding was confirmed in April 1995. The property is owned by the Suwannee River Water Management District (904/362-1001); maps may be obtained from the Florida Game and Fresh Water Fish Commission in Lake City (904/758-0525). The area is leased for private hunting in winter, but some access is available in spring and summer.

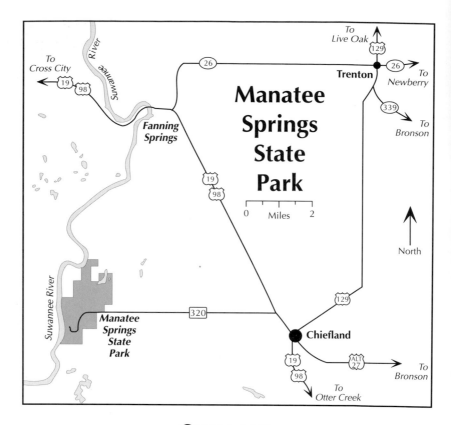

CHIEFLAND

Manatee Springs State Park (2,075 acres; standard fee) contains frontage along the famed Suwannee River. The park, located north and west of Chiefland, can be reached by turning west from US-19 onto CR-320 to the entrance (6.0). The springs discharge about 117 million gallons of water per day. Limpkins are observed in the park frequently, and manatees are seen on occasion. The park is best in fall, when migrant landbirds can be common.

Contact: Manatee Springs State Park, Route 2, Box 617, Chiefland, FL 32626; 352/493-6072.

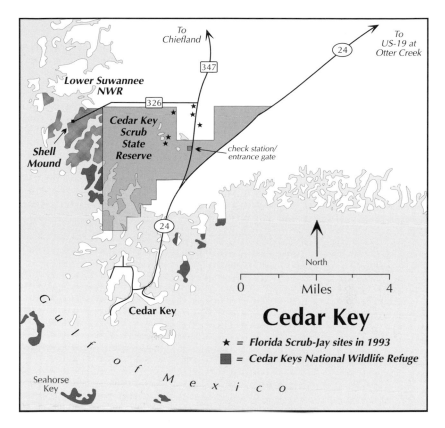

Cedar Key

★ = Florida Scrub-Jay sites in 1993
■ = Cedar Keys National Wildlife Refuge

CEDAR KEY

Located about 20 miles southwest of US-19 at the end of SR-24, Cedar Key is out of the way, but it is worth a visit if you are not traveling farther south in the peninsula. In 1867 John Muir spent three months here after completing his famous thousand-mile walk to the Gulf. Birders from Gainesville visit Cedar Key regularly, as it offers their nearest coastal birding. The causeway between the mainland and the islands attracts wading-birds, shorebirds, and larids at low tide. In winter, numerous other species such as American White Pelican and sea ducks are present. In November 1992 a Pacific Loon was observed off the fishing-pier, and Florida's third Long-billed Murrelet was observed here in March 1994. Eurasian Collared-Doves are now one of the most numerous landbirds on the islands.

Offshore from town is Cedar Keys National Wildlife Refuge (780 acres; no fee), consisting of 12 small keys that support one of the largest wading-bird rookeries in Florida. An average of 25,000 pairs nests here annually. To protect the birds, the interiors of the keys are off-limits year round. Except on Seahorse Key, which is closed completely from 1 January to 30 June, the beaches of the keys are open to those on foot.

After returning to the mainland on SR-24, bear left onto CR-347. A few Florida Scrub-Jays are found in the extensive areas of scrub along both sides of this road. Most of the birds are located from CR-326 (2.2) to about 1 mile south. The state has purchased 4,988 acres recently (and plans to purchase another 3,200 acres) as the Cedar Key Scrub State Reserve (no fee), but the area is not accessible to passenger vehicles. Besides, fire exclusion has reduced the jay population to only about 25 birds, now found mostly along the roads. A prescribed burning plan begun recently should restore the habitat, and the number of jays in the Cedar Key scrub, the northernmost population of the jays on the Gulf coast, should then increase substantially.

Contact: Cedar Key Scrub State Reserve, c/o Wacassassa Bay State Preserve, P.O. Box 187, Cedar Key, FL 32625; 352/543-5567.

At CR-326, turn left to a shell mound at the end of the road (3.5). The mound, created over hundreds of years as local Indians dumped oyster shells here, is now covered by large Live Oaks, which can be good for spring migrants. The ¼-mile Shell Mound Trail traverses hammocks. The shell mound is a small part of Lower Suwannee National Wildlife Refuge (51,365 acres; no fee), which is largely inaccessible to passenger vehicles.

A recent state acquisition in southern Levy County is Goethe (pronounced *GO-thee*) State Forest (43,614 acres; no fee), purchased in 1992 for $65 million. Public access is not currently available except on foot and by prior arrangement, but access should improve in the future. However, most of the forest is also a wildlife management area, where hunting is allowed in season. The area contains 24 Red-cockaded Woodpecker clusters and other pinewoods species. To reach the forest office from the junction of US-19/98 and CR-121 at Lebanon Station, turn right onto CR-336. The office is on the right (1.5).

Contact: Goethe State Forest, 8250 Southeast County Road 336, Dunnellon, FL 34431; 352/447-2202, or contact the Chiefland office of the Florida Division of Forestry at 352/493-6060.

Sulphur Spring is a small community south of Goethe State Forest that is a reliable spot for Florida Scrub-Jays. To reach it from US-19, turn left onto West River Road about 1 mile north of the abandoned Cross-Florida Barge Canal. For those southbound on US-19, turn right immediately after crossing the Withlacoochee River. For the final 3,000 feet of the

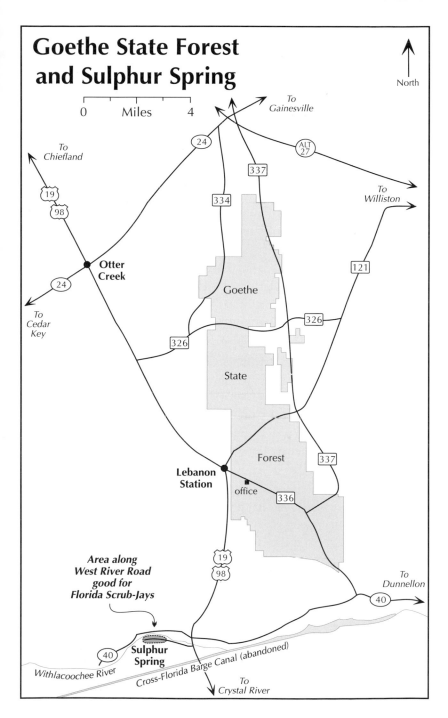

Goethe State Forest and Sulphur Spring

0   Miles   4

North

To Gainesville

To Chiefland

24

ALT 27

337

334

19

98

To Williston

Otter Creek

121

Goethe

24

326

To Cedar Key

326

State

Lebanon Station

Forest

337

office

336

Area along West River Road good for Florida Scrub-Jays

19

98

To Dunnellon

40

40

Sulphur Spring

Withlacoochee River

Cross-Florida Barge Canal (abandoned)

To Crystal River

road, the patch of scrub on both sides contains about 20 jays; watch for them perched on the powerlines along the road.

Gulf coastal areas continue on page 113.

Red-cockaded Woodpecker
Diane Pierce

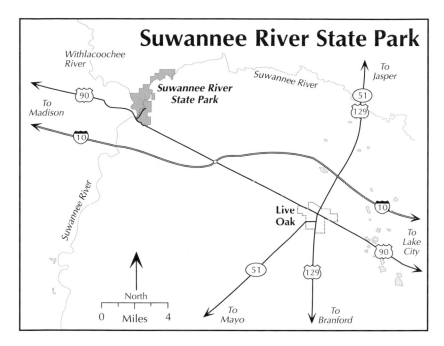

North Florida – Inland

LIVE OAK/LAKE CITY AREA

Suwannee River State Park (1,858 acres; standard fee) can be good for migrants, especially in fall. The most productive areas are along the limestone springs trail and park property on the opposite side of the river. Pine Warblers and Bachman's Sparrows are common in the Longleaf Pine flatwoods. To reach the park from SR-51 in Live Oak, drive west on US-90 to CR-132 (12.0) and turn right into the park. From I-10, exit at US-90 and go west as above (5.0).

Contact: Suwannee River State Park, Route 8, Box 297, Live Oak, FL 32060; 904/362-2746

Osceola National Forest (179,732 acres; no fee) contains some of the most extensive pine flatwoods remaining in North Florida. Characteristic species include Red-cockaded Woodpecker (52 clusters), Brown-headed Nuthatch, Eastern Bluebird, Pine Warbler, and Bachman's Sparrow. The headquarters (open Monday through Friday, 7:30 am to 4 pm) are located on the south side of US-90 in Olustee about 12 miles east of US-441. Here you can obtain a Forest Service map that shows the locations of

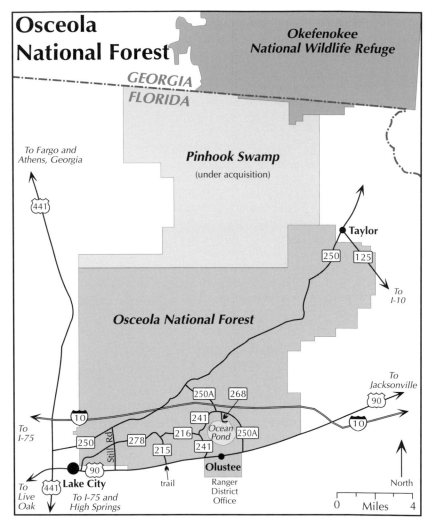

Osceola National Forest

Okefenokee National Wildlife Refuge

GEORGIA
FLORIDA

To Fargo and
Athens, Georgia

Pinhook Swamp

(under acquisition)

441

Taylor

250 125

To
I-10

Osceola National Forest

To
Jacksonville

90

250A 268

10

241

To
I-75

Ocean
Pond

250A

250

278

216

10

215

241

Olustee

90

To   441 Lake City   trail
Live
Oak   To I-75 and   Ranger   North
         High Springs   District
                               Office   0   Miles   4

some of the RCW clusters. A popular birding route of the forest is reached by driving west on US-90 from the headquarters to Still Road (7.7, or 4.4 miles east of US-441). Turn right to FR-278 (2.0) and turn right. Many RCW cavity trees (marked with white paint) are along this route, and Brown-headed Nuthatches and Bachman's Sparrows are common throughout. At FR-215 (5), turn right to return to US-90 at the Mount Carrie rest stop. A 1-mile interpretive trail is located there.

An alternate route would be to drive north on FR-215 to FR-216 and to turn east to FR-241 (2.4). Turn left to paved CR-250A (2.9) then turn right onto paved FR-268 (0.3). This road leads to Ocean Pond. Shortly after turning onto FR-268, look for the Florida National Scenic Trail. Park here and walk north on the trail to a wooded boardwalk through a cypress swamp. Typical North Florida breeding birds, including Hooded Warbler, should be seen. Ocean Pond may also be reached from US-90 by going north on CR-250A and turning left onto FR-268 (4.0).

To continue birding the forest from your stop at Ocean Pond, return to CR-250A and turn left. At CR-250 (3.5) you have a choice. You can turn right and drive almost 20 miles through the forest to the small town of Taylor. By going south on CR-125, you can eventually access I-10. To return to Lake City from CR-250A, turn left onto CR-250, which returns you to US-441 in about 12 miles.

Contact: Osceola National Forest, P.O. Box 70, Olustee, FL 32072; 904/752-2577.

North of Osceola National Forest is Okefenokee National Wildlife Refuge, located almost entirely in Georgia. Between these two large publicly owned areas is Pinhook Swamp, over 100 square miles of swamp and hydric (wet) pinewoods. The Nature Conservancy, U.S. Forest Service, and State of Florida plan to acquire the property to form a vast contiguous area of preserved land vital to protect the Threatened Florida Black Bear and other species. Breeding birds include Swallow-tailed Kites and Prothonotary Warblers. Wading-birds, including Wood Storks, are conspicuous year round. As an experiment to determine if Florida Panthers could be reintroduced into North Florida, 10 western Mountain Lions were released into Pinhook Swamp in 1993. They were then removed in June 1995.

HIGH SPRINGS

North and west of High Springs are two state parks with good riparian habitats. Both can be productive in fall for migrants and in spring and summer for Mississippi Kite, Hooded Warbler, and other species. Florida rarities to search for in winter include Winter Wren and Fox Sparrow.

O'Leno State Park (1,834 acres; standard fee) is about 7 miles north of High Springs on the east side of US-441. Adjoining O'Leno State Park on the south is River Rise State Preserve (4,182 acres), a wilderness area where the Santa Fe River travels underground for about 3 miles. Access is obtained at park headquarters by getting the combination for the lock on the gate.

Contact: O'Leno State Park, Route 2, Box 1010, High Springs, FL 32643; 904/454-1853.

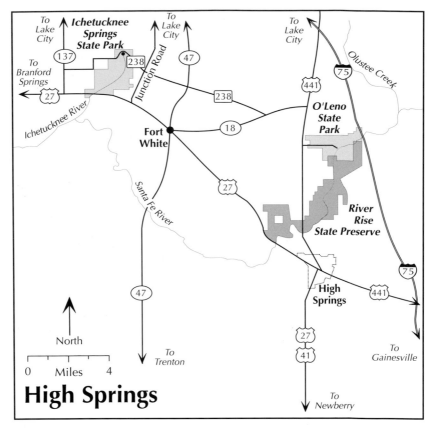

Ichetucknee Springs State Park (2,241 acres; standard fee) is located on the north side of US-27 about 12 miles northwest of High Springs. Turn right onto Junction Road about 3 miles past Fort White. At CR-238 (1.5), turn left to the park ahead (0.8). Ichetucknee is Florida's third-largest spring, releasing about 233 million gallons of water per day. Floating down the river in an inner tube is an extremely popular activity in the park, so get here early.

Contact: Ichetucknee Springs State Park, Route 2, Box 108, Fort White, FL 32038; 904/497-2511.

GAINESVILLE

Paynes Prairie State Preserve (20,224 acres), a National Natural Landmark, is one of the most popular birding sites in North Florida. William Bartram visited this wet prairie in 1774, when a large Seminole settlement was located along the shores of Alachua (pronounced *a-LA-chu-a*) Lake. Evidence shows that other Indians had lived here at least 9,000 years ago. During the Spanish years of the 1600s, the state's largest cattle ranch occupied the site.

From late November to mid-February, many birders come to see the few thousand wintering Sandhill Cranes. In addition, the preserve hosts small reintroduced populations of American Bison (released in 1975), and wild horses (released in 1985). On warm days in February and March, dozens of American Alligators bask on the canal banks along La Chua Trail. Visitors in spring and fall may be treated to a dazzling display of wildflowers.

La Chua Trail, on the north side of the prairie, offers the best birding in the preserve. To reach it from US-441 in Gainesville, go east on SR-26 to SE 15th Street (2.1) and turn right. Where the road turns sharply left (2.4), continue straight ahead onto the unpaved driveway. Drive through the gate and park across from the headquarters building (0.5). Walk past the Interpretive Center and follow the path to the prairie. (The headquarters building is open 8 am to 5 pm Monday to Friday.) If you visit on a weekend, you must park at Boulware Springs, a little farther north on SE 15th Street. Drive through the northernmost of three gates, and walk the ½-mile Rails-to-Trails path. Ranger-led tours are conducted on weekend mornings from November through April. Call 352/466-4100 for reservations.

La Chua Trail is a 1.3-mile-long levee trail that parallels a canal through open fields, extensive cattail marshes, and a lotus pond before ending at an observation tower on the shore of Alachua Lake. The best birding here is in winter, when Bald Eagles, Sandhill Cranes (hundreds or thousands may be observed distantly from the observation tower), and many other species are common. American Bitterns and Grasshopper, Lincoln's, and White-crowned Sparrows are rare but regular. In summer, Least Bitterns and Purple Gallinules breed on the lake, Mississippi Kites are often seen overhead, and Blue Grosbeaks and Indigo Buntings breed along the brushy edges of the trail.

To reach other parts of the preserve from Gainesville, go south on US-441 until you see extensive marshes on both sides of the road. Look

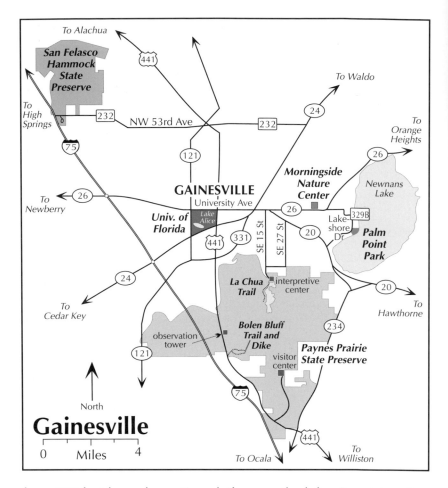

for a 200-foot-long observation platform on the left. On winter after-noons, this is a good spot for watching the flocks of cranes fly in to roost.

Continue south on US-441 to the **Bolen Bluff Trail** parking area on the left (1.3). From here, a 1.3-mile loop leads through a mixed hardwood forest to a levee that extends 3,000 feet into the prairie. The trail can be very good during fall migration; over 15 species of warblers have been reported here on some days, with Blue-winged, Golden-winged, Worm-eating, and Kentucky Warblers all regular here. Thrushes are also seen frequently. The levee offers good winter birding for Sedge and Marsh Wrens and sparrows.

Continue south on US-441 to the preserve's main entrance (standard fee) (3.5). Follow Savannah Drive to the Lake Wauberg turn-off (1.1) and turn left onto the Lake Wauberg road. This road can be good for Wild Turkeys, especially in winter. The road passes Puc Puggy campground before leading to the lake. (Puc Puggy was the Seminole name given to William Bartram.) In winter, Bald Eagles should be seen over the lake, and Orange-crowned Warblers and other species are fairly common in woods around the parking lot.

Return to Savannah Drive, turn left, and continue to the visitor center parking lot. The woods here, including the short Wacahoota Trail and the picnic area, can be good for migrant landbirds. This area is also the access point for the Cones Dike Trail. This 4-mile trail should produce King Rails year round and Soras and Marsh Wrens in winter. The trail offers your best chance for spotting Sandhill Cranes in summer and bison and wild horses year round.

Contact: Paynes Prairie State Preserve, Route 2, Box 41, Micanopy, FL 32667; 352/466-3397.

San Felasco Hammock State Preserve (6,924 acres; $2/vehicle, $1/bicycle or pedestrian) is located northwest of Gainesville. To reach it from SR-26, go north on US-441 to CR-232 (NW 53rd Avenue) (3.7), and turn left. Continue west to the parking area on the left (7.6). Mosquitoes can be a nuisance in the preserve, so be sure to bring repellent. Acadian Flycatchers, Wood Thrushes, and Hooded Warblers breed in the hardwood forests. In fall, migrant landbirds are a special attraction along the 1-mile loop trail. On the north side of the road, the sandhills contain breeding Red-headed Woodpeckers, Eastern Wood-Pewees, and Yellow-throated Vireos. About 20 miles of trails are located in the hammock north of the road, including two loop trails of about 5 and 6 miles in length, respectively. (Extensive areas of the preserve were logged in late 1994 and early 1995 to control an outbreak of bark beetles.)

Contact: San Felasco Hammock State Preserve, 4732 Millhopper Road, Gainesville, FL 32601; 352/336-2008.

Lake Alice (200 acres; no fee), located on the campus of the University of Florida, is an excellent downtown birding spot. To reach it from SR-26 (University Avenue), travel south on US-441 to Museum Drive (0.5) and turn right into the campus. The parking area for the gardens and lake is on the left (1.2). To reach the lake from SR-24, go north on SR-121 to Radio Road (1.0) and turn right. At Museum Drive (0.5) turn left to the garden parking lot on the right (0.5). The gardens and surrounding areas can be good for migrants in spring and fall. Breeding birds include Yellow-throated Warblers and Orchard Orioles. A small boardwalk offers a view of the lake, where Least Bitterns and Purple Gallinules breed. Limpkins have occurred here but are sporadic. A large wading-bird roost is located on the small islands in the western part of the lake, and hundreds of birds may be observed there in winter.

Morningside Nature Center (278 acres; no fee; open daily 9 am to 5 pm) is a good spot to pick up Brown-headed Nuthatches and other pinewoods species. From US-441, go east on SR-26 to the entrance on the left (3.7). Pick up a trail guide at the office, then take Moccasin Creek Loop Trail to the wildlife blind to check out the feeders. Other birds likely to be seen are Eastern Bluebird and Pine Warbler and, in spring and summer, Summer Tanager. There are 7½ miles of trails in the park.

From Morningside Nature Center, continue east on SR-26. Where the road veers left (1.1), continue straight ahead on CR-329B (Lakeshore Drive) to Newnans Lake. At the lake, turn right, then left after a few hundred feet. Continue to **Palm Point Park** (2.0), watching carefully for the parking lot on the left. Bird the oaks and cypresses at the point, then return to the parking lot and walk north along Lakeshore Drive. This area contains breeding Bald Eagles and Prothonotary Warblers. During fall migration the area can be excellent, with Blue-winged, Golden-winged, and Tennessee Warblers, both waterthrushes, and Scarlet Tanager among the species observed regularly.

Mississippi Kite is a fairly common breeding species (mid-April to mid-August) on the north rim of Paynes Prairie and throughout Gainesville. The birds can often be seen just by driving city streets, especially in late afternoon from mid-July to mid-August. Search especially the area bounded on the north by NW 39th Avenue, on the east by NW 13th Street, on the south by NW 8th Avenue, and on the west by NW 43rd Street.

For birders planning an extended visit to the Gainesville area, *A Birdwatcher's Guide to Alachua County, Florida* by Rex Rowan and Mike Manetz is recommended highly. (Order from Mike Manetz, 549 NW 31st Avenue, Gainesville, FL 32609; $7 plus $1.50 for postage, or order from ABA Sales.)

OCALA

Ocala National Forest (382,664 acres; no fee), established in 1908, is the southernmost national forest in the continental U.S. and was the first to be established east of the Mississippi River. It is devoted mostly to the cultivation of Sand Pine forests, which are clear-cut and used as pulpwood. The pines are endemic to xeric (extremely well-drained) sandy soils. Ocala National Forest contains the most extensive patch of xeric oak scrub remaining in the world. (About 60% of the forest is scrub.) "Islands" of Longleaf Pine flatwoods in the forest contain Red-cockaded Woodpeckers (13 clusters), Brown-headed Nuthatches, Pine Warblers, and Bachman's Sparrows. Florida Scrub-Jays are common throughout the forest in areas clear-cut 3 to 10 years previously; over 500 groups were counted in 1993, the second-largest population in the world. Because forestry practices discourage long-term occupancy of sites by the birds, jay sites are ephemeral, each lasting only about a decade until the birds must move to another, more suitable site. Search for areas with oak cover 3 to 7 feet tall and with little or no pine overstory.

To bird upland habitats, consider the following route that begins at the Forestry Center (11 miles east of Ocala) on SR-40 just inside the western boundary of the forest. (Most roads in the forest are unpaved, so be careful when pulling off onto the shoulder.) Drive east on SR-40 to paved FR-88 (13.8) and turn left. At FR-10 (5.4), turn right to Hughes Island (an island of Longleaf Pine sandhills), watching for Florida Scrub-Jays along the way. At FR-65 (2.8), turn left to FR-86 (1.5). Turn right to FR-86F (2.5) and turn left to Hopkin's Prairie (0.7). Return to FR-86 (0.7) and turn right to paved FR-88 (5.1). Turn right to paved CR-314 (4.1). (To the left is Salt Springs Island, another sandhills island that contains Red-cockaded Woodpeckers.) A few hundred feet before the intersection, marked Red-cockaded Woodpecker cavity trees are found on the right. To return to SR-40, turn left onto CR-314 to CR-314A (7.9) and turn left to SR-40 (6.8). From here, it is 5.5 miles back west to the Forestry Center.

To visit Alexander Springs for wetlands species, from CR-314A go east on SR-40, pass SR-19 (16.7), and turn right onto CR-445 (4.0). The campground is on the right (6.3). Alexander Springs release about 80 million gallons of water per day. The 1-mile loop nature trail near the swimming area is good in spring and summer for riparian woodland species such as Swallow-tailed Kite, Limpkin (year round), Acadian Flycatcher, and Prothonotary Warbler. In fall, birding can be good for migrant landbirds.

Lake George is another area good for waterbirds. To reach it from Salt Springs on SR-19, go northeast on CR-43 to the lake (7.0). To reach another part of the lake from the south, go east on SR-40 to FR-9883 (Blue Creek Road). Turn left to unmarked FR-9884 (2.5) and turn left to the lake (1.0). Bald Eagles and Ospreys nest along the lake. Look also for wading-birds and Limpkins.

The forests surrounding Rodman Reservoir at Rodman Dam (soon to be eliminated to restore habitats destroyed by damming the Oklawaha River for the now-abandoned Cross-Florida Barge Canal) contain numerous Bald Eagle nests. To reach it, go northeast on SR-19 to FR-77 and turn left. At FR-88 (4.0) turn right to the dam (1.0). Numerous ducks usually winter on the lake, and Swallow-tailed Kites are found in spring and summer.

Contact: Ocala National Forest Visitor Center, 10863 East Highway 40, Silver Springs, FL 24488; 904/625-7470. (Except for certain holidays, it is open daily from 9 am to 5 pm.) Inland areas continue on page 143.

North Florida – Atlantic Coast

JACKSONVILLE

With a population approaching 700,000, a busy commercial seaport, and a naval station, Jacksonville is a major financial, transportation, and business center for northern Florida. Nevertheless, there are productive birding areas to be found here, some along the north bank of the St. Johns River. From downtown, go north on I-95, exiting onto SR-105 (Heckscher Drive). Drive east to the ferry crossing at SR-A1A (15.3). Turn left onto Palmetto Avenue (0.6) to **Kingsley Plantation** (147 acres; no fee) on Fort George Island, an excellent spot in migration. (The homestead, with Florida's oldest plantation house, provides insights into pre-Civil-War period cotton-growing, if you have the time for a tour.) Painted Buntings are common breeders in the woods and are sometimes found around the marsh edges. Watch also for Blue Grosbeaks and Indigo Buntings. Keep right on the paved road to a former golf course, now reverting to a natural state. Follow the road as it makes a 6½-mile loop around the area, passing parklands and the Kingsley Plantation on the way. (This road is narrow and unpaved on the west side of the loop.)

Contact: Kingsley Plantation, 11676 Palmetto Avenue, Jacksonville, FL 32226; 904/251-3537.

The best spot locally for shorebirds is **Huguenot Memorial City Park** (also called Wards Bank) (449 acres; 50¢/per person), a sandspit jutting out from the north shore of the St. Johns River mouth. To reach the park from the ferry crossing, continue north on SR-A1A and turn right at the blinking light (0.8) to the guard station. Driving straight into the park from the station will lead to a short road that ends at a parking area. A short boardwalk to the right leads to an observation platform. This area may have wintering White-crowned Sparrows and other species, but generally is not especially productive. To reach the best areas of the park, turn right from the guard station and follow the paved road toward the ocean as far as possible. Park along the road and walk east across the dunes to the north jetty. A few Purple Sandpipers usually winter on the jetty; high tide is best. Lapland Longspurs and Snow Buntings occurred here formerly,

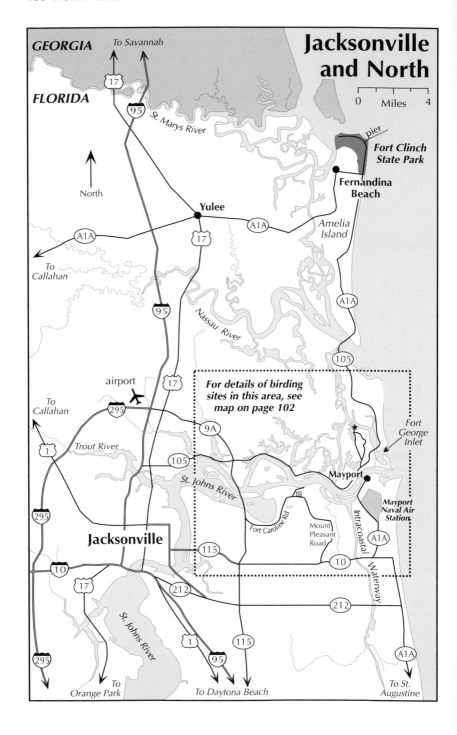

Jacksonville and North

GEORGIA

To Savannah

17

FLORIDA

95

St. Marys River

North

Yulee

A1A

To
Callahan

17

95

Nassau River

airport

17

To
Callahan

295

Trout River

1

295

105

St. Johns River

Jacksonville

115

10

17

212

St. Johns River

295

1

95

115

To
Orange Park

To Daytona Beach

0   Miles   4

pier

Fort Clinch
State Park

Fernandina
Beach

Amelia
Island

A1A

A1A

105

For details of birding
sites in this area, see
map on page 102

9A

Fort
George
Inlet

Mayport

Mayport
Naval Air
Station

Fort Caroline Rd

Mount
Pleasant
Road

Intracoastal

A1A

10

212

Waterway

A1A

To St.
Augustine

but have not been seen in recent years. Their current absence may be due to the growth of the dune vegetation (although a Snow Bunting was reported in winter 1994-1995).

Many shorebirds and various gulls and terns roost on a sandspit between the jetty and the St. Johns River. This is the most reliable local spot for "white-winged" and "black-backed" gulls. Iceland and Glaucous Gulls have occurred here, but so have partially albinistic and possibly hybrid gulls. Lesser Black-backed Gulls are becoming fairly regular in winter, while Great Black-backed Gulls are common.

Most of the shorebirds are found along the mudflats and sandbars of Fort George Inlet. During migration and in winter, a dozen or more species may be found here. Low tide is best. Reddish Egrets are often seen. You may drive from the main park road onto dirt roads through camping areas to the edge of the inlet and partly around it. *Do not drive across the dunes.* Be wary of soft sand and especially of exposed mud. It is best to park on pavement near the dunes and walk to the shore.

Contact: Huguenot Memorial City Park, 10980 Heckscher Drive, Jacksonville, FL 32226; 904/251-3335.

To reach Little Talbot Island State Park, (2,500 acres; standard fee) return to SR-A1A and go north across the Fort George River to the park on the right (3.7). The extreme north end of the beach may contain large numbers of shorebirds, an assortment of gulls and terns, and other waterbirds. The observation deck at the south end of the park road is a good spot from which to scan the ocean for Northern Gannets and sea ducks. In November and December, scoters, mergansers, and other ducks pass by in numbers.

Contact: Little Talbot Island State Park, 12157 Heckscher Drive, Fort George, FL 32226; 904/251-2320.

You might want to try a northward side-trip from the Jacksonville area to Fort Clinch State Park (1,119 acres; standard fee) at Fernandina Beach. The park is on the south side of St. Marys River, the boundary between Florida and Georgia. To reach the park from Little Talbot Island, continue north on SR-A1A until it becomes Atlantic Avenue (17.6). Turn left on Atlantic and then right (0.2) into the park. Check the Willow Pond Nature Trail on the left side of the main park road, beyond the intersection with the road to the beach. The trail is good for migrants, wintering landbirds, and, in spring and summer, for Painted Buntings. The fishing-pier is a good spot from which to scan for sea ducks and larids. Purple Sandpipers winter on the jetty alongside the fishing pier; there were 8 in 1994-1995 and 11 in 1995-1996. At high tide, they often sit on the seawall with Ruddy Turnstones.

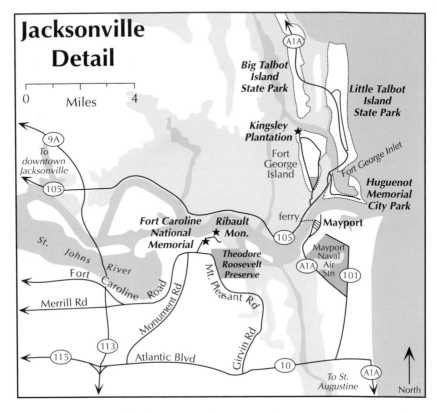

Jacksonville Detail

0 Miles 4

To downtown Jacksonville

9A

105

Big Talbot Island State Park

Little Talbot Island State Park

A1A

Kingsley Plantation

Fort George Island

Fort George Inlet

Huguenot Memorial City Park

Fort Caroline National Memorial

Ribault ★ Mon.

ferry

Mayport

105

St. Johns River

Fort Caroline Road

Theodore Roosevelt Preserve

Mt. Pleasant Rd

Mayport Naval Air Stn

A1A

101

Merrill Rd

Monument Rd

Girvin Rd

115

113

Atlantic Blvd

10

To St. Augustine

A1A

North

Contact: Fort Clinch State Park, 2601 Atlantic Avenue, Fernandina Beach, FL 32034; 904/261-4212.

To the east along the south bank of the St. Johns River, the woodlands of Fort Caroline National Memorial (no fee) and adjoining Theodore Roosevelt Preserve (no fee) can produce migrants and wintering land-birds. To reach the park from Heckscher Drive (SR-105), take SR-9A south across the impressive Napoleon Broward Bridge (known locally as Dames Point Bridge). Keep to the right on the Southside Connector and follow it to Merrill Road (0.8). Turn left on Merrill, which soon becomes Fort Caroline Road (0.7), to the memorial on the left (4.0). The nature trail and the trail by Spanish Pond are the best areas here. The overlook at Ribault Monument to the east (0.5) is a good spot from which to scan the river for ducks, a variety of gulls and terns, and other waterbirds.

Theodore Roosevelt Preserve (600 acres) contains several miles of trails through a hardwood hammock leading to salt marshes and tidal creeks. Maps are available at the Fort Caroline visitor center. As you leave Ribault Monument and pass Fort Caroline Memorial (0.5), turn right onto Fort Caroline Road to Mount Pleasant Road (0.4), and turn left. Follow Mount Pleasant Road to the preserve (1.2). Enter the road which has the sign for Trailhead Parking.

Contact: Fort Caroline National Memorial, 12713 Fort Caroline Road, Jacksonville, FL 32225; 904/641-7155.

To reach the marshes and mudflats at Mayport, go south on Mount Pleasant Road to SR-10 (Atlantic Boulevard) and turn left (5.2). Turn left at SR-A1A (3.2). As you start approaching Mayport (4.0), mudflats on the left are good at low tide for wading-birds, Clapper Rails, and shorebirds. Least Bittern, Wilson's Plover, and Black-necked Stilt have bred here. The ponds on the right, which are blocked off from tidal flow, often contain ducks in winter. Continue past the ferry landing for one block and park at the public boat ramp to scope the sandbars for gulls and terns. Check the side streets in town for Eurasian Collared-Doves and Gray Kingbirds (spring and summer).

Permission to bird the Mayport Naval Air Station may be obtained by asking at the entrance gate. To reach the station, return southward to Mayport Road (SR-101) and turn left. Along the way, you will pass Hanna County Park on the right, which is good for Painted Buntings (spring and summer) and migrants.

To visit Guana River State Park or other St. Augustine coastal areas, continue south along the coast on SR-A1A.

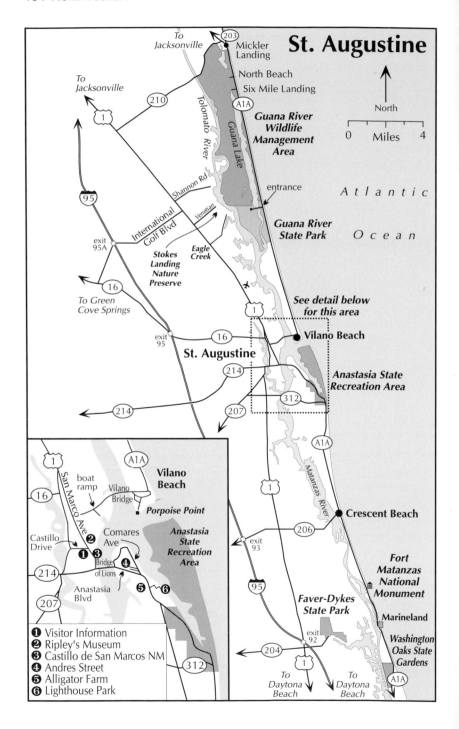

St. Augustine

To Jacksonville
203
Mickler Landing
North Beach
Six Mile Landing
A1A

To Jacksonville
210
1
Tolomato River
Guana Lake

North
0 Miles 4

Guana River Wildlife Management Area

95
Shannon Rd
International Golf Blvd
Venetian
entrance
Atlantic

exit 95A
Stokes Landing Nature Preserve
Eagle Creek

Guana River State Park
Ocean

16
To Green Cove Springs
exit 95
16
1
See detail below for this area

St. Augustine
214
Vilano Beach

312
Anastasia State Recreation Area

214
207
A1A

Matanzas River

1
Crescent Beach

206
exit 93

Fort Matanzas National Monument

95
Faver-Dykes State Park
Marineland

exit 92
204
1
To Daytona Beach
To Daytona Beach

Washington Oaks State Gardens

A1A

Detail inset

1
San Marco Ave
16
boat ramp
Vilano Bridge
A1A
Vilano Beach

Porpoise Point

Castillo Drive
❷
Comares Ave
❶❸
Bridge of Lions
❹
Anastasia Blvd
❺
❻

Anastasia State Recreation Area

214
207
312

❶ Visitor Information
❷ Ripley's Museum
❸ Castillo de San Marcos NM
❹ Andres Street
❺ Alligator Farm
❻ Lighthouse Park

ST. AUGUSTINE AREA

About 5 miles north of St. Augustine (or 20 miles south of Mayport) on SR-A1A is **Guana River State Park** (2,398 acres; $2/vehicle), another good birding site in this part of Florida. North of the park is Guana River Wildlife Management Area (9,815 acres; $2/vehicle). Combined, the two areas preserve over 11 miles of ocean frontage. Guana Lake (alternately called Lake Ponte Vedra) is a 2,200-acre lake created in 1957 when the Guana River was dammed. The northernmost entrance to the Wildlife Management Area is on the west side of SR-A1A about 6.5 miles south of the junction of SR-A1A and CR-210). The South Beach entrance is farther south (2.3). In between is Six Mile Landing on the west side; the turn-off is obscure, and parking is limited. The entrance to the state park at the Guana Dam area is farther south, just before the Trading Post convenience store on the right (4.5). Pick up a map at the park head-quarters and park at the dam (0.2). You should see wading-birds, various larids, and other waterbirds from the dam causeway. Along the grassy parts, look for migrant Bobolinks and Lark (rare), Grasshopper, and "Sharp-tailed" Sparrows in winter. Areas of the park beyond the cause-way are currently closed to vehicles. However, vehicle access on a daily basis is being considered for the future. Until then, the park and the WMA may be walked or bicycled. (A mountain bike is recommended for the sandy trails.) Vehicle access to the WMA (to the north) is available only by prior permission, which takes 2 to 3 weeks to obtain.

After crossing the dam, pick up a trail map. In the park, take the trail to the restored wetland. The trail to **Big Savannah Pond** can be excellent for wading species such as Black-crowned Night-Heron, Roseate Spoon-bill (summer), and Wood Stork. Two trails into the Wildlife Management Area may be worth hiking or biking during except hunting season. (The hunting season extends from mid-October to mid-December.) Outside hunting season, hike the trail another mile to an observation tower overlooking Capo Creek. The oak hammock before the tower should be checked during migration. A third tower, which overlooks Guana Lake, requires an additional 4-mile hike or bike. Bring insect repellent in spring and summer for Deer Flies.

Contact: Guana River State Park, 2690 South Ponte Vedra Boulevard, Ponte Vedra Beach, FL 32082; 904/825-5071.

From Guana River State Park, continue south on SR-A1A over the bridge to the T intersection at Vilano Beach (7.2). Park in the public parking lot, then walk to the beach. Go right toward the jetty and beyond it to **Porpoise Point**. This is a good spot for wading birds and larids (including large numbers of Black Skimmers), especially in winter. A few Piping Plovers should be present, along with Wilson's Plovers and Great Black-backed Gulls. In winter, be sure to check the jetty for Purple Sandpipers.

It was in this general area that Ponce de Leon is said to have begun his search for the Fountain of Youth in 1513. Founded in 1565, St. Augustine is the second-oldest continuously occupied city in the U.S. By the time St. Augustine was ceded to Great Britain in 1763, the quiet coastal town had already served as the seat of government for Spain's Florida possessions and the center for thirty missions. (The following directions to good birding sites will also bring you past some parts of St. Augustine's "Old City.")

Return to SR-A1A and cross the Tolomato River. Once on the mainland, turn left into the Vilano Beach Boat Ramp (0.1). Besides channels and inlets, there are extensive marshes and mudflats on both sides of the road. In winter, this area can be very productive for Hooded Mergansers, waterbirds, and shorebirds, including Whimbrel and Marbled Godwit. Long-billed Curlews have been found in two of the past five winters.

Just beyond the boat ramp is the bridge to the Florida School for the Deaf and Blind. The gate across the road is usually locked, but you may walk the path around the gate. Look for both night-herons in cedars to the left of the bridge.

Continue west on SR-A1A to San Marco Avenue (0.5) and turn left to head into downtown. At least four species of psittacids (Monk, Rose-ringed, Black-hooded, and Mitred Parakeets) occur in the city. Check especially around the Visitor's Information Center and Ripley's Believe It Or Not Museum at the intersection of San Marco Avenue (SR-A1A/Alternate US-1) and Castillo Drive (about 2 miles from the bridge). Eurasian Collared-Doves and Gray Kingbirds (spring and summer) can usually be found here as well; look for the kingbird also in Castillo de San Marcos National Monument. Mitred Parakeets are also sometimes found around the fort.

North of St. Augustine and inland are several good birding areas off US-1. From Business US-1 (San Marco Boulevard), go north on US-1 (Ponce de Leon Boulevard) to Eagle Creek development (6.0) and turn right. (*There is no sign at this road*). This road and side roads that branch off from it offer access to a variety of habitats, including oak hammocks, fresh water marshes and ponds, and pine flatwoods. *Do not go beyond the fence* that leads to Capo Island.

Glossy Ibis
Georges Dremeaux

Return to US-1 and turn right to Venetian (1.0), then turn right again. At Old Dixie Highway (1 block), turn right to Lakeshore Drive (0.2), and turn left. Park in the Stokes Landing Nature Preserve (300 acres; always open) parking lot just before the "Dead End" sign on the right. An observation tower overlooks a marsh at the end of the trail.

Return to US-1, continue north, and turn left onto International Golf Boulevard (1.2). Search the swamp (about 2 miles) for Barred Owls, Acadian Flycatchers, and Prothonotary Warblers. The swamp can also be good for migrants. International Golf Boulevard may also be reached by exiting (#95A) I-95 and going east.

Return to US-1, turn left to Shannon Road (0.4), and turn right. Check the pine flatwoods for Brown-headed Nuthatches and other resident species.

ANASTASIA ISLAND

From downtown St. Augustine, go east on SR-A1A across the Bridge of Lions on Anastasia Boulevard. Just before the road curves to the right, turn left onto Comares Street (0.4), and drive two blocks to Andreas Street. Three Monk Parakeet nests are located on telephone poles here. Many Black-hooded Parakeets also occur in this area, nesting in cavities in telephone poles.

Return to Anastasia Boulevard and turn left to St. Augustine Alligator Farm (0.6) on the right. The farm is a private tourist facility ($10/person), but it contains a wading-bird rookery that is worth a visit from March through May. A boardwalk allows close views of nesting Great, Snowy, and Cattle Egrets, Great Blue, Little Blue, and Tricolored Herons, and Black-crowned Night-Herons. Nests may be as close as 4 feet from the walk. During other times of the year, thousands of wading-birds roost here every night.

As you depart the alligator farm, turn right and make an immediate left onto Old Beach Road to Lighthouse Park. An oak hammock and salt water slough offer birding possibilities here. Guided tours allow you to climb to the top of the lighthouse.

Immediately beyond the turn to Lighthouse Park is **Anastasia State Recreation Area** (1,500 acres, standard fee). The entrance road passes salt marshes before leading to the main parking area. Watch for Painted Buntings in spring and summer along this road, especially around the second picnic area. Restricted beach driving is allowed; talk to a ranger for more information. Breeding species here include Wilson's Plovers, Willets, and Royal and Least Terns. In winter many shorebirds and larids are found here, especially at the north end of the beach (about 4 miles from the entrance). Northern Gannets are regularly observed from shore in late fall and winter. Peregrine Falcons and other raptors are seen in September and October.

Contact: Anastasia State Recreation Area, 1340-A SR-A1A South, St. Augustine, FL 32084; 904/461-2033 or 904/461-2000.

CRESCENT BEACH AREA

From Anastasia State Recreation Area, return to SR-A1A and go south to Fort Matanzas National Monument (298 acres; no fee) on the right (10.5). There is a ½-mile boardwalk through an oak hammock that can be good for migrants. Gray Kingbirds breed here in spring and summer.

Just past the entrance to the monument is the Matanzas Bridge. Park just north of the bridge and scan for wading-birds (including Reddish Egrets), shorebirds, and larids, especially in winter. Wilson's and Piping Plovers and Bonaparte's Gulls winter here, as does a large flock of Black Skimmers (up to 1,000 birds). A walkway across the bridge is excellent for observing the birds.

Continue south, watching for Florida Scrub-Jays in patches of scrub just south of the bridge and south of Marineland (3.3). Just before Marineland, check the small brushy island in the marsh on the right for Roseate Spoonbills in summer. As many as 45 have been seen here.

Atlantic coastal areas continue on page 174.

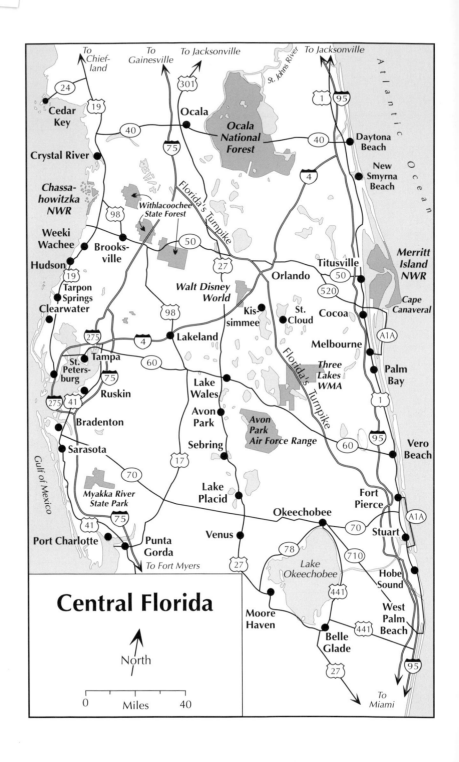

Central Florida

North

0   Miles   40

CENTRAL FLORIDA

Home of the St. Petersburg/Tampa and Greater Orlando metropolitan areas, Central Florida has become the top tourist destination in the world. The region has witnessed an incredible increase in human residents in the past four decades, causing severe habitat destruction in many areas. The subtropical influence for which Florida is famous becomes apparent here, with extensive mangrove forests along the coasts and the increased presence of Cabbage Palms in wet areas throughout. The birdlife, too, shows more of a West Indian influence, with breeding species such as Reddish Egret, Roseate Spoonbill, Snail Kite, Short-tailed Hawk, Mangrove Cuckoo, and Black-whiskered Vireo.

Many other species sought by visiting birders also occur in Central Florida. They include Magnificent Frigatebird, Wood Stork, Fulvous Whistling-Duck, Black-bellied Whistling-Duck, Mottled Duck, Swallow-tailed Kite, Sandhill Crane, Purple Gallinule, Limpkin, Snowy Plover, Wilson's Plover, Piping Plover, American Oystercatcher, Eurasian Collared-Dove, Budgerigar, Monk Parakeet, Burrowing Owl, Red-cockaded Woodpecker, Gray Kingbird, Florida Scrub-Jay, Bachman's Sparrow, Florida Grasshopper Sparrow (an endemic race), and Seaside Sparrow. Some of these species are widespread and fairly common, while others are uncommon and local. Black-bellied Whistling-Duck and Budgerigar are restricted in the state to Central Florida.

Birds that reach their southern breeding limit in the region include Cooper's Hawk, American Kestrel, Acadian Flycatcher, Carolina Chickadee, Marsh Wren, Yellow-throated Vireo, Yellow-throated Warbler, Blue Grosbeak, Indigo Bunting, Painted Bunting, and Seaside Sparrow (except the Cape Sable race).

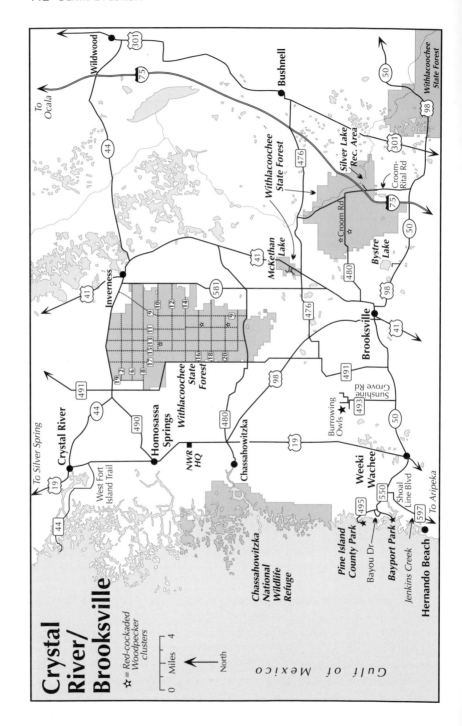

Crystal River/ Brooksville

☆ = Red-cockaded Woodpecker clusters

North

0 Miles 4

Gulf of Mexico

Central Florida – Gulf Coast

CRYSTAL RIVER AREA

Citrus County, of which Crystal River is the largest city, marks the northern boundary of the Greater St. Petersburg/Tampa area. The state is purchasing much of the sandhills in this area to protect their remnant populations of Red-cockaded Woodpeckers, Black Bears, and other rare species. The river and the largely undisturbed coastline support large numbers of wading-birds, waterfowl, larids, and West Indian Manatees. Unfortunately, access to the coast is very limited, with only one site listed below, but the forests are more accessible.

SR-44 (Fort Island Trail) runs west from US-19 in Crystal River 9 miles to the Gulf. Stop at St. Martins Aquatic Preserve (no fee) on the left (2.5), which has nature trails. Beyond the preserve, the newly acquired Fort Island Park and Recreation Area on the right (2.5) may also be worth checking. In the extensive *Juncus* marshes closer to the Gulf, breeding Marsh Wrens and Seaside Sparrows are joined in winter by Sedge Wrens and "Sharp-tailed" Sparrows. At the beach, look for wading-birds, shorebirds, and several species of gulls and terns. American White Pelican, Common Goldeneye, Hooded Merganser, and other species winter in the Gulf. Between the shore and the boat launching area is a small wooded area that can be good for migrant landbirds. Gray Kingbirds may be found in the area in spring and summer.

The small town of Chassahowitzka can be reached by going south on US-19 about 10 miles from Crystal River, then turning west onto CR-480 (Chassahowitzka Street) to its end (1.5). There, you can rent a canoe and visit Chassahowitzka National Wildlife Refuge (30,436 acres; no fee), which has a large wintering population of waterfowl and other species. Breeding species found along the river include wading-birds, Swallow-tailed Kite, Limpkin, and Prothonotary Warbler. Ospreys are common permanent residents, and Bald Eagles are usually seen. The refuge headquarters are located on the west side of US-19, 3.6 miles north of CR-480.

Contact: Chassahowitzka National Wildlife Refuge , Route 2, Box 44, Homosassa Springs, FL 32646; 352/382-2201.

Withlacoochee State Forest (128,471 acres; no fee) consists of six separate sections in Citrus, Hernando, Pasco, and Sumter counties. Most of the forest is composed of Longleaf Pine/Turkey Oak sandhills. To reach one section from Crystal River, go east on SR-44. From Homosassa Springs, take CR-490 and from Chassahowitzka, go east on CR-480. The forest contains graded dirt roads (usually passable in two-wheel drive vehicles) at one-mile intervals. East-west roads are even-numbered, starting with Trail 2 at SR-44 and ending with Trail 22 near CR-480. North-south roads are odd-numbered from Trail 19 near CR-491 to Trail 5 near CR-581. Most of the forest is good for upland landbirds, including Hairy Woodpecker, Yellow-throated Vireo, Yellow-throated and Pine Warblers, and Bachman's Sparrow. Active Red-cockaded Woodpecker clusters are located near the southwest corner of Trails 10 and 13, the southeast corner of Trails 11 and 16, and the southeast corner of Trails 11 and 20.

WEEKI WACHEE/ BROOKSVILLE AREA

To reach another part of **Withlacoochee State Forest**, from SR-50A in Brooksville travel north on US-41. At CR-480 (Croom Road) (1.2) turn right. Once in the forest (4.5), the road turns into a graded dirt road. Park at the spot where a powerline joins the road on the right (2.1) and walk north from pole #85. The trees marked with bands of red paint are Red-cockaded Woodpecker cavity trees. Pine Warblers and Bachman's Sparrows also occur here. To reach another woodpecker cluster, continue east on Croom Road to Trail 9 (1.6) and turn right. The marked cavity trees are ahead (0.3).

For a view of the Withlacoochee River, continue east on Croom Road, veering right at the fork. Silver Lake Recreation Area on the left (3.1) is not a lake but a wide portion of the river. To reach Silver Lake from SR-50 go north to Croom-Rital Road (1.0 mile east of I-75 and 3 miles west of US-301) to the area on the right (3.6). Limpkins and migrant landbirds may be found here.

McKethan Lake ($1/driver, 50¢/passenger), a part of the forest with extensive oak hammocks, is located north of Brooksville. From SR-50A, go north on US-41 to the entrance on the left (7.5). To reach it from Silver Lake turn right onto Croom-Rital Road to Croom-Nobleton Road (2.0) and turn right. When it becomes a paved road (3.3), the name changes to Edgewater Avenue, which intersects with CR-476 (Lake Lindsey Road) (0.8). Turn left to US-41 (4.9) and turn right to McKethan Lake on the left (0.5). There are many trails through the hammocks, any one of which can be good for migrant landbirds in fall.

Contact: Withlacoochee Forestry Center, 15019 Broad Street, Brooksville, FL 34601; 352/754-6777.

Bystre Lake east of Brooksville usually has a good variety of ducks in winter. To reach it from SR-50, go north on Clayton Road (2.7 miles east of SR-50A and 5.6 miles west of I-75). At the end of the road (0.5), turn right into a grassy field owned by the county. *Stay off adjacent private property.*

To try for Burrowing Owls, continue west on SR-50 to CR-493 (Sunshine Grove Road), and turn right. At Hexam Road (3.6) turn left to Eskimo Curlew Road (0.2) and turn right. The owls have been found recently within a few blocks north and west of this intersection.

To visit two small coastal parks that are best in winter, travel west from US-19 in Weeki Wachee on CR-550. At CR-495 (4.9) turn right to **Pine Island County Park** (3 acres; $2/vehicle) (2.4), the best local site to observe wintering waterbirds. The salt marshes on both sides of CR-495 between CR-550 and the park are good for wading-birds, shorebirds, rails, Marsh Wrens, and "Sharp-tailed" (winter) and Seaside Sparrows. From the park look for sea ducks, wading-birds, shorebirds (including American Oyster-catchers), and larids (including Caspian Terns). Eurasian Collared-Doves are often found along the road just before the park entrance.

Return south toward CR-550. Turn right onto Bayou Drive (2.1) for a short loop offering more salt marsh birding. Turn right onto CR-550 to reach Bayport Park (1½ acres; no fee) (1.2), which may have a few shorebirds and larids. A Surf Scoter and a Red-throated Loon were found here on the 1991 and 1995 Christmas Bird Counts, respectively.

Return to the junction of CR-550 and CR-597 (Shoal Line Boulevard) (3.2) and turn right. Proceed to Jenkins Creek fishing pier and boat ramp on the left (2.4). In the small marsh on the north side of the parking lot, look for wintering Marsh and Sedge Wrens and Swamp Sparrows. Walk over the foot-bridge and follow the creek to the west. "Sharp-tailed" (winter) and Seaside Sparrows are found in the *Juncus* marsh to the right, and there may be ducks in the creek.

Continue south on CR-597 (Shoal Line Boulevard) to Gulfview Drive (2.2). The residential roads in this area are one of the most reliable sites for Budgerigars remaining in the state. The flocks move around somewhat, but some birds usually can be found along Eagle Nest Drive, Flamingo Boulevard, Gulf Coast Drive, Gulfview Drive, and Gulf Winds Circle (left from the end of Gulfview Drive). Drive around with your car windows open to listen for the Budgie's distinctive chittering. *The entire area is private property, so please be respectful.*

To return to US-19, turn right onto CR-597 and go south to access Aripeka and points south, or turn left to return to Pine Island or Weeki Wachee via CR-550.

Birding Sites in Hernando County was published in 1995 by the Hernando Audubon Society. In addition to listing birding sites in the area, it includes an up-to-date county checklist. It may be ordered (no charge) from the Hernando County Tourist Development Bureau, 16110 Aviation Loop Drive, Spring Hill, FL 34609; 352/799-7275.

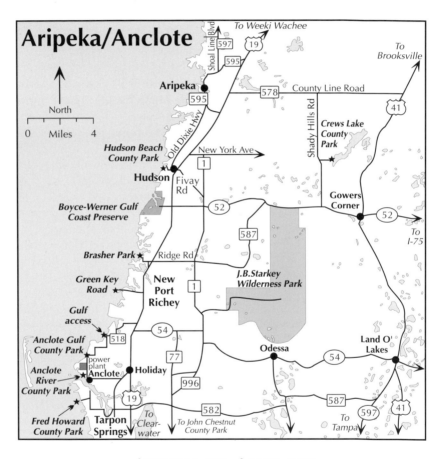

ARIPEKA TO ANCLOTE

Crews Lake County Park is an excellent spot for migrant landbirds (113 acres; no fee). This park can also be good for waterbirds year round. To reach the park from US-19, turn left onto CR-578 (County Line Road)(2.0). At Shady Hills Road (5.5), turn right. At Crews Lake Road (3.9) turn left into the park.

Since the park is off to the east, there are alternate ways to approach it. From Brooksville, go south on US-41 to County Line Road, and turn right. At Shady Hills Road (5.3), turn left and proceed as above. From the south, travel east on SR-52 past CR-587 (Moon Lake Road) to Shady Hills Road (3.8) and turn left. At Crews Lake Road (3.0) turn right to the park. From I-75, go west on SR-52, cross US-41 (10.0), and turn right onto Shady Hills Road (2.4). Proceed as above.

This park contains oak hammocks, sandhills, cypress swamps, and frontage along Crews Lake. Many trails through the woodlands can be great in fall for migrant landbirds. An observation tower affords views of the lake, which may be extensive or just a few puddles, depending on the amount of rainfall in previous months. Many locally "good" birds have been found on the lake, including Roseate Spoonbill (late summer), Fulvous Whistling-Duck, Purple Gallinule (resident but rare in winter), Limpkin, Piping Plover, Black-necked Stilt, and Black Tern. Waterfowl may be present in numbers in winter if water levels are high, and shorebirds may be common when levels are low. Brushy edges along the lakeshore may contain large numbers of wintering Sedge Wrens; over 150 were counted along a small portion of the lake on the 1994 Christmas Bird Count. To date, 191 species of birds have been seen in the park.

Contact: Crews Lake County Park, 16735 Crews Lake Drive, Spring Hill, FL 34610; 813/832-3278.

From Crews Lake County Park return to US-19 and continue southward to Hudson. Beyond the traffic light at Fivay Road, turn right onto Clark Street (0.3). Follow Clark Street to its end at Hudson Beach County Park (0.8; no fee). It is best to park south of the restaurant and walk north along the "beach" (crowded with people on most days). Look for Sanderlings and Sandwich Terns in addition to wading-birds, shorebirds, and larids. Scan the Gulf for sea ducks in winter. A small flock of Budgerigars may still frequent the trees in the parking lot, while Eurasian Collared-Doves are fairly common along Clark Street and adjacent streets.

Return to US-19 and turn right. At SR-52 (2.0) look for Budgerigars on the powerlines on the west side of US-19. If you fail to find them here, carefully check the trees in the parking lot of Perkins Restaurant at the southwest corner of the two roads. (There were 40 birds here on the 1995 Christmas Bird Count.)

Turn right onto SR-52 to its end (0.5) at Boyce-Werner Gulf Coast Preserve (no fee). There are no facilities at present, but it is permissible to enter on foot. (You may have to bushwhack through upland vegetation to get to the marsh). In the extensive *Juncus* marshes you can find Marsh

Wrens and Seaside Sparrows year round and "Sharp-tailed" and Swamp Sparrows in winter. However, be warned that walking through the marsh is difficult; needle-rush is well-named. In addition, watch out for the many ditches through the marsh that were dug years ago in an attempt to control mosquitoes.

Return to US-19 and continue south. Starting at Jasmine Boulevard (1.4), watch the wires for the next few miles for Budgerigars. They are seen most frequently at the south end of the Gulfview Square Mall parking lot on the right (1.5). Apparently, the birds roost on the large billboards facing US-19.

At Ridge Road (0.8), turn right to the end (0.1), then turn left. Go one block, then turn right onto Bay Boulevard. Proceed west to Old Post Road (0.2), then turn right to the Port Richey Recreation Center (no fee) on the left (0.4). This is another area with extensive *Juncus* marshes and mangrove forests. Marsh Wrens and Prairie Warblers breed here. At Brasher Park (0.5), numerous wading-birds, shorebirds, and several kinds of gulls and terns are found here *at low tide*. Hooded Mergansers are common in the estuaries in winter. As you leave the park, continue south on Old Post Road to US-19 (0.6), then turn right.

At **Green Key Road** (1.3; between New York Carpet Mart and Howard Johnson Inn), turn right. This area is excellent *at low tide* for wading-birds and wintering ducks, shorebirds, and gulls. This is also the best site in Pasco County for Reddish Egret. Be sure to check all the estuaries before entering Robert K. Rees County Park (no fee) at the end of the road (1.5). Check the small beach for local rarities such as Wilson's Plover, Bonaparte's Gull, and Caspian and Sandwich Terns. Scan the Gulf for sea ducks; Hooded Mergansers winter here commonly. In spring and summer, Prairie Warblers breed in the mangroves; one or two are found in most winters as well.

Return to US-19 and turn right. At CR-518 (Trouble Creek Road) (2.0), turn right. At the curve in the road (0.9), its name changes to Strauber Memorial Highway. This road winds through extensive mangrove forests, with a canal on the right side. Wading-birds, including Yellow-crowned Night-Herons, are seen frequently. A small cut in the mangroves (1.5) affords a view of the Gulf. Pull off the road here and scan the mudflats (*exposed only at low tide*).

Continue south to Anclote Gulf County Park (3.9) and turn right for another view of the Gulf. Anclote River County Park is located farther south on Strauber (1.3), on the south side of the power plant. At Anclote Boulevard (0.2), turn left to reach Alternate US-19 (2.0). From there, turn left to reach US-19 in Holiday, or turn right toward Tarpon Springs.

Jay B. Starkey Wilderness Park (15,000 acres; no fee) east of New Port Richey can be an excellent birding spot, especially in fall and winter. The park, which doubles as Pasco County's wellfield, contains extensive areas of frequently burned pine flatwoods, sandhills, hardwood hammocks, oak and Sand Pine scrub, marshes, and cypress swamps along the Pithlachascotee and Anclote Rivers. To reach the park from SR-52, go south on CR-1 (Little Road). Cross the Pithlachascotee River (6.4) and turn left onto River Crossing Boulevard (0.4). The road curves often before ending at the park (1.9). From SR-54 West, go north on CR-1 to River Crossing Boulevard (1.4), turn right, and proceed as above. Currently, a massive amount of road and housing construction is occurring near the park entrance.

The county park is a small (65 acres) portion of the wilderness park, and contains restrooms and other amenities. The cypress and bay swamp along the Pithlachascotee River just north of the main parking lot can be excellent for landbirds, especially during fall migration and in winter. Access to the remainder of the wellfield is open only to those on foot, horseback, or bicycle. In particular, the main (paved) wellfield road heading east from the park leads for several miles to the powerlines. It is permissible to walk or bike the main road east of the powerlines; birding for flatwoods species is better there.

Near or east of the powerlines, you should find Swallow-tailed Kites (spring and summer), Brown-headed Nuthatches, Eastern Bluebirds, Yellow-throated Vireos (spring and summer), Yellow-throated Warblers, Summer Tanagers (spring and summer), and Bachman's Sparrows. Wild Turkeys may be seen anywhere in the park around dawn and dusk, and Hairy Woodpeckers may be found in recently burned flatwoods. Under the powerlines you should find sparrows in winter. Look for Grasshopper Sparrows in areas with short grass and no bushes; Bachman's Sparrows should be here also. In wet areas, look for Marsh Wren and Swamp Sparrows. A Henslow's Sparrow was found here in 1990.

Contact: Jay B. Starkey Wilderness Park, 10500 Wilderness Road, New Port Richey, FL 34653; 813/834-3247.

Brown Pelican
Gail Diane Yovanovich

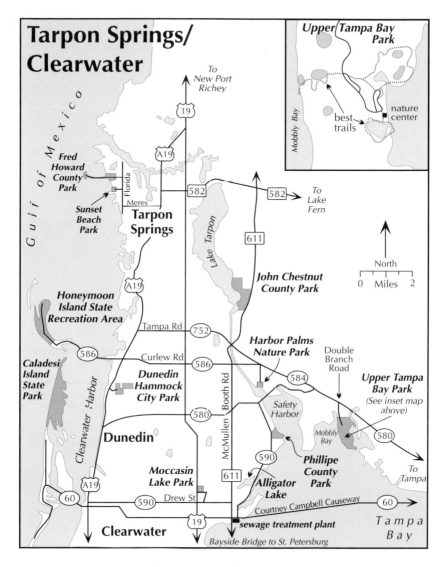

Tarpon Springs/Clearwater

TARPON SPRINGS

Fred Howard County Park (no fee) is a worthwhile spot for wintering shorebirds and migrant landbirds. To reach it from US-19 in Tarpon Springs, go west on CR-582 (Tarpon Avenue) to Alternate US-19 (1.0) and turn left. At Meres Boulevard (0.6), turn right to Florida Avenue (1.6). Turn right to Sunset Drive (1.0), and turn left to the entrance (0.2). The main park road leads to an artificial island that contains the beach. Check the causeway and the beach for wading-birds, shorebirds, gulls, and terns. Woodlands in the park can be very good for migrants, especially in fall.

Contact: Fred Howard County Park, 1700 Sunset Drive, Tarpon Springs, FL 34689; 813/937-4938.

Return to Florida Avenue and turn right. At Gulf Boulevard (0.5), turn right to Sunset Beach Park (0.3; no fee), another area good for wintering shorebirds and other waterbirds, especially at low tide.

John H. Chestnut, Jr., County Park (255 acres; no fee) is excellent for fall migrants. To reach it from US-19 in Tarpon Springs, go east on CR-582 (Tarpon Avenue). At CR-611 (East Lake Road) (3.0), turn right to the entrance on the right (4.3). To reach the park from the south, travel north from SR-752 (Tampa Road) on CR-611 to the entrance on the left (2.0). There are three nature trails through hardwood forests, cypress swamps, and along the lakeshore. At the Y in the park road, bear right, cross a bridge, and turn right. Cross another bridge and turn left into the parking lot. Walk back across the road to the boardwalk on the left. This trail goes through a mixed cypress/hardwood swamp that can be excellent for migrants in fall. The trail ends at another parking lot. To return to your vehicle, follow the road to the left.

Return to the main park road. Just before the Y, turn right into the parking lot. A trail that begins to the right of the restrooms ends at the park boat ramp and contains a tower overlooking Lake Tarpon. The third trail, the Peggy Park Memorial Trail (named after a murdered wildlife officer), is a loop trail 3,000 feet long. It is located to the left of the Y, a bit past the boat ramp on the right. Limpkins are seen occasionally along the canal on the right, but the trail is best for fall migrants.

Contact: John H. Chestnut, Jr., County Park, 3900 Sandy Point Road, Palm Harbor, FL 33685; 813/784-4686.

Return to CR-611 and turn right. Go over SR-752, where the road name changes to McMullen-Booth Road. To visit Harbor Palms Nature Park and Estuary Preserve (no fee), continue south to the traffic light at SR-586 (Curlew Road) (0.7) and turn left. At the junction with SR-752 (1.0), turn right to Oak Leaf Boulevard (0.2). Turn right to Maple Leaf Boulevard (0.9) and turn right again into the park (0.1). The park contains a boardwalk through a hardwood hammock and a mangrove forest. From the viewing platform on the bay, look north to view an active Bald Eagle nest.

Upper Tampa Bay Regional Park (2,144 acres; $1/vehicle) contains a boardwalk along a mangrove shoreline, salt marshes, estuaries, and pine flatwoods. From CR-611, go east on SR-752 or SR-586 (Curlew Road) to SR-584. Continue east to Double Branch Road (3.8) and turn right to the park on the right (0.5). (SR-584 merges with SR-580 about 1 mile before Double Branch Road.) (To reach the park from Tampa, go west on SR-580 [Hillsborough Avenue], cross SR-589 [Sheldon Road] to Double Branch Road [6.2] on the left, and proceed as above.) The best trails are the boardwalk that begins from the nature center (a Black Rail was heard calling here on the 1990 Christmas Bird Count) and the trail that heads west from the park road to Mobbly Bay. At low tide, the flats here can have numerous wading-birds (sometimes including Reddish Egrets), shorebirds (including American Oystercatchers), and the ubiquitous gulls and terns. When the tide is in, look for sea ducks and other salt water species. The oak hammock at the beginning of the trail can be great for migrant and wintering landbirds. An active Bald Eagle nest is located just northwest of the park; the birds are often seen overhead.

Contact: Upper Tampa Bay Regional Park, 8001 Double Branch Road, Tampa, FL 33615; 813/855-1765.

Return to the junction of SR-586 (Curlew Road) and CR-611 and turn left (south). At the traffic light at SR-580 (1.6), turn left onto SR-590 (Bayshore Boulevard) (1.0). Follow SR-590 as it turns right and proceed to the entrance of **Philippe County Park** (no fee) on the left. This is another park that can be good for migrant and wintering landbirds. The park is located on the west shore of Safety Harbor. The main park road ends at a tidal lagoon surrounded by a small area of mangroves and salt marsh. Look here for Yellow-crowned Night-Herons. Scope the water from along the shore for wintering ducks and other waterbirds. There are always a few Spotted Sandpipers along the seawall in winter.

CLEARWATER

Alligator Lake contains a large wading-bird rookery in spring and summer and is also a good year-round spot for Limpkins. From Philippe Park, continue south on SR-590 to 7th Street (2.0) and turn right. Go west a few blocks to Safety Harbor City Park on the left. A boat ramp at the west end offers views of the lake. You may also view the lake from near the SR-590 bridge over the lake. The heronry is located on the island in the middle of the lake. In 1994, Reddish Egrets nested here. From the bridge, it is 1.6 miles south to SR-60.

To reach Moccasin Lake Park ($2/person), go south to SR-60 and turn right. At CR-611 (McMullen-Booth Road) (0.25), turn right. At Drew Street (0.4), turn left to Fairwood Avenue (0.8), then turn right. Cross the railroad tracks (0.6) and turn left onto Park Trail to the park entrance (0.2). (To reach the park from US-19, go east on Drew Street [0.4 miles north of SR-60] to Fairwood Avenue [0.3], turn left, and proceed as above.) The park is heavily wooded and contains trails through the forest. One trail offers a view of Moccasin Lake. The park is best during fall migration. Limpkins are seen regularly near the lake.

SR-60 is one of three highways across Tampa Bay linking Clearwater/St. Petersburg with Tampa. The shoreline of Courtney Campbell Causeway (the part of SR-60 over Tampa Bay) can be excellent for a variety of waterbirds, especially in winter. From McMullen-Booth Road (CR-611) travel east and pull off onto the causeway to an unpaved parking area (0.2). Scan the bay for flocks of wintering waterfowl. Afterward, walk west to the sewage-treatment facility. In winter, a sandbar there can be full of shorebirds at low tide, and there are usually a few Bonaparte's Gulls in the area, too.

DUNEDIN

Honeymoon Island State Recreation Area (408 acres; $4 fee) is one of the outstanding birding locations on Florida's Gulf coast, especially for shorebirds. To reach it from US-19, go west on SR-586 (Curlew Road) to the entrance. Check the shorelines of the causeway for wading-birds, shorebirds, and gulls, terns, and skimmers, and scan offshore for ducks. The park is excellent also for all waterbirds and migrant and wintering landbirds. In addition to numerous common species, birds to expect here include Reddish Egret, Snowy (breeds), Wilson's (breeds), and Piping Plovers, American Oystercatcher (breeds), Whimbrel, Red Knot, "Sharp-tailed" Sparrow (*Spartina* marshes), and many other species. Winter rarities reported in the past decade include Northern Gannet, scoters, Bar-tailed Godwit, Curlew Sandpiper, Long-billed Murrelet, Ash-throated Flycatcher, and Clay-colored, Le Conte's, and White-crowned Sparrows. One or more Long-billed Curlews used to winter here regularly, but the birds have been absent for the past few years.

From the entrance station, follow the main park road a few hundred feet to a small parking area on the right. At low tide, the sandspit just offshore is often covered by a variety of wading-birds, shorebirds, and larids. Continue to the north end of the northernmost parking lot. Park at the picnic area on the right (0.9) and follow the hiking trail through the pines to the north end of the island. The woods here can be excellent for migrants in spring and fall. Gray Kingbirds, Black-whiskered Vireos, and

Prairie Warblers breed here, and Mangrove Cuckoos have occurred in late spring. There are many Osprey nests in the pines.

After leaving the picnic area, go to the north end of the beach parking lot. Walk north along the beach, watching both the ocean and the lagoon for additional water-related species. The far north end of the sandspit (a walk of over a mile) has one of the greatest shorebird concentrations in Florida throughout most of the year. This area, some of which may be under water during high tide, is also one of the most important Florida wintering sites for Piping Plovers; as many as 100 winter here annually. *Avoid areas of the beach that are posted to protect bird nesting and roosting areas.* Walking south from the beach parking area may also be productive. Check out the marshy areas for Mottled Ducks, rails, and sparrows.

Contact: Honeymoon Island State Recreation Area, 1 Causeway Boulevard, Dunedin, FL 34698; 813/469-5942.

Dunedin Hammock City Park (80 acres; no fee) is excellent for fall migrants. To reach the park from Honeymoon Island, go east on Curlew Road to Alternate US-19 and turn right (south). At Mira Vista Drive (1.3), turn left, then left again onto Douglas Avenue (0.2). Turn right onto Buena Vista Drive (0.2) to the park. A boardwalk that ends in a brackish water marsh can be reached via a bridge over the canal that leads east from the parking area. In winter, rails, Marsh Wrens, and Swamp Sparrows may be observed from the boardwalk or the observation tower. To bird the hammock for migrants, follow the many trails east or south from the parking lot. Although these trails are unmarked, they are all loops that return to the parking lot. Among many other species, Blue-winged and Golden-winged Warblers are regular here. Mosquitoes are usually a problem in fall, so bring along repellent.

Contact: Department of Leisure Services, 903 Michigan Avenue, Dunedin, FL 34698.

ST. PETERSBURG AREA

Bonner Park (no fee) in Largo is another small park that can be excellent for migrant landbirds. To reach it from US-19, go west on SR-688 (Ulmerton Road) to 143rd Street (7.6) and turn right. The park is ahead (0.5). The trail on the left at the entrance (walk back south from the parking lot) leads to a hammock and is the best trail for finding migrants. Another trail east of the entrance road is also worth birding.

Freedom Lake Park (no fee) is a small city park that offers fair birding for waterbirds. From Ulmerton Road, drive south on US-19 to 49th Street

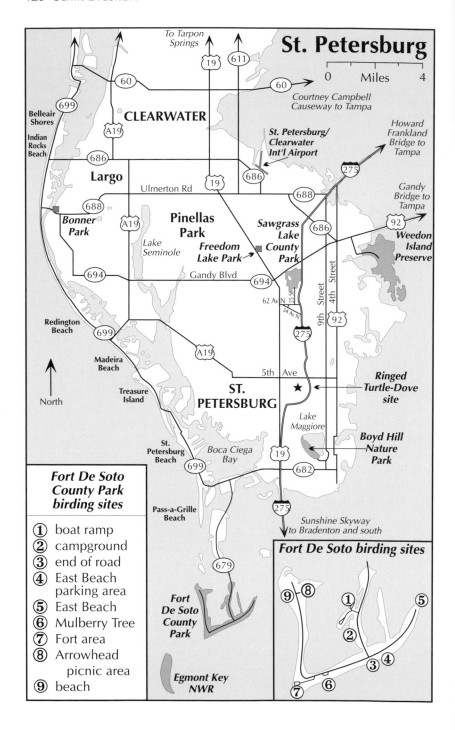

St. Petersburg

To Tarpon Springs

Courtney Campbell Causeway to Tampa

St. Petersburg/ Clearwater Int'l Airport

Howard Frankland Bridge to Tampa

Gandy Bridge to Tampa

CLEARWATER

Belleair Shores

Indian Rocks Beach

Largo

Ulmerton Rd

Pinellas Park

Lake Seminole

Bonner Park

Freedom Lake Park

Sawgrass Lake County Park

Weedon Island Preserve

Gandy Blvd

62 Av N

34 Av N

Redington Beach

Madeira Beach

Treasure Island

North

5th Ave

ST. PETERSBURG

Ringed Turtle-Dove site

Lake Maggiore

Boyd Hill Nature Park

St. Petersburg Beach

Boca Ciega Bay

Pass-a-Grille Beach

Sunshine Skyway to Bradenton and south

9th Street

4th Street

Fort De Soto County Park birding sites

① boat ramp
② campground
③ end of road
④ East Beach parking area
⑤ East Beach
⑥ Mulberry Tree
⑦ Fort area
⑧ Arrowhead picnic area
⑨ beach

Fort De Soto County Park

Egmont Key NWR

Fort De Soto birding sites

(2.6) and turn left. At Lake Boulevard (0.2) turn right and make an immediate right onto 102nd Ave. The park is on the right (0.4). (To reach the park from I-275, exit onto SR-694 [Gandy Boulevard] and go west. At US-19, turn right to 49th Street [1.8], turn right and proceed as above.) Monk Parakeets nest in the pines on the right, and until 1995 Budgerigars could usually be found in the sycamores and pines lining the road. Eurasian Collared-Doves are common in the area. At the lake, wading-birds and Muscovy Ducks are common year round. A blue-morph Snow Goose wintered here in 1995-1996. But the species which most birders visit the park to see is Limpkin. Freedom Lake is the most reliable spot in Pinellas County for finding Limpkins, despite the fact that the area is surrounded by development. On the 1994 Christmas Bird Count, 6 individuals were found here, and 5 were counted in 1995.

Sawgrass Lake County Park (400 acres; no fee) is an excellent birding spot in fall and winter. To reach it from Freedom Lake Park, return to US-19 and go south to 62nd Avenue North. Turn left onto it, and just before the overpass (0.6) turn left onto 25th Street, and proceed to the entrance (0.4). (From I-275 northbound, exit [14B] onto 54th Avenue North and go northwest. Angle right onto Haines Road [0.3], turn right sharply onto 62nd Avenue North [0.8], and turn left onto 25th Street just before the overpass [0.5]. Follow this road to the park.)

The park contains Red Maple swamps, oak hammocks, a large part of Sawgrass Lake, and other habitats. Two miles of trails wind through the forests, with over a mile of elevated boardwalk, including an observation tower overlooking the lake. During winter, the lake usually hosts Glossy Ibises, many ducks (including Green-winged Teal, Mottled Ducks, Northern Shovelers, American Wigeons, and Ring-necked Ducks), and Limpkins. Black-necked Stilts have begun to winter here recently. Woodland species that are rare in Florida in winter seem to occur more commonly in this park than in other nearby areas. Broad-winged Hawks, Black-throated Green Warblers, and Summer Tanagers have all been found nearly annually in winter recently. Florida's first verified wintering Townsend's Warbler was recorded here in 1993-1994, and the only Golden-cheeked Warbler ever recorded east of the Mississippi River was found here in August 1966. Over 200 species of birds have been reported in the park, including a Bell's Vireo found in December 1995.

Sawgrass Lake County Park is also productive during fall migration, especially from mid-August to mid-September, when early fall migrants such as Blackburnian and Cerulean Warblers occur regularly. In a typical fall season, 30 or more warbler species are reported, along with many other migrants. The best areas in the park for migrants are around the parking lot and in the oak hammock reached from the Maple Trail boardwalk (past Marker 6). After returning to the boardwalk, continue around the loop and return to the parking lot by walking along the canal. The oaks here are also good for migrants; this is where the Townsend's Warbler wintered. **Contact:** Sawgrass Lake Park, 7400 25th Street North, St. Petersburg, FL 33702; 813/527-3814.

Weedon Island State Preserve (1,300 acres; no fee) is the largest natural area remaining in St. Petersburg. Unfortunately, the birding opportunities are rather limited. To reach the preserve from I-275, go east on SR-694 (Gandy Boulevard), cross SR-92, and turn right onto San Martin Boulevard (1.1). At Weedon Island Drive (0.9) turn left to the park ahead. From the entrance gate, turn left onto the first dirt road (1.0) to the designated trail parking area. Walk the trail, bearing left at the fork, which leads to Lookout Point. A ½-mile-long trail to the left may be good for Mangrove Cuckoos and other species. **Contact:** Weedon Island State Preserve, 1500 Weedon Island Drive, St. Petersburg, FL 33702; 813/579-8360.

Since at least the early 1950s, a population of Ringed Turtle-Doves has lived in central St. Petersburg. Discovered in 1953 as three pairs, the population numbered in the low hundreds by the early 1990s. The birds frequently perch on TV antennas and telephone wires. Eurasian Collared-Doves also occur here, and apparent hybrids between the two species have been noted. Although the turtle-doves have increased in numbers, their range remains restricted to a small area of the city. The population may now be declining due to competition and interbreeding with Eurasian Collared-Doves. To reach the area, exit I-275 southbound at 5th Avenue North and go west. At 29th Street (0.8), turn left. Go one block to Dartmouth Avenue and turn right. *There is no exit for 5th Avenue North from I-275 northbound. If you are coming from the south, exit (#7) I-275 at 31st Street South and turn left to Dartmouth Avenue (1.0).*

A small population of Monk Parakeets is currently found on 13th Avenue North at 39th Street. Look for nests and birds in the *Melaleuca* trees lining the road and especially at the electrical substation.

Four blocks west, at 9th Avenue North, stop along the road to check the pond at the public library. There should be wading-birds here and a few ducks in winter. You should also see many Eurasian Collared-Doves in this area.

Boyd Hill Nature Park (800 acres; $1/person) in southeast St. Petersburg has over 3 miles of nature trails and a half-mile of boardwalks

Gray Kingbird
among mangrove islands
and Coconut Palms
Diane Pierce

through a variety of habitats, including frontage on Lake Maggiore (locally pronounced *ma-GOR-ee*). The park is best in spring and fall, but it is not usually as good as the other sites listed here. There is at least one active Bald Eagle nest in the park, though. To reach the park from either US-19 or I-275, go east on SR-682 (54th Avenue South). At 9th Street (also called Martin Luther King Street) (2.0) turn left and left again onto Country Club Way (0.6). The park is on the right.

Fort De Soto County Park (900 acres; no fee) at the mouth of Tampa Bay is productive at any season, but for migrant landbirds it is superb in spring and very good in late fall. Over 2.2 million visitors enter the park annually. To reach the park from US-19 (34th Street) or I-275, drive west on SR-682 (Pinellas Bayway; 54th Avenue South). At SR-679 (2.3) turn left (south) toward the park. You will encounter two toll-booths (50¢ and 35¢) for the bridges.

Shortly after entering the park (5.0), stop at the boat ramp on the right (0.2) to check the trees in the picnic area for migrants. Return to SR-679 and turn right to the campground on the right (0.6). It is often crowded with campers, so park along the main road and walk in if you are not camping here.

Return to the main park road and go south. Opposite the T intersection are the park headquarters; stop in for a free bird list. From the T, turn left to reach **East Beach parking area** (0.2). From the east end of the parking lot, enter the woods on the left just before the beach. The unmarked trails through the Australian Pines can be excellent for landbirds, including thrushes and Swainson's Warbler.

Return to the road and go to its very east end (1.5), where wadingbirds, shorebirds, and larids are found. In May, look for White-rumped Sandpipers here.

Go back to the T and continue southwest. At the first fishing pier on the left (0.9), park along the road and walk south past the ranger's house to a **grove of mulberry trees**. In the spring, the fruiting trees attract many hungry migrants (and eager birders).

Next, stop at the second fishing pier to scan the Gulf and to check the trees for migrants in the picnic area and around the fort.

The best area for migrants is **Arrowhead Picnic Area** (called "the family picnic area" by local birders), located opposite the North Beach parking area. From the fort, return to the main park road and turn left. As you near the end of the road, watch for the entrance to the picnic area on the right. The road winds through an oak hammock before ending at the picnic area. Unmarked paths criss-cross this area; all are excellent for birds during migration. Marked trails through adjacent woods are also productive. Single-day counts of 25+ warbler species have been made here after the passage of weather fronts.

The beach west of the main park road opposite Arrowhead Picnic Area is the best spot in the park for shorebirds, including Piping (winter) and Snowy Plovers. Wading-birds and larids are usually found here, too.

While driving through the park, watch for wintering or migrating raptors and Magnificent Frigatebirds (mostly spring and summer) overhead. Mowed grassy areas should be checked for migrant shorebirds such as American Golden-Plovers and Upland Sandpipers and for flocks of Bobolinks.

Contact: Fort De Soto County Park, 3500 Pinellas Bayway South, Tierra Verde, FL 33715; 813/866-2484.

Depart Pinellas County southbound on I-275 via the Sunshine Skyway bridge ($1/vehicle). The causeways on both sides of the bridge can be excellent for wading-birds, shorebirds, and larids, especially at low tide. From the north toll booth leaving St. Petersburg, you might check out the first scenic view (1.2). Continue to exit 2B (1.0) to the North Skyway Fishing Pier and rest area. Turn right just before USCGC Blackthorn Park to a road curving back along the shore back toward St. Petersburg. You can bird along here about a half mile. Among numerous common species, look for Magnificent Frigatebird (mostly spring and summer), American White Pelicans (winter), Reddish Egret, American Oyster-catchers, and other shorebirds and larids, predominantly in winter. (One or more Lesser Black-backed Gulls have been here in recent winters.) Farther along are other birding sites along the causeway. (On the *northbound side* of the causeway, a hiker-biker trail allows access for the causeway's entire length. It starts on Pinellas Point Drive and 34th Street South, just east of 1-275 at exit 3 [northbound] of the highway.)

After you cross over the bridge, you will be in Manatee County and may choose to bird a few sites in Bradenton (see page 136).

TAMPA AREA

McKay Bay Nature Park (no fee) is an excellent birding spot for waterbirds. To reach it from I-4, exit onto 39th Street and turn right. At CR-574 (7th Avenue) (0.4), turn right to 34th Street (0.4) and turn left. Go under the Crosstown Expressway overpass and turn left immediately at the sign. The park consists of a 1-mile boardwalk trail with points overlooking the bay and a small impoundment before ending at an observation tower. A covered platform is located near the parking area, which allows sheltered viewing of the northeast corner of the bay. The trail begins from the shelter and heads south. Just past a small bridge on the right, bear left onto a narrow trail that leads past the small impoundment before ending at a tower overlooking another part of the bay. An incoming tide is best.

Species that winter here regularly include American White Pelican, wading-birds (including Reddish Egret and Roseate Spoonbill), many ducks (including Mottled Duck, both teals, Northern Pintail, Northern Shoveler, and Ruddy Duck), shorebirds, especially American Oyster-catcher, Black-necked Stilt, American Avocet (the wintering flock num-

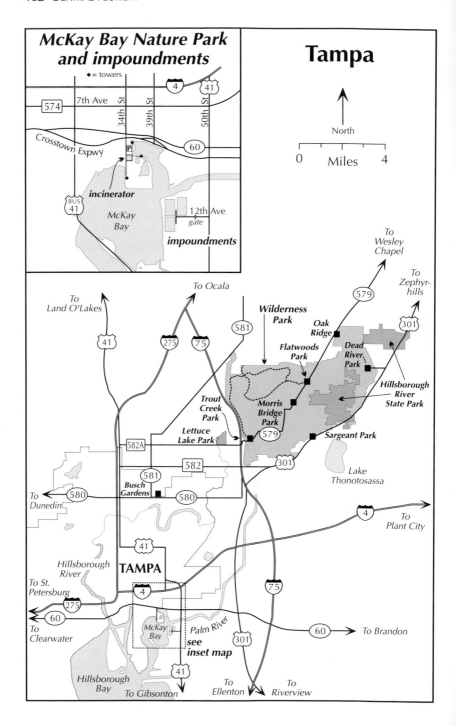

McKay Bay Nature Park and impoundments

◆ = towers

7th Ave

574

34th St
39th St
50th St

4
41

Crosstown Expwy

60

incinerator

BUS 41

McKay Bay

12th Ave
gate

impoundments

Tampa

North

0   Miles   4

To Wesley Chapel

To Zephyrhills

To Ocala

To Land O'Lakes

579

Wilderness Park

Oak Ridge

301

Dead River Park

Flatwoods Park

Hillsborough River State Park

581

41

275
75

Trout Creek Park

Morris Bridge Park

Lettuce Lake Park

582A

579

Sargeant Park

301

582

Lake Thonotosassa

581

Busch Gardens

580

To Dunedin

580

4

To Plant City

41

Hillsborough River

TAMPA

To St. Petersburg

275

4

75

60

To Clearwater

McKay Bay

Palm River

see inset map

301

60

To Brandon

To Gibsonton

41

Hillsborough Bay

To Ellenton

To Riverview

bers in the low hundreds), and Stilt Sandpiper, and Bonaparte's Gull and other larids. In summer, Gray Kingbirds and Prairie Warblers breed in the mangroves—even a Mangrove Cuckoo was found here once. Keep an eye out for the White Spoonbill seen here and at the McKay Bay impoundments since it escaped from Busch Gardens in fall 1993 (it was still present as of October 1995). Compared to a Roseate Spoonbill, this Eurasian species is larger, with all-white plumage, black legs, and a yellow-tipped black bill.

Another observation tower is at the southern end of 34th Street. This tower allows viewing of another part of the bay, where wintering Ruddy Ducks and other species are found. At low tide, Yellow-crowned Night-Heron, shorebirds, and other species will be found on the mudflats.

Note: Due to recent criminal activity in the area (including the robbery of an out-of-state birder), it is recommended that you visit the area only in groups. Lock your valuables out of sight in your vehicle.

McKay Bay impoundments (no fee), three settling-ponds built when the nearby Palm River was dredged, is another accessible area for wading-birds, wintering ducks, and shorebirds. To reach the impoundments, return to 34th Street to SR-60. Turn right to US-41 (50th Street) (1.3) and then turn right to 12th Avenue (1.0). Turn right to the yellow gate at the end of the road. Park to the side here and walk in. The ponds are above-ground impoundments contained by dikes; access is obtained by walking the tops of the dikes. The ponds are fresh water, but walking south along the west dike allows one to view the salt water mudflats along the shore of McKay Bay. Inside the ponds should be a variety of puddle ducks and shorebirds including Long-billed Dowitchers. Black-necked Stilts breed in the northern two impoundments. Wading-birds, shore-birds, and larids are found along the bay. A few dozen Stilt Sandpipers are usually found here in winter. Watch for Grasshopper Sparrows and other "grassland" species on the dikes.

Note: The impoundments are in an isolated area where some birders may not feel safe. Although there have been no incidents at this site, it may be best to visit the area only as part of a group.

Lettuce Lake Regional Park (240 acres; $1/vehicle) is located on the north side of CR-582A (Fletcher Avenue) 1.0 mile west of I-75. The park's main attraction is a 3,500-foot boardwalk that includes a 35-foot-tall observation tower. A 1-mile nature tail and paved bicycle path also provide good birding opportunities. The portion of the paved path to the right of the boardwalk entrances can be excellent for numerous migrant and wintering landbirds, especially in fall. Black-crowned Night-Herons,

Ospreys, and Limpkins are resident. In spring and summer, look for Prothonotary Warblers and Summer Tanagers.

Contact: Lettuce Lake Regional Park, 6920 East Fletcher Avenue, Tampa, FL 33592; 813/987-6204.

Recent land purchases have added 15,897 acres of protected land in the triangle between I-75 and US-301, extending northeast to Hillsborough River State Park. Thousands of additional acres northeast of the park are slated for future acquisition. Most of this recently acquired land has not been well birded, and access and facilities are still being developed. The area is known as Wilderness Park and is divided into six units. Three of the park's units are included here; each has an entrance fee of $1/vehicle.

John B. Sargeant, Sr., Memorial Park is located on the west side of US-301, 3 miles northeast of SR-582 (Fowler Avenue). The park has a short circular boardwalk along the Hillsborough River. Limpkins are often seen there.

Morris Bridge Park is located on both sides of SR-579 (Morris Bridge Road) 3.7 miles northeast of that highway's exit from I-75. The portion of the park north of SR-579 has a 1,500-foot boardwalk and a trail along the river. The southern portion of the park contains a 4,000-foot tram road that ends at the site of an old railroad bridge.

Flatwoods Park is also located on the west side of SR-579, 1.5 miles northeast of Morris Bridge Park. The park contains a 9-mile paved bicycle path and three 2,000-foot interpretive trails, all of which can all be good for fall migrants. Bachman's Sparrows are fairly common along the bicycle path.

Contact: Wilderness Park, Hillsborough County Parks and Recreation Administrative Office, 1101 East River Cove Street, Tampa, FL 33604; 813/975-2160.

Hillsborough River State Park (2,994 acres; standard fee) is good for landbirds in winter and during fall migration. The best birding is on the nature trail along the river. The park is located on the west side of US-301, 6 miles northeast of the entrance to Sargeant Park (or 9 miles from SR-582). (To reach the park from the north, turn south on US-301 from SR-54 West in Zephyrhills and proceed south to the entrance [7.2].)

Contact: Hillsborough River State Park, 15402 US-301 North, Thonotosassa, FL 33592; 813/987-6771.

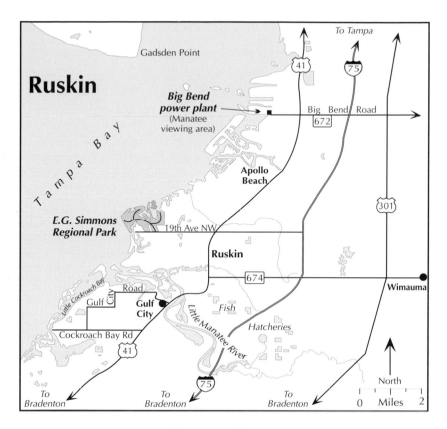

RUSKIN AREA

Tampa Electric Company offers a chance to view Endangered West Indian Manatees at the Big Bend power plant. It is located north of Ruskin on CR-672 (Big Bend Road), 1 mile west of US-41. Open from 1 December through 31 March (open 10 am to 5 pm Tuesday through Saturday, 1 to 5:30 pm Sunday, but closed Mondays), this viewing center (no fee) also offers good shorebirding at low tide, with Reddish Egrets and American Oystercatchers being observed regularly.

Contact: Corporate Relations, Tampa Electric Company, P.O. Box 111, Tampa, FL 33601; 813/228-4289.

E. G. Simmons Regional Park (458 acres; $1/vehicle) is a fine spot for wading-birds, shorebirds, and Eurasian Collared-Doves. To reach it from US-41 in Ruskin, turn west onto 19th Avenue NW to the entrance on the right (2.3).

Contact: E. G. Simmons Regional Park, 2401 19th Avenue NW, Ruskin, FL 33570; 813/671-7655.

Cockroach Bay Road is located off US-41 south of Ruskin, 4.7 miles south of the road to Simmons Park. Watch for Scissor-tailed Flycatchers in winter, especially on wires just past the orange grove on the right. In summer, Gray Kingbirds are common around the boat ramp at the end of the road (3.1 from US-41). Mangrove Cuckoos have occurred here as well and may breed regularly. For an alternate route back to US-41, turn left onto Gulf City Road (1.9 from the end). Scissor-tailed Flycatchers have wintered along this road as well. Watch also for wintering raptors, and ducks in the pond on the left.

The Gulf coast between Tampa Bay and the Fort Myers area is heavily developed and has few worthwhile birding sites. The few exceptions are listed below, and except for the Black-bellied Whistling-Duck site, even these can be bypassed if time is a factor. In that case, it is best to drive through the area from Pinellas and Hillsborough Counties on I-75. Birders who are heading to Fort Myers, Sanibel Island, or the lower east coast should continue south on I-75. Birders heading toward prairie country to look for Glossy Ibises, Crested Caracaras, Burrowing Owls, and Florida Scrub-Jays should exit I-75 at either SR-70 or SR-72 (which joins SR-70 near Arcadia). Those wishing to look for Black-bellied Whistling-Ducks should exit I-75 at SR-780 (Fruitville Road). To visit Myakka River State Park, exit I-75 at SR-72.

BRADENTON

From the south toll booth on I-275 (Sunshine Skyway), turn right onto US-19 to Terra Ceia causeway (2.6) and park before the bridge. Look for wading-birds (including Reddish Egrets), shorebirds (including Marbled Godwits), and larids. (This area is difficult to reach if you are traveling south on I-75 from Tampa or Ruskin.)

To reach the Palma Sola causeway, go south on US-41 to SR-64 (Manatee Avenue), turn right, and proceed to the causeway (5.0). The causeway bisects Palma Sola Bay and often has Reddish Egrets, Yellow-crowned Night-Herons, and other coastal species. Continue west to Perico Island. Bird the shore before you get to the bridge (1.9). In addition to common species, look for Reddish Egrets and Roseate Spoonbills here. Continue west on SR-64 to its end, at Manatee County Public Beach. Look for Monk Parakeet nests in the palms around the restrooms.

To reach Longboat Key from SR-64, go south on CR-789 (Gulf Drive). After crossing over the Longboat Key bridge (4), turn right onto Broadway

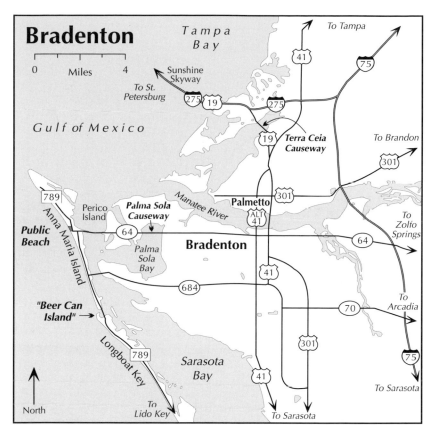

Bradenton

0 — Miles — 4

Tampa Bay

To Tampa

Sunshine Skyway

To St. Petersburg

Gulf of Mexico

Terra Ceia Causeway

To Brandon

Palmetto

789

Perico Island

Palma Sola Causeway

Manatee River

Anna Maria Island

Public Beach

64

Palma Sola Bay

Bradenton

To Zolfo Springs

"*Beer Can Island*" →

684

To Arcadia

Longboat Key

789

Sarasota Bay

To Lido Key

North

To Sarasota

To Sarasota

(0.5) to the parking area. Take the boardwalk to the beach. It is best to get here early because the beach is usually crowded with people except in the early morning. Over 200 species of birds have been reported from this area since 1977. After scanning the Gulf, look for Snowy (breeds), Wilson's (breeds), and Piping (winter) Plovers on the beach. Least Terns and Black Skimmers also nest here. Walk north to a wooded area called Beer Can Island (actually a peninsula), which can be good for migrants. In the lagoon on the east side of the "island," wading-birds (including Roseate Spoonbills and Wood Storks) and shorebirds (including American Oystercatchers) may be seen. Look for Magnificent Frigatebirds overhead, mostly in spring and summer.

Wilson's Plover
Louise Zemaitis

SARASOTA

Oscar Scherer State Park (1,384 acres; standard fee) contains the largest protected population of Florida Scrub-Jays on the Gulf coast. About 20 families are resident in this park, which also contains 3 active Bald Eagle nests. *To reach the park from I-75 southbound,* exit (#36) onto SR-681 and go southwest. At US-41, turn right and proceed to the entrance on the right (1.0). *To reach the park from I-75 northbound,* exit (#35) onto Jacaranda Boulevard and at the end of the exit ramp turn left to Venice Avenue (0.7). Turn right onto Venice Avenue and go west on it to US-41 (3.0), and turn right. The park is on the right (5.8).

Contact: Oscar Scherer State Park, 1843 South Tamiami Trail, Osprey, FL 34229; 941/483-5956.

Black-bellied Whistling-Ducks are resident near I-75 in north-central Sarasota County. Present for nearly 20 years, the birds are thought to have dispersed from Mexico or Texas and are in the midst of colonizing the Florida peninsula. The ducks are nocturnal foragers and spend the day resting around ponds. Reported in the county first at Venice in 1977 (or possibly in Sarasota in 1943!), the species is now locally common east of Sarasota (e.g., 200 observed 12 March 1993 and 250 in one flock west of I-75 on 13 November 1995). Since the early 1980s, the birds have been seen rather dependably at small ponds off Raymond Road east of Sarasota. Less regularly, they have been found at Lake Myakka and other sites in Myakka River State Park (see below). Most recently, many of the birds have moved into small ponds in residential areas west of I-75, where they are inaccessible to birders. The farming area around Palmer Boulevard can be good also for shorebirds and other waterbirds in late summer and fall.

To reach the area where the ducks may be observed, drive the dirt roads east of I-75 between SR-780 (Fruitville Road) and Bee Ridge Road. Note that all these areas are private property so *bird only from the roads*. From I-75, exit (#39) onto SR-780 (Fruitville Road) and go east. At Coburn Road (0.5) turn right. Ackerman Park on the right has a pond worth checking. The pond south of Sawgrass Road can be good for Least Bitterns and Soras (winter). The pond at Raymond Road is reached by going east on Sawgrass Road to Center Road (0.6). Turn right onto Palmer Boulevard (0.4) and turn right. At Raymond Road (0.3) turn left to the pond on the left (0.5). During winter, other waterfowl should be here also.

Myakka River State Park (28,875 acres; standard fee) southeast of Sarasota is an excellent birding spot. To reach it from I-75, exit (#37) onto SR-72 and go east to the entrance on the left (9.0). (From SR-70 in Arcadia, the park is on the right after about 27 miles. On weekends and holidays [only], a second entrance off CR-780 [Clay Gully Road] is available. It can be reached from SR-70 or SR-72.) Be sure to scan the extensive marshes where the road crosses the Myakka River and Clay Gully. Large numbers of wading-birds and wintering waterfowl can be seen here, and a few shorebirds may also be present depending on water levels. Fulvous and Black-bellied Whistling-Ducks have both been seen here.

The park has extensive oak/palm woodlands that can be good for fall migrants, but waterbirds are the big attraction. Over 12 miles of Myakka River frontage are contained in the park. Extensive shallow marshes attract waterfowl (including Fulvous and Black-bellied Whistling-Ducks and Mottled Ducks), wading-birds (including Glossy Ibises, Wood Storks, and Roseate Spoonbills on occasion), Purple Gallinules (mostly spring and summer), Limpkins (uncommon), Sandhill Cranes, and a few shorebirds. In winter, a great variety of ducks usually are present on Upper Myakka Lake (rarities have included White-cheeked Pintail, Cinnamon

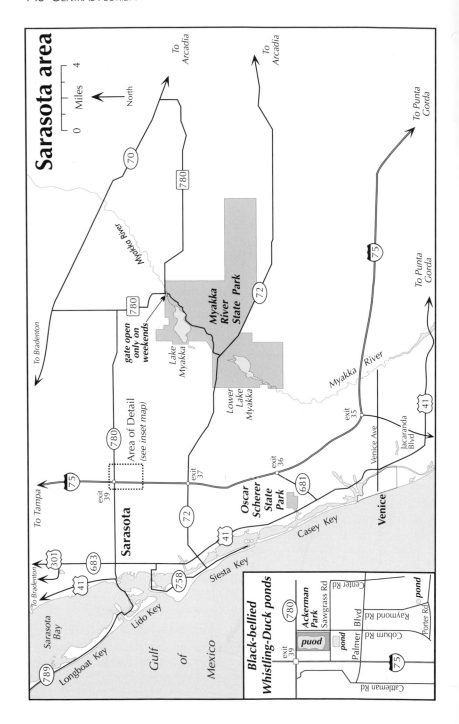

Sarasota area

North

0 Miles 4

To Arcadia

To Arcadia

To Punta Gorda

70

780

Myakka River

780

gate open only on weekends

Myakka River State Park

72

Lake Myakka

Lower Lake Myakka

Myakka River

75

To Punta Gorda

41

exit 35

Venice Ave

Jacaranda Blvd

Area of Detail (see inset map)

780

75

exit 39

exit 37

exit 36

681

Oscar Scherer State Park

72

41

Casey Key

Venice

To Tampa

Sarasota

301

683

41

758

Siesta Key

To Bradenton

To Bradenton

Sarasota Bay

Lido Key

Longboat Key

789

Gulf of Mexico

Black-bellied Whistling-Duck ponds

Ackerman Park

Sawgrass Rd

Center Rd

Porter Rd

pond

780

exit 39

puod

pond

Coburn Rd

Palmer Blvd

Raymond Rd

75

Cattleman Rd

Teal, and Eurasian Wigeon), and a few Gull-billed Terns have wintered here recently. Birds on the lake are viewed easily from the boardwalk. The *Gator Gal*, advertised as the world's largest airboat, offers one-hour tours ($6.50/person) of the lake three times a day (10 am, 11:30 am, and 1 pm). Tickets go on sale a few minutes before each tour. For more information, call 941/365-0100.

Contact: Myakka River State Park, 13207 State Road 72, Sarasota, FL 34241-9542; 941/361-6511.

Birding hotspots in Manatee and Sarasota counties, a cooperative project of three Audubon societies, was published in 1993. It has a strong coastal bias and includes many "not-so-hot" birding sites on private property, but it may be of interest to birders spending much time in the Bradenton and Sarasota areas. It may be ordered ($4) from the Sarasota Audubon Society, P.O. Box 15423, Sarasota, FL 34277-1423.

Gulf coastal areas continue on page 189.

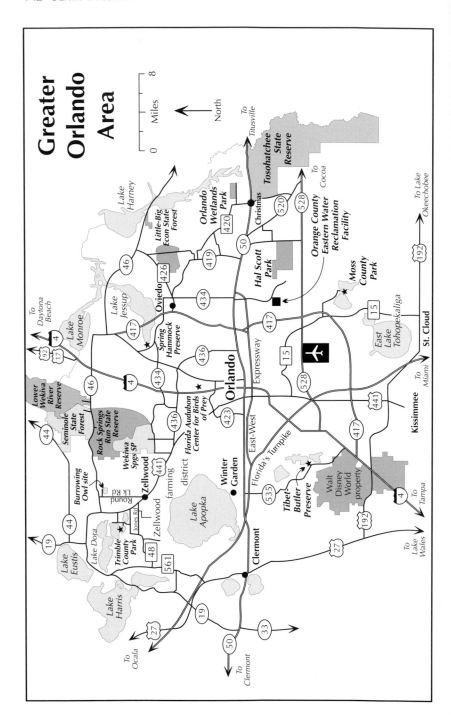

Greater Orlando Area

Central Florida – Inland

GREATER ORLANDO AREA

Birding sites in the Greater Orlando area are separated into five regions: downtown Orlando in the center and four quadrants, divided east and west by I-4 and north and south by SR-50. Because of the number of birding sites assigned to this large area, traveling from one area to another may be difficult. However, concentrating only on the bold-faced sites makes birding the Orlando area much easier, although a lot of driving may still be necessary. Deciding the starting point for directions to a given site in the Orlando area has been difficult; no one would be expected to visit all these sites in succession. Study the maps and directions carefully to determine your best route between sites. Keep in mind that the traffic on most major roads in the area can be horrendous during rush hours. Also, note that directions on road signs along I-4 are listed as east and west, even though the interstate runs roughly north-south through Orlando. To go north, follow directions *east*; to head south, go *west*.

DOWNTOWN ORLANDO

Visitors to downtown Orlando with only a few hours to spend birding may try the following route. From I-4, go west on SR-50 (Colonial Drive). At Edgewater Drive (0.2; the first traffic light), turn right to Lake Adair on the left (0.4). In winter, this lake contains numerous waterfowl and is the most reliable local spot for Canvasbacks and Redheads. Also likely to be present are Wood, Ring-necked, and Ruddy Ducks. Limpkins are present occasionally.

After circling Lake Adair, continue north on Edgewater Drive to Princeton Street (0.9; the third traffic light) and turn right. At the end of the road (1.4), turn left onto US-17/92 (Mills Avenue). Just past the first traffic light is Lake Estelle. A pair of Limpkins nests along the west side of the lake annually, and the birds are seen frequently along the edge of US-17/92, especially in spring and summer.

Continue north on Mills Avenue to Garden Drive (0.7) and turn right to **Mead Botanical Gardens** (56 acres; no fee), a city park (0.2). The park is heavily wooded and is best during fall migration. Up to 23 species of warblers have been reported here in a fall season. Breeding birds include Barred Owls and Yellow-throated Warblers.

Downtown Orlando

Maitland Blvd

Florida Audubon Center for Birds of Prey

Lake Sybelia

Horatio Avenue

East Ave

0   Mile   1

Kennedy Blvd/Lake Ave

Wymore Road

Lee Road

exit 46

Edgewater Drive

Mills Avenue

Mead Botanical Gardens

Lake Silver

Par St

Garden Drive

Lake Sue

Princeton   Street

Lake Estelle

North

Lake Adair

Edgewater Drive

To Clermont

Colonial Drive

Lake Concord

To Christmas

Birders who visit the Orlando area may wish to stop by the Madalyn Baldwin Center for Birds of Prey (open 10 am-4 pm Tuesday-Saturday; donations accepted). Operated by the Florida Audubon Society, this exceptional rehabilitation and education facility has a large collection of injured raptors that cannot be returned to the wild. Since its opening in 1979, the center has treated over 4,500 raptors and has returned 3,000 of them to the wild, including nearly 150 Bald Eagles and 8 Peregrine Falcons. Tragically, the center still receives gun-shot birds, including Bald Eagles. A pair of (wild) Barn Owls nests annually in the large oak at the entrance.

To reach the center from I-4, exit (#46) at Lee Road and turn right. Go one block, then turn left onto Wymore Road. At SR-438A (Kennedy Boulevard) (0.9; the first traffic light), turn right. (Kennedy soon becomes Lake Avenue). Watch on the left for the center's sign and turn left onto East Avenue (0.6) to the office on the left (0.2). To reach the center from US-17/92, turn west onto CR-438A (Lake Avenue) to East Avenue (0.6) and turn right to the center on the left (0.2). The Florida Audubon Society maintains a well-stocked store here with an extensive collection of bird books and related materials. Wood Ducks are often seen on Lake Sybelia from Lake Sybelia Drive just north of the center.

The center relies on outside funding to continue operating. A major source of funding is the center's popular Adopt-A-Bird program. This program allows members of the public to "adopt" a permanently injured raptor for as little as $20 per year. "Adoptive parents" receive an adoption certificate and a color photograph of "their" bird.

Contact: Madalyn Baldwin Center for Birds of Prey, 1101 Audubon Way, Maitland, FL 32751; 407/644-0190; Adopt-A-Bird: 800/874-BIRD (2473).

NORTHWEST ORLANDO

As part of a plan to preserve a large contiguous region of the Wekiva River basin northwest of Orlando, several large preserves have been established. All the parks are listed here, but access is difficult for some of them. Except for Seminole State Forest, the address is the same for all; see under Wekiwa Springs State Park. The bird list for all sites combined exceeds 200 species.

The park closest to downtown is **Wekiwa Springs State Park** (8,140 acres; standard fee). To reach it, go north on I-4 and exit (#49) onto SR-436. Proceed west to Wekiwa Springs Road (0.9) and turn right to the entrance on the right (4.1). (From US-441, go east on SR-434 to Wekiwa Springs Road [1.6] and turn left to the entrance on the left [2.9].) The park contains 8 miles of frontage along Rock Springs Run, where Limpkins may be found. The park may be excellent for migrant landbirds, especially in fall. The best trail for migrants is the trail from the main spring to Sand Lake.

Contact: Wekiva Basin GEOpark, 1800 Wekiwa Circle, Apopka, FL 32712; 407/884-2009.

Return to I-4 and go north. At SR-46, exit (#51) and go west to Lower Wekiva River State Preserve (14,538 acres; no fee) on the right (3.8). (Spellings differ here: Wekiva for the river, but Wekiwa for the springs.) From US-441, go east on SR-46 to the entrance on the left (13.9). *Access to this area is limited to those on foot or bike.* The sandhills just inside the entrance gate contain breeding Yellow-throated Warblers and Summer Tanagers in spring and summer. Red-headed Woodpeckers and a few Florida Scrub-Jays may be seen in the scrubby flatwoods. Oak woodlands can be good for migrants in fall. A bird checklist is available at the entrance.

Florida Scrub-Jay
Georges Dremeaux

To reach Seminole State Forest (10,013 acres; no fee), from Lower Wekiva State Preserve drive west on SR-46 to the entrance on the right (1.1). *The roads in the forest are also limited to foot traffic.* Eastern Bluebirds, Brown-headed Nuthatches, and Bachman's Sparrows are fairly common in the pine flatwoods along the main road. Florida Scrub-Jays are resident in the extensive scrub area across Black Water Creek. A bird checklist is available at the entrance.

Contact: Lake Forestry Station, 9610 County Road 44, Leesburg, FL 34788; 904/360-6676.

To reach Rock Springs Run State Reserve (13,850 acres; $2/vehicle), continue west on SR-46 and turn left into the reserve on (abandoned) CR-433 (1.9). Over 20 miles of trails and old roads offer birding access, but most are open only to foot traffic. At the end of the pavement (1.8), stop and look for Florida Scrub-Jays. Six families inhabit scrub along and west of the road. Swallow-tailed Kites are observed frequently in spring and summer, and Sandhill Cranes are regular breeders. Migrant landbirds may be common in fall. A bird checklist is available at the entrance gate. As you return to SR-46, notice the fence along both sides of the road. This fence was constructed to prevent Florida Black Bears from crossing the road. Instead, they are "funneled" to an underpass underneath the road. Rock Springs Run offers one of the best chances in the peninsula for sighting this Threatened mammal.

To search for Burrowing Owls, continue west on SR-46 to Round Lake Road (8.6) and turn left. At Coronado Somerset Road (0.2), turn left to South Coronado Drive on the right. Watch for the owls, which are rather numerous in this area. Drive the few roads and scan the fence-posts and fields.

From late July through September, one of the state's hot spots for shorebirds is the winter-vegetable farms at **Zellwood** (no fee). When the muck fields are flooded in late summer to destroy nematodes and to prevent subsidence, wading-birds, ducks, and shorebirds become abundant. In addition to common species, look for American White Pelicans, Glossy Ibises, Fulvous Whistling-Ducks (breeder), Mottled Ducks (breeder), American Golden-Plovers, Black-necked Stilts (common breeder), Spotted, Upland, Pectoral, Stilt, and Buff-breasted Sandpipers, Wilson's Phalaropes, and Black Terns.

To reach the farms, continue west on SR-46 to US-441 (2.0) and turn left to Zellwood. Turn right onto Jones Road (4.8), then turn left into the farm opposite Laughlin Road (0.2). (From Orlando, go west on SR-436 [Semoran Boulevard] to US-441 [Orange Blossom Trail] and turn right. At Jones Road, turn left and proceed as above.)

Another road that offers access to the fields is Canal Road, an unmarked clay road identified by the large sign for Living Carpet Sod and Nursery. This road is on the south side of Jones Road 0.9 mile west of Laughlin Road. (To reach Zellwood from Clermont and points west go north on US-27 from SR-50 in Clermont. At CR-561 [5.0], turn right to CR-48 [7.6] and turn right. At the T intersection [4.3], turn left onto CR-448A, then turn right onto Jones Road [0.5]. Canal Road is on the right [2.7], and Laughlin Road is 0.9 mile past this.)

Canal Road curves around the eastern edge of sod fields, which are good places for Black-bellied Plovers, American Golden-Plovers, and Upland, Buff-breasted, and Pectoral Sandpipers. You will soon come to the end of the road, where you may turn right or left. Drive around until you see flooded fields, then park out of the way and scan the fields. *The roads and fields here are private property but are open to birders as a courtesy. Stay out of the way of farm equipment. The clay roads are extremely slippery when they are wet, and it is easy to get stuck, so drive with extreme caution on wet roads.* Lastly, realize that the weather is likely to be stifling due to late-summer temperatures and the humidity caused by the evaporating fields. Some gates may be closed on week-ends, when the farms are patrolled by security personnel. *The farmers ask that birders call the office before visiting. It is also a good idea to ask about road conditions.*

Contact: Giles Van Dyne, Zellwood Drainage District, P.O. Box 247, Zellwood, FL 32798; 407/886-1932.

A few miles north of Zellwood is **Trimble County Park** (71 acres; no fee), well worth a stop for fall migrants after birding the farms. From Jones Road, go north on US-441 to Dudley Road (2.9) and turn left. At the end of the road (1.0), turn left onto Dora Drive. At Earlwood Drive (0.5), turn right to the park. There are two entrances; drive past the first one to the main entrance and turn left to the camping area. Follow this road to the lake, which has a short boardwalk along Lake Beauclair. Look for Black-crowned Night-Herons, Bald Eagles, and Limpkins here. At the end of the road the oak hammock can be excellent for fall migrant landbirds. For example, Cerulean Warblers are regular here in late August and September.

SOUTHWEST ORLANDO

Southwest of Orlando is Tibet-Butler Preserve (440 acres; no fee, *closed Mondays and Tuesdays*), located on Lake Tibet. To reach it from I-4, exit (#27) onto SR-535 (Winter Garden/Vineland Drive) and go north to the entrance on the right (6.1). (Alternately, from SR-50 to the north, drive south on SR-535 to the entrance on the left [9.8].) Hiking trails are available, and boardwalks will be constructed in the future. Pine Loop Trail (1-mile long) offers access to pine flatwoods, oak scrub, and a bay swamp. Screech Owl Trail (½-mile long) traverses mostly wetlands and may be closed during the summer rainy season.

Contact: Tibet-Butler Preserve, 8777 State Road 535, Orlando, FL 32836; 407/876-6696.

NORTHEAST ORLANDO

To reach Spring Hammock Preserve (315 acres; no fee) from I-4, exit onto SR-434 and go east to SR-419 (5.9). Turn left to the entrance on the right (1.9). Drive to the parking area and continue on foot to Soldier Creek. A boardwalk on the left leads through a cypress swamp where Prothonotary Warblers breed. At the end of the walk, look for wading-birds and Bald Eagles. In winter, American White Pelicans and waterfowl such as Ruddy Duck and Bufflehead may be present. Scan the water for Purple Gallinules. Return to the main road and head toward the creek. On the right is a path along the north side of the creek that is a reliable spot for Limpkins and fall migrants.

The Little-Big Econ State Forest (4,600 acres; no fee) includes 7 miles of frontage along the Econlockhatchee River. Established in 1994, the forest contains pine flatwoods, oak scrub, cypress swamps, and fresh water marshes. The forest is composed currently of two separate tracts, but over 10,000 additional acres are planned for acquisition in the future, when the forest will be one large unit. Currently, most of the area is accessible only on foot. To reach the forest from SR-434 in Oviedo, go northeast on CR-426. At Barr Street (3.4), turn right to the forest. To reach the eastern portion of the forest from Barr Street, turn right on CR-426 to Old Mims Road (3.1) and turn right. At Snowhill Road (0.2), turn right to the entrance on the right (1.9). In fall and winter, Sedge Wrens are very common in pastures and shallow marshes here.

Contact: Florida Division of Forestry; 407/262-7421 or St. Johns River Water Management District; 407/897-4311.

Orlando Wetlands Park (formerly called Orlando Wilderness Park; some signs still use that name) (1,280 acres; no fee) has many ponds that filter excess nutrients from treated wastewater before it flows into the St. Johns River. To reach the park, drive east on SR-50 past SR-520. At CR-420 (Fort Christmas Road) (4.1), turn left. At unmarked Wheeler Road (2.3), turn right to the park (1.0). Check in and out at the visitor kiosk on the left (0.5), where checklists are available. The park is closed 1 October to 20 January because of a private hunting lease on the property. Motorized vehicles are prohibited inside the park, but walking is easy on the berm roads.

Birding is best in late winter and early spring when many waterfowl and shorebirds join the resident wading-birds. The park list includes 18 species of ducks, including Mottled Duck, Northern Shoveler, and a Masked Duck that was found in November 1994. Bald Eagles are often seen overhead, Snail Kites are occasional visitors, and Limpkins are year-round residents. Some other species of interest include American White Pelican, Least Bittern, Glossy Ibis, Roseate Spoonbill, Wood Stork, and Black-necked Stilt.

Contact: City of Orlando Recreation Bureau, 649 West Livingston Street, Orlando, FL 32801; 407/246-2348 or 407/246-2288.

SOUTHEAST ORLANDO

To visit Tosohatchee State Reserve (34,000 acres; $2/vehicle; map on page 142) from Orlando Wetlands Park, return to SR-50 and turn left to Taylor Creek Road (0.3). Turn right to the reserve on the left (2.8). Sign in and out at the kiosk at the entrance. Tosohatchee contains pine flatwoods, fresh water marshes, cypress swamps, hardwood and palm hammocks, and 19 miles of frontage along the St. Johns River. Vehicle access is limited to the middle portion of the reserve. During summer, many roads may be closed due to flooding. Characteristic breeding birds include Swallow-tailed Kite, Bald Eagle, Wild Turkey, Brown-headed Nuthatch, Eastern Bluebird, Prothonotary Warbler, and Bachman's Sparrow. Organized hunts occur in season throughout most of the reserve.

Contact: Tosohatchee State Reserve, 3365 Taylor Creek Road, Christmas, FL 32709; 407/568-5893.

Hal Scott Regional Preserve and Park (4,651 acres; no fee) is southeast of Orlando along the Econlockhatchee River. It is an area of pine flatwoods, cypress swamps, and wet prairies. Some property was acquired as off-site mitigation for the construction of the southern extension of SR-417 around Orlando. Access by vehicles is not permitted, but a hiking trail is being developed. Breeding species include Brown-headed Nuthatch and Bachman's Sparrow. At least one cluster of Red-cockaded Woodpeckers occurs in the preserve, but a round-trip hike of about 4 miles is required to reach it.

To reach the preserve from SR-50 west of Christmas, go south on SR-520 to Maxim Boulevard (the entrance to the Wedgewood development) (2.2) and turn right. At the T intersection with Bancroft Boulevard (1.0), turn left and proceed to Meredith Parkway (0.1), then turn right. Drive to the end of the road (1.0) and turn left onto Dallas Boulevard. The entrance is on the right (1.6). (To reach the preserve from SR-528 [Bee Line Expressway], exit onto Dallas Boulevard, and go on to the park on the left [2.5]. *Note that the Dallas Boulevard exit—marked on the exit sign as private property—is for eastbound traffic only; you cannot exit onto Dallas Boulevard westbound.)*

Contact: Orange County Parks and Recreation Department; 407/836-4290, or St. Johns Water Management District; 407/897-4311.

The **Orange County Eastern Water Reclamation Facility** (2,062 acres; no fee) contains numerous ponds that treat wastewater before it is discharged into the Econlockhatchee River. To reach the facility from SR-50, go south on Alafaya Trail (the southern extension of SR-434) to the entrance on the right (3.3). Sign in and out at the Operations and Control Building on the right. (It is open 7 days a week, 24 hours a day.)

Around the entrance a family of Florida Scrub-Jays is resident currently, and the birds are sometimes perched on the powerlines along the road. However, because most of the scrub has been destroyed for the housing development to the north, the birds are unlikely to persist here. Around the ponds, Glossy Ibises and Mottled Ducks are residents, Bald Eagles are fairly common in fall and winter, and shorebirds are present fall through spring. Black-necked Stilts have recently begun to breed here. During winter, there usually is a good variety of ducks on the ponds, and American Pipits are found along muddy edges. It is permissible to drive along the grassy berms south to the transmission-line right-of-way. Three boardwalks have been built through three swamps on the property. Be sure to check the brushy areas for migrants.

Contact: Orange County Public Utilities Division, 1821 Alafaya Trail, Orlando, FL 32828; 407/836-7700.

Moss County Park (1,551 acres; $1/vehicle) is located southeast of Orlando between Lake Hart and Lake Mary Jane. To reach it from SR-528 (Bee Line Expressway), go south on CR-15 (Narcoossee Road) to Moss Park Road (2.8) and turn left. The park is ahead (4.5). The park contains oak hammocks, pine flatwoods, and fresh water marshes. A wading-bird rookery located on a small island in Lake Mary Jane is visible from the park. The rookery includes nesting Snowy Egrets, Little Blue and Tricolored Herons, Black-crowned Night-Herons, White Ibises, and Wood Storks.

To reach Merritt Island or other Atlantic coast birding sites from Orlando, go east on SR-50 or SR-520. Descriptions of sites in that area begin on page 174.

KISSIMMEE/ST. CLOUD AREA

For birders visiting Disney World or Orlando, Kissimmee (pronounced *kih-SIM-ee*) and St. Cloud offer many excellent birding spots within a half-hour drive of the city. In particular, Lake Tohopekaliga (usually shortened to "Toho") in Kissimmee, East Lake Tohopekaliga in St. Cloud, and the extensive flatwoods and prairies to the south are popular birding areas. To reach the area from Orlando, go south on any of the following roads: US-17/92, US-441, SR-91 (Florida's Turnpike), or SR-15. (From the west, exit I-4 at CR-532 [County Line Road] or US-192 and go east to Kissimmee.)

On Lake Tohopekaliga in Kissimmee, Brinson Park (no fee) contains a wading-bird rookery and is good for other waterbirds as well. To reach it from US-192 (Vine Street in town), drive south on US-17/92 to Drury Avenue (0.6) and turn left. At its end at Lakeshore Boulevard (0.4), turn left to CR-525 (Neptune Road) (0.2) and turn right to the park on the left. In winter the evening flight of wading-birds can be spectacular. Fulvous Whistling-Ducks nest in the marshes in the area, and American White Pelicans are seen occasionally in winter.

From US-441/17/92 (Orange Blossom Trail) in Kissimmee, go west on US-192 to CR-525 (Bermuda Avenue) (0.8) and turn left. At Emmett Street (0.9), the road becomes US-17/92; continue south to CR-531 (Pleasant Hill Road) (2.6) and turn left. At Poinciana Boulevard (7.5), turn left to Southport Park on the south shore of Lake Tohopekaliga. Although owned by Osceola County, the park is operated privately. There is a $1 fee for using the picnic area and campground, but the parking lot and boat ramp are free. The large oaks in the campground and the small swamp can be good for migrants. A pair of tame Sandhill Cranes is often found near the office. An active Bald Eagle nest is located in a cypress in the northeast corner of the park. Fulvous Whistling-Ducks and Snail Kites are seen on the lake occasionally. A pair of Crested Caracaras has nested annually north of Southport Road, and the birds may be seen from the road, especially in winter.

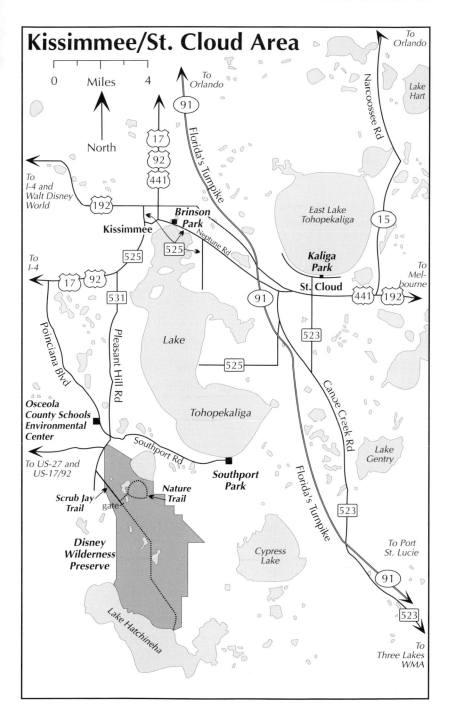

Kissimmee/St. Cloud Area

To Orlando

0　Miles　4

North

To I-4 and Walt Disney World

To I-4

To US-27 and US-17/92

91

To Orlando

17

92

441

192

Florida's Turnpike

Brinson Park

Kissimmee

525

525

Neptune Rd

525

17　92

531

Poinciana Blvd

Pleasant Hill Rd

Lake

Tohopekaliga

Osceola County Schools Environmental Center

Southport Rd

Southport Park

Scrub Jay Trail

gate

Nature Trail

Disney Wilderness Preserve

Lake Hatchineha

Cypress Lake

Narcoossee Rd

To Orlando

Lake Hart

East Lake Tohopekaliga

15

Kaliga Park

St. Cloud

441　192

To Melbourne

523

525

Canoe Creek Rd

Florida's Turnpike

Lake Gentry

523

To Port St. Lucie

91

523

To Three Lakes WMA

Return to Pleasant Hill Road and turn left to Scrub Jay Trail (1.2), which leads to Disney Wilderness Preserve (11,475 acres; no fee), an area of Longleaf Pine flatwoods, oak scrub, and wetlands. The original acreage was purchased in 1992 by the Walt Disney Company as mitigation for destroyed wetlands in a massive Disney development being built southwest of Kissimmee. Additional lands have been added to the preserve from other mitigation projects.

Characteristic flatwoods species such as Red-headed Woodpecker, Brown-headed Nuthatch, Pine Warbler, Bachman's Sparrow, and Summer Tanager (spring and summer) occur here. The preserve also contains an important population of about 40 groups of Florida Scrub-Jays and 12 Bald Eagle nests. Most of the property is not easily accessible to the public, but a nature trail on the left is provided (1.8 from Pleasant Hill Road). The trail is a loop that is 4.7 miles long. Because the road can be rough in summer and there may be controlled burns in winter, it may be advisable to call the preserve before you visit.

Contact: Disney Wilderness Preserve, 6075 Scrub Jay Trail, Kissimmee, FL 34759; 407/935-0002.

Return to Poinciana Boulevard and turn left to the Osceola County Schools Environmental Study Center (200 acres; no fee) on the left (1.0). *The center is open to the public only on weekends* (10 am to 5 pm Saturday, and noon to 5 pm Sunday). The center has an 1,800-foot boardwalk through a cypress swamp. A Bald Eagle nest is visible from this boardwalk.

Because no road travels around Lake Tohopekaliga, you must return to Kissimmee to continue birding; it is 7 miles from the environmental center to US-17/92.

ST. CLOUD

To bird the St. Cloud area from US-441/192 (Space Coast Parkway), go north on CR-523 (Vermont Avenue) to Lakeshore Boulevard (0.9) and turn right. Kaliga Park (no fee), a small park on **East Lake Tohopekaliga**, is on the left (0.6). This is a good spot for Least Bittern, Mottled Duck, Glossy Ibis, Limpkin, and Sandhill Crane. The main attraction is Snail Kite, which is resident here but easier to find in winter. Scan the marshes carefully for the kites. If you don't find them here, travel along Lakeshore Boulevard both east and west of Kaliga Park and scan the lake. Another good spot for Snail Kites is near the sewer plant to the west (1.0). A boat ramp at St. Cloud Canal (0.7 west of the sewer plant) offers another view of the lake where kites may be seen.

Return to US-192 westbound and turn south onto CR-523 (Vermont Avenue), which quickly becomes Canoe Creek Road. Canoe Creek Road parallels Florida's Turnpike for about 35 miles. On the drive from St. Cloud, you will probably see Bald Eagles and Sandhill Cranes. Crested Caracaras and Wild Turkeys are also likely, especially around dawn and dusk. Osceola County has the greatest density of Wild Turkeys in Florida. Carefully scan the pastures on the right, especially those next to woodlands and swamps. Up to 100 (!) Wild Turkeys have been observed where Canoe Creek crosses the road.

Proceed about 20 miles, then turn right onto unpaved **Joe Overstreet Road** to look for wading-birds, Crested Caracaras, Wild Turkeys, and Eastern Bluebirds. Burrowing Owls are often found in the sod field past the Sailor Hammock sign on the left (3.4). Overstreet Road ends at Lake Kissimmee (1.8). Scan the marshes and water for Least Bitterns, wading-birds (including Glossy Ibises), ducks, Snail Kites, Bald Eagles, Limpkins, and Purple Gallinules. In fall 1994, two Whooping Cranes (released from the nearby Three Lakes Wildlife Management Area) were observed frequently along the road.

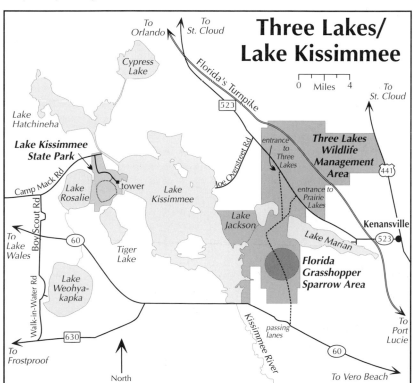

Crested Caracara
Diane Pierce

Return to CR-523 and continue southeast to the entrance of Three Lakes Wildlife Management Area (54,196 acres; no fee) on the right (3.7). From SR-60, enter the WMA on a dirt road 39.3 miles northwest of I-95, or 5.0 miles east of the Kissimmee River. The entrance (marked by a large sign) is immediately east of the beginning of the westbound passing lane. The road is best driven by high-clearance vehicles, and can be quite rough during hunting season. Three Lakes contains pine flatwoods, dry prairies, lakes, marshes, and hammocks. Currently, 34 Red-cockaded Woodpecker clusters occur in the area, including a cluster at the entrance from CR-523; look for the white bands on the cavity trees. All other pine flatwoods species are common here, including Brown-headed Nuthatch, Eastern Bluebird, Pine Warbler, and Bachman's Sparrow. Florida Grasshopper Sparrows (an Endangered endemic race) are found in the extensive dry prairies southwest of Lake Marian, and a few Florida Scrub-Jays occur in the scattered patches of scrub in the flatwoods. Many roads in the area may be impassable in two-wheel-drive vehicles, and hunting occurs from September through April. Contact the Florida Game and Fresh Water Fish Commission for more information.

Return to CR-523 and turn right into Prairie Lakes Preserve (2.0), an 8,003-acre unit of Three Lakes Wildlife Management Area with less hunting. (This is about 9 miles from US-441.) At Parker Slough (2.0) a primitive campground in an oak hammock on the right is good for birding and picnicking.

Contact: Florida Game and Fresh Water Fish Commission, 1239 SW 10th Street, Ocala, FL 34474; 904/732-1225.

From January 1993 to March 1996, about 100 Whooping Cranes have been released in the Three Lakes area in an attempt to establish a non-migratory population in Central Florida. While many of the first birds released were killed by Bobcats, new release techniques have decreased this mortality. The goal of the project is to have a minimum of 25 pairs breeding in the state by 2020.

Return to CR-523 and continue southeast for about 5 miles. There is a small restaurant (closed Mondays) on the right as the roads curves left. Turn right here onto Arnold Road toward Lake Marian, then turn right to Fred's Fish Camp, which may have Limpkins. CR-523 ends at US-441 in about 4 miles. By turning right at US-441, you can reach Florida's Turnpike or SR-60 at Yeehaw Junction (14). If returning to the Kissimmee/St. Cloud area, you may wish to take US-441 back north, which ends at US-192. Then turn left to reach St. Cloud (13.0). This road is also good for observing Bald Eagles, Wild Turkeys, and Sandhill Cranes.

LAKELAND   3/18/00

Large concentrations of wading-birds, waterfowl, shorebirds, and larids (including many rarities) have been observed in the extensive phosphate-mining district centered in Polk County. However, these sites are off-limits to the public because of ongoing mining operations and associated safety concerns. Lake Region Audubon Society is an excellent local birding group that schedules occasional trips into the mining area. For more information, contact Buck and Linda Cooper at 941/324-7304.

From August through October, **Saddle Creek County Park** (740 acres; no fee) can be an excellent spot for fall migrants (see map on next page). The park is also a reliable spot for Limpkins if you arrive early (i.e., before most park visitors). To reach the park from I-4, take SR-33 south to CR-659 (1.7) and turn left. (Note: many maps call this road CR-33A.) At US-92 (4.8) turn left and proceed to the entrance on the left (1.6). Upon entering the park, drive straight to the fenced swimming area at the back of the park. Park here and walk to the start of the trail by the wooden observation tower. The trail winds along a levee for about a mile, then ends. You must return via the same levee, but there are many side trails to explore. Bring along insect repellent in fall. Lake Region Audubon Society sponsors "warbler walks" every Saturday in September and October, at 7:30 am, starting at the swimming area.

LIMP (1)   EAPH
TUVU roost
GREG roost

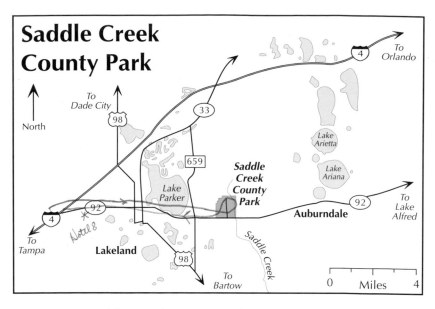

Saddle Creek County Park

To Orlando

To Dade City

North

Lake Arietta

Lake Ariana

Saddle Creek County Park

Lake Parker

Auburndale

To Lake Alfred

To Tampa

Lakeland

Saddle Creek

To Bartow

0 Miles 4

Contact: Saddle Creek County Park, 3716 Morgan Comee Road, Lakeland, FL 33801; 941/499-2613.

LAKE WALES

Lake Kissimmee State Park (5,030 acres; standard fee; map on page 155) is a good spot to see Bald Eagles throughout the year. Several pairs nest in the park; one nest is observed easily from the "Cow Camp." To reach the park from Lake Wales, go east on SR-60 to Boy Scout Road (15.0) and turn left. At Camp Mack Road (3.7) turn right to the entrance on the right (5.6). Other species found in the park include Crested Caracara, Wild Turkey, Limpkin, Sandhill Crane, Red-headed Wood-pecker, Hairy Woodpecker, Florida Scrub-Jay (at the entrance), and Bachman's Sparrow. In spring and summer, watch for Swallow-tailed Kites and Summer Tanagers. There are 13 miles of hiking trails in the park, and an observation tower at the picnic area overlooks Lake Kissim-mee.

Contact: Lake Kissimmee State Park, 14248 Camp Mack Road, Lake Wales, FL 33853; 941/696-1112.

AVON PARK

For pineland species, Lake Wales Ridge State Forest (also signed as Lake Arbuckle State Forest; 13,603 acres; no fee) is a good stop. *Be forewarned that many forest roads may not be passable in two-wheel-drive vehicles.* To reach it from the junction of US-27 and US-98, go east on CR-630. Turn left to remain on CR-630 (0.5). At the T intersection with CR-630A (1.4), bear right to North Lake Reedy Boulevard (2.6). Turn right and drive to Lake Arbuckle Road (4.8). Turn left to Rucks Dairy Road (1.4). Turn right, watching for Florida Scrub-Jays along the way. Shortly after crossing Livingston Creek (0.8), bear left onto School Bus Road. Sign in and get a map at the kiosk just ahead. Two or three pairs of Short-tailed Hawks nest in the forest annually, and the birds are seen most reliably along Reedy and Livingston Creeks from March through May. Brown-headed Nuthatches and Bachman's Sparrows are common in the flatwoods, but Red-cockaded Woodpeckers occur only irregularly. *(Note: although School Bus Road intersects with CR-64, the gate there is usually locked, so access into the forest is as described above.)*

To walk part of the Florida National Scenic Trail, park outside the forest gate and walk the trail on the left, just inside the forest. Short-tailed Hawks are frequently seen here as they forage along the creek. Watch also for Swallow-tailed Kites. To look for Brown-headed Nuthatches and Bachman's Sparrows, drive south on School Bus Road to the access road to Lake Godwin (1.0) on the right. Park at the lake and walk the road (Trail 2, which may be rough) through the pine flatwoods.

Contact: Florida Department of Agriculture and Consumer Services, Division of Forestry, Lakeland District Office, 5745 South Florida Avenue, Lakeland, FL 33813; 941/648-3163.

Avon Park Air Force Range (106,110 acres; no fee) is an active military reservation east of Avon Park. To reach it from US-27, go east on SR-64 to the entrance (9.2). Once you pass through the checkpoint, drive to the Natural Resources Office on the left at the intersection of Frostproof Grade and Smith Grade (1.5). You must sign in here and can pick up a range map. The range has a variety of habitats, including extensive Longleaf and Slash Pine flatwoods, oak and Sand Pine scrub, dry prairies, riverine and hardwood forests, and fresh water marshes. The range is open year round except from 23 October to 23 December, when public access is limited from noon Thursday through Monday evening. A recorded message tape gives more information about access; call 941/452-4223. Many of the roads in the range are very rough; only roads

was closed 3/14/00
would be good

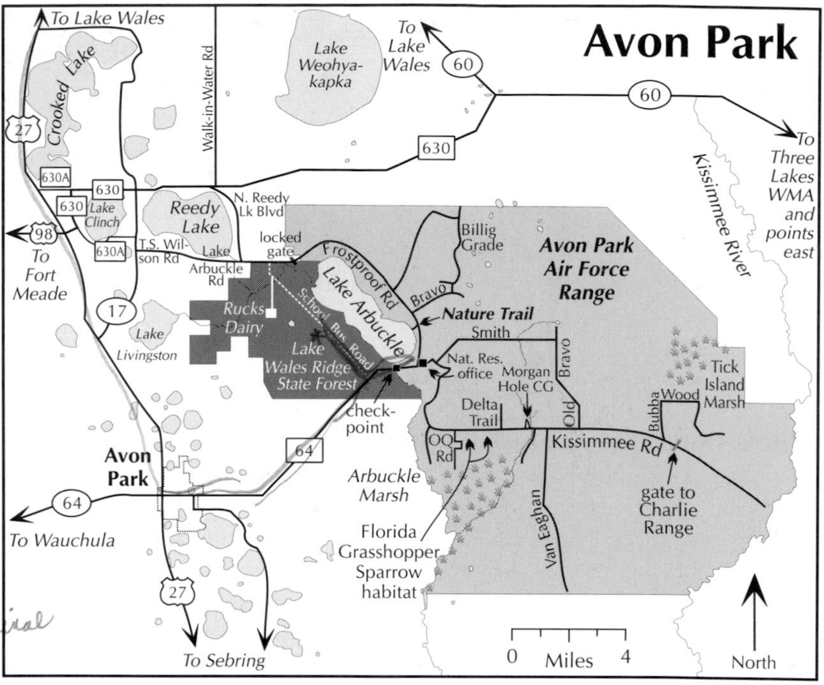

3/00

*
BGGN
NOCA cardinal
PRWA
PAWA
PIWO

that can usually be driven safely by passenger vehicles are shown on the map in this guide.

Several sought-after species are observed on the range regularly, including Swallow-tailed Kite (spring and summer), Bald Eagle, Short-tailed Hawk (spring through fall), Crested Caracara (rare), Sandhill Crane, Florida Scrub-Jay, and Florida Grasshopper Sparrow. Florida Scrub-Jays (about 300 birds, all color-banded) are common in the extensive "Bombing Range Ridge" of scrub; try along Old Bravo Road or at the intersection of Bravo Road and Billig Grade. The flatwoods support many Wild Turkeys, Red-cockaded Woodpeckers (about 20 clusters; cavity trees are marked with white paint, and the birds are color-banded), Eastern Kingbirds (spring and summer), Brown-headed Nuthatches, Eastern Bluebirds (very common), and Bachman's Sparrows. An active RCW cluster is located off Bravo Road along the north fence line east of Billig Grade. Crested Caracaras and Florida Grasshopper Sparrows occur in the extensive dry prairies on both sides of Kissimmee Road between OQ Road and Delta Trail. An active bombing range is located on the south side of the road, so keep out of this area. (Kissimmee Road through the bombing range is gated off, but the gate is usually open on weekends. *If the gate is closed, stay out: active gunnery or bombing practice is taking place.*)

To reach Arbuckle Marsh from Kissimmee Road, drive south on OQ Road. Another productive marsh is Tick Island Marsh. From Kissimmee Road, turn north on Bubba Grade to Wood Grade and turn right to the marsh on the left. At both marshes, look for American (winter) and Least Bitterns, Black-crowned Night-Herons, Wood Storks, rails, and other waterbirds.

Two areas in the range can be excellent for migrant landbirds, especially in the fall. The first, **Morgan Hole Campground**, is just north of Kissimmee Road on both sides of Morgan Creek about 3 miles east of OQ Road.

The second spot is the **Nature Trail** to Lake Arbuckle. To reach it from the office, go north on Frostproof Road. At the sand road (1.1) turn left to the parking area (0.3). The trail traverses an oak hammock and a cypress swamp and contains an observation tower on the shore of the lake. Lake Arbuckle (4,300 acres) is the largest lake remaining in Florida with an entirely protected shoreline. Waterbirds, including Purple Gallinules, are seen frequently along the lake shore, and ducks should be present in winter. Worm-eating, Blue-winged, and Golden-winged Warblers and both waterthrushes are regular here in fall.

Contact: Avon Park Air Force Range, 29 South Boulevard, Avon Park Air Force Range, FL 33825-5700; 941/452-4119.

SEBRING

With its extensive oak hammocks, **Highlands Hammock State Park** (4,694 acres, standard fee) is excellent during fall migration and is good at other seasons. In spring and summer, watch for Swallow-tailed Kites overhead; a few pairs nest in the park annually. To reach the park from US-27, drive west on CR-634. The park is straight ahead (2.6). Purchased in 1931, before the state park system was established, Highlands Hammock was saved by a group of conservationists who feared that the hammock would be cleared for agriculture. Recent land purchases by the state have added over 1,500 acres to the park's original boundaries, and 5,000 additional acres are being sought for future acquisition. Mosquitoes are usually a problem on the hammock trails, so apply insect repellent.

Southwest of the original park (in an area marked for future acquisition) occurred the last verified sighting of Ivory-billed Woodpeckers in North America. One or two birds were reported, starting in 1967. In April 1968 the roost tree of one of the birds blew down, and clear evidence of the species was provided. Two feathers of an Ivory-billed

Woodpecker (archived at the Florida Museum of Natural History in Gainesville) were collected from the cavity! Sightings persisted in the area into 1969.

There are nine trails through the park (five of these are connected); all of them can be walked in about 4 to 5 hours. Just beyond the entrance station, turn right onto the road to the campground. At the small sign that points to campground lots 105 to 138, turn right, then make an immediate

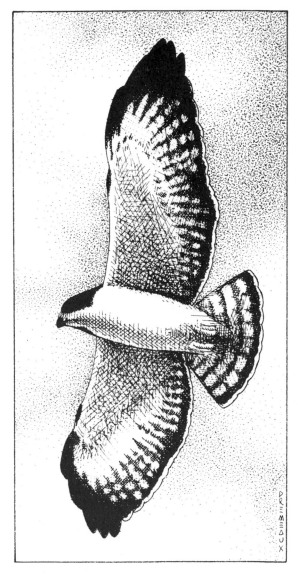

Short-tailed Hawk
Georges Dremeaux

left. The entrance to Allen Altvater Trail is on the right, opposite lot 114. (Park out of the way of campers.) The trail is a short loop through Slash Pine flatwoods (often flooded in fall) with Pine Warblers and other common woodland species. Migrants are most common in the oaks just before the small bridge.

Return to the main park road; turn right to CR-634 (0.2), and again turn right. The road traverses swamps and Slash Pine flatwoods. In the latter, look for Pine Warblers and Summer Tanagers (spring and summer). The bridge over **Charlie Bowlegs Creek** can be great for riparian migrants such as Prothonotary Warblers, waterthrushes, and other landbirds. (It is best to park on the left side of the road just beyond the bridge; be careful not to get stuck if the road is muddy.) The park ends at the junction with Hammock Road (0.5), so turn around, return to the main park road, and turn right to continue birding.

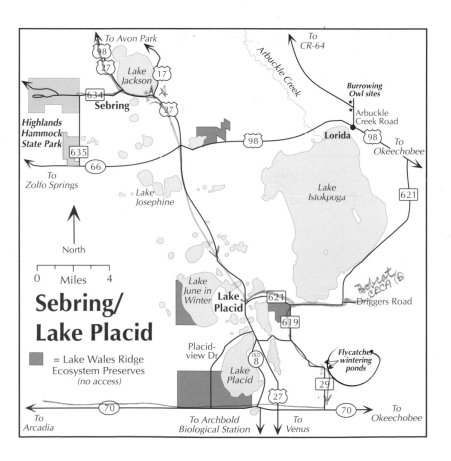

The other trails in the park traverse oak hammocks, which contain a few oaks that are over 1,000 years old and up to 38 feet in circumference. In the 1930s, surgery was performed on a few of these oaks to extend their lives. A cavity was cut into the side of a tree, and men were lowered into it. The men then removed all the dead, rotted wood from the interior of the tree. Afterward, the cavity was filled with concrete and terra-cotta tile reinforced with iron rebar to prevent future rotting of the wood. At the entrance to Lieber Memorial Trail, a large limb of one of the old oaks blew down in 1995. The broken-off portion of the limb remains on the ground to allow close inspection of the amazing "construction" of the tree's interior.

The first hammock trail, Wild Orange Trail (named for the many citrus trees naturalized in the area), begins just west of the museum on the south side of the park entrance road; *this is east of CR-634*. It crosses the park road and becomes **Alexander Blair/Big Oak Trail**. If you are not birding all the trails in the park, this trail should be one to walk, if only to view some of the magnificent old oaks. Big Oak Trail quickly becomes Hickory Trail, with its narrow "catwalk" through a bayhead. The trail ends at the park road. Cross it to bird Fern Garden Trail and Lieber Memorial Trail. Both trails include boardwalks through bay and cypress swamps, where waterthrushes and other migrants are found regularly in fall. At the end of Lieber Memorial Trail, walk *right* to return to your vehicle.

Drive to the fork and bear right. Past Lieber Memorial Trail is Young Hammock Trail, a loop trail through pine flatwoods which are succeeding, in the absence of fire, to an oak/bay hammock. Return to your vehicle and drive to the west side of the park loop to reach **Cypress Swamp Trail**, with its extensive boardwalk through a cypress swamp bordering Charlie Bowlegs Creek. This trail may be crowded with people, but it can be good for migrant birds in fall. Limpkins, Barred Owls, and American Alligators may be found on quiet days. The last trail, **Ancient Hammock Trail**, is another loop trail through a dense hammock.

Contact: Highlands Hammock State Park, 5931 Hammock Road, Sebring, FL 33872; 941/386-6094.

LAKE PLACID/VENUS AREA

Southern Highlands County offers excellent birding for many sought-after species. From Miami, the Lake Placid/Venus area represents the closest reliable site for Red-cockaded Woodpeckers, and easily accessible sites for Crested Caracaras, Sandhill Cranes, Florida Scrub-Jays, and Bachman's Sparrows. Venus is a small town with almost no facilities, but restaurants and motels are available in nearby Lake Placid. Lake Placid is about 6 miles north of the junction of US-27 and SR-70, while Venus is about 5 miles south of the junction. Birding possibilities around Lake Placid are rather limited, but Eurasian Collared-Doves and White-winged Doves are numerous and increasing in town.

One local site worth visiting in winter is located southeast of Lake Placid. From US-27 in town, go east on CR-621 to CR-619 (2.7) and turn right. At the T intersection with CR-29 (2.0), turn left to the pond on the left (2.3). From here to Old Parker Island Road (0.3), watch the fencelines and powerlines for wintering tyrannids. Since at least the early 1980s, this area has been a regular site for Western Kingbirds and Scissor-tailed Flycatchers. In December 1994 North America's first verifiable winter record of an Eastern Kingbird was established here, and a Vermilion Flycatcher was observed in February and March 1996. Check especially the small clump of Red Maples on the left side of the pond north of the road. To reach this site from Venus, go north on US-27 to SR-70 and turn right. At CR-29 (2.6), turn left to the pond on the right (2.9).

To reach **Driggers Road**, drive north on CR-29 to CR-619 (2.3) and turn right. At CR-621 (2.0) turn right to the road on the right (3.2; 0.1 mile past the sharp curve). (From US-27 in Lake Placid, simply travel east on CR-621 to Driggers Road [5.9].) There is a small pond on the left (0.1) that may be dry in summer. In winter, however, this pond can have a good assortment of puddle ducks and shorebirds, including Long-billed Dowitchers. In spring 1995 four pairs of Black-necked Stilts nested here. Watch also for numerous raptors, including Ospreys, Bald Eagles, and Crested Caracaras. White-tailed Kites have been seen from Driggers Road on two recent occasions. The wet prairies southeast of Lake Istokpoga contain good numbers of Sandhill Cranes, especially in winter. At dusk, dozens to hundreds of cranes may be seen flying in flocks to roost in the prairies. Driggers Road is one of the few public roads in the area from which it is possible to view the cranes, but note that the public portion of the road ends 0.7 mile past the pond. *Do not continue past the wooden fence.*

A site currently reliable for Burrowing Owls is located near the small town of Lorida (pronounced *lo-REE-da*), about 20 miles northeast of Lake Placid. From Driggers Road return to CR-621 and turn right. At US-98 turn left to Arbuckle Creek Road (4.6) and turn right. Park at the point where Arbuckle Creek Road angles left (1.2). Scan the fields on the left both north and south of the bend. In February 1995, 16 owls were found in these two fields, and other fields in the area contained additional owls.

Lake Placid is at the southern end of the Lake Wales Ridge, a large system of sand dunes that formed 2 to 3 million years ago when sea levels were much higher than they are presently. The ridge stretches about 100 miles to the north, and is 25 miles wide at its widest point. Around Lake Placid, however, the ridge is less than 6 miles wide. The flat area surrounding the ridge was the ocean floor before the Pleistocene Epoch.

The vast, flat area on the sides of the Lake Wales Ridge is composed of scattered bayheads, Cabbage Palm hammocks, and shallow wetlands. The wet prairies, now criss-crossed by thousands of shallow drainage ditches, have been planted to bahia and other exotic grasses and now support a large cattle industry. Because many ranches have retained much of the native vegetation, the prairie region continues to support many of Florida's unique birds. However, the citrus industry is beginning to develop large expanses of the prairies, with consequent loss of nearly all native flora and fauna.

Since the early 1900s over 85% of the scrub habitat on the Lake Wales Ridge has been lost, mostly to the citrus industry. Recently, the State of Florida, The Nature Conservancy, and the U.S. Fish and Wildlife Service have jointly committed about $40 million to purchase much of the 19,600 acres of scrub that remains. These 12 separate tracts will be managed as the Lake Wales Ridge Ecosystem Preserve, with the Federally purchased sites becoming the Lake Wales Ridge National Wildlife Refuge. Although publicly owned, many of these sites are currently off-limits to protect the rare plants which they contain. *Please do not wander into these areas.*

On SR-70 one mile west of US-27, turn left onto Old SR-8 (CR-17) to reach Archbold Biological Station (5,000 acres; no fee) (1.8). This independent research station (open 8 am to 5 pm Monday through Friday, but *closed on weekends*) preserves one of the largest patches of xeric oak scrub remaining on the Lake Wales Ridge. Much of what is known about this critically endangered ecosystem has been learned through research conducted at Archbold.

Although scientists at Archbold are studying many aspects of the scrub and its inhabitants, one project has made the station famous. Since 1969,

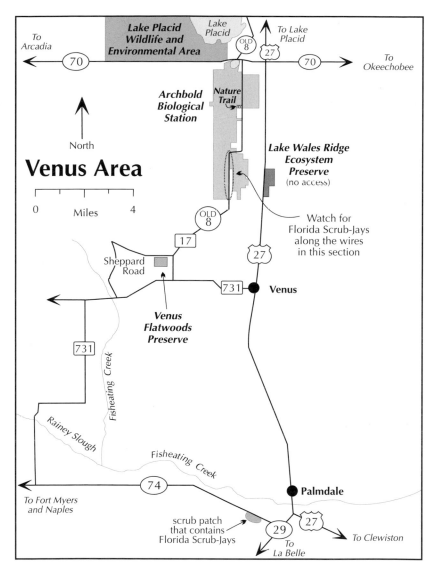

Glen Woolfenden, John Fitzpatrick, and their colleagues have studied closely a color-banded population of Florida Scrub-Jays on the station. In 1984, Woolfenden and Fitzpatrick published an ornithological monograph on the jay and continue to learn about its habitat preferences, responses to fire, dispersal characteristics, and other information critical to understanding the jay's biology. All this information is being used currently to set up a series of habitat preserves throughout the jay's range to prevent its extinction in the face of unrelenting human development and widespread fire-suppression of its habitats. The station contains 300 to 350 Florida Scrub-Jays, all but a few color-banded for individual recognition.

Because of ongoing research, most of the station is off-limits to the public, but a self-guided nature trail is provided. Stop by the office for a brochure. The trail winds through recently burned oak scrub and Slash Pine flatwoods, where the numerous dead pines attract woodpeckers. All of Florida's breeding woodpecker species, except Red-cockaded, occur along the trail. Hairy Woodpecker was also studied here; watch for color-banded birds. *Please remember that this is a private research station and not a tourist facility or a park. The scientific staff does not have time to give guided tours to birders.*

After leaving the main grounds of Archbold, continue south on Old SR-8 to where the road crosses the railroad tracks (3.0). Watch for Florida Scrub-Jays perched on powerlines along the right side of the road for the next 2 miles.

Contact: Archbold Biological Station, P.O. Box 2057, Lake Placid, FL 33862-2057; 941/465-2571.

From the railroad crossing on Old SR-8 (CR-17), continue south to Sheppard Road (5.6) and turn right. Proceed to **Venus Flatwoods Preserve** (98 acres; no fee) on the left (0.3), which consists of virgin Longleaf Pine flatwoods and seasonal ponds. This tract, long known for its cluster of Red-cockaded Woodpeckers, was purchased by The Nature Conservancy in 1992 and is accessible on foot anytime. Besides the woodpecker cluster, Eastern Bluebirds, Pine Warblers, and Bachman's Sparrows are permanent residents, and Eastern Kingbirds are found in spring and summer. Brown-headed Nuthatches are erratic at this site but may be found year round.

The RCW cavity trees are not marked, but the three trees currently active are located in the central portion of the property. All are within 200 feet of the road; one cavity tree is located right next to the road. The 1995 nest tree was located in the north-central part of the preserve; stay at least 300 feet from the nest from April to June. Before roosting, the woodpeckers often forage in the degraded pine forest to the north. To avoid missing the birds, it is best to arrive about 1 to 1½ hours before dusk, stand along the road, and listen for the birds as they approach. You may also choose to look for the birds in the tract itself. The woodpeckers frequently forage during the day in the open flatwoods west of the seasonal pond (dry six to nine months of the year) in the western third of the tract. Note that during the summer rainy season (mostly June to

August), much of the western and southern parts of the preserve may be flooded by a few inches of water.

Return to Old SR-8 and continue south to CR-731 (1.0) and turn right. At the fork in the road (3.8), bear left. The road passes through citrus groves, wetlands, and Slash Pine plantations before reaching **Rainey Slough** (7.3), a nearly undisturbed wetlands system. All the land in the area is strictly off-limits, so *bird only from the road*. If you arrive at dawn or shortly before dusk, you should see many wading-birds flying to or from their roosts to the west. A small roost of Black-crowned Night-Herons is located on both sides of the bridge. Look also for Limpkins and Purple Gallinules. King Rails are usually heard year round (especially pre-dawn), and they are joined in winter by Soras. In winter look for Marsh Wrens and Swamp Sparrows on the west side of the road and for Orange-crowned Warblers in the brush to the east. American Bitterns usually are rather easy to observe at this season around dawn or dusk as they fly around the marsh.

CR-731 ends at SR-74 (2.7), where you can turn right to the Fort Myers/Naples area or left to return to US-27. SR-74 is another prairie road excellent for finding Glossy Ibis, Mottled Duck, Crested Caracara, Sandhill Crane, and Florida Scrub-Jay. (A large patch of scrub on the south side of the road 1.3 to 2.0 miles west of SR-29 contains about 30 jays.) Additionally, a few pairs of Short-tailed Hawks breed regularly along Fisheating Creek north of the road, and you may be fortunate enough to see one of the birds spring through fall.

Depending on your travel or birding plans, you might consider returning to the intersection of SR-70 and US-27. Excellent examples of Florida prairies remain east and west of the Lake Wales Ridge, and SR-70 offers quick access to much of it. East of US-27, where the prairies are wetter, SR-70 is narrow, so it is dangerous to pull over and stop. Consequently, birders may choose to drive the side roads off SR-70, or bird the portion of SR-70 west of US-27. Because the birds occur fairly equally on both sides of US-27, one's destination after leaving the area may be the key factor in deciding which direction to drive on SR-70. To reach the Tampa Bay area, Fort Myers, or Naples, drive west; to reach Lake Okeechobee or the West-Palm-Beach-to-Miami coastal strip, go east.

There are no "scheduled" birding sites on SR-70 or on any other roads in the prairie region. Generally, most birds are large enough to be seen while driving. When they are, pull over when it is safe to do so. Characteristic birds of the region that are usually fairly easy to see are wading-birds (including Glossy Ibis and Wood Stork), Mottled Duck,

Swallow-tailed Kite (spring and summer), Crested Caracara, and Sandhill Crane. Scattered reports of White-tailed Kites have occurred recently, mostly in fall and winter.

OKEECHOBEE

The small town of Okeechobee is located at the junction of US-441 and SR-70. It takes its name from the huge lake just to the south, well-known for its immense ecological value, including as one of the best bass-fishing lakes in the world. Historically, the lake was part of the vast Kissimmee River/Everglades wetlands system. Water from the chain of dozens of interconnected lakes in Central Florida flowed north (beginning with tiny Lake Annie in Archbold Biological Station) all the way to Orlando. The water then flowed south through another chain of lakes before flowing into the Kissimmee River, with a floodplain up to 5 miles wide. The river meandered slowly southward before emptying into the northwest corner of Lake Okeechobee. Along its 102-mile length, the river nourished 35,000 acres of wetlands. During years of high water, Lake Okeechobee overflowed its southern banks, whereupon the water would flow south through the Everglades and eventually into Florida Bay, over 100 miles to the south.

To speed drainage of the region, the Kissimmee River was converted in the 1960s to the C-38, a canal 300 feet wide, 30 feet deep, and 56 miles long. As the river floodplain was drained, predominately for cattle ranching, wintering waterfowl populations along the river decreased by 92%.

Even worse, a dike 35 feet tall and 140 miles long had been built around Lake Okeechobee in the 1930s. At 700 square miles, Okeechobee is the second-largest fresh water lake in the U.S., but it is relatively shallow. (Its deepest part is only 20 feet deep.) In the 1920s, two hurricanes passed over the lake. The tidal surges from the storms killed over 2,000 people living in Clewiston and Moore Haven. The Herbert Hoover Dike was built to prevent this tragedy from recurring, but the dike isolated the lake from the Everglades, and it remains isolated today.

Lake Okeechobee is now used predominately as a source of drinking-water for the 4.5 million people who live along Florida's southeast coast, and as an irrigation source for the Everglades Agricultural Area (EAA) on the lake's southern shore. The EAA is 1,100 square miles of drained marshland now grown to sugar cane, rice, and vegetables. Water levels in the lake are therefore maintained for human uses, not for wildlife. In drought years, when water is needed most in the Everglades, it is kept in the lake to avoid water shortages for humans. In flood years, when wildlife is already stressed, additional water is released into the Everglades to prevent flooding in agricultural and other developed areas. This water-management scheme has caused serious disruptions to the Everglades ecosystem in the past two decades.

John Ogden reports that wading-bird populations have declined from at least 205,000 birds in the 1940s to 22,000 birds in the 1980s, nearly a 90% reduction in numbers. Still other problems plaguing the Everglades are two exotic plants (namely, Australian Punk Tree, *Melaleuca quinquenervia,* and Brazilian Pepper, *Schinus terebinthifolius*) that are rapidly invading a vast amount of land. Control of these noxious plants is currently insufficient, and they continue to increase in range and numbers. (It has been estimated that over 1 million acres of South Florida now contain *Melaleuca,* and some fear that it could cover the entire region within the next 30 years.) Another threat to the Everglades is high levels of mercury. The source of the contamination is currently unknown, but mercury has been found in the water, the soil, and the tissues of wading-birds, Raccoons, Florida Panthers, and many other aquatic and terrestrial species.

Fortunately, a major reclamation project is being implemented to allow the present-day Everglades to function more like the historic ecosystem. In 1994 the U.S. Army Corps of Engineers, the State of Florida, South Florida Water Management District, The Nature Conservancy, National Audubon Society, and a host of other governmental and environmental agencies proposed a massive restoration effort of the 50% of the original Everglades that remains undeveloped. Among the ambitious plans in the proposal are filling in much of the C-38 Canal and returning flow to the Kissimmee River, filling in several other drainage canals, building impoundments in the EAA to filter chemicals out of the water that is discharged into the Everglades, and returning key portions of farmland in western Palm Beach and southern Dade Counties to marshland to restore more natural water-flow to Everglades National Park and Florida Bay. Over the next 15 years, 43 miles of the Kissimmee River and almost 30,000 acres of wetlands are planned to be restored. Given the current political climate in Washington, the future of this $3.5+-billion proposal may be in jeopardy. Time will tell.

Because of the Hoover Dike, Lake Okeechobee is not visible from the ground except from the few public access points. Four of these access points are listed below. One is south of the city of Okeechobee, two are

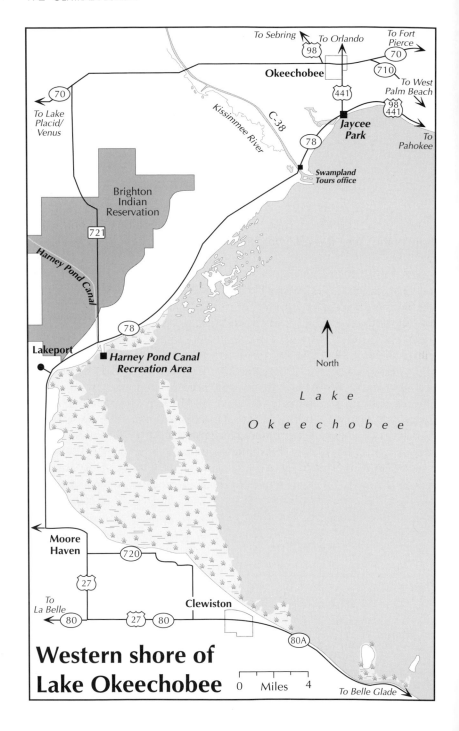

To Sebring To Orlando To Fort
Pierce

98 70

Okeechobee 710

441 To West
Palm Beach

70 98
441

To Lake
Placid/
Venus

Kissimmee River C-38 78 Jaycee
Park To
Pahokee

Swampland
Tours office

Brighton
Indian
Reservation

721

Harney Pond Canal

78

Lakeport

Harney Pond Canal
Recreation Area

North

Lake

Okeechobee

Moore
Haven

720

27

To
La Belle

80 27 80 Clewiston

80A

**Western shore of
Lake Okeechobee**

0 Miles 4

To Belle Glade

along the northwest and west shores of the lake, and the last is west of Belle Glade on the south side of the lake.

From SR-70 in Okeechobee, drive south on US-441. Cross SR-78 (3.2) to **Jaycee Park** (no fee). From the boat ramp at the far end of the park, waterbirds are common year round. There is a large wading-bird rookery in the willow thicket across the boat channel; Anhingas are one of the most common nesters. Also look for Purple Gallinules and Limpkins, both resident. In winter, ducks may be common away from the boating areas. Larids and other birds often rest on the abandoned fishing pier.

Return to SR-78 and turn left. Just before the bridge over the Kissimmee River (4.4), turn right to **Swampland Tours** ($17.50/person), a pontoon boat that offers 2-hour tours of the marshes along the northwest shore of the lake. *It is recommended that you call the office before your visit.* Two tours depart the dock daily (at 10 am and 1 pm) and travel about 25 miles through wetlands leased by the National Audubon Society since the beginning of this century. Species seen on many trips include wading-birds (including Glossy Ibis), waterfowl (including Fulvous Whistling-Duck and Mottled Duck), Snail Kite (may be hard to find in spring when the birds are nesting), Purple Gallinule, Limpkin, and Black-necked Stilt. American Alligators are also seen frequently.

Contact: Swampland Tours, 10375 Highway 78 West, Okeechobee, FL 34974; 941/467-4411.

Continue southwest on SR-78 to Lakeport Plaza on the left (look for the BP gas station) (16.0), opposite CR-721. From the plaza parking lot, take the access road to the right to **Harney Pond Canal Recreation Area** (no fee). Although birding this area in summer and fall can be decidedly dull, an elevated boardwalk at the far end offers the best ground view of Lake Okeechobee. In winter, large flocks of ducks may be seen from here, and Purple Gallinules are seen along the shore year round.

From the Harney Pond Canal, you have several choices. To go north, return to Okeechobee via SR-78. To reach the Lake Placid/Venus area, go north on CR-721 to SR-70, then go west. (CR-721 is a lightly traveled road, and good for spotting Crested Caracaras.) Continuing south on SR-78 leads to US-27 in Moore Haven. About 6 miles south of town, turn west on SR-80 to reach Corkscrew Swamp Sanctuary (via SR-29 in Immokalee) or the Fort Myers/Naples area. Traveling east on SR-80 brings you to the Belle Glade area (great for shorebirds from July to September if you can find an accessible site), and after about 30 more miles, the West Palm Beach area.

Vast areas of the EAA are planted to sugar cane, a rather sterile habitat for birds. Although mature cane fields and unmowed road edges are ideal for Smooth-billed Anis, it is not advisable to spend much time in the EAA looking for anis for two reasons. First off, Smooth-billed Anis are a declining species unpredictable in their occurrence. You could spend hours in perfect habitat and not find any birds. Secondly, the economies of towns like Clewiston and Belle Glade are strongly dependent on the Federally price-supported sugar industry. Recent battles between the sugar producers who want to continue "business as usual" and environmentalists who want to tax the industry as part of the larger effort to restore the remaining Everglades will probably intensify in the future. Unfortunately, some local residents are therefore somewhat hostile to birders and other environmentalists.

Inland areas continue on page 202.

Central Florida – Atlantic Coast

NEW SMYRNA BEACH

Ponce de Leon Inlet forms the northern terminus of the Indian River Lagoon, an estuary known widely for its diversity of aquatic life. There is no bridge over the inlet, so you must return to the mainland to travel between Daytona Beach and New Smyrna Beach. County parks are located on both sides of the inlet and provide access to lagoon marshes, dunes, and beaches. Birding around the inlet can be very good, especially in winter. Northern Gannets, Piping Plovers, and Great Black-backed Gulls are present in winter, along with many other wading-birds, shorebirds, and larids. On the jetties, look for Purple Sandpipers, which are rare in winter; watch also for Northern Gannets, sea ducks, and jaegers offshore. During fall, watch for Peregrine Falcons and other migrant raptors. Least Terns and Black Skimmers nest on the south side of the inlet from April to July.

To reach **Lighthouse Point Park** (55 acres; $1.50/driver, 50¢/additional person) on the north side of the inlet, exit (#85) I-95 onto SR-421 (Dunlawton Avenue) and go east. At its end at SR-A1A (4.9), turn right to the park (5.5). As you cross the Intracoastal Waterway on SR-421, check both sides of the causeway for roosting shorebirds, gulls, terns, and skimmers. Inside the park you can drive to the base of the jetty, which has a paved pathway along the top. Check for Purple Sandpipers and other shorebirds.

Smyrna Dunes Park (250 acres; $3/vehicle) is located on the south side of the inlet. To reach it from I-95, exit (#84) onto SR-44 and go east and merge into SR-A1A south. At Peninsula Avenue (5.7) turn left to the park (2.8) next to the Coast Guard station. The park contains a 1½-mile-long boardwalk through a remnant coastal hammock and over dunes and spoil fill. Take the boardwalk to the second exit on the left (marked W2). Follow a separate boardwalk around a small pond that may have Sedge Wrens and "Sharp-tailed" Sparrows in winter. Take the second right to the inlet, watching for larids and other birds. Turn right and follow the shore to the south jetty, which may have Purple Sandpipers in winter. Scan offshore for Northern Gannets and jaegers in fall and winter. Rejoin the boardwalk at the base of the jetty and turn right to return to your vehicle.

To reach **Turtle Mound**, a part of **Canaveral National Seashore** (57,661 acres; no fee), return to the junction of SR-A1A and Peninsula Avenue and continue south along the seashore (8.7). Turtle Mound is 40 feet tall and was created by Indians dumping oyster shells there for centuries. Because it is the highest point in the area, it has served as a landmark for mariners since the 1500s. For the same reason, the mound is great for birding. In fall, numerous raptors can be seen from the two platforms here, including Merlins and Peregrine Falcons. It also serves as the best land-site in Florida for observing pelagic species.

Harry Robinson, an Orlando birder, has put Turtle Mound on the birding map with his unprecedented fall counts of pelagic species (especially jaegers), mostly on days with strong north to east winds. From 23 October to 29 November 1991, Harry counted 6,171 jaegers (4,579 Pomarine, 1,591 Parasitic, and 1 Long-tailed), and on 9 November 1992, he counted 2,226 Pomarine Jaegers! In addition to jaegers, Harry has reported Cory's, Greater, Sooty, Manx, and Audubon's Shearwaters, Wilson's, Leach's, and Band-rumped Storm-Petrels, Brown and Red-footed Boobies, Northern Gannets, South Polar Skua, Black-legged Kittiwakes, Sabine's Gull, Arctic Tern, and Red-necked and Red Phalaropes, all from Turtle Mound!

In addition to birding Turtle Mound, also check Mosquito Lagoon for waterfowl and other species. For migrant landbirds, try the Windy Ridge Trail across from Parking Area 3 or the trails at Eldora Hammock at Parking Areas 7 and 8.

Contact: Canaveral National Seashore, 308 Julia Street, Titusville, FL 32796-3521; 407/267-1110.

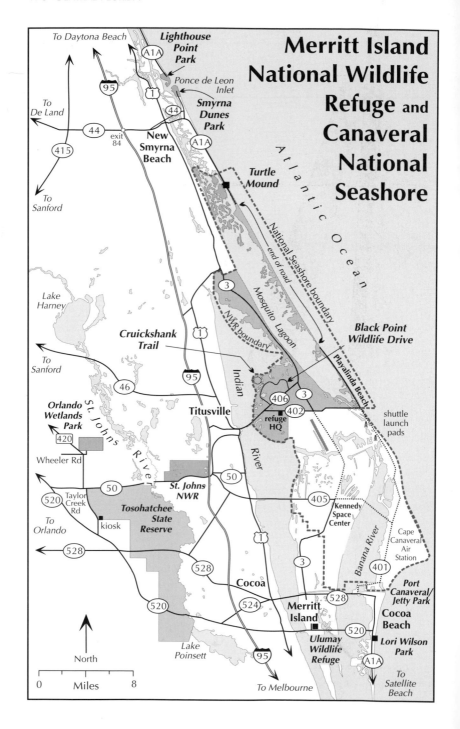

Merritt Island National Wildlife Refuge and Canaveral National Seashore

To Daytona Beach

Lighthouse Point Park

Ponce de Leon Inlet

Smyrna Dunes Park

New Smyrna Beach

To De Land

To Sanford

Turtle Mound

Atlantic Ocean

National Seashore boundary
end of road

Mosquito Lagoon

NWR boundary

Lake Harney

Cruickshank Trail

To Sanford

Black Point Wildlife Drive

Playalinda Beach

Indian River

Titusville

refuge HQ

shuttle launch pads

Orlando Wetlands Park

Wheeler Rd

St. Johns River

Taylor Creek Rd

To Orlando

kiosk

St. Johns NWR

Tosohatchee State Reserve

Kennedy Space Center

Banana River

Cape Canaveral Air Station

Cocoa

Port Canaveral/Jetty Park

Merritt Island

Cocoa Beach

Lori Wilson Park

Ulumay Wildlife Refuge

Lake Poinsett

To Melbourne

To Satellite Beach

North

0   Miles   8

exit 84

TITUSVILLE AREA

Merritt Island National Wildlife Refuge (83,796 acres; no fee) is one of the top birding sites on the Florida Atlantic coast, especially for wintering waterfowl, shorebirds, and larids. The refuge contains 21 Threatened and Endangered animals, more than any other U.S. refuge outside Hawaii. Combined with Canaveral National Seashore, the refuge contains the world's largest population of Florida Scrub-Jays. Insect repellent is needed in much of the refuge in spring and summer (Mosquito Lagoon is well-named!). All of the refuge lands were purchased in the 1960s by the U.S. Government to develop the Kennedy Space Center. Non-essential parts of the property became the refuge; most of the Kennedy Space Center remains off limits because of ongoing NASA and military activities.

To reach the refuge from US-1 in Titusville, go east on SR-406 across the Indian River. Upon reaching the island, turn right onto a dirt road just beyond the guardpost (0.8 mile from the drawbridge). The road circles an impoundment for 1.6 miles. Just before rejoining SR-406, turn sharply right to circle a second impoundment for 1.4 miles. These two impoundments can be exceptional for wading-birds, waterfowl, and shorebirds; for example, over 200 White-rumped Sandpipers were seen here one May morning. Three impoundments on the other side of SR-406 should also be checked. To reach them from the first impoundment, simply cross SR-406. From the second impoundment turn left onto SR-406 and turn right to the ponds (0.8). Follow the water's edge on the right to the pump-house. Park here and check the impoundments behind the pump-house. Continue on the dirt road to SR-406 and turn left to the entrance of **Black Point Wildlife Drive** (1.2). This one-way driving loop, which travels in a clockwise direction, is 6.3 miles long and is one of the most productive parts of the refuge. Wading-birds, waterfowl, shore-birds, gulls, and terns are features of the drive. An active Bald Eagle nest is visible in a tall Slash Pine on the east side of SR-406 just north of the entrance to the drive. The road follows dikes built in the 1950s to control salt-marsh mosquitoes. By impounding the marshes (i.e., maintaining high water levels in summer), natural tidal flow was eliminated, so many of the marshes succeeded to shallow pools. The refuge is now returning tidal flow to some of the marshes in order to restore them.

Unfortunately, this restoration project is decades too late to save the Dusky Seaside Sparrow, which was endemic to salt and brackish marshes on Merritt Island and along the St. Johns River on the mainland. The species (later downgraded to a race of the Seaside Sparrow) was discovered in 1872 west of present-day Titusville and later on Merritt Island. The original Merritt Island population was estimated at about 2,000 pairs, but it had been reduced to about 600 pairs by 1957. A mere 6 years later, only 30 pairs were estimated to remain, and the last Dusky on Merritt Island was seen in 1977. The last wild birds (6 males) were observed in the St. Johns marsh in 1980. An attempt to breed the few remaining birds at Walt Disney World with females from another race ended in failure when the door to the sparrows' enclosure was accidentally left open one night, allowing a predator to enter the enclosure and kill all the birds.

About halfway through the drive is an observation tower at the beginning of the 5-mile Cruickshank Trail, which honors famed birder, conservationist, and wildlife photographer Allan D. Cruickshank, who lived in the area and who strongly influenced the establishment of the refuge. After completing the wildlife drive, turn left to SR-3 (1.7) and turn right. Watch along the road for Florida Scrub-Jays for the next 7 miles. At the traffic light at SR-402 (3.2), turn left to the ranger station at **Canaveral National Seashore** (57,661 acres; no fee). Because this road is so close to the Space Shuttle launch pads, *you must remain in your vehicle at all times, and you may not stop along the road.* Furthermore, parts of the seashore are closed from 3 days before to 1 day after a shuttle launch; call NASA at 407/867-2805 for information on shuttle launch dates. After a few miles, the road goes north for about 5 miles before ending at a NASA camera pad. To the right of the road is a dune covered by Saw Palmettoes and other plants of this coastal strand habitat. This dune prevents viewing the Atlantic Ocean, but there are many board-walks over the dune to unspoiled **Playalinda Beach**. About 3,000 to 4,000 sea turtles nest annually along the seashore's 24 miles of beaches. The Eddy Creek crossover between Parking Areas 7 and 8 also affords a good view of Mosquito Lagoon to the west.

Although the beach contains wading-birds, shorebirds, and larids (including Great Black-backed Gulls), the main draw here is the possibil-ity of pelagic birds in fall and winter. On days with strong east or northeast winds, boobies, shearwaters, storm-petrels, and especially Northern Gannets and jaegers may be seen in large numbers. Also in fall (especially October), watch for migrating raptors. In addition to common species, Merlins and Peregrine Falcons are seen here regularly; a few of each winter at the seashore and the refuge.

Return to SR-402 and cross SR-3 (re-entering the refuge) to the parking lot on the right (1.7). Two trails through an oak/Cabbage Palm hammock originate here. Oak Hammock Trail (a ½-mile walk) should be taken, but Palm Hammock Trail is less productive.

American White Pelicans
Gail Diane Yovanovich

Return to SR-402 and turn right to the visitor center on the left (1.3), which offers displays and a small bookstore.

The remainder of SR-402 has several pull-offs to allow for wildlife observation. In winter, waterfowl and American Coots are usually abundant in the marshes and impoundments here; this is also one of the best sites in Florida for Northern Pintails. Be sure to scan the duck flocks carefully; 1 or 2 Eurasian Wigeons are found here almost annually, and Cinnamon Teals occur occasionally.

Once you reach SR-406, the basic refuge/seashore tour is completed, but two additional roads may be driven if time permits. Both are rough unpaved roads but are passable in passenger vehicles. The first trail originates from Black Point Wildlife Drive; turn left just beyond Marker 11. At the first open water, the road splits. The left road is better overall, but a White-cheeked Pintail was observed down the road to the right in 1990. When water levels are favorable, large numbers of waterfowl and shorebirds can be seen there. The road to the left is about 8 miles long and ends at SR-3. Turn right to return to SR-402.

The second road is located on the north side of SR-402, 2.0 miles west of Playalinda Beach, and follows Mosquito Lagoon until it ends at SR-3.

In winter, waterfowl, shorebirds, larids, and other waterbirds can be common here.

Contacts: Merritt Island National Wildlife Refuge, P.O. Box 6504, Titusville, FL 32782-6504; 407/861-0667 and Canaveral National Seashore, 308 Julia Street, Titusville, FL 32796-3521; 407/267-1110.

COCOA AREA

From US-1 in Cocoa, go east on SR-520 toward Cocoa Beach. Watch for a Dennys Restaurant on the left; turn left there onto Sykes Creek Parkway (4.8). After crossing the first bridge (1.0), turn left at the Ulumay Wildlife Sanctuary sign. Turn right into the sanctuary and park (0.3). By walking the dikes, you should see many wading-birds, shorebirds, and larids. The dike to the left of the entrance has a lookout tower from which you can scan the marshes. Large concentrations of waterbirds are found in winter, including American White Pelicans and Ruddy Ducks.

Continue east on SR-520 to SR-A1A (4.8) and turn left. Bear left at the fork (2.0) to remain on SR-A1A. At George King Boulevard (1.6) turn right onto SR-401 (North Atlantic Drive) (1.0). Turn left to Jetty Drive (0.3), then turn right to Jetty Park ($1/vehicle). In addition to common waterbirds, Northern Gannets and jaegers may be seen from the observation platform. Numerous fishing boats dock here, and you may wish to join one to look for pelagic species offshore.

Return to SR-A1A and turn right. The road soon curves to the left. Turn right onto SR-401 (0.3), then turn right again onto Grouper Street (1.6). At Cargo Road (0.5) turn left to check out the impoundments, then return to Grouper Street and turn left to the canal and two turning basins. This area can be very good for wading-birds, shorebirds, and larids, especially at low tide. One or more Common Eiders have been seen here recently.

Return to SR-A1A because SR-401 is gated off to the east (where it leads to Cape Canaveral Air Station).

To reach **Lori Wilson Park** (32 acres; 50¢ parking), a small oceanfront park in Cocoa Beach, go south on SR-A1A, pass by SR-520 (Merritt Island Causeway), to the park on the left just south of the Hilton Hotel (1.5). The park preserves a remnant wind-pruned coastal oak hammock that can be excellent for landbirds during spring and fall migrations. Painted Buntings frequent the feeder near the start of the trail. During other seasons, birding in the park may be dull, although common species are routinely found on the beach. One family of Florida Scrub-Jays inhabits the northern part of the park.

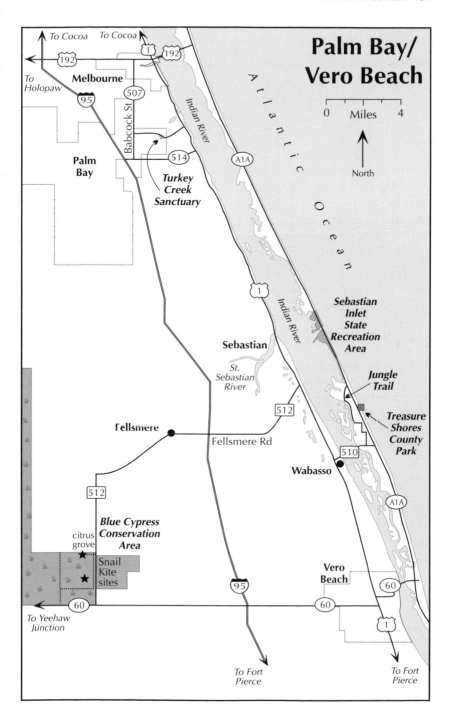

Palm Bay/ Vero Beach

To Cocoa

To Cocoa

To Holopaw

Melbourne

Palm Bay

Babcock St

Indian River

Turkey Creek Sanctuary

Atlantic Ocean

Miles

0   4

North

Indian River

Sebastian

St. Sebastian River

Sebastian Inlet State Recreation Area

Jungle Trail

Treasure Shores County Park

Fellsmere

Fellsmere Rd

Wabasso

Blue Cypress Conservation Area

citrus grove

Snail Kite sites

Vero Beach

To Yeehaw Junction

To Fort Pierce

To Fort Pierce

PALM BAY

Turkey Creek Sanctuary (77 acres; donations accepted) can be excellent for migrants, especially in fall. To reach it from I-95, exit at SR-514 (Malabar Road) and go east to SR-507 (Babcock Street) (0.5). Turn left, go to Port Malabar Boulevard (1.3), and turn right. At Santiago Drive (1.1), turn right to the sanctuary on the right. An Ash-throated Flycatcher wintered here in both 1994-1995 and 1995-1996.

VERO BEACH AREA

Sebastian Inlet State Recreation Area (578 acres; standard fee) is the most heavily used state park in Florida (with over 1 million visitors annually), but it can still be good for birds. Sebastian Inlet divides the park into two sections. Enter the north section along SR-A1A; check the cove near the parking area for wading-birds (including Reddish Egrets and Roseate Spoonbills), Wilson's and Piping (winter) Plovers, other shorebirds, and larids. Wooded areas may contain landbirds during migration. The fishing pier is a good spot from which to scan for Northern Gannets, scoters, and jaegers in winter, especially on days with strong east winds. Watch for Purple Sandpipers on the jetty in winter. Cross the inlet and turn right to reach the south entrance of the park (0.6). Follow the road to its end at the Indian River. At low tide the area contains wading-birds, shorebirds, and larids. Marbled Godwits are regular in August and September. Sea turtles nest along the park's three miles of beaches.

Contact: Sebastian Inlet State Recreation Area, 9700 South SR-A1A, Melbourne Beach, FL 32951; 561/984-4852.

To reach an area good for migrants, go south on SR-A1A to Jungle Trail (3.3) and turn right. Jungle Trail is a 4.6-mile-long road between SR-A1A and the Indian River. It is unpaved but well maintained. To reach Jungle Trail from US-1 at Wabasso, drive east on CR-510, cross the Indian River, and turn left onto Jungle Trail (2.1). The road passes through oak hammocks, citrus groves, and residential areas along the eastern shore of the Indian River. Because it is less than a mile from the Atlantic Ocean, the road is best during spring migration. Worm-eating Warblers and other Caribbean-wintering species are regular here in spring; even a Kirtland's Warbler was found on 22 April 1993. In fall look for Peregrine Falcons and other migrant raptors.

At the north end of Jungle Trail, 0.1 mile before it ends at SR-A1A, there is a small road to the left that leads to an impoundment built for mosquito control. Depending on the water level in the impoundment, waterfowl and shorebirds may be present in winter. The dike surrounding the impoundment may be walked; it is 2½ to 3 miles around. The property is publicly owned, and permission to walk it is not required. Bring insect repellent in spring and summer.

Treasure Shores County Park (no fee) is located on the east side of SR-A1A, 4.5 miles south of Sebastian Inlet. During migration, thousands of Northern Gannets stream by offshore, and migrant landbirds may be found in brushy areas.

To reach an area of the St. Johns Marsh that usually is good for Snail Kites, travel west from Vero Beach on SR-60. Pass under I-95 and turn right onto CR-512 (7.5). (Drive this road with caution; the large citrus trucks are a potential hazard.) Watch for a small dirt road over the dike on the left (1.5) used by boaters to get to the marsh. This area is part of **Blue Cypress Conservation Area** (47,800 acres; no fee). The dike may be walked west for about 2 miles. Kites are seen here regularly, especially in early morning and before dusk. Look also for wading-birds (including Least Bittern), Fulvous Whistling-Duck, Mottled Duck, King Rail, Purple Gallinule, and Limpkin.

If you do not find kites here, return to CR-512 and go north to another access point on the left (2.5) just before the citrus groves. Park off the road and walk in past the spillway.

FORT PIERCE

Some of the best local birding spots are on North Hutchinson Island north of Fort Pierce. From I-95 or SR-91 (Florida's Turnpike), go east on SR-70 to US-1 and turn left. At North Beach Causeway, the part of SR-A1A north of Fort Pierce Inlet (3.2), turn right and cross the Indian River. At the east end of the bridge (0.9), park and check the mudflats and mangrove islands for wading-birds and shorebirds.

Continue east on SR-A1A and turn right into Fort Pierce Inlet State Recreation Area (340 acres; standard fee) (1.4). Inside the park, turn right onto the first paved road to Dynamite Point. Look here for wading-birds, shorebirds, and larids. Low tide is best. A telescope is helpful, because most of the birds will be across the channel on Coon Island. Return to the main park road, turn right, and then turn left into the parking lot. Near the north end of the parking lot is Coastal Hammock Trail, a half-mile-long nature trail that can be good for migrants.

Contact: Fort Pierce Inlet State Recreation Area, 905 Shorewinds Drive, Fort Pierce, FL 34949; 561/468-3985.

Return to SR-A1A and turn right. At the traffic light, turn left to Jack Island Boulevard (1.1), then turn left to Jack Island State Preserve (958 acres; no fee). Park and walk across the foot-bridge, where you may pick up a trail map. The island is mostly mangroves, with patches of hardwood hammock, and is criss-crossed by dikes. Marsh Rabbit Trail (1 mile long) is the best trail, with an observation tower overlooking the Indian River. Roseate Spoonbills are present spring through fall, and Black-whiskered Vireos have bred here. The area is also good for migrant and wintering landbirds.

Between Fort Pierce and Port St. Lucie is an extensive area of fresh water marshes and wet prairies known as the Savannas, to which there are several points of access. From SR-70, go south on US-1 to CR-712 (Midway Road) (3.6). Turn left to Savannas Recreation Area (600 acres; $1/vehicle) on the left (1.4). Drive to the end of the road, cross the foot-bridge, and walk to the left to an observation tower. Across the marsh is a rookery used by Anhingas and wading-birds. Least Bitterns, King Rails, and Purple

Great Egret
Gail Diane Yovanovich

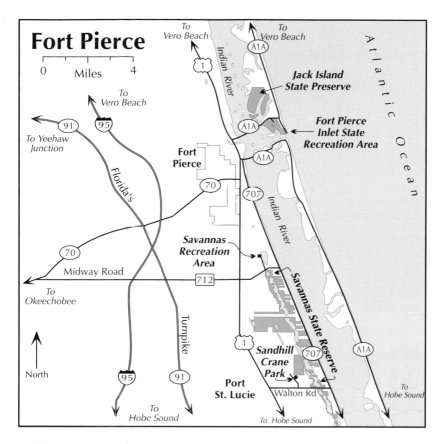

Gallinules are resident, many ducks are found in winter, and Snail Kites are seen occasionally.

Contact: Savannas Recreation Area, 1400 Midway Road, Fort Pierce, FL 33482; 561/464-7855.

South of CR-712 (Midway Road) is Savannas State Reserve (4738 acres). One part can be reached by going south from Midway Road on US-1. At Walton Road (5.6), turn left to Lennard Road (1.6). Turn left again toward Sandhill Crane Park. At the information sign on the right (0.5), look for a trail into the preserve. The trail leads through pine flatwoods with Brown-headed Nuthatch, Pine Warbler, Summer Tanager, and Bachman's Sparrow. Depending on the water level, you may be able to walk to areas that afford views of the marsh. For a guided walk, contact the Department of Environmental Protection at 561/340-7530.

Atlantic coastal areas continue on page 207.

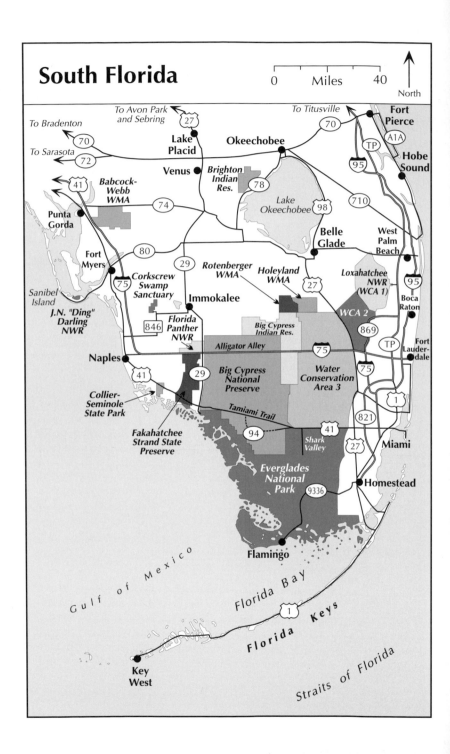

South Florida

0   Miles   40

North

To Avon Park and Sebring
To Titusville
Fort Pierce

To Bradenton
70
Lake Placid
27
Okeechobee
70
TP
A1A

To Sarasota
72
Venus
Brighton Indian Res.
78
Lake Okeechobee
98
95
Hobe Sound

41
Babcock-Webb WMA
74
Belle Glade
West Palm Beach
710

Punta Gorda
80
29
Rotenberger WMA
Holeyland WMA
27
Loxahatchee NWR (WCA 1)
95

Fort Myers
75
Corkscrew Swamp Sanctuary
Immokalee
WCA 2
Boca Raton

Sanibel Island
J.N. "Ding" Darling NWR
846
Florida Panther NWR
Big Cypress Indian Res.
869
TP
Fort Lauderdale

Naples
41
29
Alligator Alley
75
Big Cypress National Preserve
Water Conservation Area 3
75
1

Collier-Seminole State Park
Tamiami Trail
94
Shark Valley
41
821
27
Miami

Fakahatchee Strand State Preserve
Everglades National Park
9336
Homestead

Flamingo

Gulf of Mexico

Florida Bay
1
Florida Keys

Key West

Florida Keys

Straits of Florida

SOUTH FLORIDA

One of the few truly subtropical regions in North America, mainland South Florida has some birds found nowhere else in the country. The number of specialties is limited to only two native birds (Greater Flamingo and Cape Sable Seaside Sparrow) and three countable exotics (Canary-winged ["White-winged"] Parakeet, Red-whiskered Bulbul, and Spot-breasted Oriole). Monk Parakeet is locally very common in South Florida but also occurs elsewhere in the state. Non-countable species breeding in the region include Rose-ringed Parakeet, Red-masked Parakeet, Mitred Parakeet, Dusky-headed Parakeet, Chestnut-fronted Macaw, Red-crowned Parrot, Orange-winged Parrot, Common Myna, Hill Myna, and literally dozens more. Some of these will likely become established in the future if current population trends continue. The status of Yellow-chevroned Parakeet is explained in the Introduction. All of these species can be found in the Greater Miami area; a few also occur in the West Palm Beach and Fort Lauderdale areas. Rose-ringed Parakeets are also found in Naples.

The best birding spots in the region are Greater Miami, Everglades National Park, and the Fort Myers/Sanibel Island area. These areas can be birded easily in about a week, often including Corkscrew Swamp Sanctuary, Big Cypress National Preserve, Fakahatchee Strand State Preserve, or other excellent sites (such as the Lake Placid/Venus area in Central Florida).

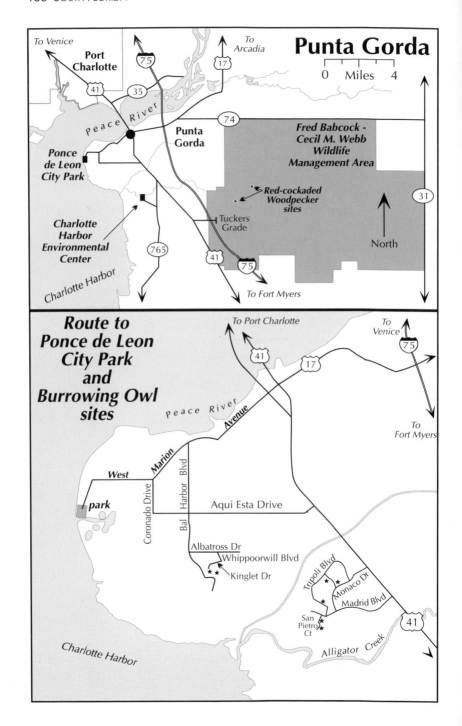

Punta Gorda

To Venice

Port Charlotte

To Arcadia

0 Miles 4

Peace River

75

35

17

41

74

Punta Gorda

Fred Babcock - Cecil M. Webb Wildlife Management Area

31

Ponce de Leon City Park

Red-cockaded Woodpecker sites

Charlotte Harbor Environmental Center

765

41

Tuckers Grade

75

North

Charlotte Harbor

To Fort Myers

Route to Ponce de Leon City Park and Burrowing Owl sites

To Port Charlotte

To Venice

75

41

17

To Fort Myers

Peace River

Avenue

Marion

West

Coronado Drive

Bal Harbor Blvd

park

Aqui Esta Drive

Albatross Dr

Whippoorwill Blvd

Kinglet Dr

Tripoli Blvd

Monaco Dr

Madrid Blvd

41

San Pietro Ct

Charlotte Harbor

Alligator Creek

South Florida – Gulf Coast

PUNTA GORDA

To reach a few birding sites in town, exit (#29) I-75 onto US-17 (Marion Avenue) and go west. (The road name changes to West Marion Avenue west of US-41). At Marion Court (3.0) bear left to Ponce de Leon City Park. The park contains a wildlife rehabilitation facility (guided tours available) and a boardwalk through mangroves where Prairie Warblers breed and where Mangrove Cuckoos may be found. In winter look for shorebirds and larids on the mudflats (at low tide) and Hooded Mergansers and other waterbirds offshore.

As you return to Punta Gorda, turn right onto Bal Harbor Boulevard (1.4). At the stop sign at Aqui Esta Drive (1.0), check out the lake behind the shopping center at the southwest corner of the two roads. The lake is used as a night roost for Hooded Mergansers in winter, and other ducks and waterbirds should also be seen. Also in this area are several Burrowing Owls. Most of the burrows are marked with wooden stakes to prevent mowers from crushing them.

South of Punta Gorda is the Alligator Creek portion of Charlotte Harbor Environmental Center (3,000 acres; donation requested). The center is open weekdays 8 am to 3 pm, Saturdays 8 am to noon, but it is closed Sundays. To reach it from Bal Harbor Boulevard, drive east on Aqui Esta Drive to US-41 (1.7) and turn right. At SR-765 (Burnt Store Road) (1.6), turn right to the entrance on the right (1.1). Pick up a map at the entrance. There are two trails through the area; one goes through pine flatwoods, and the other through *Juncus* salt marsh and mangrove forest. Bald Eagles nest on the property. Guided tours are available November to April. The center offers the only easy access to the Charlotte Harbor State Preserve (no facilities at present).

Contact: Charlotte Harbor Environmental Center, 10941 Burnt Store Road, Punta Gorda, FL 33955; 941/575-4800.

East of Punta Gorda is Fred Babcock/Cecil M. Webb Wildlife Management Area (65,770 acres; *$25 annual fee/person*). To reach it from US-41 or I-75 (exit #27), go east on Tuckers Grade to the entrance. (Tuckers Grade is 3.1 miles south of SR-765 on US-41.) Much of the area has Slash Pine flatwoods with breeding birds such as Sandhill Cranes, Eastern Kingbirds, Brown-headed Nuthatches, Pine Warblers, Summer Tanagers, and Bachman's Sparrows. The big attraction is the Red-cockaded Woodpecker, with 27 clusters onsite (some cavity trees are marked). Because of the fee (waived for Florida residents 65 and older), few birders visit the area, but some birds can be found along SR-74 and SR-31, two main roads that serve as the north and east boundaries of the area. (Also note that hunting is permitted throughout the area in winter.)

A recreation area (11,000 acres) near the entrance offers about 15 miles of unpaved roads usually passable in regular vehicles. Two Red-cockaded Woodpecker clusters occur in the recreation area, along with most other birds of the management area.

Contact: Fred Babcock/Cecil M. Webb Wildlife Management Area, 29200 Tuckers Grade, Punta Gorda, FL 33955; 941/639-1531.

FORT MYERS AREA

Fort Myers is an excellent base from which to bird the southern Gulf coast and the western Everglades. Southwest Florida Regional Airport east of the city is modern, convenient, and much less crowded than the airports at Tampa, Orlando, or along the southern Atlantic coast. I-75 is just a few miles from the airport and offers a speedy, non-congested way to move around the region. In the city CR-869 (Summerlin Road) provides a bypass around busy downtown areas. You should avoid CR-867 (McGregor Boulevard), which is narrow, congested, and full of traffic lights.

Many Burrowing Owls inhabit the huge development of Cape Coral west of Fort Myers. To reach an area with many owls, travel west from North Fort Myers on SR-78 (Pine Island Road) to Chiquita Boulevard (7.5) and turn left. At Beach Parkway (4.5) turn right and proceed to Sands Boulevard (1.6), watching along the way for the owls or the stakes that mark their burrows. From Sands Boulevard turn left onto Cape Coral Parkway (0.8). Owls are easy to find in this area, west to SW 29th Avenue. (To reach this area from the south, exit I-75 at Daniels Road and drive west to Summerlin Road [5.8]. [Daniels Road becomes Cypress Lake Drive west of US-41.] Turn right and proceed to College Parkway [0.7; the second light], then turn left. After you cross the Cape Coral bridge [$1/vehicle], the road name changes to Cape Coral Parkway. Go west to Sands Boulevard [9.1] and the area mentioned above.)

Lakes County Park ($3/vehicle) is good for wading-birds year round and migrant landbirds in fall. To reach it from Summerlin Road, go east on Gladiolus Drive (1.8 south of Daniels Road) to the entrance on the left (1.0). The park contains a variety of habitats, including shallow lakes, a cypress swamp, and pinewoods. Trails access the woodlands, and a boardwalk provides views of the lake. A large heronry of egrets, herons, and ibises is found along the lake edge at the east side of the park. For

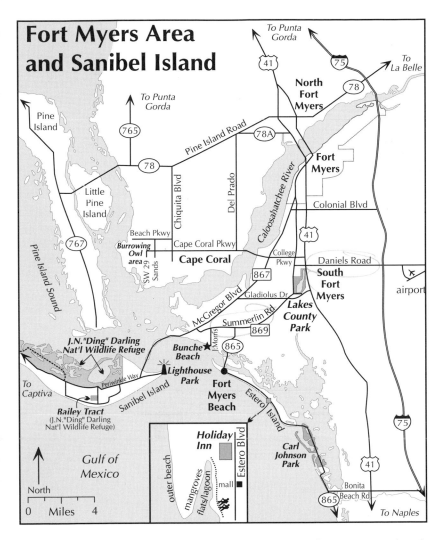

Fort Myers Area and Sanibel Island

To Punta Gorda

To La Belle

North Fort Myers

Pine Island

To Punta Gorda

765

Pine Island Road

78A

Fort Myers

78

Little Pine Island

Chiquita Blvd

Del Prado

Caloosahatchee River

Colonial Blvd

767

Pine Island Sound

Beach Pkwy

Burrowing Owl area

Cape Coral Pkwy

Cape Coral

College Pkwy

Daniels Road

41

South Fort Myers

airport

SW 29 Sands

867

Gladiolus Dr

McGregor Blvd

Summerlin Rd

Lakes County Park

869

J.N."Ding" Darling Nat'l Wildlife Refuge

J.Morris

865

Bunche Beach

To Captiva

Periwinkle Way

Lighthouse Park

Sanibel Island

Fort Myers Beach

Estero Island

75

Bailey Tract (J.N."Ding" Darling Nat'l Wildlife Refuge)

Gulf of Mexico

Holiday Inn

Estero Blvd

Carl Johnson Park

North

outer beach

mangroves flats/lagoon

mall

0   Miles   4

Bonita Beach Rd

865

41

To Naples

the past few years, a Scarlet Ibis of unknown origin has associated with White Ibises at the colony. The boardwalk provides excellent views of the birds.

Contact: Lakes County Park, 7330 Gladiolus Drive, Fort Myers, FL 33908; 941/432-2000.

Sanibel Island

To reach **Sanibel Island**, return to Summerlin Road and go south to the Sanibel Causeway toll plaza. (Summerlin Road merges with McGregor Boulevard just before the causeway.) The flats beside the Sanibel toll plaza and the causeway to Sanibel Island are great for wading-birds, shorebirds, and an excellent variety of gulls and terns, especially in winter. Beach parking is reached by a turn-off on the left just before the toll booth. After passing the toll station ($3/vehicle), pull off anywhere on the two causeway islands. (Low tide is best.) Wilson's Plovers, American Oystercatchers, and Willets are resident. Snowy Plovers formerly were regular here but are now unpredictable. Some better shorebirds here in winter include Whimbrels, Long-billed Curlews, Marbled Godwits, and Red Knots. Flocks of larids usually contain a few Sandwich Terns.

Upon reaching the island, continue to Periwinkle Way (3.5 miles from the toll booth) and turn right. At Tarpon Bay Road (2.8), turn right, then left onto Sanibel-Captiva Road (0.3). The entrance to the main portion

White Ibis   Georges Dremeaux

of **J. N. "Ding" Darling National Wildlife Refuge** (6,000+ acres; $4/vehicle) is on the right (2.0). *The use of tape recordings to attract wildlife in the refuge is prohibited.* The refuge was established in 1945 and renamed, in 1967, after Jay Darling, the Pulitzer Prize-winning political cartoonist, conservationist, creator of the Duck Stamp program, and head of the U.S. Biological Survey (now the U.S. Fish and Wildlife Service) during the Franklin D. Roosevelt administration. The visitor center is open 9 am to 4 pm Monday through Thursday and Saturday but is *closed on Friday.* The most popular birding attraction is the 5-mile **wildlife drive**, open 7:30 am to 7:30 pm, but also *closed on Friday.* This excellent one-way drive traverses hammocks, mangrove forests, mosquito-control impoundments, and coastal estuaries. It is one of the most-visited birding spots in Florida. The wildlife drive is best from October to early March, when wintering American White Pelicans, ducks, shorebirds, and landbirds augment the resident wading-birds. Many birds are tame and allow close approach for observation and photography. Reddish Egrets, Roseate Spoonbills, and Ospreys usually are easy to find year round. Be sure to bring insect repellent in spring and summer.

During the spring and summer, three Florida specialties breed in the refuge. Gray Kingbirds and Black-whiskered Vireos usually are found easily, but Mangrove Cuckoo is much more of a challenge. There should be a few cuckoos along the wildlife drive, where they may be heard calling in early morning in spring and early summer, but the birds are very secretive. Walk the roadside through the dense mangrove forests, especially near Red Mangrove Overlook, and from miles 2.5 to 4.0 (measured from the entrance gate).

Shell Mound Trail, on the left 0.3 mile before the end of the wildlife drive, allows access into a tropical hardwood hammock growing on an old Indian shell midden. The hammock includes many plants of West Indian origin, including Gumbo Limbo and Spanish Stopper. This trail can be very good for migrants in spring and fall, but mosquitoes may be a problem. Shell Mound Trail can also be reached from Sanibel-Captiva Road via Wulfert Road (3.4 miles west of the refuge entrance) and is open even on Fridays.

Another trail accessible when the rest of the refuge is closed is Indigo Trail, which can be good in the early morning in spring for Mangrove Cuckoo. The trail begins on the west side of the visitor center and follows a dike for 2 miles through mangrove forests. The trail continues to the wildlife drive via Cross Dike, but the latter two trails are closed on Fridays.

The **Bailey Tract** (no fee) is a small separate part of the refuge. To reach it from Periwinkle Way, travel south on Tarpon Bay Road to the entrance on the right (0.4). The area contains thickets, marshes, and ponds, all reached by many short trails. In spring and summer, Gray Kingbirds and Black-whiskered Vireos breed here; the latter are easy to find in the tall Australian Pines along the canal at the south edge of the tract. American Alligators and Black-necked Stilts breed in the ponds in spring and early summer.

Contact: J. N. "Ding" Darling National Wildlife Refuge, #1 Wildlife Drive, Sanibel, FL 33957; 941/472-1100.

Return to Periwinkle Way and go east. Drive past Causeway Boulevard to the end of the road (1.4) into **Lighthouse Park** at Point Ybel (75¢/hour parking). The hammock and Australian Pines between the parking lot and the lighthouse offer an excellent site for fall migrant landbirds in southwestern Florida. Pileated Woodpeckers are easy to find and exceptionally tame here. To return to the mainland drive back to Causeway Boulevard and turn right.

If time permits, two other areas on the island are worth visiting. Bailey-Matthews Shell Museum ($4/person) is located on the south side of Sanibel-Captiva Road 0.8 mile west of Tarpon Bay Road (1.2 miles east of the entrance to Ding Darling refuge). The museum is an educational facility with interpretive displays of seashells and habitat dioramas to broaden the public's appreciation of marine environments.

The Sanibel-Captiva Conservation Foundation Nature Center (1,100 acres; $2/person) is also located on the south side of Sanibel-Captiva Road, 0.2 mile west of the museum. This private refuge (open 9 am-4 pm, *closed Sundays, and closed Saturdays from June through October*) also educates the public about the island's natural history. The center has exhibits, a bookstore, and 4 miles of trails crossing marshes, thickets, and hammocks. Trails may be walked independently or as part of a guided tour. Most of the birds here can also be found at the Bailey Tract.

Once you return to the mainland, Bunche Beach is an easily reached small park at the end of John Morris Road. From the Sanibel toll plaza, travel northeast on McGregor Boulevard, bear right onto Summerlin Road, then turn right onto John Morris Road (2.8 miles from the toll plaza or 1.5 miles west of San Carlos Boulevard). The park is at the end (1.2) and is good for wading-birds, shorebirds, and larids during migration and in winter. Here, too, low tide is best.

Fort Myers Beach is excellent for migrant and wintering shorebirds. To reach it, go south on SR-865 (San Carlos Boulevard) from Summerlin Road (4.3 from the toll plaza, or 1.5 from John Morris Road). (To reach this junction from the north, go southwest from Daniels Road on Summerlin Road and turn left onto SR-865 [5.8].) Once on the barrier island,

San Carlos Boulevard continues southeast as Estero Boulevard. Park at the Holiday Inn on the right (4.4) and walk around the south side of the hotel to the beach. *(Keep in mind that the hotel is private property and that we do not want to lose access to this premier birding site. If the hotel parking lot is crowded, it may be better to park at the shopping mall on the left, about 500 feet farther south, and then walk back to the Holiday Inn.)*

Wading-birds (including Reddish Egrets and Roseate Spoonbills) and many shorebirds can be viewed closely by following the footpath along the edge of the lagoon to the flats at the south end of the point. (August through October is best.) A variety of shorebirds use the area as a migratory staging area, and many winter here as well. In addition to common species, look for Wilson's (resident), Piping (winter), and Snowy (uncommon resident) Plovers, American Oystercatcher (resident), Whimbrel, Marbled Godwit, Long-billed Curlew (perhaps the most reliable site in the state), and large numbers of Red Knots. Florida's second Surfbird was found here in February 1978. A Curlew Sandpiper wintered here in 1993-1994 and was again observed on 25 June 1995. Gulls, terns, and other waterbirds are also common. Again, low tide is best.

Birders wishing to visit the Naples area or Corkscrew Swamp Sanctuary should continue south on SR-865, which turns east (becoming Bonita Beach Road) and thus connects with I-75. (Those visiting Corkscrew will exit I-75 at CR-846, the first exit south of SR-865, in about 3.5 miles.)

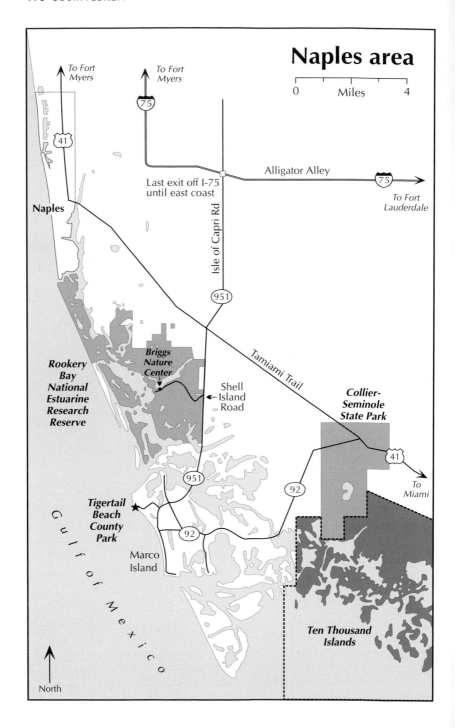

Naples area

0   Miles   4

To Fort Myers

To Fort Myers

75

Alligator Alley

75

To Fort Lauderdale

Last exit off I-75 until east coast

Isle of Capri Rd

41

Naples

951

Tamiami Trail

Briggs Nature Center

Rookery Bay National Estuarine Research Reserve

Shell Island Road

Collier-Seminole State Park

41

To Miami

951

92

Tigertail Beach County Park

Marco Island

92

Gulf of Mexico

Ten Thousand Islands

North

NAPLES AREA

The area surrounding Naples contains much of the habitat remaining for the Threatened Florida Black Bear and Bald Eagle and Endangered Florida Panther and Red-cockaded Woodpecker. Many of these vital lands are protected in areas such as Everglades National Park, Big Cypress National Preserve, Rookery Bay National Estuarine Research Reserve, Collier-Seminole State Park, Cape Romano/Ten Thousand Islands Aquatic Preserve, Corkscrew Swamp Sanctuary, Corkscrew Regional Ecosystem Watershed, and Florida Panther National Wildlife Refuge. Other areas, such as the massive Golden Gate Estates South development (about 80 square miles of roads and canals but few houses) and the undeveloped area west of it, are currently being acquired as a state forest. For local birding information, contact the Collier County Audubon Society at 941/649-9754 or Briggs Nature Center (below) at 941/775-8569.

Rookery Bay National Estuarine Research Reserve (12,500 acres) is located about 12 miles south of Naples. Because the majority of the reserve is mangrove forests, much of it is accessible only by boat. The Conservancy's Briggs Nature Center serves as the interpretive center for the reserve and is a good source of local birding information ($2/person; open year round Monday-Friday 9 am-4:30 pm; from October through June open on Saturdays from 9 am-4:30 pm; from January through March open Sundays from 1 pm-4:30 pm). To reach the center from I-75, exit at SR-951 (Isle of Capri Road) and go south. Cross US-41 (8.0) and turn right onto unpaved Shell Island Road (2.0). The center is ahead (1.0). (To reach the center from Naples, take US-41 southeast to SR-951, turn right, and proceed as above.)

The nature center features a ½-mile boardwalk trail through an oak hammock and mangroves before ending at a coastal pond, which may have wintering waterfowl, including Hooded Mergansers. In April and May, when the pond may be mostly dry, it attracts large concentrations of wading-birds, including Reddish Egrets and Roseate Spoonbills. The feeders around the center have been reliable for Shiny Cowbirds in recent winters. The reserve contains two groups of Florida Scrub-Jays which were introduced here in 1989 as an experiment to learn whether or not jays can be located to unoccupied scrub sites. This tiny population has twice been supplemented with additional birds in order for it to persist. Two other trails (Catclaw and Monument) traverse mangrove forests, where Mangrove Cuckoos, Black-whiskered Vireos, and Prairie Warblers breed. Birding boat tours and guided canoe trips are also available during winter months; call the center for more information.

Contact: Briggs Nature Center, 401 Shell Island Road, Naples, FL 33962; 941/775-8586.

After exploring Rookery Bay, return to SR-951 and turn right to **Tigertail Beach County Park** ($3/vehicle) on Marco Island, about 6 miles to the south. After you cross the bridge to Marco Island, the name of the road becomes Collier Boulevard. Go through the third traffic light at Bald Eagle Drive and turn right onto Tigertail Court (0.5). Turn left onto Hernando Drive to a 3-way stop sign. The park is straight ahead. Tigertail Beach is an important wintering site for shorebirds. The best areas in the park are on the emergent sandbars 1 mile to the right and on the peninsula ½ mile to the left. Species to search for include Reddish Egret and Snowy, Wilson's, and Piping Plovers. Low tide is best for shorebirds. Snowy Plovers breed here, as do Least Terns and Black Skimmers. Some areas are roped off year round as Critical Wildlife Areas.

Return to SR-951 and turn right to San Marco Boulevard (SR-92) (1.0), then turn left. After about 12 miles, SR-92 ends at US-41 (Tamiami Trail). At this point, you may turn left to return to Naples or turn right to continue east toward Big Cypress National Preserve, Everglades National Park, and the Miami area. *You cannot access I-75 from US-41 east of SR-951 (and vice versa) until you reach Miami.*

Collier-Seminole State Park (6,423 acres, standard fee) is at the junction of SR-92 and US-41. On the north side of US-41 is a 6-mile hiking trail through the cypress swamp. Ask at the ranger station about conditions on the trail (it is often under water) and for the combination of the lock. Mosquitoes can be bad in spring and summer.

Contact: Collier-Seminole State Park, Route 4, Box 848, Naples, FL 33961; 941/394-3397.

BIG CYPRESS REGION

Birders continuing east on US-41 may stop at **Fakahatchee Strand State Preserve** (61,962 acres; no fee). (A "strand" is an elongated swamp aligned with water flow.) Fakahatchee Strand is 3 to 5 miles wide and 20 miles long. It is the largest strand forest remaining in the U.S. and contains such Threatened and Endangered species as Florida Panther, Black Bear, Mink, Mangrove Fox Squirrel, and Wood Stork. Fakahatchee also preserves the largest Royal Palm hammock in the United States. Because of the preserve's immense ecological value, its facilities are limited. The most accessible part of the preserve is the boardwalk at **Big**

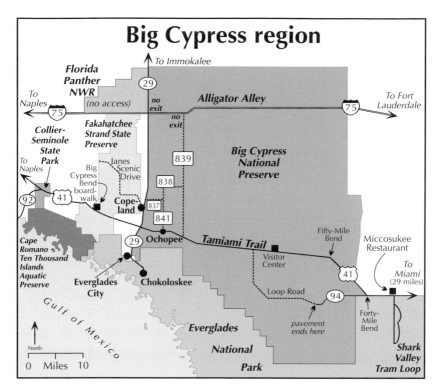

Big Cypress region

To Immokalee

Florida Panther NWR (no access)

29

no exit

Alligator Alley

To Naples

75

To Fort Lauderdale

75

Collier-Seminole State Park

Fakahatchee Strand State Preserve

To Naples

Janes Scenic Drive

Big Cypress Bend boardwalk

Cope-land

no exit

839

838

837

841

Big Cypress National Preserve

Cape Romano Ten Thousand Islands Aquatic Preserve

29

Ochopee

Tamiami Trail

Visitor Center

Fifty-Mile Bend

Miccosukee Restaurant

To Miami (29 miles)

41

Everglades City

Chokoloskee

Loop Road

94

pavement ends here

Forty-Mile Bend

Gulf of Mexico

North

0   Miles   10

Everglades National Park

Shark Valley Tram Loop

Cypress Bend. It is located on the north side of US-41, 2 miles east of Port of the Islands resort. Park next to the Seminole village. The trail is 2,000 feet long and extends into a swamp with huge virgin Bald Cypresses. Species that may be encountered here include Limpkin, Barred Owl, and other swamp species. The trail can also be good for migrant and wintering landbirds. (Big Cypress Bend is especially recommended to those who do not plan to visit Corkscrew Swamp Sanctuary.)

To reach the other accessible portion of the preserve, continue east on US-41 to SR-29 and turn left. At the first road on the left (2.5) proceed to the stop sign and turn right. The preserve office is next to the fire tower (1.1). The road quickly becomes **W. J. Janes Scenic Drive** (open daily, dawn to dusk), an 11-mile drive through the preserve. The road continues through Golden Gate Estates South (a massive unbuilt development now being acquired as a state forest) to SR-846, but because of the maze of unmarked and occasionally flooded roads, it is recommended that you turn around at the west boundary of the preserve and return to SR-29. From here you can go south to Everglades City (bordering Everglades National Park), or return to US-41 and continue east, or turn left to visit

Big Cypress National Preserve, or continue north to Immokalee. *Again, you cannot access I-75 from SR-29.*

Contact: Fakahatchee Strand State Preserve, P.O. Box 548, Copeland, FL 33926; 941/695-4593.

Florida Panther National Wildlife Refuge (26,000 acres) is located at the northwest corner of I-75 and SR-29, adjacent to Fakahatchee Strand State Preserve and Big Cypress National Preserve. Purchased in 1989, the refuge preserves essential habitat for the critically Endangered Florida Panther, believed to number fewer than 50 animals. It is closed to all public use.

The northwest corner of **Everglades National Park** encompasses the Ten Thousand Islands region, named for the hundreds of mangrove-covered keys just offshore. This portion of the park can be visited only by boat. The Everglades National Park Gulf Coast Ranger Station offers boat tours from Everglades City on an hourly basis ($9/person). The best trip lasts about 2½ hours, including a ½-hour walk on the beach at Kingston Key. Wading-birds, including Roseate Spoonbills, are the highlight of the boat trips. Everglades City is located on SR-29 about 5 miles south of US-41. The visitor center is open daily.

Contact: Everglades National Park Gulf Coast Ranger Station, P.O. Box 120, Everglades City, FL 33939; 941/695-3311.

Most of **Big Cypress National Preserve** (729,000 acres; no fee) is inaccessible to passenger vehicles, but a few well-maintained gravel roads offer a 12-mile driving tour through the western section. From SR-29, go east on US-41 to CR-841 (Birdon Road) (3.0) and turn left. (From Janes Scenic Drive, you may choose to go north on SR-29 to CR-837 [Wagon Wheel Road] [1.0] and turn right. At the junction with Birdon Road, turn left.) Beyond Wagon Wheel Road, the road turns to the right before ending at CR-839 (Turner River Road). Stop frequently along this road to look for wading-birds, including both of the night-herons and American Bitterns (winter), Snail Kites, and Purple Gallinules. At CR-839, turn right to return to US-41.

Continue east on US-41 through two "bends" in the road. At the second bend (Forty-Mile Bend), turn right onto SR-94 (Loop Road), a 24-mile loop through the southern part of the preserve. The first 8 miles are paved, but the rest is unpaved and usually very rough. The pavement ends just beyond an environmental education center on the left. On the right opposite the center is a short nature trail through a West Indian hardwood hammock. Those who wish to drive Loop Road all the way to Monroe Station should first check at the visitor center for current road conditions.

*Wood Stork
with Water Lettuce
and Pickerel Weed*
Diane Pierce

Contact: Big Cypress National Preserve, HCR 61, Box 11, Ochopee, FL 33943; 941/695-4111.

From Forty-Mile Bend, continue east on US-41 to the **Miccosukee Indian Restaurant** (3.6). Just west of the restaurant (that is, north of the water-control structure) is an active Snail Kite roost. The birds are viewed easily shortly after dawn and before dusk. During the day, the kites forage in the extensive marshes well to the north and south of the road and usually are difficult to locate from US-41.

Shark Valley is just east of the restaurant (0.1) and is a northern access point to Everglades National Park. A 15-mile paved loop road is available for hiking, biking, or via a two-hour guided tram ($7.30/person) supplied by the Park Service; it cannot be driven by private vehicle. The road ends at a 65-foot-tall observation tower that overlooks the great "River of Grass" ecosystem. Anhingas, wading-birds, Snail Kites, Limpkins, American Alligators, and other wildlife may be seen from the trail. During wet years, as in winter 1994-1995, the loop trail may be inundated. Call 305/221-8455 for more information. (To reach Shark Valley from I-95 in Miami, go west on US-41 [Tamiami Trail] to the entrance on the left [35.0].)

South Florida – Inland

IMMOKALEE AREA

Immokalee is a small farming town located in the northwestern Everglades. The following 60-mile loop that begins and ends in town is a good way to sample Florida prairie country. All the property along this route is privately owned, so bird only from the roads. From CR-846 in town, go north on SR-29 to CR-832 (Keri Grade) (12.3) and turn right. This lightly traveled road traverses pine flatwoods, Cabbage Palm hammocks, Okalacoochee Slough, marshes, and cattle pastures for about 19 miles before ending at CR-833. The sugar cane field on the left (10.9) frequently contains a huge roost of Tree Swallows in winter and early spring. In February and March, when the cane is tall, over 1 million birds have roosted here in the past. At CR-833, turn right to CR-846 (12) and turn right to Immokalee.

Birds likely to be seen along the route include species typical of southern Florida flatwoods and wet prairie habitats. Look for wading-birds (including Glossy Ibises and Wood Storks), Mottled Ducks, other puddle ducks (winter), Swallow-tailed Kites (spring and summer), Crested

Caracaras, Purple Gallinules, Limpkins, and Sandhill Cranes. In spring and summer you may be lucky enough to see Great White Heron, Roseate Spoonbill, or Short-tailed Hawk.

Between Immokalee and the Gulf coast is **Corkscrew Swamp Sanctuary** (10,720 acres, $6.50/person), owned and operated by the National Audubon Society. It is worth a visit if only to view the huge cypress trees, but the birds can make it a special treat. To reach the sanctuary from SR-29 in Immokalee, travel west on CR-846. At CR-849 (Sanctuary Road) (15), turn right and follow this road to the sanctuary. (From the Gulf coast, exit [#17] I-75 onto CR-846 and go east. At CR-849 [17.0], turn left and continue to the park.) *The use of tape recordings in the sanctuary is prohibited.*

The main attraction is the 2¼-mile boardwalk that loops through a variety of habitats, including the largest old-growth stand of Bald Cypresses remaining in the state, with some trees that are nearly 500 years old. Corkscrew is home to a Wood Stork rookery that is often the largest in the nation; a few nests are usually visible from the boardwalk. (The birds nest in late winter and early spring.) Like other colonies of this Endangered species, breeding success varies considerably from year to year according to local water levels and related supplies of food. In 1992, 1,200 pairs of Wood Storks at Corkscrew fledged 2,750 young; in 1993,

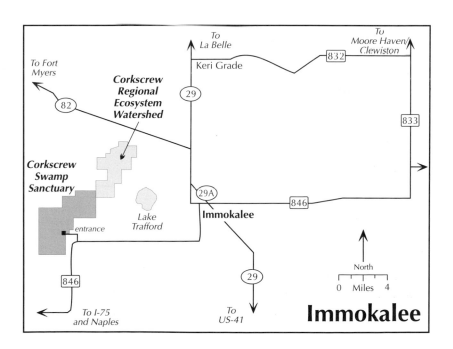

To La Belle

To Moore Haven/ Clewiston

To Fort Myers

Keri Grade

832

Corkscrew Regional Ecosystem Watershed

29

82

833

Corkscrew Swamp Sanctuary

29A

846

Lake Trafford

Immokalee

entrance

846

29

North

0   Miles   4

To I-75 and Naples

To US-41

Immokalee

420 pairs nested, but no young fledged; in 1994, only 42 young fledged from 434 nests; and in 1995, 913 nests were built, but only about 200 young fledged.

Other birds of special interest include Swallow-tailed Kite (spring and summer), Limpkin, and Pileated Woodpecker. Barred Owls may be cooperative here. These species and American Alligators are all accustomed to people on the boardwalk. As a result, they are tame and may allow close study. Also, Cottonmouths (Water Moccasins) are less wary here than in most places; they are frequently sighted from the boardwalk. Painted Buntings are fairly common winter residents and visit the feeders near the gift shop and in the picnic area regularly. Short-tailed Hawks occasionally are seen in spring and summer.

Contact: Corkscrew Swamp Sanctuary, 375 Sanctuary Road, Naples, FL 33964; 941/657-3771.

The state is purchasing much land surrounding the sanctuary as part of the Corkscrew Regional Ecosystem Watershed (CREW) project. Eventually, a corridor may link the sanctuary with Florida Panther National Wildlife Refuge and Fakahatchee Strand State Preserve to the south.

BELLE GLADE AREA

Birders traveling south along the east side of Lake Okeechobee have only a few good birding sites between Okeechobee and Belle Glade. In Pahokee, SR-715 splits off US-441 and parallels the Hoover Dike. Brushy areas along the road may contain Smooth-billed Anis, but use caution when pulling off the road. SR-715 and US-441 both continue south to Belle Glade. At SR-717 (West Canal Street North) (10.2), go west to the levee (2.0). Drive up the levee road and cross the one-lane bridge to the **Belle Glade Marina and Campground**. *This site is privately owned, so bird it discreetly.* Beyond the bridge, follow Canal Street to the gate. Park here and walk the road to look for Indigo Buntings, Painted Buntings, Blue Grosbeaks, and Orchard Orioles, which have all wintered here in recent years. Return to your vehicle and turn left to the end of the campground. From here, American (winter) and Least Bitterns, ducks, Purple Gallinules (numerous and almost tame here), and Limpkins can be seen on the lake. A Couch's Kingbird was reported from February to April 1991.

From late July to early September, **vegetable fields** in the Belle Glade and South Bay areas are flooded to prevent subsidence and to kill nematodes. Migrant shorebirds and larids gather by the thousands! In addition to common species, look for Buff-breasted Sandpiper, Long-

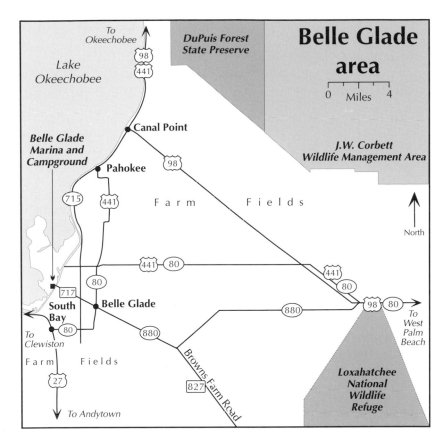

Belle Glade area

0 Miles 4

To Okeechobee
98 441

Lake Okeechobee

DuPuis Forest State Preserve

Canal Point

Belle Glade Marina and Campground

Pahokee 98

J.W. Corbett Wildlife Management Area

715 441

Farm   Fields

North

441 80

441
80

80

717

South Bay

To Clewiston

80

Belle Glade

880

98 80

To West Palm Beach

880

Farm   Fields

27

827

Browns Farm Road

Loxahatchee National Wildlife Refuge

To Andytown

billed Dowitcher, Wilson's Phalarope, and Black Tern. Breeding species include Mottled Ducks, Fulvous Whistling-Ducks (common), King Rails, Black-necked Stilts (abundant), Gull-billed Terns, and even Black Skimmers (the latter two are rare). Some flooded fields also may contain huge numbers of wading-birds. In recent years, flocks of hundreds or thousands of egrets, Glossy Ibises, and Wood Storks have been reported, and 60 Roseate Spoonbills were seen here in August 1994.

Unfortunately, most fields in this area are private property and are off-limits to the public. Many farmers prohibit trespassing because of past vandalism of equipment or because of liability concerns. The few farmers who do allow birders access to their fields do so only to specific local birders, rather than to anyone who wishes to get onto the property. Therefore, this guide does not specify which farms are "open" to birding. Visiting birders are recommended to drive *public* roadways in the area until flooded fields are visible. *Do not drive through any gates, even those that are open.* You may get into trouble for trespassing or get locked *inside* a farm.

One public road that may allow access to flooded fields is Brown's Farm Road (CR-827), south of SR-880 about 6 miles east of Belle Glade. Besides shorebirds, watch along the roadside for Barn Owls and Smooth-billed Anis.

Smooth-billed Ani
Louise Zemaitis

South Florida – Atlantic Coast

HOBE SOUND AREA

Jonathan Dickinson State Park (11,383 acres; standard fee) contains the largest diversity of habitats remaining along Florida's southeast coast. The entrance is on the west side of US-1 about 3½ miles north of Jupiter Inlet, or 4.7 miles south of CR-708 in Hobe Sound. Although not directly on the ocean, the park's acreage represents the largest protected coastal area between Hobe Sound and Miami, about 90 miles to the south. The park contains 2 miles of frontage along the Loxahatchee River, part of which is the only river in the state designated a National Wild and Scenic River. Ospreys and Bald Eagles nest here. Another feature of the park is that it contains the sixth-largest protected population of Florida Scrub-Jays. About 50 groups were estimated to occur here in 1993. The birds are common in low oak scrub in the northeastern part of the park. Prescribed burns are set to maintain the scrub in the early successional stage required by the jays. The rest of the park is composed of pine flatwoods, Sand Pine scrub, cypress domes, sloughs, wet prairies, and floodplain and riverine wetlands. Bachman's Sparrows are found in the flatwoods, but Red-cockaded Woodpeckers have been extirpated from the park since 1984. The park has four short-to-medium-length nature trails good for finding wading-birds, Pileated Woodpeckers, and other landbirds. The road to Hobe Mountain offers a panoramic view of the park.

Contact: Jonathan Dickinson State Park, 16450 Southeast Federal Highway, Hobe Sound, FL 33455; 561/546-2771.

Hobe Sound National Wildlife Refuge (968 acres; $5/vehicle or $1/pedestrian) is located between Jonathan Dickinson State Park and the Indian River. There are two main access points to the refuge. The first is on the mainland on the east side of US-1, 2.4 miles north of the entrance to Jonathan Dickinson State Park. The refuge headquarters and Hobe Sound Nature Center are located here. There is no fee at this entrance, which features the **Sand Pine Scrub Nature Trail** (½-mile long), where Florida Scrub-Jays can usually be found. The trail winds along a dune ridge overlooking Indian River and is especially good for viewing migrant landbirds.

The second part of the refuge is a few miles north on the barrier island. It features dunes, ocean frontage, and mangrove forests bordering the Indian River. From the nature center, drive north on US-1 to CR-708 (Bridge Road) (2.3) and turn right to the ocean (1.3). At CR-707 (Beach

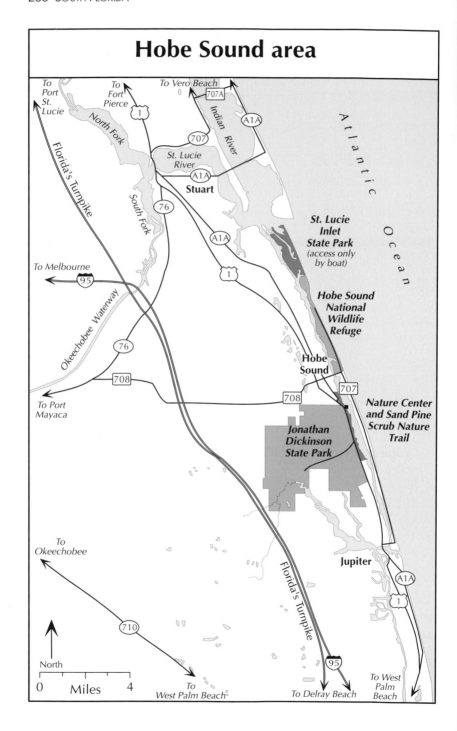

Hobe Sound area

Road), turn left to the refuge ahead (1.8).   Hobe Sound Refuge extends 3½ miles north to St. Lucie Inlet State Park (accessible only by boat), which continues another 2½ miles to St. Lucie Inlet. This undeveloped stretch of beach provides one of the few remaining areas in southeast Florida where Least Terns still nest on the beach. The beach, closed

Snail Kite   Shawneen E. Finnegan

nightly, is a major sea turtle nesting area from April through September. Up to 100,000 turtle hatchlings may be produced in good years.

Contact: Hobe Sound National Wildlife Refuge, P.O. Box 645, Hobe Sound, FL 33475; 561/546-6141; Hobe Sound Nature Center, 561/546-2067.

The Indian River, including spoil islands next to the Intracoastal Waterway and the sandbars near St. Lucie Inlet, offers birders many views of wading-birds, shorebirds, and larids. Check especially areas along Stuart Causeway (SR-A1A) and the Jensen Beach Causeway (CR-707A). Besides many common species, look for Roseate Spoonbills year round and Bonaparte's Gulls in winter.

NORTH PALM BEACH
TO BOCA RATON

John D. MacArthur Beach State Park (225 acres; standard fee) contains wading-birds and larids but is visited mostly for migrant landbirds. To reach it from US-1, go east on CR-708 (Blue Heron Boulevard) to SR-A1A (Ocean Drive) (1.8) and turn left to the park (2.0). Satinleaf Trail at the north end of the park and the area around the entrance station are the best places to search for migrants. Rarities reported in the park recently include a La Sagra's Flycatcher in April 1993 and a Stripe-headed Tanager in August and September 1995.

Contact: John D. MacArthur Beach State Park, 10900 State Road 703 (A1A), North Palm Beach, FL 33408; 561/624-6950.

An excellent place to find Snail Kites is the **Solid Waste Authority facility** (no fee) in West Palm Beach. To reach it, exit (#54) I-95 onto SR-702 (45th Street) and go west. *There is no exit off Florida's Turnpike at SR-702.* At Jog Road (3.1) park by the side of the road and watch for kites flying to and from the roost on the property. Shortly after dawn and before dusk are the best times. From 1987 to 1991, the monthly average of kites that used the roost was about 30 birds, but 212 were present in May 1989 during a severe drought. Numbers of kites using the roost are highest from April to September. For more information, call the facility at 561/640-4000.

John Prince Park on Lake Osborne in Lake Worth can be good for migrants; it is also an excellent spot for Limpkins. To reach the park from I-95, exit (#47) onto South 6th Avenue and go west to SR-807 (Congress Avenue) (0.8; the second traffic light). Turn left to the entrance on the left (0.8). At the crossroads (0.2) turn right, then left to follow the road along the canal. Check the lake on the left for Limpkins. Look also for

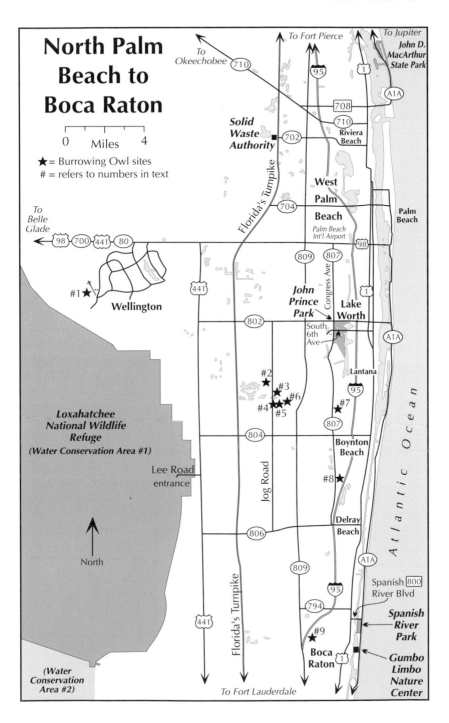

North Palm Beach to Boca Raton

0 | Miles | 4

★ = Burrowing Owl sites
= refers to numbers in text

To Okeechobee

To Fort Pierce

To Jupiter

John D. MacArthur State Park

710

95

1

708

710

A1A

Solid Waste Authority

702

Riviera Beach

West Palm Beach

704

Palm Beach Int'l Airport

Palm Beach

To Belle Glade

98 700 441 80

98

#1 ★

Wellington

441

809

807

John Prince Park

Lake Worth

Congress Ave

1

802

South 6th Ave

A1A

#2 ★

#3 ★

#6 ★

#4 ★ #5 ★

Lantana

95

#7 ★

807

Loxahatchee National Wildlife Refuge
(Water Conservation Area #1)

804

Boynton Beach

Lee Road
entrance

Jog Road

#8 ★

Delray Beach

806

North

809

A1A

Florida's Turnpike

95

794

Spanish 800 River Blvd

Spanish River Park

#9 ★

441

Boca Raton

1

Gumbo Limbo Nature Center

(Water Conservation Area #2)

To Fort Lauderdale

Atlantic Ocean

Black-crowned Night-Herons, Purple Gallinules, and Smooth-billed Anis. From the parking lot, walk back to the canal and cross the foot-bridge to check the other lakes. Because of the crowds of people that use the park during weekends, it is best to visit on a weekday.

Arthur R. Marshall Loxahatchee National Wildlife Refuge (147,368 acres; $5/vehicle or $1/pedestrian) contains the only natural habitats remaining in the northern Everglades. Much of the refuge (which includes Water Conservation Area 1) is off-limits to the public, and parts are accessible only by motorboat, but an excellent section west of Boynton Beach is accessible by passenger vehicle. To reach it from either I-95 (exit #44) or Florida's Turnpike (exit #86), travel west on SR-804 (Boynton Beach Boulevard) to US-441 and turn left. At Lee Road (2.0) turn right to the entrance. The visitor center on the right is open daily from 9 am to 4 pm from mid-October to mid-April. During the rest of the year, the center is closed Mondays and Tuesdays.

The refuge has two nature trails. The Cypress Swamp boardwalk begins next to the visitor center. It is 2,000 feet long and traverses a cypress swamp. The Marsh Trail on the south side of Lee Road is 4,000 feet long and circles one of the ten impoundments. Since water levels vary between impoundments, all should be searched. In or around the impoundments, look for Anhingas, wading-birds, Fulvous Whistling-Ducks, Mottled Ducks, King Rails, Purple Gallinules, Limpkins, Black-necked Stilts, and Smooth-billed Anis. American Alligators are numerous. In winter, ducks and shorebirds can be common when water levels are favorable, and Painted Buntings may be found in shrubbery along Marsh Trail. Florida's first verified Cassin's Kingbird spent the winter of 1989-1990 here, and a Fork-tailed Flycatcher was observed in July 1992. Smooth-billed Anis may also be found by walking the dike north and south of the boat ramp at the western end of the main refuge road. A 5½-mile-long canoe trail begins and ends at the boat ramp; call ahead to insure that the trail is open. Snail Kites formerly were common around the impoundments, but the birds more often use the interior of the refuge, where higher water levels are maintained.

Contact: Arthur R. Marshall Loxahatchee National Wildlife Refuge, 10216 Lee Road, Boynton Beach, FL 33437-4796; 561/734-8303.

BOCA RATON

Spanish River Park can be great for migrants and West Indian strays. This city park is very popular, so it is best to arrive early. The parking fee inside the park, designed to discourage tourists (!), is *$8 ($10 on weekends)*, but limited (free) parking is available along Spanish River Boulevard west of SR-A1A. To reach the park, exit (#40) I-95 onto SR-794 (Yamato Road) and go east. At US-1 (0.8) turn right to CR-800 (Spanish River Boulevard) (0.6). Turn left onto it, cross over the Intracoastal Waterway (0.5), and park on the right. Walk south through the Australian Pines into the park. A Bananaquit and two Stripe-headed Tanagers were found here in April 1994, North America's first verified Cuban Pewee spent almost a month here in March and April 1995, and a Bahama Mockingbird was found in April 1995.

Also worth a look during migration is the Gumbo Limbo Nature Center (1.25 miles south of Spanish River Boulevard) on the west side of SR-A1A. Short nature trails through a hardwood hammock are located north and south of the center.

There are still many scattered sites in coastal Palm Beach County that contain small populations of Burrowing Owls. It is recommended that you purchase a detailed road map of eastern Palm Beach County to locate the specific sites easily. Please keep in mind that all the properties in which the burrows are located are privately owned, so *observe the birds only from the road edges.* Also, please avoid the school sites when classes are in session. The sites are listed from north to south (see the map on page 211).

1) Aero Club development in Wellington: 15 burrows; the 2 most accessible are located along Take Off Place west of Aero Club Drive.

2) Manatee Elementary School on Hypoluxo Road 0.2 mile west of Jog Road: burrows in the faculty parking lot and the large open field.

3) Christa McAuliffe Middle School on LeChalet Boulevard 0.2 mile east of Jog Road: burrows inside the bus circle and in the field at the rear of the school.

4) Gateway Boulevard and Jog Road: 1 burrow 150 feet southeast of the junction of the two roads.

5) Crystal Lakes Elementary School on Gateway Boulevard 0.3 mile east of Jog Road: burrows in the parking lot, bus circle, and field.

6) Gateway Boulevard 0.1 mile west of Military Trail: 1 burrow on the south side of the road.

7) Boynton Canal south of Gateway Boulevard and east of Congress Avenue: 2 burrows in a pasture on the south side of the canal, visible from Congress Avenue.

8) Caloosa Park on the east side of Congress Avenue north of West Atlantic Avenue: burrows along the outfield fences of the baseball field.

9) Florida Atlantic University, Boca Raton campus: many burrows, all marked by numbered stakes.

Burrowing Owl   Georges Dremeaux

POMPANO BEACH/
FORT LAUDERDALE AREA

The Pompano Beach landfill is closed to public access, but the surrounding undeveloped areas are excellent for wintering gulls. To reach the area, exit (#36) I-95 at SR-834 (Sample Road) and go west. At SR-845 (Powerline Road) (1.7), turn right. Between SR-834 and SR-869 (Sawgrass Expressway; SW 10th Street) (2.0), check the lakes and open areas for gulls in this area. Rarities that have been found in the area include Franklin's, Thayer's, Lesser Black-backed (over 20 birds at times), Glaucous, and Great Black-backed Gulls.

Easterlin Park (46 acres; $1/person weekends and holidays) is reached by exiting (#31) I-95 at SR-816 (Oakland Park Boulevard) and going east. At NW 9th Avenue (Powerline Road) (0.3), turn left to NW 38th Street (0.5) and left to the park on the left. The mixed cypress/hardwood hammock can be good for landbirds. In winter look for Broad-winged Hawks, Yellow-throated Vireos, and Orange-crowned, Cape May, Black-throated Blue, and Black-throated Green Warblers.

Contact: Easterlin Park, 1000 NW 38th Street, Oakland Park, FL 33309; 954/938-0610.

Hugh Taylor Birch State Recreation Area (180 acres; standard fee) is the best local spot for migrants. From I-95 exit (#30) onto SR-838 (East Sunrise Boulevard) and go east to the park on the left (just past the Intracoastal Waterway). Spot-breasted Orioles are observed regularly from late August through early October and may also be seen at other seasons. Key West Quail-Dove, La Sagra's Flycatcher, Bahama Mockingbird, and Stripe-headed Tanager are among the rarities that have been found here.

Contact: Hugh Taylor Birch State Recreation Area, 3109 East Sunrise Boulevard, Fort Lauderdale, FL 33304; 954/564-4521.

John U. Lloyd State Recreation Area (251 acres; standard fee) is also worth exploring for migrants and West Indian strays. To reach the park from US-1 in Dania, drive east on SR-A1A (Dania Beach Boulevard) and follow the signs north to the entrance (2.2). In winter Northern Gannets, Magnificent Frigatebirds, and Great Black-backed Gulls may be observed from the jetty at the northernmost tip of the park. Barrier Island Nature Trail is good for migrants and West Indian strays. La Sagra's Flycatcher, Bahama Mockingbird, and Bananaquit have all occurred in the park in recent years.

Contact: John U. Lloyd State Recreation Area, 6503 North Ocean Drive, Dania, FL 33004; 954/923-2833.

Pompano Beach/Fort Lauderdale Area

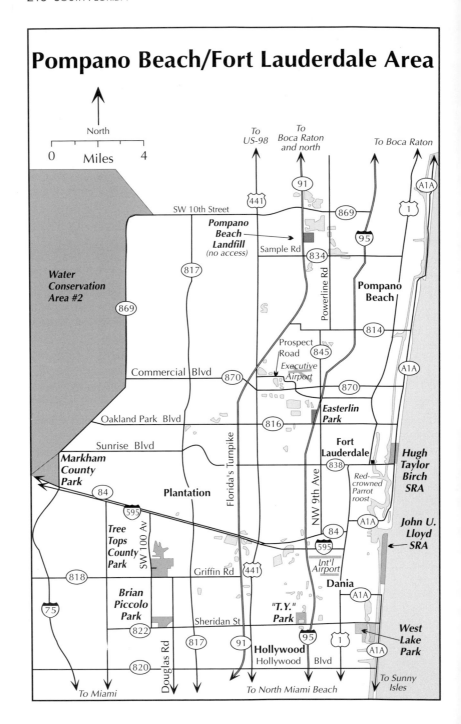

Along SR-A1A between SR-822 and SR-820 (Hollywood Boulevard), look on the wires for Gray Kingbirds in spring and summer. Monk Parakeets, resident in this area, are often found in the Coconut Palms along the beach and SR-A1A in Hollywood Beach.

Topeekeegee Yugnee (Seminole for "meeting place") Park (150 acres; $1/person weekends and holidays) in Hollywood has a large oak hammock and a 40-acre lake. To reach the park, usually shortened to "T.Y." Park, exit (#24) I-95 at SR-822 (Sheridan Street) and go west. At North Park Road (0.6), turn right to the park on the right (0.2). Look for migrant and wintering landbirds in the oak hammock; a Black-throated Gray Warbler wintered here in 1993. Short-tailed Hawks are seen occasionally.

Contact: Topeekeegee Yugnee Park, 3300 North Park Road, Hollywood, FL 33021; 954-985-1980.

Tree Tops County Park (358 acres; $1/person weekends and holidays) contains a 1,000-foot boardwalk through a fresh water marsh. To reach the park, exit (#26) I-95 at SR-818 (Griffin Road) and go west. At SW 100th Avenue (7), turn right to the entrance on the right (0.5). Follow the road to the boardwalk sign (0.6) and park. Walk the trail to the marsh, which may have American (winter) and Least Bitterns, wading-birds, ducks (mostly Mottled Duck), and Purple Gallinules. In winter 8 to 10 species of warblers may be observed along the oak hammock trails, including Black-throated Green Warblers. In January 1993 a Black-throated Gray Warbler was present in the hammock, and a La Sagra's Flycatcher wintered near the visitor center in 1994-1995.

Contact: Tree Tops County Park, 3900 SW 100th Avenue, Davie, FL 33328; 954/370-3750.

Since the 1970s a flock of Red-crowned Parrots has been present (and possibly established) in Fort Lauderdale. The location of the roost changes, but from 1993 to 1995 some parrots roosted regularly in the Australian Pines at the southwest corner of US-1 and 13th Street NE.

Two areas in the Fort Lauderdale area still contain a few Burrowing Owls. One site is Fort Lauderdale Executive Airport, which has active burrows marked with plastic perches. To reach the airport, exit (#32) I-95 at SR-870 (Commercial Boulevard or NW 50th Street) and go west. At 31st Avenue (2.1), turn right to Prospect Road (0.5). Turn right, then left onto Executive Airport Perimeter Road (0.1). The burrows are in the field ahead.

Burrowing Owls are also found in Brian Piccolo Park (180 acres; $1/person weekends and holidays) on the north side of SR-822 (Sheridan Street) 6.5 miles west of I-95. Burrows are located near the park entrance and office and around the ballfields.

Markham County Park (665 acres; $1/person weekends and holidays) borders Water Conservation Area 2B, where Snail Kites can usually be observed year round (depending on water levels). To reach the park, exit (#1) I-595 at NW 136th Avenue and immediately turn left onto SR-84 (Weston Road). The park is on the right (1.9). Turn left after the park entrance and park at the Everglades Nature Trail sign. Walk the narrow road that leads to the L-35 levee which separates the park from the Everglades. When water levels in the conservation area are low, causing fish to become concentrated in shallow pools, spectacular concentrations of wading-birds can occur. In addition to common species, look for Wood Storks and Limpkins. During migration, the nature trail may also be worthwhile.

Contact: Markham County Park, 16001 West State Road 84, Sunrise, FL 33326; 954/389-2000.

GREATER MIAMI AREA

Dade County, the home of the crowded and heavily urbanized Greater Miami area, is laid out as a grid, a system which allows any site in the county to be located easily. Streets (16 to the mile) run east and west, and avenues (10 to the mile) run north and south. Most of the streets and avenues are numbered, using the junction of Flagler Street (just north of US-41 [8th Street]) and Miami Avenue (between I-95 and US-1) as the center point. Streets and avenues are numbered outward from this point; thus 3rd Street is close to Flagler Street, while 162nd Street would be 10 miles away. All streets and avenues to the northwest of this intersection are labeled NW, those to the southwest are labeled SW, and so on. Because the intersection of Flagler Street and Miami Avenue is so near the coast, most of the streets and avenues are either NW or SW.

Birding sites within the Greater Miami area are scattered widely, so for the purposes of this guide the area has been divided into five regions. Areas north of US-41 (Tamiami Trail) are listed as North Miami. Areas south of US-41 are split into four areas: Key Biscayne, South Miami, Kendall, and Homestead/Florida City. Greater Miami is comprised of many suburban towns and unincorporated areas (e.g., Hialeah, Coral Gables, Opa-Locka, Kendall) that once were separated by pinelands, but are now combined as one continuous sprawling region. The divisions used in this guide are merely for the sake of convenience; visitors will notice few differences from one area to the next.

US-41 (Tamiami Trail) offers direct access to Shark Valley (Everglades National Park), Big Cypress National Preserve, Fakahatchee Strand State

Preserve, and points farther west. A reliable Snail Kite site is located near the Miccosukee Indian Restaurant on US-41; see the Big Cypress section (page 202) for more information.

Tropical Audubon Society operates a birding hotline that normally is updated every Wednesday evening; call 305/ 667-PEEP (7337).

Lastly, be assured that the Miami area is not as dangerous a place as it may appear to be from the media reports. All the sites listed here should be safe, assuming that normal precautions are taken.

Spot-breasted Oriole
Gail Diane Yovanovich

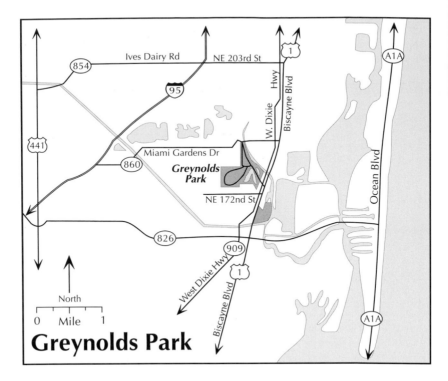

Greynolds Park

NORTH MIAMI

Greynolds Park (no fee) in North Miami Beach contains a rookery (and year-round roost) of numerous wading-birds, but the Scarlet Ibises introduced there in July 1961 no longer occur. The park is good also for migrant landbirds and Spot-breasted Orioles. To reach it, go north on US-1 (Biscayne Boulevard) to NE 172nd Street. On the right is the east section of the park, but turn left, cross the tracks, and turn right onto West Dixie Highway (one block). The entrance is on the left (0.3). From I-95, exit (#20) at Ives Dairy Road and go east on NE 203rd Street. At West Dixie Highway (1.1; just before the railroad tracks), turn right to the entrance (2.0). Shortly after entering the park, turn left and stop in the first parking area. Several trails lead off from this point, but you should walk the road, turn left at the tower, and go about a block to the golf course. Look for the flowering trees straight ahead. Turn left and follow a small road down to the rookery. Spot-breasted Orioles feed in flowering trees, such as the big *Bombax* tree near the clubhouse. Orioles may also be found around the first parking lot near the stone bridge.

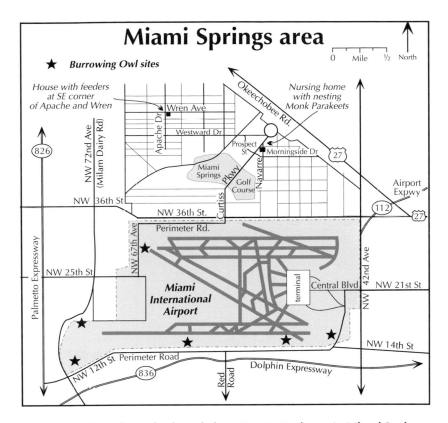

Miami Springs area

★ **Burrowing Owl sites**

0   Mile   ½   North

House with feeders
at SE corner
of Apache and Wren

Nursing home
with nesting
Monk Parakeets

Okeechobee Rd.

Wren Ave

Apache Dr

Westward Dr

NW 72nd Ave
(Milam Dairy Rd)

826

Prospect
St

Morningside Dr

27

Miami
Springs

Golf
Course

Navarre

Pkwy

Airport
Expwy

NW 36th St

NW 36th St.

Curtiss

112

27

Perimeter Rd.

NW 67th Ave

Palmetto Expressway

NW 25th St

**Miami
International
Airport**

terminal

Central Blvd

NW 42nd Ave

NW 21st St

NW 14th St

NW 12th St

Perimeter Road

836

Red
Road

Dolphin Expressway

Many psittacids can be found along Curtiss Parkway in **Miami Springs**, a residential area just north of Miami International Airport. From SR-826 (Palmetto Expressway), exit onto NW 36th Street and go east to the light at Curtiss Parkway (2.0). Turn left (north) and follow the road as it curves to the right through the Miami Springs Golf Course. Park on Navarre Drive at the Fair Haven Nursing Home on the right (1.0). Bird the block around the nursing home first, then walk the median of Curtiss Parkway back to the golf course. Hundreds of Monk Parakeets nest in the *Melaleuca* trees on the nursing home grounds, and other psittacids also occur regularly. Curtiss Parkway is a divided roadway with a wide, landscaped median between the lanes. Check the oaks, figs, and other trees in the median for psittacids, Spot-breasted Orioles, and wintering and migrant landbirds. Psittacids that have occurred here include Maroon-bellied, Black-hooded, Red-masked, Mitred, Canary-winged ("White-winged"), and Yellow-chevroned Parakeets and Red-crowned, Blue-fronted, Orange-winged, and Yellow-headed Parrots. Gray Kingbirds may be present in spring and summer.

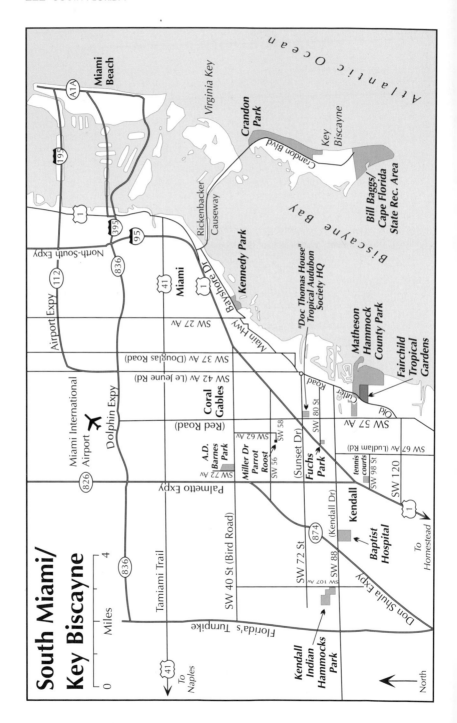

South Miami/
Key Biscayne

To visit another area nearby that usually is good for psittacids, go south on Navarre Drive one block to Morningside Drive, turn right, and follow it across Curtiss Parkway. Morningside Drive curves to the right and becomes Prospect Street. Turn left onto Westward Drive (0.4) to Apache Drive (0.8, the first traffic light) and turn right. Go three blocks and park just beyond a large *Poinciana* tree on the right. The house on the southeast corner of Apache Drive and Wren Avenue has several feeders visited by many parakeets. Monk Parakeets are the most common, but sometimes also present are Red-masked, Mitred, White-eyed, Dusky-headed, Yellow-chevroned, Maroon-bellied, Green-cheeked, Blue-crowned, Green, and Orange-fronted Parakeets. This area is also a good spot for Spot-breasted Orioles. Look for them in the Bottlebrush trees along the alley crossing Apache Drive. Since mid-1995 this area has lost some of its appeal, but it is still worth a stop.

A few pairs of Burrowing Owls inhabit grassy areas in the southern part of Miami International Airport. From Curtiss Parkway return to NW 36th Street and turn right. At NW 72nd Avenue (Milam Dairy Road) (1.5), turn left to NW 12th Street (1.6), which becomes Perimeter Road. Turn left again and continue to the parking area on the right (1.3). From here, walk the airport fence east to NE 57th Avenue (Red Road). Owls should be seen between the fence and the runway. To return to a major roadway from the parking lot, travel east on Perimeter Road to NW 57th Avenue (0.4) and turn right to reach SR-836. (Airport officials are considering building a new runway in the area that contains most of the owl burrows.)

KEY BISCAYNE

Going south from downtown Miami, US-1 crosses over the Miami River and becomes Brickell Avenue. Continue past US-41 (Tamiami Trail) at SW 7th and 8th streets. After passing under an overpass, turn left onto Rickenbacker Causeway ($1/vehicle) to reach Key Biscayne.

You come first to Virginia Key, which formerly offered excellent birding but is not as productive at present. On the left side of the key (opposite Seaquarium) is the entrance to Virginia Beach ($3/vehicle). Follow the road as it curves left, then right. Park near the sewage treatment facility (look for Black-necked Stilts here) on the left and walk past the gate for about ¼ mile. Brushy vegetation on the left may have sparrows in winter, migrants in spring and fall, and Smooth-billed Anis year round. Where the pavement ends, walk to the rocky beach and continue another ¼ mile or so. Turn onto a trail through Australian Pines before ending at the north point of the key. At low tide, the mudflats to the left can be good year round for wading-birds, including Great White Herons, Reddish Egrets, and Roseate Spoonbills, and shorebirds, including Wilson's and Piping (winter) Plovers. Greater Flamingoes that may be seen here are believed to be escapes from Hialeah Race Track. Another exotic currently present is one or more Great Black-Hawks (apparently of the South American race) reported in the area since 1972 and still present as of November 1995, presumably from birds that escaped from Crandon Park Zoo.

After crossing Bear Cut, you come to Key Biscayne, where the road name changes to Crandon Boulevard. Upon entering the key, pull into the marina on the right to scope the sandbars exposed at low tide. Return to Crandon Boulevard and turn left into **Crandon County Park** (960 acres; $3.50/vehicle). Park in the north parking area and walk the beach north. The park contains almost 3½ miles of ocean frontage; shorebirding here may produce Wilson's and Piping Plovers, Whimbrel, and other species. The wooded area on the left, north of the northernmost parking lot entrance, has a dirt road and a paved bicycle path through it that parallel the beach. This area is good for migrants, and a La Sagra's Flycatcher was found here in April 1995. Another good birding area is the gardens area at the south end of the park. The gardens now occupy the site of the former Crandon Park Zoo, which was responsible for the releases of many exotic birds (Black-bellied Whistling-Duck, Great Black-Hawk, and Red-crested Cardinal are three examples). Some of these birds may no longer occur, but Green Iguanas native to the Neotropics are still present. Migrant landbirds can be common here in spring and fall.

After leaving Crandon Park, continue south to the end of Key Biscayne to Bill Baggs/Cape Florida State Recreation Area (406 acres; standard fee) (2.6), formerly an excellent birding site during migration. Most of the area was covered by exotic Australian Pines, which attracted many landbirds, but all vegetation in the park was destroyed by Hurricane *Andrew* in 1992. Caribbean strays such as Key West Quail-Dove, Bahama Mockingbird, Thick-billed Vireo, and Stripe-headed Tanager have occurred here, and the park was excellent for viewing fall raptor migration that included less common species such as Cooper's Hawks, Merlins, and Peregrine Falcons. The park is being replanted with native vegetation, and it may soon again offer excellent birding opportunities. In October 1994 a Northern Wheatear was photographed here.

Contact: Bill Baggs/Cape Florida State Recreation Area, 1200 South Crandon Boulevard, Key Biscayne, FL 33149; 305/361-5811.

SOUTH MIAMI

From Rickenbacker Causeway, go south on US-1 (Brickell Avenue) to South Miami Avenue (0.2) and turn left. (This road soon becomes South Bayshore Drive.) Kennedy Park is on the left (1.4). A flock of 25 to 30 Canary-winged ("White-winged") and Yellow-chevroned Parakeets sometimes occurs here, and other psittacids may also be present.

Miami City Hall, at the end of Pan American Drive on the left (0.3 past Kennedy Park), may also have psittacids and Hill Mynas.

South Bayshore Drive ends a few blocks past Pan American Drive at McFarlane Avenue. Turn right, go one block, then turn left onto Main Highway, which ends at SW 37th Avenue (1.0). Turn left onto SW 37th Avenue, then turn right onto Ingraham Highway (0.2). Ingraham Highway ends at SW 42nd Avenue (LeJeune Road), where you turn left. Go halfway around the circle to Old Cutler Road, then continue south to **Matheson Hammock County Park** (100 acres) (1.8). Turn left at the light toward the beach and marina. The park sustained heavy damage from Hurricane *Andrew*, especially in the loss of dead trees used by cavity nesters like psittacids, Pileated Woodpeckers, and Hill Mynas. Park on the left upon entering the park and check the picnic area for White-crowned Pigeons, Canary-winged ("White-winged") and Yellow-chevroned Parakeets, and Hill Mynas. The picnic area is especially good for migrant and wintering landbirds and has had its share of rarities, including a Sulphur-bellied Flycatcher (Florida's first verified record) in October 1995. Mangrove Cuckoos may occur, especially during spring and fall, and Short-tailed Hawks are seen regularly in fall and early winter. Across Old Cutler Road from the south end of the picnic area, an undeveloped section of the park preserves a West Indian hardwood hammock. Besides the birds mentioned above, look for migrant and wintering landbirds and Black-whiskered Vireos, which have bred here in spring and summer.

Farther into the park (after the fee station, $3.50/vehicle), the road forks. The left fork leads to the marina and the right one to an impressive Red Mangrove forest, damaged severely by *Andrew*. Prairie Warblers breed here, and other warblers winter. At the end of the road, wading-birds and shorebirds (including a few Piping Plovers) frequent the beaches, especially at low tide. In 1994-1995, a Purple Sandpiper wintered around the swimming pond.

Contact: Matheson Hammock County Park, 9610 Old Cutler Road, Miami, FL 33156; 305/666-6979.

Roseate Spoonbill
Shawneen E. Finnegan

Fairchild Tropical Gardens (83 acres; $7/person) (0.4), next to the south end of Matheson Hammock County Park, contains a large collection of exotic plants. The dense vegetation attracts Short-tailed Hawks, White-crowned Pigeons, psittacids, Gray Kingbirds, Hill Mynas, Black-whiskered Vireos, Spot-breasted Orioles, and migrants. Although the park was damaged heavily by *Andrew*, a major replanting project has restored the gardens. Because of the fee, however, few birders stop here.

Continue south on Old Cutler Road to the T intersection with SW 57th Avenue (Red Road). To bird inland sites in South Miami, drive north to SW 40th Street and turn left.

A. D. "Doug" Barnes Park (no fee) is an area "discovered" recently by Miami birders after *Andrew* destroyed many popular birding sites. The park, which contains a hardwood hammock, pine rocklands, and fresh-water ponds, is best during migration and in winter. To reach it from SW 40th Street (Bird Road), drive north on SW 72nd Avenue to the entrance on the right (0.2). At the T intersection just past the entrance, turn left to a group of buildings on the left (0.2) and park on the right. Behind the buildings is a mixed pine and hardwood hammock reached by a nature trail. (The hammock is fenced, but a gate north of the first building is usually left unlocked.) Check this area, especially during migration; 20+ warbler species have been seen here in fall, including Swainson's and Worm-eating Warblers. Florida's southernmost Red-breasted Nuthatch was found in the park in October 1993. Eurasian Collared-Doves are resident, and a pair of Spot-breasted Orioles has nested here. To the right of the parking lot is a pineland picnic area. Return to the T and continue south to a hardwood picnic area with two cattail ponds that are good for Least Bitterns.

To reach a psittacid roost, exit SR-826 (Palmetto Expressway) at SW 56th Street (Miller Drive) and go east. At SW 62nd Avenue (1.5) turn right. After two blocks (0.1) turn right onto SW 58th Street. Just beyond the 5-way intersection, the road crosses a canal (0.3). Park here and watch for the birds as they come to roost about ½ hour before dark. White-crowned Pigeons also occur in this area in spring and summer. In late 1995, many of the Australian Pines used as roost sites by the psittacids were cut down or trimmed, and the birds now roost in large *Ficus* and *Poinciana* trees south of the canal. You may have to walk around the neighborhood a bit to find them. *Be aware that some birders have experienced crime problems in this neighborhood.*

Another psittacid roost, smaller than the one above, is located near **Fuchs Park** on the southeast corner of SW 80th Street and US-1. (*Note that the same birds use both roosts; the birds move from one to the other. Sometimes both roosts are in use simultaneously; at other times, all the birds are at one roost or the other.*) Check the area near the apartment buildings just northeast of the park, starting about ½ hour before dusk. The nightly cast varies, but Red-masked Parakeets and Orange-winged and White-fronted Parrots usually are most common; Blue-fronted and Lilac-crowned Parrots are less frequent, and many other species are possible.

The Doc Thomas House is the headquarters of the Tropical Audubon Society, an active local birding chapter. It is located on the south side of SW 72nd Street (Sunset Drive) just east of SW 57th Avenue (Red Road) in South Miami. The offices and a small shop are open 9 am to 4 pm daily, but birders should call ahead before visiting. On the grounds, Monk, Yellow-chevroned, and Canary-winged ("White-winged") (least common) Parakeets are observed almost daily, Red-whiskered Bulbuls are nearby, and Spot-breasted Orioles nest almost annually. Native species are also represented, with Gray Kingbirds breeding in the area. Many migrants have occurred here, including Black-whiskered Vireos and Golden-winged, Connecticut, and Swainson's Warblers.

Contact: Tropical Audubon Society, 5530 Sunset Drive, Miami, FL 33134; 305/666-5111, FAX: 305/667-9343.

KENDALL

This suburban district of Greater Miami is known among birders as the home of the Red-whiskered Bulbul, of which a few birds escaped in August 1960. The species appears marginally established in the Kendall area, although its range remains limited to a small section of the district. The birds are most common within the triangle created by US-1 on the north and west, SW 57th Avenue (Red Road) on the east, and SW 120th Street on the south, but birds occur south to SW 186th Street and west to SW 100th Avenue.

Bulbuls currently are fairly easy to find around the Royal Palm Tennis Courts at the northeast corner of SW 98th Street and SW 72nd Avenue just east of US-1. Check the wires along SW 98th Street, the side streets to the south, and the entrance to the courts. Watch the tree-tops and wires; bulbuls often sit in exposed places. Drive around the area, and you should see one eventually. Early morning is best.

A couple of blocks behind the tennis courts is the home of Art and Betty Furchgott (6901 SW 96th Street), who are very friendly to visiting birders. Red-whiskered Bulbul, Spot-breasted Oriole, and Yellow-chevroned and Canary-winged ("White-winged") (least common) Parakeets are in the area. In summer 1995 the Furchgotts' feeders became swamped by Rock Doves, and the other birds have been seen less dependably since then. The area in and around Kenwood Elementary School at 9300 SW 79th Avenue is another area good for bulbuls, Spot-breasted Orioles, and other landbirds in fall and winter.

A large Monk Parakeet colony is located on the grounds of Baptist Hospital on the south side of SW 88th Street (North Kendall Drive) just west of SW 87th Avenue. The birds are easiest to find in trees near the westernmost pond. Look in the *Melaleuca* trees for the nests. Other birds possible here include Canary-winged ("White-winged") Parakeets, Red-whiskered Bulbuls, and Hill Mynas. Check the ponds for wading-birds, Ring-necked Ducks (winter), and other waterbirds. A White-cheeked Pintail of unknown origin was photographed here in January 1996.

Kendall Indian Hammocks Park (no fee) is a long narrow park north of SW 88th Street (North Kendall Drive) between SW 107th and SW 114th avenues. To reach it from Kendall Drive, take SW 107th Avenue north to the entrance on the left at SW 84th Street (0.4). Park on the left next to the ball fields (0.6). A hardwood hammock on the right contains trails through the hammock that can be good for migrant and wintering landbirds. Connecticut Warblers were found here in May 1994.

New Tamiami Airport (just off the map) also contains a few Burrowing Owls. To reach it, take SW 128th Street west from SW 137th Avenue. Some active burrows are marked by plastic perches; one pair of owls nests at the Weeks Air Museum.

HOMESTEAD/FLORIDA CITY AREA

Castellow Hammock Park (60 acres; no fee) had an extensive hardwood hammock, but it was largely destroyed by Hurricane *Andrew*. To reach the park from US-1, drive west onto SW 216th Street (Hainlin Mill Drive). Turn left onto SW 162nd Avenue (Farm Life Road) to the entrance on the left (0.5). The park is still closed because of damage from the hurricane, but it is permissible to park at the gate and walk in. The park's main attractions now are the bird feeders along the edge of the woods that are still being stocked during the winter months. Painted Buntings frequent the feeders regularly; Indigo Buntings may also be present. White-winged Doves are common year round, and Swallow-tailed Kites and Black-whiskered Vireos may be found in spring and summer.

In 1987 P. William Smith discovered **Cave Swallows** of the West Indian race (or perhaps a full species) nesting under highway overpasses and bridges north of Homestead. The birds continue to nest in the area and are observed most easily from April through early September. To reach the largest colony, go east on SW 216th Street (Hainlin Mill Drive) to Florida's Turnpike. Go under the overpass and turn left immediately onto the northbound service road that parallels the turnpike. Park on the grass strip on the right side of the road next to the canal. *(If you leave your car, be advised that there have been some auto break-ins here.)* Cave Swallows usually can be observed easily from this point. They are most obvious during the breeding season, but birds arrive earlier in the year. (Cave Swallows only roost here when they begin returning in late January and are not likely to be seen then except at dawn and dusk.)

The Chekika section of Everglades National Park is located on SW 237th Avenue north of SW 168th Street (Richmond Drive) about 6 miles west of SR-997 (Krome Avenue). The area was damaged heavily by Hurricane *Andrew*, but the hammock is still good for migrant and wintering landbirds. White-tailed Kites have been reliably seen recently

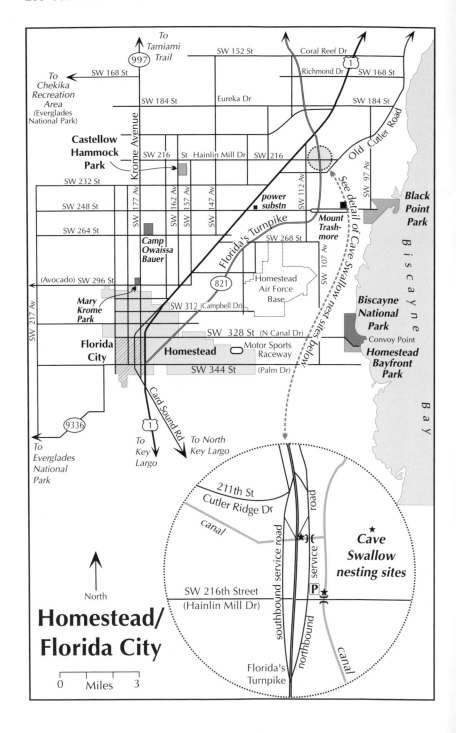

To
Tamiami
Trail
997

To
Chekika
Recreation
Area
(Everglades
National
Park)

SW 152 St
Coral Reef Dr
1
SW 168 St
Richmond Dr
SW 168 St
SW 184 St
Eureka Dr
SW 184 St

Krome Avenue

Old Cutler Road

Castellow
Hammock
Park

SW 216 St
Hainlin Mill Dr
SW 216

SW 232 St

SW 177 Av
SW 162 Av
SW 157 Av
SW 147 Av
SW 112 Av
SW 97 Av

power
substn

Black
Point
Park

SW 248 St

SW 264 St

Camp
Owaissa
Bauer

Florida's Turnpike

Mount
Trash-
more

SW 268 St

SW 107 Av

See detail of Cave Swallow nest sites below

Biscayne

(Avocado) SW 296 St

821

Homestead
Air Force
Base

Biscayne
National
Park

SW 217 Av

Mary
Krome
Park

SW 312 (Campbell Dr)

SW 328 St (N Canal Dr)

Convoy Point

Homestead
Bayfront
Park

Florida
City

Homestead

Motor Sports
Raceway

SW 344 St (Palm Dr)

Bay

9336

Card Sound Rd

1

To
Key
Largo

To North
Key Largo

To
Everglades
National
Park

211th St
Cutler Ridge Dr

canal

Cave
Swallow
nesting sites

southbound service road

motor service road

North

SW 216th Street
(Hainlin Mill Dr)

P

Homestead/
Florida City

Florida's
Turnpike

northbound
service

canal

0   Miles   3

about three miles south of the park entrance, along SW 237th Avenue. In winter 1994-1995, 4 adults were seen here.

Continue south on US-1 to SW 248th Street (Coconut Palm Drive) and turn left. A power substation on the left (0.5) contains Monk Parakeet nests. Check at the turnpike overpass (2.3) in spring and summer for Cave Swallows, which have nested here in previous years. "Mount Trashmore", the huge local landfill on the left (1.8), can be good for gulls and sometimes has Bald Eagles and shorebirds. The road ends at Black Point Park (no fee) (0.5). Turn left before the parking lot, cross the bridge, turn right at the stop sign at the extension of SW 97th Avenue, and go to the small parking area. Walk along the channel that leads to the bay. At the end is a rock jetty that can be good for wading-birds, shorebirds, and larids. Purple Sandpiper and Lesser Black-backed Gull have been seen here.

Contact: Biscayne National Park, P.O. Box 1369, Homestead, FL 33090-1369; 305/230-7275.

Return to Krome Avenue and turn right to SW 264th Street (Bauer Drive). Turn right to Camp Owaissa Bauer (109 acres; no fee) (10.3), which contains a large hammock damaged by *Andrew*. The hammock and pinelands can be good for migrant and wintering landbirds, including Whip-poor-wills. In spring and summer look for Swallow-tailed Kites and Black-whiskered Vireos. In winter check the feeders near the office for Painted Buntings and possibly Indigo Buntings. For more information, call 305/247-6016.

Return to SR-997 (Krome Avenue, SW 177th Avenue) and turn left. Drive south to SW 296th Street (Avocado Drive) (2.0). Park on Krome Avenue south of this intersection and walk back to small, unmarked Mary Krome Bird Sanctuary (3 acres; no fee) at the northwest corner of Krome Avenue and Avocado Drive. *Avoid the avocado and mango groves to the west and north; they are private property.* This park is most famous for the Bahama Woodstar that was present here from July to August 1981. Ruby-throated Hummingbirds are regular from fall through spring, and Rufous Hummingbirds have also occurred regularly (3 were here in October 1995). The park may also contain other wintering and migrant landbirds.

About 4 miles south of Black Point Park, at the east end of SW 328th Drive (North Canal Drive), are Homestead Bayfront County Park and the Convoy Point visitor center for Biscayne National Park. (The visitor center is north of the road, and the county park is to the south.) Because most of Biscayne National Park (181,500 acres; no fee) is offshore, a boat is needed to visit most of it. Hurricane *Andrew* passed directly over the park and caused extensive damage to the park facilities, mangrove forests, and hammocks, but most facilities have been rebuilt. A private concessioner operates boat tours from Convoy Point (305/230-7275). A smaller visitor center is located on Elliott Key, about 8-9 miles offshore, which was also damaged heavily by the hurricane. The key contains West Indian hardwood hammocks that can be good for landbirds; the first North American record of La Sagra's Flycatcher was found here in December 1982. The park also contains a coral reef that may be explored by a glass-bottom-boat tour or by snorkeling. (This park is far less crowded than John Pennekamp Coral Reef State Park on Key Largo.) The jetty at Convoy Point can be good for wading-birds, shorebirds, and larids.

Return to SR-997 (Krome Avenue) and go south through downtown Homestead to SR-9336 (Palm Drive; SW 344th Street) (3.0) and turn right. With several turns along the way (follow the signs), this road leads to Everglades National Park, but there are a few birding sites before heading to the park that may be worth a stop in winter and early spring.

At the C-111E Canal (5.2 miles from SR-997), wooded areas north of the road can produce a variety of sparrows and buntings, and the canal itself could have a few wading-birds and possibly Mottled Ducks or Limpkins. Continue past the canal to SW 209th Avenue (0.4; usually unmarked) and turn right. Make a loop by continuing north to a T intersection (0.2), turning left at another T (0.2), then returning to SR-9336 (0.2) on SW 212th Avenue. Watch powerlines, fencelines, sprinkler heads, or dead limbs in this area from November to April for wintering Western Kingbirds and Scissor-tailed Flycatchers. A Cassin's Kingbird was found here in 1992 and 1995-1996. Check the blackbird flocks here and in the surrounding neighborhood for rarities like Yellow-headed Blackbird, Shiny Cowbird, or Bronzed Cowbird. Other birds that may be present are raptors (including Swainson's Hawks) in winter, Upland Sandpipers and Bobolinks in fall, Smooth-billed Anis (year round), Painted Buntings (fall through spring), and various sparrows (including Clay-colored, Lark, Grasshopper, and White-crowned) in winter. Exploring the roads in this whole area could produce many good birds in the winter months. *But be sure to remain on the roadway: in this area trespassing on farmlands is not tolerated!*

To visit Everglades National Park, return to SR-9336 (Palm Drive) and go west to the park entrance. If not visiting the park, return to SW 344th Street, cross US-1, and continue east. The road ends in about 8 miles at the Turkey Point nuclear power plant. In fall and winter this area can be good for raptors, and Smooth-billed Anis may be present year round.

On US-1 just south of SW 344th Street, look for Common Mynas in the parking lots of the various fast-food restaurants, especially the Burger King.

As you drive along SR-9336 toward Everglades National Park, you pass through some of the most valuable farmland in the U.S., supplying the country with the bulk of its winter vegetables, such as tomatoes. You will notice two unique characteristics about this region: the "soil" is composed of small pieces of rock, and the native vegetation has been almost totally obliterated. (You will know that you are approaching Everglades National Park by the line of Slash Pines visible from a great distance.)

Most of southern Dade County is low-lying and was frequently inundated prior to drainage. Upland vegetation grows on "outcroppings" of limestone deposited about 1 million years ago. The limestone is at ground level or just a few inches below it. The "rock plow," a combination bulldozer and plow, was invented to break up the soft limestone into small pieces to allow farming.

The pinelands on these limestone outcroppings comprise a unique ecosystem called Miami Rockland. Although the pines are the same variety of Slash Pines that are found elsewhere in southern Florida, the understory contains many shrubs of West Indian affinity, and the herbaceous layer contains several endemic species. Originally, 180,000 acres of Miami Rockland could be found in Dade County. Today, fewer than 4,000 acres remain outside Everglades National Park, a 98% reduction in this century. Many pinelands that remain in private hands are small parcels that are heavily overgrown with exotic plants, especially Brazilian Pepper and Australian Pines. Furthermore, as is clearly evident along SR-9336, most mature Slash Pines were killed by a combination of Hurricane *Andrew*'s intense winds and a subsequent infestation of wood-boring beetle larvae. A $90 million land-acquisition program enacted recently in Dade County will purchase and restore the most significant tracts of Miami Rockland remaining. Exotic plants will be eradicated from the pinelands, and a regular fire regime will be implemented to restore and maintain the habitat.

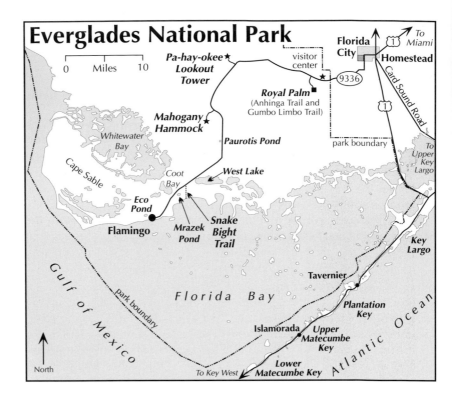

Everglades National Park

0 Miles 10

Pa-hay-okee ★
Lookout
Tower

Mahogany ★
Hammock

Whitewater
Bay

Cape Sable

Coot
Bay

Eco
Pond

Flamingo

Mrazek
Pond

Snake
Bight
Trail

Paurotis Pond

West Lake

Royal Palm ■
(Anhinga Trail and
Gumbo Limbo Trail)

visitor
center

Florida
City

To Miami

Homestead

9336

park boundary

To
Upper
Key
Largo

Card Sound Road

Key
Largo

Tavernier

Florida Bay

Plantation
Key

Islamorada
Upper
Matecumbe
Key

Lower
Matecumbe Key

To Key West

Gulf of Mexico

park boundary

Atlantic Ocean

North

EVERGLADES NATIONAL PARK

With so much written about the Everglades, everyone has pre-con-
ceived ideas about what is to be found there. First-time visitors are
amazed to discover that Everglades National Park is not what they thought
it would be. Having heard about subtropical Florida, some come looking
for "jungles," but find that the cypresses are stunted and grow on islands
surrounded by marshes. Other people expect a great "river of grass", but
find that during dry years there is almost no fresh water in the park.
Almost no one is prepared for the flat terrain that stretches for miles.

Dedicated in 1947 by President Harry S Truman, Everglades National
Park was the first national park to be established at the mouth of a river
rather than at its source. Since then, it has been designated an International Biosphere Reserve, a World Heritage Site, and a Wetland of
International Significance. Today, it is visited annually by over 1 million
people, of whom about a third are from other countries. Although only
a few Florida bird specialties are found here, Everglades National Park is
one of Florida's most-visited birding spots. Without doubt, the park and

the entire Everglades ecosystem are associated throughout the world with Florida and its wading-birds.

The Seminoles called this area *Pa-hay-okee,* meaning "grassy waters." In her monumental book, Marjory Stoneman Douglas also refers to the Everglades as a great "River of Grass." Unlike any other river, the Everglades are a vast, shallow expanse of water moving slowly south through sawgrass and cypress prairies. Sawgrass, the dominant plant of the Everglades, is not a grass but a sedge, so, technically, the Everglades are a "River of Sedge." Because of the extreme flatness of the region, the "river" is 50 miles wide and only inches deep. The water drops only about 15 feet over its 100-mile flow from the southern shore of Lake Okeechobee to Florida Bay.

Less than 20% of the original Everglades is contained within the boundaries of Everglades National Park. (Another 30% is protected in other parks and water conservation areas, and about 50% has been destroyed.) In 1989 over 107,000 acres of the "East Everglades" region were authorized to be added to the park, and additional lands are sought for future acquisition. At 1,506,309 acres, Everglades is the largest national park east of the Mississippi River; it contains almost 150 miles of coastal shoreline.

Except for the Everglades City and Shark Valley regions listed earlier in this guide, the only land access to the park is from SR-9336 in Florida City. From the park entrance station, it is 38 miles to the end of the main park road at Flamingo. (Make sure that your vehicle has sufficient fuel.) For the entire drive, the elevation of the road never exceeds 6 feet above sea level. In fact, the area is so flat and shallow that Harold Wanless et al. state that much of Everglades National Park will become a shallow salt- or brackish-water estuary within the next 50 years if the current rate of sea level rise continues.

Florida specialties to search for in the park include Greater Flamingoes (mostly at high tide at Snake Bight), Short-tailed Hawks (fairly common over uplands anywhere in winter), Smooth-billed Anis (irregular, but possible at Eco Pond), Painted Buntings (fairly common but often hard to see in brushy areas throughout), and Cape Sable Seaside Sparrows (uncommon and secretive; most reliable near the road to Mahogany Hammock). A few Lesser Nighthawks have been found in the park in recent winters, and Whip-poor-wills (regular in winter) and Barn Owls (unpredictable year round) may be seen along the main road at night. Other wading-birds, including Wood Storks and Roseate Spoonbills, are widespread year round.

Because Everglades National Park consists of sawgrass and cypress prairies, West Indian hardwood hammocks, and mangrove forests, it should be expected to have mosquitoes, especially in summer. What most visitors are unprepared for is the sheer number of mosquitoes (and their ferocity), especially at places like Snake Bight Trail and Eco Pond. At times, venturing outside your vehicle is impossible without strong insect repellent, and even this defense only lessens the misery. *Be forewarned: parts of Everglades National Park may be unbearable in summer because of mosquitoes.* At other seasons mosquitoes are less often a problem, depending on recent rains.

Although lodging is found easily outside the park, there is only one motel (with 102 rooms and 24 cottages) inside the park, at Flamingo. The rates are most expensive from 15 December to 30 April and are cheapest 1 May to 31 October, when food service is minimal. For information, call the Flamingo Lodge at 941/695-3101. Additionally, Everglades National Park has three campgrounds, at Chekika, Long Pine Key, and Flamingo.

To reach the park from the Homestead/Florida City area, go west on SR-9336 (Palm Drive) from SR-997 (Krome Avenue), US-1, or SR-821 (Florida's Turnpike). (The Turnpike ends just north of SR-9336, so turn right *immediately* after merging with US-1.) Along SR-9336, you will probably see on the wires Eurasian Collared-Doves and possibly White-winged Doves.

Once inside the park ($5/vehicle), drive to the visitor center (open 8 am to 5 pm daily) on the right beyond the toll booth (0.6). The center contains a large selection of natural history books, a 15-minute movie about the Everglades, and a logbook for recording interesting sightings. *The use of tape recordings is prohibited in the park.*

Drive to the bridge over Taylor Slough (1.0). This site is good for wading birds; watch especially for American Bitterns in winter. Cape Sable Seaside Sparrows may also be found here, but they are more reliable near Mahogany Hammock.

Continue to the road to Royal Palm Hammock (0.5) and turn left onto it. Royal Palm Hammock was a state park before the national park was established. The most popular birding site here is **Anhinga Trail**, a ½-mile boardwalk over Taylor Slough. Formerly an excellent birding spot, it is now less productive but still worth a stop. The wooden boardwalk was destroyed by Hurricane *Andrew* and has been rebuilt, partially with recycled plastic. Because birds and other wildlife are accustomed to people on the boardwalk, the animals have become quite tame. As a result, Anhinga Trail offers excellent photographic and nature-study opportunities when water levels are attractive. Some birds that may observed are wading-birds like American (winter) and Least Bitterns, both night-herons (Yellow-crowned is the more common), and Purple Gallinules. American Alligators are common year round. It will not take long for you to realize why this is called Anhinga Trail; those birds are numerous here, and in spring, they nest within a few feet of the boardwalk. A few Great White Herons (mostly immatures) should also be present along the trail. Swallow-tailed Kites may be seen overhead.

Gumbo Limbo Trail enters the hammock from the south end of the Royal Palm visitor center, just to the right of the Florida Panther monument. It is ½-mile long and is named for the tree characterized by reddish, peeling bark. Like most other trees in the hammock, the Gumbo Limbo is of West Indian origin, restricted in the U.S. to South Florida. The trail can be good for tree snails and migrant and wintering landbirds. Wintering *Myiarchus* flycatchers should be examined closely, because Brown-crested Flycatchers occur here occasionally, in addition to Great Crested Flycatchers, which are regular. Many warblers may be found along the trail in winter, including Black-throated Green, Worm-eating, and Magnolia Warblers. Also in winter, Short-tailed Hawks are often seen over the hammock; mid-morning (9:00 to 9:30 am) is best. Where the trail crosses the Old Ingraham Highway, you can walk about a mile from the visitor center area through excellent hammock habitat.

Return to the main park road and turn left. At the road to Long Key (2.2), turn left. Long Key is not a key is the true sense of the word, but an island of Miami Rockland pinewoods surrounded by sawgrass prairies. Pinelands Nature Trail (2.1 miles from the campground) on the right side of the main road can be good for migrants and wintering landbirds such as Barn Owls and Whip-poor-wills. Pine Warblers breed here, but four other characteristic species of Florida's pinewoods no longer occur. Red-cockaded Woodpecker, Brown-headed Nuthatch, and Eastern Bluebird have been extirpated from Everglades National Park since about the 1960s. Although the pine forests have recovered from the extensive logging that occurred before the park was established, the birds died out anyway. Recently, Hairy Woodpecker became the fourth species to become extirpated from the park; the last one was sighted in 1991.

Pa-hay-okee Overlook on the right (6.3) is not particularly good for birds, but a 1,000-foot-long boardwalk and overlook offers visitors views of the extensive sawgrass prairie community that dominated the original Everglades ecosystem. Sometimes a pair of Sandhill Cranes is present here. The Pa-hay-okee area is the start of the dwarf cypress forest. Many Pond-Cypresses in this region are stunted due to a shallow water level.

Although the trees are only 10 to 20 feet tall, they may be well over a century old.

Mahogany Hammock (7.1), located to the right off the main road, is good for Barred Owls, Pileated Woodpeckers, and tree snails. In winter, the hammock is a good spot for White-crowned Pigeons and can be excellent for wintering warblers. There are usually a few Magnolia and Black-throated Green Warblers here, and Hooded Warblers have been found on rare occasions. The road to the hammock can have Western Kingbirds in winter.

The best area in the park to search for Cape Sable Seaside Sparrows is a zone centered on the road to Mahogany Hammock. From about 1½ miles before this road to about 1½ miles beyond it, look for the sparrows in the marshes on both sides of the main park road. The best single site is located about 1.1 miles past the turn to Mahogany Hammock. The best time to find the birds is before 10 am from March to July, when singing males are conspicuous. Otherwise, these birds are difficult to locate.

Paurotis Pond on the right (4.4 miles from the road to Mahogany Hammock) is the first of five roadside ponds. Wood Storks have nested here in late winter the past few years. Nine Mile Pond on the left (2.0) is worth a stop for wading-birds, Mottled Ducks (and other ducks in winter), Swallow-tailed Kites (spring and summer), Limpkins, and White-crowned Pigeons.

West Lake on the left (4.4) was formerly great for wintering ducks and coots, but it has been barren in recent years. The boardwalk along the Mangrove Trail can still be good. White-crowned Pigeons should be seen here at dusk, Mangrove Cuckoos may be present in spring, and migrant and wintering landbirds can be common.

The 1.8-mile **Snake Bight Trail** on the left (1.6) is the best of several trails in this area. The trail goes through a mangrove forest and ends at a boardwalk providing a panoramic view of Snake Bight (a bight is a bay formed by a curved coastline). Mangrove Cuckoos occur here in spring and summer and occasionally in winter. The boardwalk is very productive for shorebirds (best at low tide, when extensive mudflats are exposed), and this is the most reliable site in the U.S. for Greater Flamingoes (best at high tide). In January 1979 a Key West Quail-Dove was found along the trail, and a Stripe-headed Tanager spent two weeks here in December 1990. *Be aware that mosquitoes here can be horrendous.* You may find it preferable to ride a bicycle (rentals available at Flamingo) rather than to walk the trail. Additionally, the Park Service operates a

Greater Flamingo
Georges Dremeaux

tram service along the trail from December to April; again, contact the visitor center for information.

Mrazek Pond on the left (1.6) can be disappointing from late spring through early winter, but from January to April when the water level may be low, concentrating the fish, the pond attracts hundreds of wading-birds, including Wood Storks and Roseate Spoonbills. Opportunities for nature study and photography then are excellent.

The 2½-mile Rowdy Bend Trail (1.1) and 2-mile Christian Point Trail (1.9) cross coastal prairies and mangrove forests, but you will probably find more birds along the 2-mile Bear Lake Trail, starting from the end of Bear Lake Road (0.4). *This trail has been closed since Hurricane* Andrew *and is currently inaccessible,* but check at the park office; it should reopen in the future. The trail goes through a tropical hardwood hammock that may have Mangrove Cuckoos, White-crowned Pigeons, and other land-birds. Swallow-tailed Kites breed here. In winter look for Scissor-tailed Flycatchers along the first few hundred feet of the trail.

Flamingo (0.4) is a small commercial area at the end of the park road, containing a visitor center, marina, motel, restaurant, and campground. A Bald Eagle nest (active in winter) in mangroves in the bay is visible from the restaurant. At low tide, the mudflats south of the visitor center may contain American White Pelicans, wading-birds (including Great White Herons and Reddish Egrets), shorebirds, gulls, and terns. Check the tern flocks for Gull-billed Terns, which winter here in small numbers. In April and May 1987 Florida's second Black-tailed Godwit was found here. Check the blackbird flocks for Shiny Cowbirds, and the Sea Grapes and other scrubby trees for migrant and wintering landbirds, including Ruby-throated Hummingbirds, Cape May Warblers, and Baltimore and Bul-lock's Orioles. Yellow-throated Warblers are found in the palms from fall through spring. In the canal behind the marina, you may be lucky enough to see an Endangered American Crocodile. (Be aware that American Alligators may also be present.)

On the right toward the campground is **Eco Pond**, a small pond once used to recycle treated wastewater. There is a short boardwalk and observation platform overlooking the pond, and trails around it. Rarities seen around the pond have included Fulvous Whistling-Duck, White-cheeked Pintail, Black Rail, Groove-billed Ani, Lesser Nighthawk, and Lazuli Bunting (several on 14 November 1995). White Ibises abound here, and other wading-birds roost on the pond's island, including Roseate Spoonbills. In winter watch for Short-tailed Hawks overhead and keep an eye out for Smooth-billed Anis, which still occur here from time to time. Least Bitterns are often seen year round. Migrant and wintering landbirds (including Painted Buntings) are found in brushy areas around the pond.

Enter the campground (watch for Scissor-tailed Flycatchers in winter). Coastal Prairie Trail begins off Campground Loop B and cuts through coastal marshes for 7 miles. It can be a rough walk because of the vegetation and the mosquitoes, but Sedge Wrens and numerous "Sharp-tailed" and Swamp Sparrows winter in the marsh. (To search for the birds, it is often best to leave the trail and hike through the marsh.)

Several boat trips start at the marina, but most are not particularly good for birding. Since these trips vary widely from season to season, it is wise to check with a park naturalist about which one to take. Greater Flamingoes have been seen in winter on Sandy Key, about 7 miles southwest of Flamingo. When they are present in the park but are not found at Snake Bight, it may be possible to charter a boat from the marina to search for them.

Contact: Everglades National Park, 40001 SR-9336, Homestead, FL 33034; 305/242-7700.

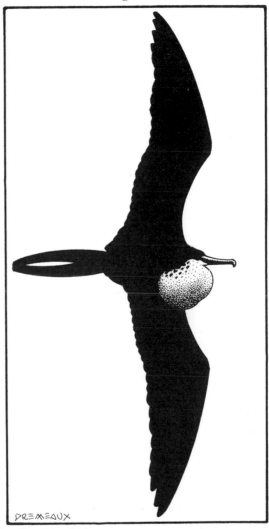

Magnificent Frigatebird
Georges Dremeaux

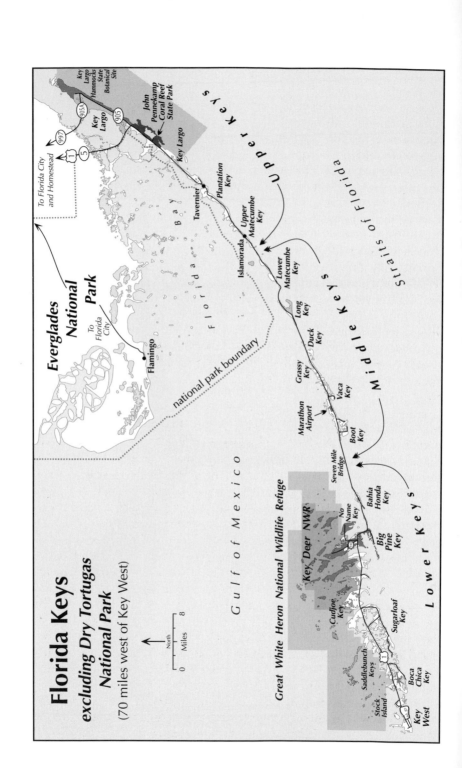

Florida Keys
excluding Dry Tortugas National Park
(70 miles west of Key West)

North
0   Miles   8

Everglades National Park

Gulf of Mexico

Florida Bay

national park boundary

To Florida City

Flamingo

To Florida City and Homestead

997
1
5
905A
905

Key Largo

Key Largo Hammocks State Botanical Site

John Pennekamp Coral Reef State Park

Key Largo

Plantation Key

Tavernier

Upper Matecumbe Key

Islamorada

Lower Matecumbe Key

Long Key

Duck Key

Grassy Key

Vaca Key

Marathon Airport

Boot Key

Seven Mile Bridge

Bahia Honda Key

No Name Key

Big Pine Key

Key Deer NWR

Great White Heron National Wildlife Refuge

Cudjoe Key

Sugarloaf Key

Saddlebunch Keys

Stock Island

Boca Chica Key

Key West

Upper Keys

Middle Keys

Lower Keys

Straits of Florida

FLORIDA KEYS

The Florida Keys are one of the few places in the U.S. with native birds not easily found elsewhere. Breeding specialties of the keys include Masked Booby, Magnificent Frigatebird, Great White Heron, Reddish Egret, Roseate Tern, Bridled Tern, Sooty Tern, Brown Noddy, White-crowned Pigeon, Mangrove Cuckoo, Antillean Nighthawk, Gray Kingbird, Black-whiskered Vireo, and Cuban Yellow Warbler. Nearly all are relatively easy to find from April through July, provided that the Dry Tortugas are included in the trip. The cuckoo is the only species that is usually difficult to locate. Other birds more-or-less restricted to the Keys are White-tailed Tropicbird (usually 1 to 2 annually), Brown Booby, Red-footed Booby (usually 1 or 2 annually), Black Noddy (1 to 3 annually), Short-eared Owl (West Indian race), and Shiny Cowbird (may be breeding regularly; generally rare elsewhere in the state). A spring or summer pelagic trip into the Gulf Stream should produce Audubon's Shearwater, Brown Booby, Bridled Tern, and possibly Band-rumped Storm-Petrel.

To date, 19 West Indian species have strayed to the Keys: Least Grebe, Masked Duck, Scaly-naped Pigeon, Zenaida Dove, *Leptotila* dove, Key West Quail-Dove, Ruddy Quail-Dove, Antillean Palm Swift, La Sagra's Flycatcher, Loggerhead Kingbird, Cuban Martin, Bahama Swallow, Bahama Mockingbird, Thick-billed Vireo, Bananaquit, Stripe-headed Tanager, Yellow-faced Grassquit, Black-faced Grassquit, and Tawny-shouldered Blackbird. Most of these species are casual or accidental in Florida, but the mockingbird, flycatcher, and vireo now occur annually. Other birds are represented by West Indian races that differ from North American birds: Mourning Dove, Short-eared Owl, Cave Swallow, and Yellow Warbler. Some of these races may be split into full species in the future. Other rarities found in the Keys include the only North American record of European Turtle-Dove (9-11 April 1990), the third North American record of Variegated Flycatcher (15 March 1991), the only North American record of Southern Martin (14 August 1890), and Florida's only Golden-crowned Sparrow record (21 June 1990). Exotics like Eurasian Collared-Dove, Monk Parakeet, and Blue-crowned Parakeet are common in some areas.

In winter, small buteos often perch on powerlines throughout the Keys. Most will be Broad-winged Hawks, with lesser numbers of Red-shouldered Hawks. Broad-wings tend to perch on the wires and Red-

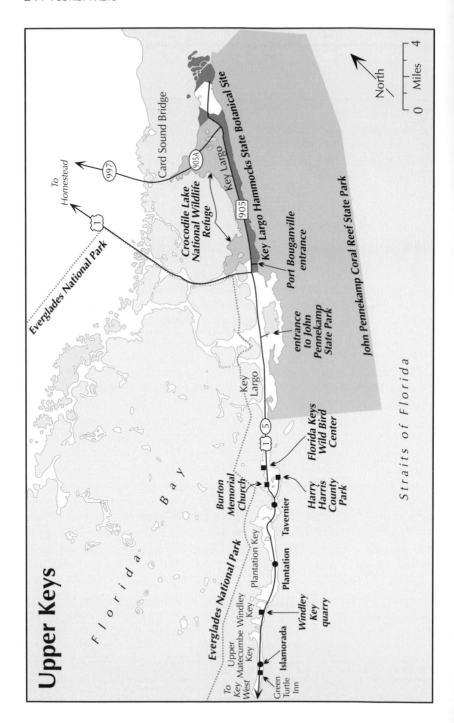

Upper Keys

shoulders more often on the poles. (Most are immatures, so identification can be tricky.) A few Short-tailed Hawks also winter in the Keys but are seldom seen perched; they spend the days soaring above the hammocks.

The middle and lower Florida Keys probably are the best under-publicized areas in North America for fall raptor migration. The season lasts from late September to early December, with peak movements the first three weeks in October. Several sites are described below, but any spot with an unobstructed view of the sky can be rewarding. Fifteen species of raptors are resident or regular migrants into or through the Keys (although Swallow-tailed Kites leave before the others arrive), and 3 or 4 additional species occur occasionally. All day count totals of 10 to 14 species and 1,000+ individuals are regular in early October. The best sites in the Keys record higher peak daily totals of Peregrine Falcons than Cape May, New Jersey, or Assateague Island in Maryland and Virginia. More Swainson's Hawks are reported here than from any other location east of the Mississippi River.

Access through the Keys is along US-1, which follows Henry Flagler's old Overseas Railroad. (A few sections of the original railway bridges with the first highway later built on top still exist.) The roadway, rebuilt in the 1980s, is 128 miles long with 43 bridges. The longest bridge is Seven Mile Bridge (now only 6.7 miles long) between Knight Key and Little Duck Key. While the Keys are largely developed, the two predominant upland habitats on the island chain—West Indian hardwood hammocks and mangrove forests—are evident. Both have been destroyed extensively for gas stations, fast-food restaurants, strip malls, motels, and subdivisions. Fortunately, the state has prioritized the purchases of all significant tropical hammocks remaining in the Keys, including the magnificent forests on North Key Largo. (Mangrove forests are now protected from development by laws protecting wetlands.)

Beyond Key West is Dry Tortugas National Park, located about 70 miles to the west. Breeding Masked Boobies, Brown Noddies, and Sooty Terns, along with a "migrant trap" and the potential for West Indian vagrants, all combine to make Dry Tortugas National Park the most exciting birding spot in Florida, and certainly one of the top sites in North America.

As you start your trip toward Key West, you will probably want to call the rare bird alert for the Lower Keys: 305/294-3438.

UPPER KEYS

To start your trip down the Keys from the end of SR-821 (Florida's Turnpike) in Florida City, go south on US-1 and bear left onto Card Sound Road (1.0). The first part of the road is bordered by a line of unproductive Australian Pines damaged heavily by Hurricane Andrew. It is also narrow, with few pull-offs, so it is best to continue to the toll booth just before the Card Sound Bridge ($1/vehicle) (11.5).

Pull off between the toll booth and the bridge to check the shallow mangrove-dotted waters for Reddish Egrets, Wilson's Plovers, Sandwich Terns, and many other wading-birds and shorebirds. At low tide, a mud bar on the left side of the road is favored. At high tide the birds perch on the bases of the large power poles. Cuban Yellow Warblers have been found in the mangrove clumps just off the road here, particularly near the restaurant just before the toll booth.

After you cross the Card Sound Bridge, you are on **North Key Largo**. In the early 1980s the state ranked purchases of all undeveloped property on Key Largo as essential to preserving the tropical hardwood hammock ecosystem in the Keys. Since 1982 the state has purchased 2,907 acres on Key Largo (at a cost of $66.3 million) and intends to purchase the remaining 303 acres that are still privately owned. Two large areas purchased have become Crocodile Lake National Wildlife Refuge (6,800 acres; *no access*) and Key Largo Hammocks State Botanical Site (2,100 acres; no fee). Because tropical hardwood hammock habitat is so rare in the United States, *public access to most of the area is forbidden*. Furthermore, the area contains many rare or endemic species, such as tree snails, Schaus's Swallowtail, American Crocodile, Key Largo Woodrat, and Key Largo Cotton Mouse. Because of drug-smuggling and poaching activities, these areas are patrolled regularly by law-enforcement personnel. *Under no circumstances should birders trespass into areas on North Key Largo that are off-limits!* Trespassing here violates all birding ethics. Besides, you might get arrested.

On Key Largo, Prairie Warblers are common year round and Black-whiskered Vireos are common in spring and summer in the mangroves. Card Sound Road runs through mangrove forests and a series of shallow lagoons now a part of Crocodile Lake National Wildlife Refuge. This area is used extensively by wading-birds and shorebirds, but fences constructed recently to prevent crocodiles from getting killed on the road now make birding difficult.

At the end of Card Sound Road, turn right onto CR-905 and head southwest through the largest West Indian hardwood hammock remain-

Black-whiskered Vireo
with Red Mangrove
Diane Pierce

ing in North America. Most of the plants here will be new to you. This area has the highest tree diversity in the United States, and about 80% of the plants are of West Indian origin. *Bird this area only from the road.* From mid-April to mid-August stop anywhere alongside the hammock, and you can squeak out Black-whiskered Vireos and Prairie Warblers. White-crowned Pigeons are found year round but are most common in spring and summer. Watch the tree-tops between here and Key West and you are bound to see them.

Along CR-905 between Card Sound Road and US-1, Crocodile Lake National Wildlife Refuge is on the right, and **Key Largo Hammocks State Botanical Site** and a few private inholdings are on the left. A nature trail through the botanical site (open 8 am to 5 pm daily) is located at the site of the failed Port Bougainville development on the left (8.6 from Card Sound Road or 0.4 from US-1). *Bird only from the paved roads and the marked nature trail.* La Sagra's Flycatchers and Thick-billed Vireos have occurred here. Black-whiskered Vireos and Prairie Warblers are common breeders, and Mangrove Cuckoos are possible. For access to other areas in the botanical site, contact John Pennekamp Coral Reef State Park (305/451-1202) to request a back-country permit.

Continue along CR-905. After passing US-1 on the right, look for Mile Marker 106 (0.4). All directions along US-1 in the Keys are in relation to these small green mile markers (abbreviated "MM"), a convenient system. The markers begin at the County Courthouse in Key West and end in Florida City, for a total of 124 miles. *Note that as you head toward Key West, the MM mileage decreases. Note also that for mileages listed in tenths of a mile, you must subtract the correct amount from the previous marker (e.g., MM 82.3 is 0.7 mile beyond MM 83).*

The entrance to **John Pennekamp Coral Reef State Park** (2,350 upland and 53,661 submerged acres; standard fee) is on the left (MM 102.4). The park, which is 8 by 21 miles in size, preserves the only living coral reef in the continental United States and receives over 2 million visitors annually. Excellent displays, including a 30,000-gallon salt water aquarium, introduce the coral reef environment to visitors. Glass-bottom-boat tours offer views of the reef; snorkeling equipment is also available. The reef contains over 650 species of fishes (!), 40 species of coral, and many other reef inhabitants. Two short nature trails are available for birding, one through a mangrove forest and the other through a tropical hardwood hammock. Breeding birds include White-crowned Pigeons, Gray Kingbirds, Black-whiskered Vireos, and Cuban Yellow Warblers. The hammock can be good for landbirds during migration.

Contact: John Pennekamp Coral Reef State Park, P.O. Box 487, Key Largo, FL 33037; 305/451-1202.

From US-1 to Marathon, the Keys are narrow and heavily developed. The few remaining patches of hammocks and the residential areas can be good for landbirds and White-crowned Pigeons, but the aesthetics and ethics of birding here are like those in any town. The keys beyond Marathon are less developed and more pleasing to bird.

The **Florida Keys Wild Bird Center** on the right (MM 93.8; no fee, donations accepted) is a rehabilitation facility. Besides the caged amputees and recovering "patients," numerous free-flying wading-birds are fed daily, including "Great White" and "Wurdemann's" Herons and Reddish Egrets. A short nature trail through a hammock can be good for migrant landbirds. The boardwalk past the cages leads to a small salt water pond where wading-birds (including Roseate Spoonbills) can be seen in season and Black-necked Stilts have bred.

Behind Burton Memorial Methodist Church on the left (MM 93.0) is a mangrove lagoon, great in early morning and late afternoon for wading-birds and shorebirds, and in winter for Roseate Spoonbills and ducks.

Harry Harris County Park (no fee) usually is worth a stop. Turn left onto Burton Drive (MM 92.8) and follow the signs to the entrance. Birding along the shore at low tide is good for wading-birds, shorebirds, and larids. A La Sagra's Flycatcher was found here in December 1992. For the past few years, a pair of Swallow-tailed Kites has nested in the Australian Pines on the right side of US-1 at MM 89.2.

The National Audubon Society maintains a small research department in Tavernier. At Indian Mound Trail (MM 89.0) turn right (just past Florida Keys Native Nursery). The office, in the second house on the left, is open Monday through Friday 8:30 am to 4:30 pm. Stop by for their excellent booklet *Birdfinding in the Florida Keys* ($1; $2 by mail).

Contact: National Audubon Society, 115 Indian Mound Trail, Tavernier, FL 33070; 305/852-1542.

At Windley Key on the right is the small parking area to Windley Key Quarry (no fee), a recent state acquisition (MM 85.2). The site includes three quarries where fossil coral was mined for fill and building material. The quarry walls and floor show cross-sections of several coral species. Antillean Nighthawks have been found here but are more dependable closer to Key West. About 2 miles of nature trails wind through the hardwood hammock, where Mangrove Cuckoos sometimes occur and Yellow-throated Vireos have wintered. Black-whiskered Vireos (spring and summer) and Prairie Warblers are common. *You must currently call 305/664-4815 or go to Long Key State Recreation Area (see below) to get a key for the gate,* but this situation may improve in the future.

On Upper Matecumbe Key, the vicinity of the Green Turtle Inn on the left (MM 81.3) is the site of 3 of the 4 U.S. records of Loggerhead Kingbird, but none has been found since 1976. This general area also has produced Bahama Mockingbirds, Thick-billed Vireos, and Florida's only Golden-crowned Sparrow record. Check powerlines and woodlots for a mile or so around the inn, but *bird discreetly and only from the roads.*

MIDDLE KEYS

On Lower Matecumbe Key, Caloosa Beach on the left (MM 73.1) has a short boardwalk and restroom facilities. If it's not too crowded, it can have good numbers of shorebirds, larids, and sometimes Reddish Egrets. The best area is nearest the bridge over Channel Two.

Long Key State Recreation Area (849 upland and 117 submerged acres; standard fee) on the left (MM 67.5) offers a 2-mile nature trail along the beach and a boardwalk through a mangrove-lined lagoon. The Australian Pines in the campground at the western end of the park are popular roosts for migrant raptors. The end of Long Key (MM 65.6) at the foot of the Dante Fascell bridge is also an excellent spot for watching raptor migration.

Contact: Long Key State Recreation Area, P.O. Box 776, Long Key, FL 33001; 305/664-4815.

Farther along, on Grassy Key, is Lake Edna. To reach it, turn right onto Tropical Avenue (MM 57.9) to the ponds (0.2). Reverse direction and turn right onto an unnamed paved side road one block, then turn right onto Peachtree Street (0.1) to the main ponds on the left. Continue to the end of Peachtree, turn left onto Morton Street, and left again onto Kyle Avenue to reach the other side of the ponds. Reddish Egrets and shorebirds (including Wilson's Plovers and Black-necked Stilts) are present in spring and summer, and many Least Terns roost here in late summer.

Curry Hammocks (no fee) on Fat Deer Key is another recent state park acquisition. Turn left at MM 56.1 to a substantial grassy clearing with an automated weather station. This is a good hawk migration site and may have nesting Antillean Nighthawks in spring and summer.

On the left at the stoplight at MM 53.8 is Key Colony Beach Causeway. Follow the signs to the municipal golf course. Turn right at West Ocean Drive (0.7) and right again onto 8th Street (0.2). Check out the small golf course for Burrowing Owls, especially where the road loops around to become 7th Street, which returns you to West Ocean Drive.

The *Marathon Lady* and several other charter boats dock at Vaca Cut (MM 53.0). Their half-day fishing trips may go out far enough to be worthwhile for pelagic birds. Talk to the captains first to see which boats are going out to deeper water in the Gulf Stream, beyond the edge of the continental shelf (about 10 miles).

At the Marathon Airport on the right (MM 52.5-51.0), check the wires for wintering Western Kingbirds and Scissor-tailed Flycatchers, especially toward the far end (MM 51.0). At MM 51.0, between the Disabled American Veterans building and the large orange windsock, is a retention pond. When it contains water, the pond may have wading-birds, ducks, and shorebirds, including species otherwise difficult to see in the Keys, such as Glossy Ibis, American Golden-Plover, Whimbrel, and Solitary, White-rumped, Pectoral, and Buff-breasted Sandpipers. September tends to be the best month. Antillean Nighthawks call over the airport at dusk from May to August.

Turn left at the traffic light onto CR-931 (MM 50.0) beside Nations Bank and follow it to Sombrero Beach County Park at the end of the road

Mangrove Cuckoo
Gail Diane Yovanovich

(1.8). Two or three pairs of Burrowing Owls are resident here, and the park can be good for raptor migration in fall.

The Florida Keys Museum of Natural History (open 9 am to 5 pm Monday through Saturday, and noon to 5 pm Sunday; $5/person) is on the right, across from CR-931 (MM 50.0). A short nature trail through a West Indian hammock may contain Black-whiskered Vireos, migrant landbirds, and possibly Mangrove Cuckoos.

Turn left at the second segment of CR-931 (MM 48.1). The cellular-phone tower on the left (just off the highway) occasionally has a Bald Eagle perching on it. In fall it is used regularly as a roost by Peregrine Falcons (9 were present at dawn on the 1995 hawk watch).

Across the CR-931 drawbridge is **Boot Key**, the premier raptor migration site in the Keys and one of the best—yet little-known—hawk-watching sites in North America. *The entire key is private property, so bird only from the road.* In fall, exceptional numbers of Sharp-shinned Hawks, Merlins, and Peregrine Falcons move through; Cooper's Hawk as well as Short-tailed and Swainson's Hawks are regular. (A couple of Short-tails may also spend the winter on Boot Key.) The best place for raptor-watching is about 0.9 mile past the drawbridge. Set up a lawn

Middle Keys

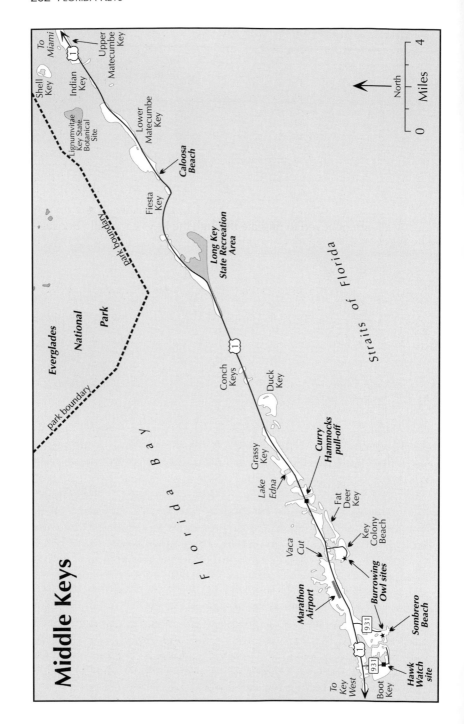

chair on the roadside, put on sunscreen, bring along plenty of liquids and snacks, set up your scope, and be prepared for hundreds of raptors. Wayne Hoffman, an ornithologist with the National Audubon Society, is responsible for bringing Boot Key to the attention of the birding world. Beginning in 1989, Wayne has organized a one-day count on Boot Key, usually in the second week of October. With Wayne's permission, the results of the six October raptor counts from Boot Key, 1989 to 1994, are reproduced in the table below. (The 1995 count was conducted on a day with strong SE winds and intermittent rain—the remnants of Tropical Depression *Pablo*—and was called off at 2:30 pm.) Keep in mind that these are daily totals only; *seasonal totals far exceed these numbers.* As a case in point, the highest daily count of Peregrine Falcons is 190, but about 2,000 are believed to migrate through the Keys each fall. Because many hawks will be flying over at high altitude, especially at midday, a telescope is recommended.

Species	*1989*	*1990*	*1991*	*1992*	*1993*	*1994*
Turkey Vulture	25	1	12	16	3	18
Osprey	34	26	21	24	26	48
Bald Eagle	0	0	0	2	1	2
Northern Harrier	17	4	46	21	9	8
Sharp-shinned Hawk	99	66	993	630	98	91
Cooper's Hawk	0	1	12	10	14	17
Red-shouldered Hawk	0	0	0	1	0	1
Broad-winged Hawk	197	111	415	66	219	150
Short-tailed Hawk	0	0	0	1	4	1
Swainson's Hawk	0	0	0	8	0	0
Red-tailed Hawk	0	0	0	1	0	0
American Kestrel	56	39	159	82	65	50
Merlin	20	37	33	44	42	15
Peregrine Falcon	57	45	129	97	190	119
Species	8	9	9	14	11	12
Individuals	505	330	1820	1003	671	520

Boot Key may also be birded (*from the road*) for landbirds. A patch of upland vegetation on the west side of the road 0.1 mile south of the bridge can be good for migrants; a Thick-billed Vireo was found here in October 1993. The area at the east end of the road can be good for Mangrove Cuckoos, and a Key West Quail-Dove remained here for several months in 1987. (There is talk of closing the drawbridge, which would severely restrict future access to Boot Key).

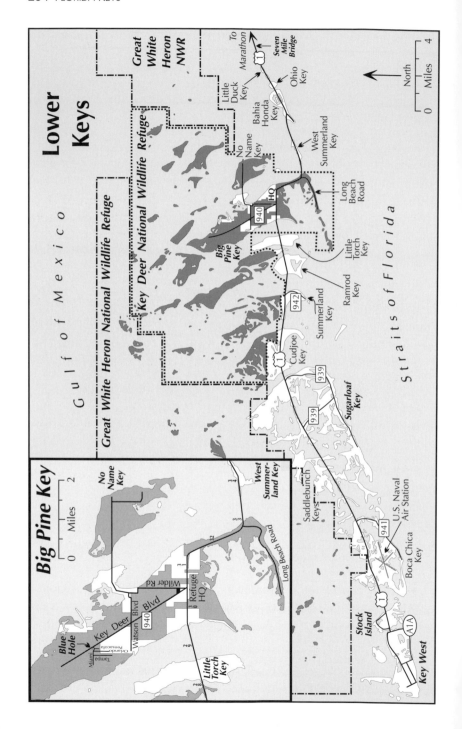

LOWER KEYS

Beyond Seven Mile Bridge the traffic gets somewhat lighter and the birding better. Check any of the numerous beaches for wading-birds, shorebirds, and larids. You will probably see a Magnificent Frigatebird or two overhead along this stretch. The first pair of keys beyond the long bridge (Little Duck and Missouri) and the bridges connecting them can be good for migrant raptors in fall. Birds crossing from Boot Key are often much lower and thus closer when they reach these keys.

After crossing the Missouri/Ohio channel onto **Ohio Key** (also called Sunshine Key) (MM 41.2), look to the left opposite the campground. This intertidal lagoon is a critical shorebird staging area in the Keys. From August to April, over two dozen Piping Plovers may be present. Contact the attendant at the campground guardpost for access, or scope the birds from the highway.

Bahia Honda State Recreation Area (635 acres; standard fee) on both sides of the road (MM 39.1) has wading-birds and shorebirds. Silver Palm Nature Trail at the far eastern picnic area may have migrants in spring and fall. A variety of warblers winter in and around the campgrounds; 1 or 2 Cape May Warblers usually winter near the old bridge.

Contact: Bahia Honda State Recreation Area, Route 1, Box 782, Big Pine Key, FL 33043.

Big Pine Key offers some of the nicest birding in the Keys, yet few birders stop there. The island has a variety of habitats: beaches, mudflats, mangrove forests, pinelands, and West Indian hardwood hammocks. Big Pine is one of the few keys with a permanent source of fresh water. Antillean Nighthawks can be found almost anywhere on the island from mid-April to September. As you enter the key, turn left onto Long Beach Road (MM 32.9), the first paved road to the left, past a private camp-ground. After approximately 0.5 mile, the road curves to the right. After the curve park your vehicle at a gated trail on the left. Walk behind the gate and bear left. A berm road will become visible; it extends to the shore. In winter Northern Gannets and jaegers can sometimes be scoped from here. This also is a good area for watching raptors. Walk to the left along the shore trail to the east, curving to the north. Most of this land is part of **Key Deer National Wildlife Refuge** (also called National Key Deer Refuge) (8,005 acres; no fee), where *the use of tape recordings is prohibited.* The shoreline usually has wading-birds and shorebirds. Wintering landbirds include Cape May and Black-throated Green Warblers, American Redstarts, and Northern Waterthrushes, besides more-common wintering species. White-crowned Pigeons are resident, and

Mangrove Cuckoos and Black-whiskered Vireos breed here. The trail brings you to a campground.

Other productive areas in the refuge can be reached by returning to US-1 and turning left. Turn right onto CR-940 (Key Deer Boulevard) (MM 30.5). Watch the roadsides for Key Deer, a tiny, endemic race of the White-tailed Deer about the size of a very large dog. The current population numbers 250 to 300 animals that are threatened by residential and commercial development, collisions with vehicles, and *illegal* feeding by misguided humans. *Do not feed the deer.* Fortunately, recent land acquisitions have purchased most of the remaining private property on Big Pine and neighboring keys, and the rest is planned for acquisition in the future.

The refuge headquarters are located in the Big Pine Shopping Plaza just north of US-1 between Key Deer Boulevard and Wilder Road. A maintenance facility (closed to the public) on Watson Boulevard is a good spot for Antillean Nighthawks. To reach it, go north from US-1 on Key Deer Boulevard to Watson Boulevard (1.7) and turn left to the gate (0.6). From late April through August, nighthawks occur here regularly, and Reddish Egrets and other wading-birds are also found.

Turn around from the maintenance facility and go east on Watson Boulevard. Cross Key Deer Boulevard and continue to the stop sign at the end of Watson Boulevard. Turn left and go across the hump-backed bridge. After 0.9 mile you will cross a larger bridge onto No Name Key. Most of the land on No Name Key is part of the refuge and is open to foot traffic, but *tapes are prohibited here, too.* Past the bridge, a dirt road to the right (Paradise Drive) (1.2) leads through a hammock that can be good for Mangrove Cuckoos and other landbirds. At the end of the pavement (1.4 from the bridge), a muddy trail leads south for several hundred feet along the beach berm. This area also has Mangrove Cuckoos and a variety of wintering warblers.

Return to Key Deer Boulevard on Big Pine Key and turn right to Blue Hole (1.3), a shallow fresh water pond on the left. Masked Ducks have been found here, and a Least Grebe was present in October 1988. On the left side of Key Deer Boulevard beyond Blue Hole is 3,000-foot-long **Watson Nature Trail** (0.3). From early October to late November, kettles of raptors form in the morning around Blue Hole and soar over the pine forests. Turkey Vultures and Broad-winged Hawks are most common, but Swainson's and Short-tailed Hawks are regular. In October 1994 a Key West Quail-Dove was found here.

Turn around and turn right onto Higgs Lane (immediately past Blue Hole) and quickly turn right onto Pensacola Road to a stop sign. Turn right onto Orlando Road, which soon curves left and becomes Miami Boulevard. Continue a short distance to the point where the road can no longer be driven. Park and follow the road, which becomes the trail into **Watson Hammock**. In winter, the hammock contains Great Crested Flycatchers, warblers, and other landbirds. In summer, look for White-crowned Pigeons, Mangrove Cuckoos, Gray Kingbirds, and Black-whiskered Vireos. Watson Hammock is a confusing area to negotiate. Also, it contains Eastern Diamondback Rattlesnakes. *The hammock is closed from 1 April through 31 May to protect Key Deer during fawning season.* For the botanist, the hammock is an excellent area to view Manchineel, Poisonwood, Gumbo Limbo, Cupania, Strangler Fig, and other tropical trees.

From the parking spot, return east to Tampa Road (0.2) and turn right. At 0.4 mile the road emerges from pinelands into a shrubby marsh known as the *Strumpfia* patch, for a rare Bahamian shrub. Turn right onto a short gravel road that ends next to a long narrow borrow-pit in the marsh. Antillean Nighthawks have nested here, and the marsh occasionally attracts Glossy Ibises, Common Snipes, and other marsh birds rare in the Keys. This is a particularly good spot for watching raptors overhead. Return to Miami Boulevard, for the road beyond this point quickly becomes very rough.

Contact: Key Deer National Wildlife Refuge, Big Pine Key Plaza, Big Pine Key, FL 33043; 305/872-2239.

Continuing down US-1 from Big Pine Key, you will see on the right side numerous small keys that are part of Great White Heron National Wildlife Refuge (2,087 land acres; no fee). The refuge stretches from Marathon to Key West and covers an area of 8 by 40 miles. Key West National Wildlife Refuge (2,019 land acres; no fee) starts near Key West and stretches west through the Marquesas Keys. This refuge is 15 by 25 miles in area. A private boat is needed to visit either refuge.

On **Sugarloaf Key** turn left onto the second part of CR-939 opposite the Sugarloaf Lodge (MM 17.1). At the end of the road (2.6), turn right and go over the bridge to Saddlebunch Key. A well-known site for Mangrove Cuckoos is between the bridge and the end of the paved road (0.9). You can walk down the dirt road past the gate, but only the first few hundred yards are good cuckoo habitat. Prairie Warblers are common breeders, with lesser numbers of Cuban Yellow Warblers. Sugarloaf Key is also famous for its salt-marsh mosquitoes, so be sure to bring along a strong insect repellent. *Because this is probably the most-visited Mangrove Cuckoo site in the United States, it is recommended that you use tapes here only sparingly or preferably not at all.*

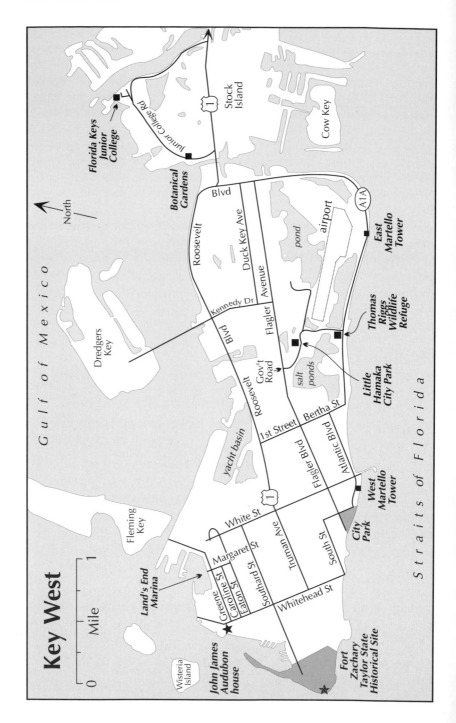

Key West

On US-1 at Big Coppitt Key (MM 10.7), turn left onto CR-941 to explore Boca Chica Key Beach behind the Key West Naval Air Station. It is a good spot to look for Reddish Egrets and other species. Do not watch the military planes with your binoculars. In the past, some birders have been hassled for "spying."

Beyond CR-941 are several shallow ponds along US-1 (MM 7.2) where Reddish Egrets are found regularly.

On Stock Island, go past the golf course and turn right onto Junior College Road (MM 4.2). (This is the last road before the bridge to Key West.) The **Key West Botanical Gardens** are on the right (0.2; no fee) (look for a row of posts). The gardens are a good spot for White-crowned Pigeons and Black-whiskered Vireos, and can be excellent during migration. Farther along Junior College Road (1.1), the junior college on the left is a good place at dusk for Antillean Nighthawks.

Murray Marina, on the left just before the junior college, is one of the places where you get a seaplane ride to Dry Tortugas National Park (Key West Seaplane Service: 305/294-6978.)

KEY WEST

Over the short bridge at Stock Island is Key West, often called the "southernmost city" or the "capital of the Conch Republic." Only about 4 miles by 2 miles in extent, the place is packed with historic homes and plenty of tourists.

Upon entering Key West, turn left onto SR-A1A (Roosevelt Boulevard). Watch on the right for a row of large power poles along Duck Key Avenue (0.3). Western Kingbirds and Scissor-tailed Flycatchers can often be found along this street in winter. At the T intersection with Kennedy Drive, turn left to Flagler Avenue (0.1) and turn right. At Government Road (1.5), turn left to Little Hamaka City Park. A series of mangrove-fringed pools on the right known as the salt ponds are good for wading-birds, ducks, and shorebirds in season. In spring and summer continue along the back side of the Key West Airport for Antillean Nighthawks. Shortly after the road curves left is a small parking lot. A nature trail and a boardwalk here pass through low hammock and mangrove areas, good for migrant and wintering warblers, including Northern Waterthrushes. This park may be the last place in Key West that regularly has Mangrove Cuckoos, and a Black-faced Grassquit was found here 6 May 1993.

Return to Roosevelt Boulevard and turn right to circle the south side of the airport. Beyond the airport watch on the right for the Thomas Riggs Wildlife Refuge. (This is at the south end of the ponds described above under Little Hamaka Park.) Smooth-billed Anis are possible here, and Reddish Egrets and Clapper Rails are resident. The highway turns inland at Bertha Street. Turn left onto Atlantic Boulevard (one block). At White Street (0.6), an old pier extends into the ocean. Just before White Street is (fenced) Key West Indigenous Park on the right, which can be excellent for migrants when it is open. The city park on the right just beyond White Street is the area of Key West's formerly resident Bahama Mockingbird, present in spring and summer from 1991 to 1994. At the county beach just beyond the West Martello Tower (a Civil War fortification) is a broken pier which always has larids.

Fort Zachary Taylor State Historical Site (fee) is worth a visit, especially in spring. Built during 1845-1866 as part of Florida's coastal defense system, it has armaments and other historic artifacts. The site, at the southwest corner of the island, is reached from Whitehead Street by turning west onto Southard Street to the entrance. In addition to common shorebirds, the park is a good place to see Roseate Terns offshore; they breed on nearby rooftops. During spring migration, the park may contain rarities such as West Indian Short-eared Owls or Upland Sandpipers.

Contact: Fort Zachary Taylor State Historical Site, P.O. Box 289, Key West, FL 33041; 305/292-6713.

While in Key West, be sure to call the local RBA (305/294-3438). It may tell you in spring and summer where Shiny Cowbirds could be on the island, or in winter where Short-tailed Hawks might occur.

Before leaving Key West, you might want to stop by Audubon House and Gardens. (205 Whitehead Street, at the corner of Green Street; 305/294-2116; fee $7). Audubon stayed here when he visited the Lower Keys in 1832. The house was restored in 1960, and includes period antiques, a garden, Audubon artwork, and a gift shop.

DRY TORTUGAS NATIONAL PARK

The highlight of a spring birding trip to Florida is a visit to **Dry Tortugas National Park** (formerly Fort Jefferson National Monument; no fee), seven small keys located about 70 miles west of Key West. The islands are open to the public year round, but are accessible only by seaplane or boat. (By most standards, transportation by boat is better than by seaplane; see below.) Because there is no naturally occurring fresh water on the islands, and because they also lack insects and other food, the Dry Tortugas support limited birdlife in summer and winter. But during spring (especially) and fall migration, these keys are home to a dazzling assortment of migrant landbirds. Additionally, many West Indian species have strayed to the Dry Tortugas, including Ruddy Quail-Dove, Variegated Flycatcher, Loggerhead Kingbird, Bahama Swallow, Bahama Mockingbird, Thick-billed Vireo, and Yellow-faced Grassquit. On 6-7 April 1995 a dove in the tropical genus *Leptotila* was photographed on Garden Key. As yet unidentified to species, it is almost certainly a first record for North America.

Despite the West Indian vagrants, it is its seabirds that make the Tortugas such a birding magnet. Besides the islands' breeding species (Magnificent Frigatebird, Masked Booby, Sooty Tern, and Brown Noddy), rarities such as White-tailed Tropicbird, Brown and Red-footed Boobies, and Black Noddy are regular here, or nearly so. Roseate Terns are fairly common in spring and summer but no longer nest in the park.

Whether arriving by boat or by seaplane, you will usually first encounter **Garden Key**, only 16 acres in size, but the Tortugas' second-largest island. Most of the key is contained inside the remains of massive Fort Jefferson, begun in 1846 but never completed. Over 16 million bricks went into the fort's construction, with its three stories of walls up to eight feet thick. The 19th-century architecture of the fort is impressive. During the Civil War the fort was used by the Union Army as a prison, and it remained a prison until 1874. (The most famous prisoner was Dr. Samuel Mudd, an accused "Lincoln Conspirator" who was later pardoned for helping to fight the 1867 yellow fever epidemic which swept through the fort.) Today, rooms in the fort contain living quarters of the park rangers and a small interpretive center and store. Most of the fort is accessible to birders during daylight hours (the top serves as a great lookout post for White-tailed Tropicbirds), but the fort is closed at night.

Outside the fort on the southern part of the key is a small campground shaded by coconut palms. *You must provide your own food and water* and your own tent, but restrooms, picnic tables, and cooking grills are provided. Inside the fort is a large expanse of mowed lawn with numerous trees and shrubs, mostly of West Indian origin. Check all these trees for migrants. As you enter the fort across the moat, angle left to reach a bird fountain that has been installed inside a small copse. The fountain is an excellent place to sit quietly and watch the birds as they come to drink and bathe. The fountain is also the spot to observe a famous Tortugas spectacle. Cattle Egrets that are moving north in spring often land on the lawn inside the fort. The egrets soon discover that insects are scarce on the keys, so they turn to stalking warblers and other small passerines at the water fountain. (Or sometimes the egrets visit the fountain to soak other birds to aid in swallowing them.) Despite this

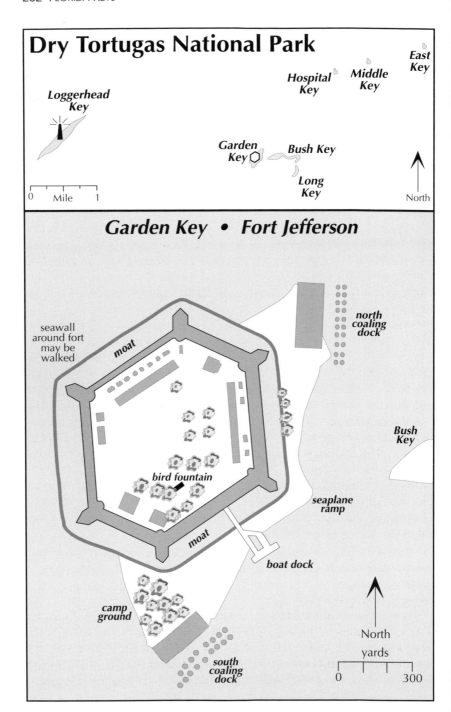

Dry Tortugas National Park

East Key

Hospital Key   Middle Key

Loggerhead Key

Garden Key   Bush Key

Long Key

0   Mile   1

North

Garden Key • Fort Jefferson

seawall around fort may be walked

moat

north coaling dock

Bush Key

bird fountain

seaplane ramp

moat

boat dock

camp ground

North

yards

south coaling dock

0   300

improvisation, many Cattle Egrets that reach the Tortugas die of starvation. Directly east of Garden Key are Bush and Long Keys—*both off limits from 1 March to 1 October to protect the nesting birds.* These keys are easily observed from the fort. An estimated 40,000 pairs of Sooty Terns and about 2,000 pairs of Brown Noddies nest on Bush Key. About 100 pairs of Magnificent Frigatebirds nest on Long Key, their only breeding colony in North America.

Two to five miles northeast of Garden Key are three tiny sandbars known as Hospital, Middle, and East Keys. East Key is not visible from Fort Jefferson, but a very powerful telescope may offer somewhat satisfactory views of Hospital and Middle Keys. Since 1984 small numbers of Masked Boobies have nested in late winter and early spring on Hospital Key, their only rookery in the continental U.S. In April 1995, 60 Masked Boobies, including 3 nestlings, were seen on Hospital Key. Middle Key washes over every summer, but reappears in fall.

The last island in the Tortugas chain is the largest. **Loggerhead Key**, located about three miles west of Garden Key, is well known for its tall U.S. Coast Guard lighthouse and its Australian Pines. These fast-growing exotic trees have created a dense forest on the island with very little understory except yuccas and cactus. This tall, open, wooded habitat is unique on the Tortugas and attracts many birds not usually observed on Garden Key. (The National Park Service is currently eradicating the pines and replacing them with native plants.) Numerous landbirds seek shelter in the dense foliage. Thrushes, Swainson's, Kentucky, and Connecticut Warblers, and other ground-dwelling species forage in the litter of pine needles. This abundance of landbirds attracts numbers of accipiters and falcons, including Cooper's Hawks, Merlins, and Peregrine Falcons.

Perhaps nowhere else in North America can "feather puddles" be so prevalent as on Loggerhead Key. It is quite a challenge to identify birds by the piles of feathers which are all that remain of raptor kills. Yellow-billed Cuckoos seem to be the most-preyed-upon species, but a variety of other puddles can also be found, including such diverse species as Least Bittern, Sharp-shinned Hawk (Peregrine Falcon kill!), Purple Gallinule, Yellow-bellied Sapsucker, Prothonotary Warbler, Scarlet Tanager, and Bobolink.

As mentioned above, there are two ways of getting to the Tortugas: boat and seaplane. The seaplane flight offers impressive views of coral reefs, a shipwreck, the Marquesas Keys, and the Tortugas, but the birder is then restricted to Garden Key. Nesting Masked Boobies on Hospital Key can at best be seen distantly, as can buoy-roosting Brown Boobies

Brown Noddy
Georges Dremeaux

and Roseate Terns. The many raptors and landbirds on Loggerhead Key are completely inaccessible. The standard seaplane tour is brief: 45 minutes each way for the flight, with only two hours at the fort. Extended visits of any duration are also possible, but the fee is almost doubled because the plane must make two round-trip flights. The standard tour costs about $160; a full-day tour (with about 6 hours on land) costs about $275; and the extended visit (with a future scheduled pick-up) is about $300.

The much-preferred method of taking a boat is usually more expensive than a seaplane, but is much more advantageous. Most boat trips are three days in duration, but single-day trips that are less expensive than a seaplane flight were begun in 1995. While single-day trips allow one to sample the Dry Tortugas, birders will almost certainly want to spend more than a few hours on Garden Key. Every major North American birding tour company (and many minor ones) regularly schedules one or more 3-day birding trips to the Tortugas between early April and mid-May. The birding schedule differs little between tour companies once at the Tortugas, but there are differences on the trips to and from Key West. Most boats depart Key West (usually from the Land's End Marina by Margaret Street) at dawn and arrive at Garden Key around noon, but some trips depart at midnight and arrive at dawn. Trips depart around dawn on the third day and arrive back at Key West in the early afternoon. Most pelagic trips produce fair to good numbers of Audubon's Shearwaters and Bridled Terns. A few Band-rumped Storm-Petrels have been seen on several trips recently.

Once at the Tortugas, some tour companies offer the option of sleeping on the boat (usually in a sleeping-bag on deck, but occasionally in a bunk below deck) or camping on Garden Key. Because food cannot be purchased at the Tortugas, the boat will supply your meals.

The main advantage that boat tours to the Tortugas have over seaplane trips is access to the other islands. Invariably, the boat tour will visit Loggerhead Key for a few hours of birding the Australian Pine forests for raptors and landbirds, and will cruise the boundary of the park to observe Brown Boobies and Roseate Terns roosting on the buoys and channel markers. Afterward, the boat will briefly anchor off Hospital Key one evening to watch the Masked Boobies fly in to roost. Boat tours also supply a small dinghy or Zodiac used for close-up views of Bush and Long Keys. Because the keys are off-limits during the seabird nesting season, the dinghy offers the closest views possible of nesting Magnificent Frigatebirds, Sooty Terns, and Brown Noddies, together with the opportunity to search for a Black Noddy roosting on Bush Key.

Although many companies schedule spring trips to the Tortugas, reserve your space early because it is a *very* popular birding destination. Accommodations vary, but most boat trips cost between $450 to $600 for three days. Many groups also provide an optional South Florida/Keys birding extension tour before or after the Tortugas trip for an additional charge.

Presently, no birding company offers single-day Tortugas trips by boat, so interested birders should contact the Yankee Fleet directly at 800/634-0939 or 305/294-7009 (Key West). The boat departs Key West at 8 am and returns at 7 pm on Monday, Wednesday, and Friday (and other days by appointment). About 6½ hours are spent in transit and 4½ hours are spent at Fort Jefferson. Garden Key is the only key visited, and the boat does not visit the buoys and channel markers in the park for boobies and terns—but you do get two daytime pelagic trips. Currently, the trip costs about $82 per adult (including tax). Because the boat leaves Key West on a regular schedule, you may take the boat to Garden Key, camp there for almost any length of time, and return on another of their scheduled boat trips (about $97 per adult, including tax, for this option).

SPECIALTIES OF FLORIDA

L isted below are birds of particular interest to many birders in Florida. The concept of Florida specialties here is a broad one, combining different categories and including birds usually not associated at all with the state (e.g., Pacific Loon, White-faced Ibis, Long-billed Murrelet, Sprague's Pipit, and House Finch). All West Indian vagrants and all other species whose regular North American range is largely or exclusively restricted to the state are included, as well as many common and widespread species that are also sought by visitors to Florida or birders living in the state. Some species (e.g., King Rail and Eastern Bluebird) are included for the benefit of western birders, others (e.g., White-winged Dove and Scissor-tailed Flycatcher) are included for eastern birders, while still others (e.g., Yellow-breasted Chat and wintering ducks) are included for Europeans visiting the state or for Florida residents. Also included are a number of exotics not on the AOU and ABA lists, but apparently increasing in range and numbers and that might be considered as established in the future (e.g., Muscovy Duck, Black-hooded Parakeet, and Common Myna). A few other exotics (e.g., Hill Myna) are included because they are well known, even though their populations are small. Identification tips are included for only those species not illustrated in the National Geographic *Field Guide to the Birds of North America*, second edition (Scott 1987) (e.g., Yellow-chevroned Parakeet, La Sagra's Flycatcher, and Shiny Cowbird).

Some West Indian species are illustrated in Peterson's *A Field Guide to the Birds East of the Rockies*, in Bond's *Birds of the West Indies*, or in Downer and Sutton's *Birds of Jamaica*. The publication of a new West Indies guide by Raffaele, Wiley, Garrido, and Keith is expected by mid-1998 and will be a welcome aid to birders seeking vagrant birds in Florida.

Although references are listed only rarely in the species accounts, all information contained in this section is based on information published in recent ornithological and birding publications. Literature sources for these accounts are contained in Duncan (*The Birds of Escambia, Santa Rosa, and Okaloosa counties*, 1991), Robertson and Woolfenden (*Florida Bird Species: An Annotated List*, 1992), Stevenson and Anderson (*The Birdlife of Florida*, 1994), Kale et al. (*The Atlas of the Breeding Birds of Florida*, 1992), and the Florida Ornithological Society's Field Observations Committee seasonal bird reports. For comprehensive summaries of the seasonal and regional distributions of all of Florida's birds, consult Robertson and Woolfenden or Stevenson and Anderson.

This guide follows Robertson and Woolfenden and Stevenson and Anderson in using the term *record* for a sighting only if it is backed up by a specimen, photograph, or audio or video tape. A sight-only observation is termed a *report.*

Red-throated Loon—A rare but regular coastal winter resident. Reported most often along the northern Atlantic coast, rare in the Panhandle, and irregular south to the Keys.

Pacific Loon—Believed to be a rare winter resident of Gulf coastal areas throughout, but probably overlooked. Reported most often from the Panhandle, but it has occurred south to the Keys. Reported much less frequently in the Atlantic.

Least Grebe—A casual straggler (6 reports, 4 probably valid) from the West Indies to the southern peninsula and Keys. Accepted reports are from Miami (November 1970 and April 1992), Big Pine Key (October 1988), and Marco Island (March to April 1990).

Eared Grebe—First verified in 1959, but now a regular winter resident throughout.

Tubenoses (petrels, shearwaters, and storm-petrels)—Unlike some other coastal states, Florida has no regularly scheduled pelagic trips (outside of those which are by-products of boat trips to Dry Tortugas National Park). This lack of trips is mainly due to the fact that pelagic birding in the state is considered generally fair to poor. Additionally, much of the ocean floor is shallow far offshore, requiring boats to travel long distances to reach water of sufficient depth to attract pelagic birds in numbers. Pelagic trips into the Gulf of Mexico must usually go out about 80 miles, while trips into the Atlantic vary in the distance to deep water (the Gulf Stream). The Gulf Stream is only about 5 miles off Palm Beach County, but it is over 50 miles off Jacksonville. Pelagic trips from the Keys need to travel south into the Florida Straits only about 10 miles.

Charter fishing boats operate out of nearly every marina in the state, and experienced pelagic birders may choose to tag along. (Some boats charge less for passengers who do not fish, so talk to the captains first.) Inexperienced birders should probably wait for a pelagic trip organized by the Florida Ornithological Society or a local Audubon Society rather than go on a fishing boat because on a fishing excursion there will ordinarily not be any experienced observers available to help you identify the birds you see. (Pelagic birding is nothing like land birding, and it takes many boat trips before you become accustomed to the different birding elements at sea.)

Another alternative to pelagic birding in Florida is to follow Harry Robinson's lead and watch the Atlantic Ocean from Turtle Mound, a part of Canaveral National Seashore. Since 1990, Harry has reported 5 shearwaters (Cory's, Greater, Sooty, Manx, and Audubon's), 3 storm-petrels (Wilson's, Leach's, and Band-rumped), 2 boobies (Brown and Red-footed), Northern Gannet, Red-necked and Red Phalaropes, all 3 jaegers (Pomarine, Parasitic, and Long-tailed), South Polar Skua, Black-legged Kittiwake, Sabine's Gull, and Arctic Tern—all while sitting on shore!

Black-capped Petrel—A rare but regular visitor in Gulf Stream waters of the Atlantic Ocean and the Florida Straits. Very rare in the Gulf of Mexico. Most reports are from April to October.

Cory's Shearwater—A fairly common to occasionally abundant visitor offshore. Occurs much more frequently in the Atlantic than in the Gulf, and is most common from July through November.

Greater Shearwater—A rare to uncommon visitor offshore, more frequent in the Atlantic. Occurs almost year round but is reported most often from May to October.

Sooty Shearwater—A rare but regular year-round visitor offshore, reported more frequently in the Atlantic.

Manx Shearwater—An occasional visitor (about 20 reports) offshore, reported more often in the Atlantic. Has occurred in every month except July but is usually reported in winter.

Audubon's Shearwater—An uncommon to locally common visitor offshore. Most common off the southeast coast and Keys, especially from April to October. Uncommon to rare elsewhere and at other seasons. Seen on most spring boat trips between Key West and Dry Tortugas National Park.

Wilson's Storm-Petrel—An uncommon visitor offshore, more common in the Atlantic. Reported from April to November.

Leach's Storm-Petrel—A rare visitor off both coasts, usually far offshore. Reported from April to November.

Band-rumped Storm-Petrel—Considered a rare visitor offshore, but Chris Haney found it to be rather common 45 to 60 miles off the Atlantic coast from Daytona Beach northward (especially off Jacksonville) from late April to early September. It has recently been reported fairly regularly on spring boat trips between Key West and Dry Tortugas National Park.

White-tailed Tropicbird—A rare but usually annual spring and summer visitor to the Dry Tortugas, but its occurrence there has declined in the past few years. Elsewhere, an irregular visitor off both coasts from March to October.

Masked Booby—An uncommon resident at the Dry Tortugas, breeding annually in late winter and early spring since 1984. In April 1995, 57 adults and 3 chicks were observed. Nesting sites on Hospital Key are not easily visible from Fort Jefferson, although the birds may be viewed with a very powerful telescope. Unlike the Brown Booby, the Masked Booby does not perch on buoys and channel markers, but it often sits on the water. Elsewhere, a rare but regular visitor off both coasts.

Brown Booby—An uncommon to fairly common non-breeding resident at the Tortugas, perching on buoys and channel markers. Elsewhere, rare but regular off both coasts, with two anomalous reports from Lake Okeechobee.

Red-footed Booby—An occasional spring and summer visitor (about 25 reports), reported most frequently at the Tortugas. Florida reports have occurred from March to October. The brown morph is the form most expected to occur in the state, but birds in intermediate plumage have also been observed.

Northern Gannet—An uncommon to abundant winter resident off both coasts, mainly from November to April. Observed frequently from shore (often in large numbers) from Santa Rosa Island, Cape San Blas, St. George Island, Cape Canaveral, and other barrier islands, including those from West Palm Beach to Miami.

American White Pelican—An uncommon to abundant, local winter resident of the peninsula (10,000 to 12,000 birds), occurring coastally and at select inland sites such as large lakes and phosphate-mine impoundments. Some birds remain through the summer. Found primarily in spring and fall in the Panhandle and Keys.

Brown Pelican—A common to abundant coastal resident throughout, but less common in the Panhandle, especially in winter. Inland occurrences in Central Florida are increasing, and the species has bred recently at Lake Okeechobee.

Great Cormorant—An occasional to rare winter visitor (about 50 reports), mostly along the Atlantic coast. Very rare inland and in the Keys. Florida reports range from October to June.

Anhinga—A common resident of the peninsula, but rare in the western Panhandle and the Keys. Most birds withdraw from the eastern Panhandle in winter. Strongly prefers fresh water habitats. Easy to find in peninsular Florida.

Magnificent Frigatebird—A common resident at the Tortugas. About 100 pairs nest on Long Key, the only breeding colony in North America.

Elsewhere, a common to locally abundant non-breeding resident of the Keys and South Florida coasts, decreasing in abundance northward, where it occurs mostly from April to October. Forms large roosts of up to hundreds of birds on offshore islands (over 1,100 roosted on Marco Island in August 1995). Irregular in the western Panhandle, along the northeast coast, and inland, usually after storms.

Wading-birds—Perhaps no other family of birds represents the image of Florida to most people more than its wading-birds. Although current populations are greatly reduced from numbers up to about 1870, wading-birds remain a highly visible and widespread component of all wetlands in the state, even stormwater retention ponds in urban areas. Nearly all species are common throughout, although numbers in the Panhandle are diminished in winter. In many areas (Zellwood, Belle Glade, phosphate-mine impoundments, and coastal areas at low tide), spectacular numbers of wading-birds can be seen.

Great Blue, Little Blue, and Tricolored Herons and Great and Snowy Egrets are common to abundant residents throughout. White Ibises are abundant in the peninsula, but rare in parts of the Panhandle. They are declining rapidly statewide and especially in South Florida and were declared a Species of Special Concern in 1994. Green Herons are uncommon throughout, but are rather rare in the Keys. Black-crowned and Yellow-crowned Night-Herons are uncommon to locally common residents throughout (Yellow-crowns withdraw from the Panhandle in winter). The Black-crowned is usually more common inland, while the Yellow-crowned is more common coastally, especially along the Gulf coast.

American Bittern—An uncommon winter resident of marshes and other wetlands of the mainland, occasional in the Keys. Infrequently seen because of its secretive habits and inaccessible habitats. Reports of breeding in Florida are poorly documented. Among other sites, wintering birds are observed regularly at Rainey Slough.

Least Bittern—An uncommon to locally common spring and summer resident of fresh water marshes throughout, less common in salt water and brackish water marshes and mangrove forests. Most common in Lake Okeechobee and the Everglades. Winters from Central Florida southward.

Great White Heron—A fairly common resident of South Florida, considered currently to be a white morph of Great Blue Heron. Almost certain to be seen along US-1 from Key Largo to Key West, and fairly common also in Everglades National Park. The state's population is about 800 pairs. During post-breeding dispersal (late summer-early fall), birds may occur anywhere along the coasts, and a few are found inland. Stevenson and Anderson consider Great White Heron to be a separate species.

"Wurdemann's Heron"—is intermediate in plumage between Great Blue and Great White Herons. Present in coastal areas of southern Florida (mostly in the Keys), it looks like a Great Blue Heron, but has the white head and neck and yellowish legs of a Great White Heron. It is thought to be a hybrid between mixed pairings of Great Blue and Great White Herons. It is considered rare, but according to William B. Robertson most of the breeding Great Blue Herons in the Lower Keys appear to be Wurdemann's Herons.

Reddish Egret—A fairly common Gulf coastal resident from Tampa Bay southward through the Keys, less common on the Atlantic Coast north to Merritt Island. Post-breeding dispersal carries the birds northward increasingly to the eastern Panhandle and even inland, especially immatures. About 400 pairs breed in the state. The red morph is much more common than the white morph except in the Lower Keys, where, as Bill Smith has observed, the white morph predominates. Occurs regularly at Honeymoon Island State Recreation Area, Merritt Island National Wildlife Refuge, J.N. "Ding" Darling National Wildlife Refuge, Fort Myers Beach, and along US-1 in the Keys, among many other places. In winter, a few are found in Gulf Islands National Seashore (Pensacola area) and St. Marks National Wildlife Refuge.

Cattle Egret—A common to abundant resident throughout, except rare to uncommon in the Keys. Withdraws partially in winter, especially from the Panhandle and North Florida. It is now the most abundant wading-bird in the state, even though it did not occur in Florida until the early 1940s. Unlike other wading-birds, it forages primarily in upland sites such as pastures and fields.

Scarlet Ibis—Current status uncertain. An 1874 specimen from Central Florida and another specimen reportedly taken in the state in 1883 presumably represent stragglers from Trinidad or South America. Recent reports may also represent naturally occurring vagrants, but many Scarlet Ibises have escaped from captivity in Florida. The issue is clouded further by the 1961 introduction of 22 Scarlet Ibis eggs taken from Trinidad and placed into White Ibis nests in Greynolds Park, Miami. Seventeen Scarlet Ibises fledged from these nests, and in subsequent years, the birds hybridized with White Ibises, producing pink or orange offspring. (It should be noted that *pink or orange ibises are not Scarlet Ibises; they are hybrid ibises*). Bright-red birds and immatures have appeared in southern Florida since the late 1970s, but their origins cannot be determined.

Since 1991, one has been present in the Fort Myers area, where it is frequently seen roosting in Lakes County Park.

Glossy Ibis—A locally common and increasing resident of marshes and wet prairies throughout the peninsula, generally rare in the Panhandle and Keys. Rare to uncommon along the coast. The state's population numbers 2,000 to 3,000 pairs. Usually easy to find at Zellwood, in marshes along the St. Johns River west of Titusville, Myakka River State Park, the prairie region west of Lake Okeechobee, and the Belle Glade area.

White-faced Ibis—A casual visitor and breeder, represented by only 5 records in the past 100+ years (April 1886 nesting in Brevard County, April 1937 nesting at Lake Okeechobee, June 1960 at Flamingo, April 1966 at Pensacola, and October 1994 at Fort Walton Beach). Possibly overlooked in Florida; immatures may be indistinguishable from immature Glossy Ibises.

Roseate Spoonbill—An uncommon to locally common resident along both coasts. About 1,000 pairs currently breed in the state, and this number is increasing. Nests in winter (January-February) in southern Florida north to Tampa Bay and Merritt Island. Post-breeding dispersal carries the birds northward to the Panhandle, along the entire Florida Atlantic coast, and inland (mostly hatching-year birds). Almost sure to be seen year round in J.N. "Ding" Darling National Wildlife Refuge. Regular also in McKay Bay, at Flamingo (Everglades National Park), the Florida Keys, and many other coastal areas (and a few inland sites).

Wood Stork—An uncommon to locally abundant resident of the peninsula, rare in the Panhandle and Keys. An Endangered species, it had a Florida population numbering 4,400 pairs in 1993, 3,588 in 1994, and 5,523 in 1995. Nests in late winter and early spring and disperses widely afterward. Flocks of hundreds or even thousands may be seen at Zellwood, the Belle Glade area, phosphate-mine impoundments, and other areas. A large rookery exists in Corkscrew Swamp Sanctuary, where a few nests may be visible from the boardwalk. Another accessible rookery is at Paurotis Pond in Everglades National Park. Nesting success is dependent upon receding water levels that concentrate fish and other prey, and is highly variable.

Greater Flamingo—Up to the late 19th century, a common to abundant winter resident of Florida Bay (now a part of Everglades National Park) and other areas from breeding colonies in the West Indies. This wintering population disappeared as the species' breeding range contracted eastward because of human pressures.

In the 1930s, Greater Flamingoes from Cuba were released at Hialeah Race Track near Miami in an attempt to establish a local breeding flock. The original birds were not pinioned, and many of them flew away. Eventually, a breeding population of several hundred birds was established at the race track; they are still present and breeding. These birds are also not pinioned or banded, and all are capable of sustained flight.

Since the 1950s a flock of up to 40 birds (adults and immatures) has been found in the southwest portion of Everglades National Park (especially at Snake Bight) throughout the year, but mostly in fall and winter. High tide is best for viewing. Up to 16 birds wintered at Snake Bight in 1995-1996.

The origin of the flamingoes currently present in Florida is not known. Birds banded in the southeast Bahamas are known to regularly disperse long distances, but there is no direct evidence that any of these birds account for the Florida flock. It is also widely argued that the Florida flock consists of birds that "dispersed" from Hialeah Race Track, but there is no direct evidence to support this theory, either. Those who believe in the latter theory have never explained why the birds, if they are escapes, regularly winter exclusively in Everglades National Park, a traditional flamingo wintering site, especially since the site is about 60 miles southwest of Hialeah. (Escaped birds tend to remain in the area from which they escaped.)

Birds observed elsewhere in the state are usually presumed to be escapes, although Bill Smith points out that "essentially all other captive flamingoes in the state are pinioned and incapable of flight." Numerous reports of one or more birds along the eastern Panhandle coast a few days after Hurricane *Allison* in June 1995 probably involved storm-driven birds from the West Indies.

Robertson and Woolfenden state that "recent observations probably include wild birds from the Bahamas or Cuba, as well as local escapees." Stevenson and Anderson comment that of flamingoes in Florida, "probably the great majority are escapes, but occasional emigrants from the Bahamas or Cuba would not be surprising."

Lastly, note that *flamingoes seen in Florida are not necessarily Greater Flamingoes*. There are two reports of Chilean Flamingoes (*Phoenicopterus chilensis*) in Florida, both presumed escapes. The presence of exotic flamingoes in the state is probably under-reported, as most observers would likely assume that all flamingoes seen in the state are Greater Flamingoes.

Waterfowl—Only 5 species of waterfowl breed widely in Florida, and 2 of these are exotics. During winter, however, 22 species occur regularly in the state, and about 14 others occur less frequently. St. Marks National Wildlife Refuge is probably the best site in the state to observe wintering waterfowl, but numerous other sites are also excellent. A few species of ducks return to Florida in August, but most waterfowl do not arrive until late November or early December, and most depart in February or March.

Regular in winter are Snow Goose (rare to uncommon; mostly in the Panhandle), Green-winged Teal (uncommon to common throughout), American Black Duck (uncommon; mostly in St. Marks refuge), (wild) Mallard (common in the Panhandle, rare to uncommon south to Central Florida; feral birds are resident throughout), Northern Pintail (local; mostly in St. Marks refuge, Merritt Island National Wildlife Refuge, and McKay Bay), Blue-winged Teal (common throughout; probably the most widespread wintering duck in the state), Northern Shoveler (uncommon to common throughout), Gadwall (local; common only in the Panhandle), American Wigeon (uncommon to common throughout), Canvasback (local; mostly coastal), Redhead (local; mostly coastal), Ring-necked Duck (common throughout), Greater Scaup (coastal; common in the Panhandle, rare to uncommon in the peninsula), Lesser Scaup (mostly coastal; common to abundant), Black Scoter (rare to locally common; mostly along the Panhandle and North Florida coasts), Surf Scoter (rare to uncommon; mostly along the Panhandle and North Florida coasts), White-winged Scoter (rare; mostly along the Panhandle and North Florida coasts), Common Goldeneye (uncommon; mostly along the Panhandle coast), Bufflehead (mostly coastal; common in the Panhandle, uncommon south through Central Florida), Hooded Merganser (uncommon to common throughout), Red-breasted Merganser (mostly coastal; common throughout), and Ruddy Duck (rare to locally common throughout). One or more Cinnamon Teal and Eurasian Wigeons are usually reported in Florida annually.

Canada Goose—Formerly an abundant winter resident in the St. Marks area but now rare or irregular. However, in the late 1960s, the Florida Game and Fresh Water Fish Commission began releasing birds of the non-migratory race *Branta canadensis maxima* (the Giant Canada Goose) into the state, predominantly in the Tallahassee area, but also south to the central peninsula. Additional birds have been released by others, and Canada Geese have now bred as far south as Hialeah Race Track in Miami. It is extremely difficult if not impossible to distinguish wild wintering Canada Geese from resident feral birds; the latter presumably account for the vast majority of birds that now occur in the state.

Fulvous Whistling-Duck—An uncommon to abundant, local resident of fresh water marshes and flooded farmlands (especially rice fields) of Central and southern Florida. Irregular in the Panhandle and Keys. Rather easy to find from July to October at Zellwood and Belle Glade when agricultural fields are flooded. The birds may also be found at Lake Okeechobee and in Loxahatchee National Wildlife Refuge, especially in late winter.

Black-bellied Whistling-Duck—An uncommon to common, very local resident of the central peninsula, predominantly southeast of Sarasota. Discovered as a small flock in the early 1980s, the birds are believed to have dispersed from Mexico or Texas and are now in the midst of what is probably a natural colonization of Florida. The population in Sarasota currently numbers over 250 birds. Presumed dispersers from the flock have been reported north to Hernando, Hamilton, Lake, and Orange Counties and east to the extensive phosphate-mining region in Polk and Hardee Counties and to the St. Johns Marsh in Indian River County. Other reports from the 1960s and 1970s (some known to be escapes) occurred in the Belle Glade area and along the southeast coast. In September 1993 2 birds were reported in St. Marks National Wildlife Refuge. Because of its increasing and dispersing population, the species may show up anywhere in the central peninsula or beyond.

Muscovy Duck—An uncommon to locally abundant resident of residential areas throughout, but least common in the Panhandle and North Florida. Native to Mexico south through South America. Individuals in Florida are released birds or their progeny, and the establishment of the species in the state is in dispute. Robertson and Woolfenden consider Muscovy Duck to be an established exotic, but Stevenson and Anderson do not. The species is also considered not established in Florida by the AOU and the ABA checklist committees.

The Florida Breeding Bird Atlas project mapped the breeding ranges of all Florida birds from 1986-1991. *Muscovy Duck was the fourth most-widespread exotic in the state*, behind European Starling, House Sparrow, and Rock Dove. It was found in 274 (26%) of the state's 1,028 quadrangles, compared to 100 quadrangles (9%) for Eurasian Collared-Dove, 52 quadrangles (5%) for Monk Parakeet, and only 2 quadrangles (0.18%) for Red-whiskered Bulbul. The latter three species are considered by the AOU and the ABA to be established exotics, while Muscovy Duck is not. It is time for birders to deliberate following Robertson and Woolfenden, and Kale et al. in viewing Muscovy Duck as an established exotic in Florida.

Mottled Duck—A common resident of marshes, lakes, and fresh water (rare in brackish water) of the peninsula from about Gainesville south to about Lake Okeechobee. Most common around Lake Okeechobee and uncommon farther south, (e.g., in much of the Everglades). In 1991, Johnson et al. determined that the statewide population was stable at 14,000 pairs. However, hybridization with exotic Mallards is a growing concern; Moorman and Gray reported in 1993 that at least 5% of all Mottled Ducks in Florida exhibited Mallard plumage characteristics. If measures to contain releases of exotic Mallards into Florida are not enacted, we may eventually lose the Mottled Duck in Florida due to genetic swamping by Mallards.

White-cheeked Pintail—An occasional visitor (about 20 reports) from the West Indies, mostly to southern Florida. Most Florida sightings occur from November to May. The species is commonly kept in captivity in the state, and some birds seen in Florida have been proven to be escapes. Some recent Florida reports (for example, Pensacola, March 1995, and Tampa, April 1995) have been determined to be escapes.

Masked Duck—An occasional visitor from the West Indies mostly to South Florida, with about 30 reports since the first one in 1955. About half of all reports are from Loxahatchee National Wildlife Refuge, where breeding in February 1977 was reported by Maggie Bowman. The most recent Florida report was in Orlando Wetlands Park in November 1994.

Osprey—An uncommon to locally common resident throughout, occurring coastally and inland. Most birds withdraw from northern Florida in winter. Their large nests are frequently seen in trees and on man-made structures such as power poles, TV antennas, and specially constructed nesting platforms. Osprey is designated a Species of Special Concern in the Keys because of its poor nesting success there. A 1978 estimate put the state population at a minimum of 1,500 to 2,000 pairs. Lake Istokpoga east of Lake Placid hosts over 100 active nests. According to Mike McMillian, this is believed to be the highest density of Ospreys in the state. Not hard to find.

Swallow-tailed Kite—A fairly common spring and summer resident, primarily of the peninsula. The state's population is estimated at 500 to 800 pairs, which makes up most of the U.S. population. It forms communal roosts in late summer before migrating out of the country. One publicly inaccessible roost in eastern Glades County (according to Ken Meyer) has contained up to 2,200 birds at once and up to 3,000 birds in a season! Rather easy to find in the peninsula from March through July.

White-tailed Kite—Formerly a resident of the prairie region, apparently rare and local. Since the 1960s reported more frequently throughout much of the state, but absent from the Keys. Most reports occur fall through spring. In 1984, an adult and a juvenile observed west of Fort Lauderdale suggested its return as a breeding species. Breeding was confirmed in 1986, with three nests in Broward County, and in 1988 breeding was successful in Dade County. The species continues to breed in the Everglades region of Broward and Dade Counties, with breeding probably occurring in other areas as well. In the 1990s birds have also been reported in Brevard, Collier, Franklin, Glades, Highlands, Lafayette, Manatee, Okaloosa, Osceola, Palm Beach, Sarasota, and Wakulla Counties. In spring and summer 1995, four adults frequented the area around the main entrance to Everglades National Park.

Snail Kite—A rare to locally common *nomadic* resident of fresh water wetlands of the central and southern mainland. According to Rob Bennetts, the state's population numbered 996 birds in November-December 1994, a 17% increase over that of 1993. The birds move around eastern South Florida according to local water conditions. Differing water levels affect the availability of the kite's chief prey, the Apple Snail (*Pomacea paludosa*), forcing the birds to move from site to site.

In the late 1960s, most birds were found in Water Conservation Area 2A, but they moved to Water Conservation Area 1 (= Loxahatchee National Wildlife Refuge) by the early 1970s. Water Conservation Area 3A contained most of the kites from the mid-1970s to 1993, but the current hotspot is Water Conservation Area 2B. A few birds are resident in Central Florida, at Lakes Kissimmee, Tohopekaliga, and East Tohopekaliga.

An easily observed roost site is currently located just northwest of the Miccosukee Indian Restaurant on US-41 in western Dade County. It is best to arrive shortly after dawn or about an hour before dusk to see the birds. The Palm Beach County Solid Waste Authority's incinerator and landfill site in West Palm Beach is also a reliable site, but arrangements to visit the site must be made in advance—call 561/640-4000. Another site currently reliable for the birds is the Blue Cypress Conservation Area north of SR-60 about 15 miles west of Vero Beach.

A special issue (November 1983) of the *Florida Field Naturalist*, devoted entirely to the Snail Kite in Florida, is still available ($3 plus $1 postage). (Order from Glen Woolfenden, Editor of Special Publications, Archbold Biological Station, 123 Main Drive, Venus, Florida 33960.)

Mississippi Kite—An uncommon to rather common spring and summer resident of Panhandle and North Florida forests, except rare in northeast Florida. Breeds south to Gainesville, where it is locally uncommon. Usually found rather easily from mid-April to September. Rarely observed farther south during migration, but a few fall and winter reports exist from the Keys.

Bald Eagle—A rather common *and increasing* resident throughout the eastern Panhandle and peninsula, but rare in the western Panhandle and uncommon in the Keys. Florida's breeding population, the largest of any state outside Alaska, numbered 667 pairs in 1993, 831 in 1995, and continues to increase. The greatest density of nesting eagles in the state is located in the Lake Kissimmee area, with over 100 active territories. Including non-breeding immatures, the state's population of eagles exceeds 3,000 birds. *To prevent vandalism of nest trees, specific directions to Bald Eagle nests are generally avoided in this guide, though a few well-known sites are mentioned.*

From late May through July (i.e., after the breeding season), most of Florida's eagles migrate north out of the state, and then the species can be difficult to locate in many areas. (In Florida Bay, only young of the year migrate north; the adults are resident or wander locally). During other months, Bald Eagles are not hard to find in the peninsula.

Cooper's Hawk—A rare to uncommon migrant and winter resident throughout. Breeds south to south-central Florida, generally uncommonly, but locally commonly in some areas of North Florida (e.g., Tall Timbers Research Station).

Red-shouldered Hawk—A common resident over most of the state, less common in the western Panhandle and the Keys. Florida's most widespread diurnal raptor, it is found in swamps and other wooded habitats and is often seen perched on powerlines. The South Florida race of Red-shouldered Hawk is particularly pale and small. Vocal, and difficult to miss.

Broad-winged Hawk—A rather common breeder in the Panhandle and North Florida. Generally rare in migration, but common in fall in the western Panhandle and the Keys. In winter, fairly common in the Keys and rare but regular in the southern peninsula north to St. Petersburg.

Short-tailed Hawk—Generally a rare resident but more common locally. Winters in South Florida, when it is easiest to locate. One or two days in Everglades National Park between November and February should result in a few sightings of the species; small numbers also winter in the Keys. Northward migration begins in February. Breeds sparingly throughout the peninsula, and irregularly west to the eastern Panhandle. Migrants are regular in small numbers in the Keys. The dark morph outnumbers the light morph about 3-1 or 4-1.

Breeding habitat consists of large areas of undisturbed riparian wood-lands and cypress swamps, especially near open habitats. Unlike Red-tailed and Red-shouldered Hawks, Short-tails do not hunt from perches. Rather, they forage while soaring, then dive on their prey, primarily birds. Recent observations suggest that exotic White-winged Doves and Eur-asian Collared-Doves comprise an important part of their winter diet in South Florida. In Key West, a few birds have actually become backyard residents in recent winters.

Swainson's Hawk—A rare to locally common winter resident of the extreme southeast mainland and Keys. Kettles of a few hundred birds are reported occasionally. Irregular elsewhere in winter and during migration.

Crested Caracara—An uncommon resident of the prairies west and north of Lake Okeechobee. According to Jim Layne, the state's popula-tion of this Threatened species seems stable at about 150 pairs, despite extensive loss of habitat in recent years. Sure to be seen if one drives roads in the region long enough. The following roads are among those that are good for finding the species: US-27 (south of SR-70), SR-29, SR-70, SR-74, SR-78, SR-80, SR-84, and CR-721.

Peregrine Falcon—An uncommon to locally common coastal fall migrant, most common along the Atlantic coast and Keys during the first half of October. Generally rare along the coasts in winter and during spring migration, and inland at any season. Peak daily totals recorded at Boot Key have exceeded 100 birds, and 2,000 are thought to pass through the Keys every fall.

Wild Turkey—An uncommon to locally common resident of the peninsula, except absent from the region southeast of Lake Okeechobee. The greatest concentration of turkeys in the state is located from about Orlando south almost to Lake Okeechobee. Prefers areas with a mix of open fields and oak hammocks or swamps. Birds are most active and conspicuous within a few hours after dawn and before dusk.

Northern Bobwhite—An uncommon to common resident of wooded areas throughout, except absent from the Keys. Rare or absent from many developed areas. Usually not too hard to find.

Black Rail—A secretive and little-known resident of scattered areas throughout the peninsula, rare to locally uncommon. Breeds in coastal marshes along the northern Gulf coast, in brackish marshes west and east of Titusville, and possibly in fresh water marshes inland at sites such as Paynes Prairie State Preserve, Lake Woodruff National Wildlife Refuge, and the northern Everglades. Reported in the past at other sites, including

Merritt Island National Wildlife Refuge. Migrates throughout the state, including the Keys. Winters from Central Florida southward.

A survey conducted recently by Doug Runde et al. located presumed breeding birds on the following public lands: St. Vincent National Wildlife Refuge offshore from Apalachicola (no vehicle access), St. Marks National Wildlife Refuge and vicinity (many sites), Big Bend Wildlife Management Area (especially the end of CR-361 south of Steinhatchee), St. Johns National Wildlife Refuge (no public access), and Lake Woodruff National Wildlife Refuge. As many as 20 rails have been heard calling in St. Johns National Wildlife Refuge, where radio-tagged birds currently are being studied by Michael Legare and others.

The species responds well to tape recordings of its calls, *but avoid overuse of the tape*, especially on CR-361. Although Black Rails may respond to tapes during the day, Doug McNair states that the ideal time for searching for the species is on calm nights between midnight and 2 am.

Clapper Rail—A common resident of coastal salt and brackish marshes and mangrove forests throughout. Rarely seen, but vocalizes frequently, often throughout the day.

King Rail—An uncommon resident of fresh water marshes throughout the mainland. Occasional in the Keys during migration. Rarely seen, but vocalizes often, chiefly around dawn and dusk.

Purple Gallinule—A fairly common but local spring and summer resident throughout, though nesting at only a few sites in the Keys. Migrants are found throughout, even in Dry Tortugas National Park, where birds are found regularly in April. Winters locally from Central Florida southward. Found in shallow fresh water wetlands covered with floating vegetation such as water lilies, water lettuce, and water hyacinth. Among literally hundreds of breeding sites statewide are Wakulla Springs State Park, Zellwood, Myakka River State Park, Lake Okeechobee, Belle Glade, and Everglades National Park (especially Shark Valley).

Limpkin—An uncommon to locally common resident of marshes and swamps throughout much of the peninsula. Rare to absent in the western Panhandle and rare in the eastern Panhandle (except in Wakulla Springs State Park, where it is almost sure to be found), the southern Everglades, and the Keys. Extremely vocal, especially at night. In addition to Wakulla Springs, may be found in Freedom Lake Park (St. Petersburg), Saddle Creek Park, Rainey Slough, Corkscrew Swamp Sanctuary, Lake Okeechobee (Swampland Tours boat trip), Loxahatchee National Wildlife Refuge, John Prince Park (Lake Worth), Shark Valley (Everglades National Park), and numerous other sites.

Sandhill Crane—An uncommon to abundant resident of the peninsula, rare in the Panhandle and Everglades, and absent from the Keys
(except for a few Dry Tortugas reports). About 2,000 pairs of the resident
endemic race *Grus canadensis pratensis* breed in the peninsula, most
commonly in Central Florida. About 25,000 birds of the migratory race
G. c. tabida winter in the peninsula, with numbers decreasing southward.
A large population winters in Paynes Prairie State Preserve, with birds
scattered throughout open areas of the peninsula, especially the prairie
region of Highlands and Glades Counties. The species becomes quite
tame in some areas (e.g., eating corn out of human hands) and is not hard
to find in the central peninsula.

Whooping Crane—Formerly an occasional winter visitor (possibly
resident) at a few sites in the peninsula; extirpated for over 50 years. In
1993 biologists from the U.S. Fish and Wildlife Service and the Florida
Game and Fresh Water Fish Commission initiated a project to release into
Central Florida at least 200 birds over the next 10 years. The release sites
are located in Three Lakes Wildlife Management Area in southwestern
Osceola County. These sites are off-limits to the public, but the birds
have begun to make exploratory flights around Central Florida. Cranes
have been observed as far north as Okahumpka (Lake County) and
Zellwood. Steve Nesbitt has noted that—unlike Whooping Cranes elsewhere, which forage primarily in marshes—the birds released into Florida
spend much time foraging in dry fields, a habit shared with Florida
Sandhill Cranes. Birds are released while in juvenal plumage, which is
molted into full adult plumage the following year. The cranes are
color-banded, fitted with radio transmitters, and monitored by aircraft
daily.

It is premature to determine whether this experiment will succeed, but
many released birds have been killed by Bobcats (including 80% of the
first 40 birds released). Birders throughout the central peninsula, especially those in western Osceola County, should be aware of the potential
presence of Whooping Cranes nearby. (Recently, Whooping Cranes
have been observed foraging in marshes around Lake Kissimmee, including 21 birds in late February 1996.)

Shorebirds—As might be expected in a state with over 1,200 miles of
shoreline (750 miles of sandy beaches and 450 miles of salt marshes or
mangrove forests), Florida is a major migratory and wintering area for
shorebirds. Important shorebird staging and wintering areas are Lanark
Reef (no vehicle access), Honeymoon Island State Recreation Area,
McKay Bay, Merritt Island National Wildlife Refuge, Fort Myers Beach,
and Ohio Key, among many others. During fall migration (mid-July to

late October), inland sites such as phosphate-mine impoundments and flooded agricultural fields at Zellwood and Belle Glade can also contain thousands of birds. Holding-ponds at sewage treatment facilities can provide additional habitat for shorebirds, especially at inland sites, where the ponds may be the only available habitat.

Of the 47 species of shorebirds verified in Florida, only 7 breed in the state. Six of the breeding species are included in the following accounts (the widespread Killdeer is excluded). Of the 40 non-breeding species, 33 occur more-or-less annually. The 7 irregularly occurring species are Mountain Plover, Black-tailed Godwit, Hudsonian Godwit, Bar-tailed Godwit, Surfbird, Sharp-tailed Sandpiper, and Curlew Sandpiper.

Some shorebirds are restricted to coastal habitats, but most occur inland as well, especially during migration. Shorebirds not found inland regularly are Snowy, Wilson's, and Piping Plovers, American Oyster-catcher, Whimbrel, Long-billed Curlew, Red Knot, and Sanderling. Migrant species more-or-less restricted to inland (or at least upland) sites are American Golden-Plover, Upland, Pectoral, and Buff-breasted Sandpipers, Long-billed Dowitcher, and Wilson's Phalarope.

In winter, few shorebirds winter inland; exceptions are Killdeer, Black-necked Stilt (local), both yellowlegs, Western and Least Sandpipers, both dowitchers (Short-billed is local), Common Snipe, and American Woodcock. A few individuals of other species (e.g., Spotted Sandpiper) may also be found inland in winter. Except for Long-billed Dowitcher, Common Snipe, American Woodcock, and Red-necked and Red Phalaropes (both pelagic), all of Florida's wintering shorebirds occur along the coast. To observe the largest diversity of wintering shorebirds in the state, visit any of the coastal sites listed above, where one may observe 6 species of plovers, American Oystercatcher, and 13 species of sandpipers (including Whimbrel, Long-billed Curlew, Marbled Godwit, and hundreds of Red Knots).

Snowy Plover—A rare to uncommon, local resident of less-disturbed sandy beaches along the Gulf Coast. Fewer than 200 pairs breed in the state, mostly in the Panhandle. It can usually be found on Santa Rosa Island, the Fort Pickens section of Gulf Islands National Seashore, St. George Island State Park, Honeymoon Island State Recreation Area, Fort De Soto Park, and Fort Myers Beach, among other sites.

Wilson's Plover—An uncommon to locally common resident of coastal areas throughout, rare to uncommon in the western Panhandle, and uncommon on the Atlantic coast. Most birds in the Panhandle and North Florida move south to winter in the southern half of the peninsula.

Found at most sites listed above for the Snowy Plover and other areas such as the Atlantic coast and the Keys.

Piping Plover—An uncommon to locally common winter resident of sandy beaches, chiefly on the Gulf coast. Easiest to find in Honeymoon Island State Recreation Area, where as many as 100 birds winter annually. Also found on St. George Island, Lanark Reef, Fort De Soto Park, Fort Myers Beach, Ohio Key, and at other sites.

American Oystercatcher—An uncommon to locally common coastal resident, most common along the central Gulf coast. Rare in the western Panhandle, the extreme southern mainland, and the Keys. Easy to find in Honeymoon Island State Recreation Area, at Fort Myers Beach, and elsewhere. Lesser numbers are found along the eastern Panhandle and in the Indian River. It is a Species of Special Concern in the state.

Black-necked Stilt—An uncommon to abundant, local spring and summer resident of the peninsula and Keys. Occurs throughout but is more common at inland sites such as flooded agricultural fields and phosphate-mine impoundments. Easy to find at Zellwood and the Belle Glade area. Winters locally at a few sites in the central and southern peninsula. Occurs chiefly as a migrant in the Panhandle (especially the western half), but has recently begun breeding at a few sites in the region.

American Avocet—A very local winter resident of the southern half of the peninsula, but common where it occurs. Flocks that include many dozen to a few hundred birds winter in McKay Bay, Polk County phosphate-mine impoundments, Merritt Island National Wildlife Refuge, and a few other mainland sites. Elsewhere, a very rare to uncommon migrant throughout, reported mostly along the coasts.

Willet—A fairly common resident of coastal marshes and mudflats throughout; locally abundant in winter. Rare but regular inland in fall.

Whimbrel—A rare to fairly common winter resident of coastal areas throughout, usually easy to find at Honeymoon Island State Recreation Area, Merritt Island National Wildlife Refuge, and Fort Myers Beach, among other sites.

Long-billed Curlew—A very rare but regular coastal winter resident, occurring much more frequently along the Gulf coast. A few (1 to 3) birds winter regularly at Fort Myers Beach, and until recently, in Honeymoon Island State Recreation Area.

Marbled Godwit—A local winter resident of the eastern Panhandle and peninsula, more common along the Gulf coast. Irregular in the western Panhandle and Keys and rare inland in fall. Usually easy to find in winter at Lanark Reef, in Honeymoon Island State Recreation Area,

McKay Bay, Merritt Island National Wildlife Refuge, and Everglades National Park (Flamingo).

Red Knot—An uncommon to locally abundant winter resident of sandy beaches. Rare in the western Panhandle and Keys and most common along the central Gulf coast. Found at Lanark Reef, Honeymoon Island State Recreation Area, Fort De Soto County Park, and Fort Myers Beach.

Stilt Sandpiper—An uncommon to locally abundant migrant throughout, especially inland at flooded farmlands (e.g., Zellwood and Belle Glade) and phosphate-mine impoundments. In winter, locally common in the southern half of the peninsula. McKay Bay impoundments and Merritt Island National Wildlife Refuge are two wintering sites.

Long-billed Dowitcher—An uncommon to locally abundant migrant and winter resident of freshwater wetlands throughout, but rare in the western Panhandle and virtually absent from the Keys. It is believed to avoid salt water habitats in Florida.

Short-billed Dowitcher—A common to abundant winter resident along the coasts, this species also occurs inland during migration and in winter. The two species of dowitchers are best identified by voice.

American Woodcock—A rare to uncommon, secretive winter resident throughout the mainland. Breeds in late winter and early spring south to at least north-central Florida, with a few reports in South Florida. Because the species is active from dusk to dawn, it is usually difficult to observe.

Phalaropes—All 3 of the world's phalaropes occur in Florida. Wilson's Phalarope is an irregular spring migrant but rare to uncommon in fall, mostly at flooded farmlands and phosphate-mine impoundments. Try Zellwood and Belle Glade. Red-necked and Red Phalaropes are regular migrants and winter residents offshore, mostly in the Atlantic Ocean. Both species are irregular inland, usually following storms.

Skuas—Casual visitors to offshore waters (about 10 Florida reports, many of them questionable). There is only one record: a South Polar Skua found alive on the beach at Melbourne on 17 June 1993. Other skua reports (1 reported as a Great Skua and others not identified to species) have been reported in the Atlantic (6 reports), off the Keys (3+ reports), and in the Gulf (1 report). Reports range from September-March, with two June reports.

Jaegers—As a group, jaegers are uncommon winter residents and locally abundant fall migrants off both coasts, but large numbers of birds are seen only on the Atlantic coast. Pomarine Jaeger is the most common jaeger in the state; Long-tailed is the rarest. Although many Atlantic coast sites in Florida are good for observing jaegers in fall, the best site is Turtle

Mound, a part of Canaveral National Seashore. From mid-October through November, hundreds (occasionally thousands) of jaegers can be seen from shore (a telescope is helpful), especially on days with strong east or northeast winds.

Gulls—Fifteen species of gulls have been recorded in Florida. Only one of these, Laughing Gull, breeds in the state. All others are winter residents, although individuals of many species remain through the summer. In addition to Laughing Gull, 8 other species occur in Florida annually or nearly so: Franklin's (rare; mostly Gulf coast), Bonaparte's, Ring-billed, Herring, Lesser Black-backed (generally rare but increasing), Glaucous (rare; mostly Atlantic coast), and Great Black-backed Gulls and Black-legged Kittiwake (mostly pelagic). Irregular stragglers to Florida are Little, Black-headed, Band-tailed, Thayer's, Iceland, and Sabine's Gulls. Most species are limited to coastal areas, but 4 species (Laughing, Bonaparte's, Ring-billed, and Herring [rare] Gulls) also occur inland at dairies, flooded farm fields, large lakes, and landfills.

Laughing Gull—A common to abundant permanent coastal resident, locally common inland (non-breeding). One of the most common larids in Florida.

Band-tailed Gull (*Larus belcheri*)—One captured in the late 1960s in Pensacola; a few reports (mostly winter) from Marco Island in the 1970s. This is a species of coastal South America, and these birds' origins are uncertain.

Lesser Black-backed Gull—A rare to locally uncommon, increasing winter resident of coastal areas almost throughout, with a few inland reports. Most common at landfills. Huguenot Park (Jacksonville) and the area around the Pompano landfill have attracted the largest numbers of Lesser Black-backed Gulls in the state: over 20 birds on a few occasions.

Great Black-backed Gull—An uncommon to common winter resident of the Atlantic coast from about Merritt Island northward, generally rare farther south and on the Gulf coast. Summer reports are increasing.

Terns—Fourteen species of terns have been recorded in Florida. Of these, only the Arctic Tern is not found annually. Eight of the regular species breed regularly in the state: Gull-billed, Caspian, Royal, Sandwich, Roseate, Least, Bridled, and Sooty Terns and Brown Noddy. Common Tern has bred occasionally in Florida. Except for Least Tern, all breeding species have extremely limited ranges. Caspian and Sandwich Terns breed only at the mouth of Tampa Bay, Roseate and Bridled (rare) Terns breed only in the Lower Keys, and Sooty Terns and Brown Noddies breed only on Bush Key in Dry Tortugas National Park. One or more Black Noddies should be present at the Tortugas in spring and summer (non-breeding). Outside the breeding season, Common Terns are uncommon to locally abundant along the coasts during migration and are rare in winter, Black Terns are uncommon to common throughout, Forster's Terns are common along the coasts and uncommon inland, Royal and Sandwich Terns increase along the coasts and are rare inland, and Caspian Terns occur throughout, but are more common coastally.

Gull-billed Tern—A rare to uncommon, local spring and summer resident at a few coastal and inland sites in the peninsula; many sites are ephemeral. Breeds in the Panhandle only in the Apalachicola area. Winters in the extreme southern mainland; look for it in Everglades National Park (Snake Bight and Flamingo).

Roseate Tern—An uncommon to fairly common spring and summer resident of the Lower Keys, numbering about 300 to 350 breeding pairs. Rare elsewhere offshore and coastally. Can usually be found in spring and summer resting on beaches, buoys, and channel markers in Dry Tortugas National Park, and on channel markers at Fort Zachary Taylor State Park in Key West. Seen on most spring and summer pelagic trips in the Lower Keys.

Least Tern—An uncommon to common spring and summer resident of coastal areas throughout. A local breeder inland around Tallahassee, Orlando, and the Polk County phosphate-mining district; elsewhere generally rare inland. Many Florida colonies have moved to gravel rooftops as beach nesting sites are used increasingly by humans. Although reported often in winter (especially on Christmas Bird Counts), the species is unverified in Florida from mid-October to mid-March. *In winter plumage, the bills of Least Terns are blackish, not yellow with a black tip as in breeding plumage.*

Bridled Tern—An uncommon to common visitor offshore. Most numerous in the Gulf Stream off the southeast coast and Keys, especially from April to October. Less common elsewhere and rare in winter. Seen on most spring boat trips between Key West and Dry Tortugas National Park. Since 1987, a very rare breeder (1 to 3 pairs) on Pelican Shoal near Key West, its first North American breeding site.

Sooty Tern—An abundant spring and summer resident on Bush Key in Dry Tortugas National Park, numbering 25,000 to 40,000 breeding pairs. Elsewhere, a rare summer visitor off both coasts. Occasionally inland, especially after storms.

Brown Noddy—An abundant spring and summer resident on Bush Key, numbering about 2,000 pairs. Rare elsewhere in summer off both coasts and occasional inland after storms.

Black Noddy—A very rare but regular non-breeding spring and summer resident at the Tortugas, numbering 1 to 3 birds almost annually. Otherwise unreported in the state or in North America!

Black Skimmer—An uncommon to abundant resident of coastal areas nearly throughout, but in the Keys solely a winter resident. Usually withdraws from the Panhandle in winter. Also occurs inland, at times abundantly (occasionally breeding), at phosphate-mine impoundments, flooded agricultural fields, and large lakes.

Long-billed Murrelet—Unknown in the state until 27 December 1986, when a freshly dead specimen was found at Honeymoon Island State Recreation Area. Another was found dead in Fort De Soto County Park 4 December 1993, and a live bird was observed at Cedar Key 16-28 March 1994. Florida's fourth record was established 28 November 1994, when a bird was captured off St. Petersburg. This species is not illustrated in any North American field guide, but is identified from the Marbled Murrelet by the proportionately longer bill and more extensive white eye crescents. Apparently, all "Marbled Murrelets" recorded in North America away from the Pacific coast are Long-billed Murrelets. Although the species must be regarded as casual or accidental in Florida, finding 4 records along the Gulf coast in the past 9 years (with 3 of these occurring in less than 12 months!) is astonishing.

White-crowned Pigeon—A common to abundant spring and summer resident of the Keys and extreme southern mainland, numbering about 5,000 pairs. Usually easy to find along US-1 in the Keys and along the main road through Everglades National Park. Many birds winter in the Bahamas and Cuba, when the species is uncommon and may be difficult to locate in Florida. Feeds on *Ficus* (fig), Poisonwood, and other tropical fruiting trees. According to Allan Strong and Tom Bancroft, continued destruction of tropical hardwood hammocks on the mainline Keys threatened its survival in the U.S. (Fortunately, the state is purchasing nearly all remaining tropical hammocks in the Keys.)

Ringed Turtle-Dove—Exotic, believed to be a long-domesticated form of the African Collared-Dove (*Streptopelia roseogrisea*). A population that numbers in the low hundreds of birds is easy to find in one St. Petersburg neighborhood, where the species was first noted as a few pairs in 1953. Ringed Turtle-Doves are the white doves used by magicians, and those released during weddings and other events, so birds may be found anywhere because of local escapes or releases. However, many reports of Ringed Turtle-Doves outside St. Petersburg are misidentified Eurasian Collared-Doves. *Ignore erroneous accounts which state that Ringed Turtle-Doves are established in Tampa and Miami.* In 1994 this species was delisted by the AOU and ABA and is no longer officially countable in North America.

European Turtle-Dove (*Streptopelia turtur*)—One was on Lower Matecumbe Key 9 to 11 April 1990. Although a flight across the Atlantic is certainly possible, the ABA Checklist Committee has treated this as a species of uncertain origin.

Eurasian Collared-Dove—Exotic, native to India, Asia Minor, and the Balkans, but colonized much of central and western Europe in the 20th century. A few birds escaped from captivity in the Bahamas in 1974 and soon colonized the southeast Florida coast and Keys. Its numbers and range increased at a stunning pace: in 1991 Bill Smith estimated the population in Dade and Monroe counties at 100,000 birds! The species continues to increase and spread and appears to be colonizing all of Florida: as of January 1996, it has been reported from 43 of the state's 67 counties. *The presence of this species anywhere in Florida should not be considered surprising.*

Still somewhat local in many areas (especially outside South Florida), but the population is expected to continue to increase in range and numbers. It tends to colonize coastal areas first, then establishes small outposts elsewhere, and finally fills in unoccupied areas in between.

Because *Streptopelia* doves are covered insufficiently in North American field guides, comments here should allow the birder to distinguish these two species. Ringed Turtle-Doves may be seen in a variety of plumages because they are cage birds that are often cross-bred. Those in St. Petersburg are seen in at least three plumage types. The least common plumage is an albino, with pure white plumage and pink bill, eyes, and legs. "Pied" birds have a somewhat random, mottled appearance of white and tawny feathers on the back and wings. Most birds in St. Petersburg are very pale to whitish, with slightly darker primaries. A black crescent is present on the back of the neck on all Ringed Turtle-Doves except some that are all white.

Eurasian Collared-Doves are chunkier and a bit larger than the slimmer, smaller Ringed Turtle-Doves. (Collared-Doves resemble White-winged Doves in body shape, while Turtle-Doves look like Mourning Doves). Collared-Doves are also darker in plumage, almost as brownish-gray as Mourning Doves, with blackish primaries, and a very conspicuous white border around the black collar. Eurasian Collared-Doves have dark gray undertail coverts, while those of Ringed Turtle-Doves are white. Eurasian Collared-Doves also have a peculiar habit of perching on the *tops* of telephone poles in addition to perching on wires. Vocalizations between the 2 birds are distinctive. Eurasian Collared-

Doves sing a flat, monotonous trisyllabic *coo-COO-coo*, often repeated for long periods, and have a cat-like *mew* call, usually given in flight. Ringed Turtle-Doves have a rolling, varied song similar to *coo-ca-ROOOOOO-aw*, and give a *heh-heh-heh* call, usually while perched. Songs of both species are included on the cassette tape *Voices of the New World Pigeons and Doves* by Hardy et al. (Bill Smith wrote an excellent article in *American Birds*, on separating the *Streptopelia* doves, with many color photographs of both species.)

Assume that all Streptopelia *doves observed in Florida outside central St. Petersburg are Eurasian Collared-Doves, unless all field-marks of Ringed Turtle-Doves are noted.* Ringed Turtle-Doves may be found anywhere in the state because of local escapes, but the only population of any size is in St. Petersburg.

Scaly-naped Pigeon—An accidental visitor, probably from Cuba. There are only 2 Florida (and North American) records, both from Key West: 24 October 1898 and 6 May 1929. (Bond calls this species Red-necked Pigeon.) It is a large dark-gray pigeon with a reddish-purple nape and breast, and red eyes, orbital rings, and feet. Dark "scaling" on the nape gives it its name.

White-winged Dove—A rare to uncommon migrant and winter resident along the entire Gulf coast from western-breeding birds that move eastward to winter in the peninsula. A separate, breeding population of White-winged Doves was first noted in Homestead in the 1950s and has increased in numbers and range steadily since then. Birds now occupy residential areas along the Atlantic coast north to the Vero Beach area. The origin of these birds is debated. Many claim that birds from Mexico were intentionally released from private collections. However, the birds appear to more closely resemble West Indian forms, so natural colonization from the Bahamas or elsewhere is also possible. Recent observations of White-winged Doves in the Keys, especially Dry Tortugas National Park, may support the theory of natural colonization from the West Indies. Whatever the origin of the Homestead birds, the Florida Game and Fresh Water Fish Commission released some of these birds into the citrus belt of Central Florida in the 1970s (to provide hunters with another avian target), and this population has also expanded into residential areas. The species is now locally abundant in areas of Polk and Highlands Counties, and some birds are found as far north as Apopka.

Zenaida Dove—An accidental visitor from the West Indies to the Keys, with only two verified Florida records during this century: Plantation Key (2 birds December 1962 to March 1963) and Key Largo (June 1988). For a recent summary see Bill and Susan Smith's report of the 1988 bird in

Florida Field Naturalist. Reportedly a common breeder on a few of the Keys in Audubon's time. (ID hint: This species appears very chunky due to its short tail. You don't think of a Mourning Dove when you see a Zenaida Dove, despite the similarities in plumage.)

Common Ground-Dove—An uncommon to fairly common resident throughout. Prefers open habitats such as fields, pastures, pine flatwoods, sandhills, and coastal dunes. Declining almost throughout its North American range and becoming hard to find in many areas of Florida.

Key West Quail-Dove—An occasional visitor from the West Indies to the southeast coast and Keys, with about 15 reports in the past century. Recent accepted reports have come from Boot Key (March to June 1987), Key Largo (June 1990), Bill Baggs/Cape Florida State Recreation Area (October 1991), Hugh Taylor Birch State Recreation Area (April to May 1992), Palm Beach County (2 reports in April and May 1992), and Big Pine Key (October 1994). Reportedly bred on Key West in Audubon's time.

Ruddy Quail-Dove—An accidental visitor from the West Indies to the Keys, with only 3 verified records this century: Key West (May 1923), and Dry Tortugas National Park (spring 1962 and December 1977). Another was reported at the Dry Tortugas 18 September 1995.

Psittacids—As of March 1996, 68 species of exotic parrots have been reported in the wild in Florida, but only 3 of these are considered by the AOU and ABA to be established. Two of the 3 established species have declined significantly in range and numbers in the past 15 years, while the other continues to increase. Of the remaining 65 species, most are represented by only a few reports which represent local escapes that briefly existed in the wild. Because all psittacids originate from birds that accidentally escape or are intentionally released, *virtually any of the world's species may be encountered in Florida, as well as natural and captive-bred hybrids that may be impossible to identify conclusively.* Most have been reported in the Miami area (62 of the state's 68 species!), but many other cities in the state have recently reported breeding parrots (besides the 3 established species), including St. Augustine, Cedar Key, Crystal River, Clearwater, St. Petersburg, Tampa, Bradenton, Sarasota, Orlando, Naples, Fort Lauderdale, and Marathon.

Because so few species are illustrated in North American field guides, two books will help the birder greatly in identifying Florida's psittacids. *Parrots of the World* by Joseph Forshaw includes a superb color painting by William T. Cooper of every species in the world, but it is large, heavy, and expensive. A much less comprehensive but far more manageable source is *Simon and Schuster's Guide to Pet Birds* by Matthew Vriends, a small paperback book ($14) that contains a color photograph of 206 species of cage birds, including 98 psittacids.

The following accounts include the 3 species considered established, plus another 6 that seem to be increasing in range and numbers, and that may in the future be considered to have become established.

Budgerigar—An established exotic, native to Australia. From the early 1960s to the late 1970s, it was an abundant resident of residential areas within a mile or two of the Gulf coast from southwestern Hernando County south to Sarasota County. In 1978, one roost in Pasco County contained 6,000 to 8,000 birds! By the mid-1980s, the population had declined severely, possibly due to increasing competition with European Starlings over nesting cavities. (The increase of the European Starling as a widespread breeding bird in Central Florida corresponds rather well with the decline of the Budgerigar). By December 1995, Budgies were essentially extirpated from Pinellas County (Clearwater, St. Petersburg, and the barrier islands) and areas to the south (Bradenton and Sarasota). Perhaps 100 or fewer birds can still be found in southwest Hernando County (Hernando Beach) and northwest Pasco County (Hudson to Port Richey). Local escapes may be found anywhere. The natural color morph of Budgies is yellowish-green, but aviculturists have created white, blue, and yellow varieties, and a few of these artificial color morphs can be seen in the wild.

Rose-ringed Parakeet—An unestablished exotic, native to Africa and Asia. Although present in the Miami area since at least the 1930s, according to Wes Biggs, the population there remains small. Other tiny to small populations are (or were) located in St. Augustine, Cedar Key, Crystal River, and Clearwater. John Douglas believes that the rather sizable population in the Naples area is currently declining. Illustrated in the National Geographic guide, but note that the species is extremely similar to other *Psittacula* parakeets.

Monk Parakeet—An established exotic, native to southern South America. A locally abundant resident, mainly of urban areas in many cities of the peninsula. The largest numbers are located in the Greater Tampa Bay area and from Fort Lauderdale to Miami. Over 500 birds were counted on the 1992, 1994, and 1995 St. Petersburg Christmas Bird Counts; hundreds have also been reported on recent CBCs in Fort Lauderdale and Miami. Breeds communally in large stick nests built in trees, on power poles, electrical substations, and other structures. (All other psittacids nest in cavities.) A popular cage bird, it may be found anywhere, and range expansion into new areas is likely.

Black-hooded Parakeet (*Nandayus nenday*)—An unestablished (?) exotic, native to South America. Reported from many widely scattered areas (St. Augustine, Bradenton, Sarasota, West Palm Beach), but most numerous (and possibly established) in the St. Petersburg area. On the 1992 St. Petersburg CBC, 100 birds were counted, and 117 were seen on the 1994 Count. (Photographed in Vriends, but not illustrated in National Geographic.) As its name suggests, the front portion of the head is blackish. A pale blue patch is present on the breast, and the feathers on the "thighs" are bright red. Easy to identify if seen well.

Blue-crowned Parakeet (*Aratinga acuticauda*)—An unestablished exotic, native to South America. Since the late 1980s, flocks of 20 or more birds have been reported from St. Petersburg, Key Biscayne, Key Largo, Islamorada, and Marathon. (Photographed in Vriends but not illustrated in National Geographic.) The species is green overall, with a yellowish bill and a bluish tint to the face and crown, offset by a large white orbital-ring.

Red-masked Parakeet (*Aratinga erythrogenys*)—An unestablished exotic, native to South America. Numerous in the Miami area, with local escapes reported from Winter Park (Orlando area) and St. Petersburg. (Photographed in Vriends but not illustrated in National Geographic.) It is a green parakeet with red on the crown and the front of the face (red surrounds the eyes), on the leading edge of the folded wing, and on the "thighs." Compare carefully with the Mitred Parakeet, below.

Mitred Parakeet (*Aratinga mitrata*)—An unestablished exotic, native to South America. Reported recently from St. Augustine, Sarasota, Miami, Key Largo, and Key West. (Not listed in Vriends or National Geographic; consult Forshaw.) A green parakeet with red on the forehead and front of the face (but usually not surrounding the eyes) and scattered red feathers on the head, breast, and belly. Unlike Red-masked Parakeet, it lacks the red trailing edges to the wings.

Canary-winged ("White-winged") Parakeet (*Brotogeris versicolurus*)—An established exotic native to South America. It is currently known as Canary-winged Parakeet, but its common name might change as a result of the 1997 split of this species by AOU. Noted first in Miami in the 1960s, its range increased along the Atlantic coast north to West Palm Beach. By 1972, the Miami population alone was estimated at 1,500 to 2,000 birds. All Florida specimens from the 1970s are of this species, which is pictured in most North American field guides. By the 1980s, this species had declined substantially, but still occur in numbers in Dade County and possibly elsewhere.

Yellow-chevroned Parakeet (*Brotogeris chiriri*)—Formerly considered a race of the Canary-winged ("White-winged") Parakeet, but elevated to a species by the AOU in 1997. Native to South America, it was first noted in Florida in the Miami area in the late 1980s and remains limited to Dade County. It has not been documented to breed in the wild in Florida, and its establishment is undetermined. The distribution of both species overlaps in Dade County, although many areas are dominated by one or the other species, while other areas seem to have both species in fairly equal numbers. This reprinted edition distinguishes between Canary-winged ("White-winged") and Yellow-chevroned Parakeets in Florida.

Yellow-chevroned Parakeets are similar to Canary-wingeds ("White-wingeds"), but lack the large white wing patch, showing instead only the yellow patch on the secondary coverts. Photographed in Vriends and Smith and Smith, but not illustrated in Scott. See Smith and Smith for a thorough summary of the occurrence of the Canary-winged ("White-winged") and Yellow-chevroned Parakeets in Florida.

Red-crowned Parrot—An unestablished (?) exotic, native to Brazil. In the 1970s and 1980s, it was a rather common resident of the Fort Lauderdale and Miami areas. Presently, it is rare in Miami but still occurs in numbers in Fort Lauderdale. Recent numbers on the Fort Lauderdale CBC were 100 (1990), 45 (1991), 6 (1992), 80 (1993), and 24 (1994). Stevenson and Anderson consider the species to be established in the Fort Lauderdale area.

Mangrove Cuckoo—A rare to uncommon, *inconspicuous* coastal resident of mangrove and tropical hardwood forests of the southern mainland and Keys. Reported regularly north along the Gulf coast to St. Petersburg and to Miami on the Atlantic coast (but may stray north as far as the Vero Beach area). It is either less common or simply harder to find in winter. Responds well at certain times of the year to recorded Mangrove Cuckoo calls, *but the use of tapes from April to July (especially on the mainline Keys) is strongly discouraged, given the bird's extremely limited range and the potential negative effects of using tapes on the same few nesting individuals.* The use of tapes is prohibited altogether in J. N. "Ding" Darling National Wildlife Refuge, Everglades National Park, and Key Deer National Wildlife Refuge.

Smooth-billed Ani—Up to the late 1970s, a locally common and widespread resident of brushy areas of the southern third of the peninsula, less common north to Central Florida. It declined sharply in range and numbers by the mid-1980s and is now limited largely to southeastern Florida and scattered sites in the Keys. Loxahatchee National Wildlife Refuge may be the most reliable accessible site in the state, but anis still occur also in other water conservation areas, the sugar cane region southwest, south, and southeast of Lake Okeechobee, Everglades National Park (especially Eco Pond), and elsewhere. Responds well to recorded Smooth-billed Ani calls.

Groove-billed Ani—A rare but regular coastal winter resident of the Panhandle, especially the western half. Elsewhere, an irregular winter visitor, usually near the coast. Has occurred as far south as Everglades National Park.

Barn Owl—A rare to uncommon resident of open habitats throughout, but, according to Wayne Hoffman, decreasing in the Keys apparently because of collisions with vehicles. More common in winter with the influx of northern-breeding birds, when the species may be locally common in the southern peninsula. Strictly nocturnal, it is easiest to see by driving farm roads after dark and watching for the birds perched on powerlines and poles. The species is sometimes rather easy to see in winter along the main road through Everglades National Park.

Burrowing Owl—An uncommon to locally very common resident of the peninsula and Keys. The state's population was estimated recently by Elizabeth Haug et al. at 3,000 to 10,000 birds. Burrowing Owls have significantly expanded their range in Florida this century, coincident with widespread clearing of forests and draining of wetlands by humans. Many small populations are ephemeral. Reliable sites include Cape Coral west of Fort Myers, near Lorida northeast of Lake Istokpoga, many small sites in Palm Beach County, Fort Lauderdale Executive Airport, Miami International Airport, and a few sites near Marathon. In 1993 a population was discovered in the western Panhandle which may consist of birds from the western U.S.

Barred Owl—A fairly common resident of riparian forests, oak and palm hammocks, bayheads, and swamps throughout, except generally absent from the Keys. Responds well to tape recordings and imitations of its *Who-cooks-for-you, who-cooks-for-you-all* call. Because it is active during the day and becomes acclimated to humans, it can often be seen in Highlands Hammock State Park, Corkscrew Swamp Sanctuary, Everglades National Park (especially Mahogany Hammock), and other similar areas. Usually fairly easy to locate with a tape, but the use of tapes is forbidden in Corkscrew Swamp Sanctuary and Everglades National Park.

Short-eared Owl—A rare to uncommon, *unpredictable* winter resident of open areas of the Panhandle and northern half of the peninsula, irregular farther south. Since 1990 spring and summer observations on the Keys (especially Key West and the Dry Tortugas) are apparently dispersers from expanding West Indian populations. Compared with birds from North America, those from the West Indies are somewhat smaller, have less streaking on the belly, and are buffier below. The taxonomy of the West Indian races is being studied; these birds may be good candidates to be split into one or more species in the future.

Antillean Nighthawk—An uncommon spring and summer resident almost exclusive to the Lower Keys, but it may occur north to Homestead and Florida City. First noted in the state in 1941. There is evidence that it is now declining in Florida. From late April to August, it should be found near the Key West airport, near the junior college on Stock Island, on Big Pine Key, near the Marathon airport, and in other open areas in the Lower Keys. Occurs during spring migration in Dry Tortugas National Park. Although slightly smaller and buffier than the Common Nighthawk (difficult to see at dawn and dusk), it is best identified by its one- to four-note *pit* calls, usually written as *killy-ka-dick* or *pitty-pit-pit*, but frequently bearing no resemblance to these "translations." Note, however, that Common Nighthawks may also utter a two-note call that sounds like *crick-et* or *pip-et*.

Lesser Nighthawk—A rare migrant predominately along the Gulf coast and an irregular winter resident in Everglades National Park (and probably elsewhere in South Florida). Of the 25 reports through the fall of 1995, 16 were in spring (14 April to 17 May), 4 in fall (23 October to 14 November), and 5 in winter (26 November to 16 March). Most of the winter reports and a few others represent multiple birds (2 to 12), so the species may migrate and winter in small flocks. *No nighthawk has been verified to winter in Florida, so any nighthawk observed in the state from December through February should be photographed (and tape-recorded if it is vocalizing).*

Chuck-will's-widow—A fairly common to common spring and summer resident nearly throughout, but it does not breed on the Keys. Due to its crepuscular habits, it is much more likely to be heard than seen. Winters in small numbers in the southern third of the peninsula and the Keys. Elsewhere, it arrives from late February to mid-March and usually ceases singing in June or July. Its song, delivered at night, is characteristic of Florida's oak and pine woodlands.

Antillean Palm Swift—An accidental visitor from the West Indies (probably Cuba) to the Keys. There is only one verified North American record: 2 birds at Key West 7 July to 17 August 1972. The species is illustrated in color in Peterson, as a black-and-white sketch in Bond's *Birds of the West Indies*, photographed distantly in Downer and Sutton's *Birds of Jamaica*, but not included in National Geographic. It is black above and white below, with a white rump and a conspicuous black breast band. In size, it is smaller than a Chimney Swift.

Vaux's Swift—A rare and local winter resident of North Florida, reported thus far only from Apalachicola, Tallahassee, and Gainesville, but unidentified *Chaetura* swifts have been reported elsewhere. Very few of the Florida reports have been verified; specimens or audio recordings of its calls are mandatory. *Any small grayish-brown swift observed in Florida from mid-November through the end of February should be studied carefully and reported to other observers, because Chimney Swifts are not known to occur in the state in winter.*

Cuban Emerald—Apparently a casual visitor from the Bahamas or Cuba to the southern half of the peninsula and the Keys, but verifiable evidence that supports its occurrence in the state (and in the country) does not exist. There are about 14 reports, from all months except December and February, but many of these are probably erroneous. *Any hummingbird potentially of this species in Florida should be photographed and/or videotaped.*

Bahama Woodstar—A casual visitor from the Bahamas to the southeast coast, with only 4 accepted Florida reports, all in the past 35 years. Three of the birds remained for many weeks after their initial discoveries. All sightings so far have been of females or immature males. Reported in Miami (January 1961); Lantana, Palm Beach County (August to October 1971); and Homestead (April to June 1974 and July to August 1981).

Black-chinned Hummingbird—A rare to locally uncommon winter resident throughout, especially in the Panhandle. Apparently more likely to occur in winter from Central Florida northward than is the Ruby-throated Hummingbird, but most observers are not familiar with the subtle field marks that distinguish the two species. Ruby-throated Hummingbirds are uncommon winter residents in South Florida and the Keys, but reports from elsewhere should be closely examined. Females and some immature males of the two species are virtually identical in plumage; Black-chinned Hummingbirds seem to have a behavioral trait that helps to distinguish them from Ruby-throated Hummingbirds. When hovering, Black-chins seem to bob their tails almost continuously. By contrast, Ruby-throats and other similar species will flick their tails only occasionally. According to Kenn Kaufman (in *A Field Guide to Advanced Birding*), the possibility that the two species can be separated by this behavioral trait "merits further study."

Rufous Hummingbird—A rare to uncommon fall migrant and winter resident throughout, except unreported from the Keys. Because most plumages are indistinguishable in the field from Allen's Hummingbird, *Selasphorus* hummingbirds in Florida should be closely scrutinized and preferably captured for banding to identify them specifically. There have been 3 or 4 male *Selasphorus* hummingbirds in Florida with all-green backs suspected of being Allen's Hummingbirds, but documentation was lacking or inconclusive.

Red-headed Woodpecker—An uncommon to fairly common resident nearly throughout, but an irregular visitor to the extreme southern peninsula and the Keys. Prefers open pinelands, sandhills, and oak woodlands. Withdraws in winter from some areas in northern Florida and may be irruptive elsewhere, with numbers varying considerably from year to year.

Red-bellied Woodpecker—A very common resident throughout, less common in the Keys. The most common and widespread woodpecker in Florida, it is virtually impossible to miss.

Hairy Woodpecker—A rare to locally uncommon resident almost throughout, but virtually extirpated from South Florida and absent from the Keys. The most difficult to find of Florida's woodpeckers, it is attracted to, and possibly dependent upon, recently burned areas and other sites with many dead and dying trees (especially pines). Avon Park Air Force Range and Archbold Biological Station are two reliable sites in south-central Florida.

Red-cockaded Woodpecker—An uncommon but very local resident of mature open pinewoods of the Panhandle and northern half of the peninsula, rare south to Big Cypress National Preserve. In their 1983 statewide study of the species, Don Wood and Anne Wenner listed 1,139 clusters in Florida, but additional clusters have been located subsequently. RCW sites in this guide include three national forests (Apalachicola, Ocala, and Osceola), three state forests (Blackwater, Goethe, and Withlacoochee), two air force bases (Avon Park and Eglin), two wildlife management areas (Three Lakes and Babcock-Webb), Venus Flatwoods Preserve, and Big Cypress National Preserve, among others.

Red-cockaded Woodpeckers are dependent upon mature (60 years old) Longleaf or Slash Pines for cavity excavation. With few exceptions, the birds laboriously excavate a cavity into a living pine infected with Red-heart, a fungal disease that rots the heartwood. The birds drill resin wells around the cavity entrance, which causes sap to flow down the trunk. These coatings of resin are believed to repel tree-climbing snakes. The resin also allows active cavity trees to be distinguished easily; sap on inactive trees ceases to flow and turns grayish. Most Red-cockaded Woodpecker cavities face in a westerly direction, probably because the afternoon sun is hotter than the morning sun and would cause more sap to flow.

Most cavity trees on protected lands are painted with a band of paint (often white) 4 to 5 feet above the ground. Active cavity trees should be watched from a non-obtrusive distance (remember that the species is

Federally Endangered) 1 to 1½ hours before dusk. Red-cockaded Wood-peckers are vocal when foraging and when flying in to roost. Their call is a somewhat squeaky single note, quite unlike that of any other woodpecker in the state.

Pileated Woodpecker—A fairly common resident nearly throughout, but absent from the Keys (except rare on Key Largo). Vocal, especially in late winter, and usually not hard to find.

***Empidonax* flycatchers**—All 5 species of eastern-breeding *Empidonax* flycatchers are believed to have occurred in Florida. Except for many Acadian Flycatchers, most empids in Florida are silent and may be impossible to identify conclusively. Acadian Flycatcher is a fairly com-mon spring and summer resident of swamps and riparian forests south to the central peninsula. During migration it is uncommon throughout. Yellow-bellied Flycatcher is a rare migrant throughout. Alder and Willow Flycatchers are probably regular fall migrants, but separating the two species during migration is usually impossible. (Even most specimens can be identified only as "Traill's Flycatchers".) Least Flycatcher is a rare to uncommon migrant and a rare to locally uncommon winter resident of South Florida, irregular farther north.

Cuban Pewee (*Contopus caribaeus*)—A casual or accidental straggler from the Bahamas or Cuba to South Florida, represented by 3 reports. The first was a bird observed on Hypoluxo Island in Palm Beach County on 2 October 1984. Although the bird was photographed, it never vocalized and was not verified. In March 1995, a calling Cuban Pewee was videotaped in Spanish River Park, also in Palm Beach County. The bird remained about a month and was observed by hundreds of birders from throughout North America and elsewhere. A third bird was ob-served at Dry Tortugas National Park on 20 May 1996.

Until recently, Cuban Pewee was one of three races of the Greater Antillean Pewee, but was elevated to a species by the AOU in 1995. (The other species—Jamaican Pewee and Hispaniolan Pewee—are not likely to stray to Florida.) Cuban Pewee is best distinguished by its rapid *see-see-see-see* calls; the Spanish River Park bird called incessantly. The Tortugas bird never vocalized, but was described as being "extremely brown" in plumage and had a "half eye-ring."

Cuban Pewee is not illustrated in any North American field guide, but a Greater Antillean Pewee is illustrated in Bond, and a Jamaican Pewee is photographed in Downer and Sutton. Cuban Pewees are very similar to other small flycatchers, but the birds have a small light spot behind the eye. Vocalizations are probably essential for conclusive identification. See identification hints by Kaufman.

Ash-throated Flycatcher—An occasional fall and winter visitor (about 20 reports) from the western U.S. Reported most often from the Panhandle, but has occurred nearly throughout (no Keys reports, though).

Great Crested Flycatcher—A common spring and summer resident throughout. Uncommon in winter in South Florida and the Keys, increasing north to the Tampa Bay area and irregular farther north. *Because Ash-throated, Brown-crested, and La Sagra's Flycatchers also occur in Florida, all Myiarchus flycatchers observed in winter should be closely examined, especially those from the Tampa Bay area northward.*

Brown-crested Flycatcher—An occasional winter resident (about 40 reports) of South Florida and the Keys, with migrants reported elsewhere.

La Sagra's Flycatcher (*Myiarchus sagrae*)—A rare but increasingly-found species from Cuba or the Bahamas, first recorded in 1982. There are now about 15 accepted reports, from the Dry Tortugas northward along the Atlantic Coast to Palm Beach County. The most recent reports were from Fort Lauderdale (November 1994 to January 1995), Miami (April 1995), and Spanish River Park (May 1995). There are two seasonal peaks when the species is reported reliably in Florida: December-January and April-May.

This is one of the few vagrants to Florida which is not illustrated in any standard North American field guide. La Sagra's Flycatcher was formerly considered a race of another West Indian *Myiarchus*, Stolid Flycatcher (*M. stolidus*). The Bahamian race of *M. stolidus* is illustrated in Bond. It is this bird that is now recognized as a separate species, La Sagra's Flycatcher. Compared with a Great Crested Flycatcher, *M. sagrae* is smaller, mostly white below and dull brown above, with an all-black bill. Some primaries and tail feathers may have a rusty tinge, but it is not conspicuous. Yellow on the underparts is highly restricted or lacking entirely. Its voice is similar to the *wheep!* of a Great Crested Flycatcher, but it is higher in pitch, lacks the burry quality, and is not as loud. See Robertson and Biggs (from *American Birds* in 1983) and Smith and Evered (from *Birding* in 1992) for more information, including many color photographs in the latter article.

Tropical and **Couch's Kingbirds**—Occasional migrants and winter residents throughout, with about 20 reports. Both species have been reported in Florida, but only Couch's Kingbird has been verified in the state (one specimen from Palm Beach County in March 1996). Based on call notes or bill size, most of the few reports identified to species have been Couch's Kingbirds, but 2 reports were identified as Tropical Kingbirds, including one report by Dennis Paulson that was convincingly detailed. Reports have occurred from September to May. *Call notes of birds observed in Florida should be tape-recorded.*

Cassin's Kingbird—A casual migrant and winter resident from the western U.S., represented by 5 reports: Fort De Soto County Park (October 1984), Loxahatchee National Wildlife Refuge (December 1988 to May 1989), Homestead/Florida City (March to April 1992 and winter 1995-1996), and Fort Walton Beach (May 1992).

Western Kingbird—A rare to uncommon winter resident from Central Florida southward, irregular farther north. Migrants occur along the entire coastline, especially in fall. *Tropical, Couch's, and Cassin's Kingbirds may also be present in Florida in winter, so be careful when identifying yellow-bellied kingbirds.*

Gray Kingbird—An uncommon to locally very common spring and summer resident along the coast, but local in the Panhandle and northeast Florida. Not hard to find from April to September, especially in the Keys. Occurs inland south of Lake Okeechobee, including as a breeder in suburban areas from West Palm Beach to Homestead, and throughout Everglades National Park. Common also at Fort De Soto County Park, J.N. "Ding" Darling National Wildlife Refuge, and elsewhere. In the Panhandle, it is found most reliably at Alligator Point, but a few pairs breed as far west as Fort Pickens.

Loggerhead Kingbird—A casual visitor probably from Cuba to the southeast coast and Keys. Only 4 verified Florida records exist, from Islamorada (December 1971 to January 1972, winter 1972-1973, and November to December 1976) and Miami (March 1976).

Scissor-tailed Flycatcher—Status mirrors that of the Western Kingbird. Winters most regularly in South Florida and the Keys, but locally uncommon north to about Ruskin. Migrants occur widely, but most are seen along the Gulf coast. Reported in Florida in every month, but most common from September to April.

Cuban Martin—A casual or accidental visitor from Cuba and the Isle of Pines to the southern half of the peninsula. There are only 3 Florida (and North American) records: Cape Florida (18 May 1858), Clearwater (no date, but in the latter 1800s), and Key West (9 May 1895).

Southern Martin—An accidental visitor from southern South America. There is only 1 North American record: 1 female collected at Key West 14 August 1890, but not identified correctly until 1963.

Bahama Swallow—A casual visitor from the Bahamas to South Florida and especially the Keys. From 1988 to 1992, an adult spent five consecutive breeding seasons at a Cave Swallow colony in the Homestead area, until it became a traffic casualty in April 1992. Except for two reports in winter, Bahama Swallows have been reported in Florida from March to mid-August. Some birds (e.g., the Homestead bird) have remained for many weeks after their initial discoveries. Breeding in the state is purely speculative. See Bill and Susan Smith's *Birding* article for a complete history of the Bahama Swallow in Florida, including four color photographs.

Cave Swallow—Formerly a casual visitor from Central America or the West Indies to coastal areas almost throughout, but reported most frequently from the Keys. Since 1987, small numbers have nested under highway bridges and overpasses in the Homestead area. Smith et al. have pointed out that these birds are of the West Indian race *Hirundo f. fulva*, possibly a species distinct from *H. f. pelodoma*, the race that breeds in northern Mexico and the southwestern United States. Florida's breeding Cave Swallows have returned as early as early January and depart by late September.

Florida Scrub-Jay—An uncommon to common, but *extremely local* resident of the peninsula. Occurs in low oak scrub in hundreds of scattered subpopulations, mostly on relic dune systems, from Levy, Marion, and Putnam Counties south to Collier, Glades, and Palm Beach Counties (but 1 bird persists in Pompano Beach in northern Broward County). In 1994, Fitzpatrick et al. estimated the state's population at 4,000 groups, believed to be a 90% reduction of its original size. The decline in the past 15 years is estimated to be 25% to 40% of the total loss, and the species is continuing to plummet in numbers, especially in the northern portion of its range.

Because it is a Threatened species restricted to Florida, is dependent on a rare and severely diminished habitat, is sedentary, breeds cooperatively, occupies a low-growing open habitat, and can be easily tamed for research purposes, the Florida Scrub-Jay is the subject of numerous studies, most notably the 28-year study at Archbold Biological Station in southern Highlands County. In fact, the Florida Scrub-Jay is one of the most thoroughly studied vertebrates in the world.

Protected (but not necessarily managed) populations of Florida Scrub-Jays occur in Ocala National Forest (about 450 groups), Merritt Island National Wildlife Refuge/Canaveral National Seashore/Cape Canaveral Air Station (about 500 groups estimated), Oscar Scherer State Park near Sarasota (about 20 groups), Avon Park Air Force Range (about 90 groups), Archbold Biological Station (about 110 groups), Jonathan Dickinson State Park (about 50 groups estimated), and elsewhere. Unless scrub is burned every 10 to 15 years, it becomes overgrown, and the density of jays decreases until they may die out entirely.

Fish Crow—A common to abundant resident of the state, but absent in the Keys except for a small group near Key West. Most common along the coasts and absent from much of the interior (but abundant around Lake Okeechobee), where it is replaced by the American Crow, which is absent from most coastal areas (although common at Flamingo). Virtually impossible to miss. Its distinctive call is a nasal *huh-uh.*

White-breasted Nuthatch—Formerly a fairly common and widespread resident in the Panhandle and northern half of the peninsula, with winter reports south to Everglades National Park and Miami. The species' range has declined severely since the mid-1930s, for reasons still not understood, and is now virtually restricted to Leon and Jefferson Counties, with scattered winter reports elsewhere in northern Florida. Phipps/Overstreet Park and Tall Timbers Research Station, both in Tallahassee, are among the most accessible sites in the state to observe the species.

Brown-headed Nuthatch—An uncommon to common resident of open pinewoods throughout, except rare and local in South Florida and absent from the Keys. Listen for their characteristic high, squeaky "rubber ducky" calls. Responds well to Eastern Screech-Owl calls.

Red-whiskered Bulbul—An established exotic, native to India. A few birds that escaped from a Miami "bird farm" in 1960 began breeding shortly afterward. The species is now established marginally in residential areas of Kendall, a suburban area south of Miami, but its range does not seem to be expanding. It is fairly easy to find in the neighborhood surrounding the Kendall tennis courts. Its population probably numbers in the low hundreds of birds but is not being studied or censused currently. Its voice is a series of loud whistles that rise and fall.

Carolina Wren—A common to abundant, widespread resident throughout, but absent from the Keys (except local on Key Largo). Its loud, variable, ringing song is one of the most common avian sounds of Florida.

Winter Wren—A rare to locally uncommon winter resident of the Panhandle and North Florida, very rare or absent farther south. Reports from Central and South Florida are often questioned. Prefers brushy areas along streams and rivers. Regularly found in Florida Caverns State Park and Torreya State Park, both in the Panhandle.

Marsh Wren—An uncommon to locally common resident of coastal marshes from Apalachicola to New Port Richey on the Gulf coast and along the Atlantic coast south only to about Jacksonville. During migration and in winter, northern-breeding races occur throughout Florida in fresh, brackish, and salt marshes.

Eastern Bluebird—An uncommon to locally common resident throughout, except rare or absent in the extreme southern peninsula and the Keys. Prefers pine flatwoods, pastures, and similar open areas with scattered trees. Usually not hard to find.

Thrushes—All six species of North American *Catharus* thrushes occur in Florida. Wood Thrushes breed fairly commonly south to about Gainesville, and the species is a rare but regular migrant throughout. Hermit Thrush is a fairly common winter resident throughout. The remaining 4 species (Veery and Gray-cheeked, Bicknell's, and Swainson's Thrushes) occur only in migration.

Bicknell's Thrush—From its description in 1882 until 1995, this thrush was considered a race of the Gray-cheeked Thrush. Its breeding range is limited to southern Quebec, the Maritime Provinces, and higher elevations in the New England states; it winters in the West Indies (Cuba, Dominican Republic, Haiti, Puerto Rico, etc.). Citing differences in plumage, voice, measurements, breeding range and habitat, and genetics, as well as a failure to respond to songs from other races of the Gray-cheeked Thrush, Ouellet suggested elevating Bicknell's Thrush (*C. bicknelli*) to species status. The AOU Check-list Committee accepted Ouellet's recommendations and split the species in 1995. (DNA evidence suggests that the two species diverged about 1 million years ago).

The identification of Bicknell's Thrush presents a challenge to birders. In the hand, Bicknell's Thrush differs from both races of the Gray-cheeked Thrush by its warmer brown upperparts, buffier throat, chestnut (rather than olive or olive brown) tail, and soft-parts colors (e.g., a bright yellow base to the lower mandible), but these characteristics are extremely difficult to observe in the field except under ideal viewing conditions. In fact, Bicknell's Thrush closely resembles the eastern races of Swainson's Thrush; look for the gray cheeks of Bicknell's Thrush. Ian MacLaren wrote an excellent article on the identification of Bicknell's Thrush in the October 1995 issue of *Birding* which includes several color photographs.

Specimen data confirm that Bicknell's Thrush migrates along the Atlantic coast of the U.S. between its breeding and wintering grounds. Based on recordings of nocturnal flight calls obtained in May 1989 and May 1991 in Brevard County (and Volusia County?), Evans identified many Bicknell's Thrushes, but no Gray-cheeked Thrushes. Insofar as the Gray-cheeked Thrush winters exclusively in Central and South America, it is likely to be more common along the Gulf coast of Florida in spring, whereas Bicknell's Thrush is probably restricted to the Atlantic coast. The distribution of the two species in Florida in fall is less certain.

Bahama Mockingbird—First noted in 1976, but now a rare and increasingly regular visitor from the Bahamas to the southeast coast and Keys, with about 30 reports through 1995. It has occurred from February through September, but most reports are from March to May. In 1991, a male summered in Key West and built a nest. Presumably the same bird returned for three subsequent summers and may have nested successfully in 1994.

Sprague's Pipit—A very rare but regular winter resident of short-grass areas along the Panhandle coast, occasional elsewhere. Has wintered for the past 7 years at Apalachicola Airfield and also occurs rather frequently (but not annually) on the causeway to St. George Island.

Loggerhead Shrike—An uncommon to locally common resident of open areas north of the Everglades, local or absent in the extreme southern peninsula and Keys. Although declining throughout its range, it is still easy to find in open country throughout most of Florida.

Common Myna (*Acridotheres tristis*)—An unestablished (?) exotic, native to Asia but introduced into many areas. First noted in the state in Miami in 1983, it has been reported north to Clewiston (present since the late 1980s) and Cocoa Beach (first noted in 1990), and west through parts of Everglades National Park to Fort Myers and Everglades City. Although it remains uncommon and locally distributed, chiefly in the Greater Miami area, it seems to be becoming established.

The species is illustrated in Peterson's western guide (Hawaii section) but not in the National Geographic guide. Common Mynas are starling-sized birds with a rich brown body offset by a black head and tail. The belly is white, and there are white patches in the wings and tail. The bill, eyes, and legs are yellow, and yellow patches of bare skin are present below the eyes.

Hill Myna—An unestablished exotic, native to India, Southeast Asia, and Indonesia. It has been present in suburban areas of the southeast coast since at least the 1960s but has not become established. Its breeding range is now much reduced and limited mostly to coastal areas of Delray Beach/Boca Raton and Coconut Grove/Old Cutler (Miami). Reports elsewhere are probably local escapes.

White-eyed Vireo—A fairly common resident virtually throughout. The species may be locally common during migration, especially at coastal areas in spring. In winter, when generally silent, it can be somewhat difficult to find. Responds well to pishing and Eastern Screech-Owl recordings.

Thick-billed Vireo—A very rare but increasing visitor from the Bahamas to the southeast coast and Keys. First reported in 1961 but not verified until 1989. There are now about 10 accepted reports from August to May, with peaks occurring in spring and fall. The largest number reported in Florida was 3 birds in Bill Baggs/Cape Florida State Recreation Area in September and October 1989.

Although included in the National Geographic guide and in Bond's *Birds of the West Indies*, the birds illustrated display the yellow breast and belly of Thick-billed Vireos inhabiting the southern Bahamas. The form most likely to occur in Florida inhabits the northern Bahamas and usually has very pale yellow underparts that may appear almost grayish. Unlike White-eyed Vireos, which typically have black mandibles, the bill of Thick-billed Vireos is paler, appearing gray or brownish, occasionally pinkish. (Five color photographs of Thick-billed Vireos appeared in the fall 1990 issue of *American Birds*; the photos and accompanying article should be consulted before reporting this species in Florida.)

Black-whiskered Vireo—Until the early 1980s, a fairly common to common, widespread spring and summer resident of mangrove and hardwood forests of the southern half of the peninsula and the Keys. Most common in the Keys and southern peninsula, but bred north to St. Petersburg and Merritt Island. Rare but almost regular along the entire Gulf coast to Pensacola, usually in spring. Since the mid-1980s, the species has been declining and is now virtually extirpated as a breeder on the Gulf coast from Sarasota northward and locally on the Atlantic coast. This decline may be due to brood parasitism by Brown-headed Cowbirds. The species is still numerous in the Keys and along the southwest coast north to about Sanibel Island.

Wood-warblers—Perhaps as compensation for its relative lack of breeding species, Florida witnesses an abundance of migrant warblers in spring and fall. As of March 1996, 42 species have been verified to occur in the state. Excluding the probably extinct Bachman's Warbler (once a locally common migrant in Florida) and 5 irregularly occurring species (Black-throated Gray, Townsend's, Golden-cheeked, Kirtland's, and Mourning Warblers), 36 species occur in Florida annually or nearly so. Eleven of these breed regularly in the state, but the remainder are migrants or winter residents. Only the breeding species are included here.

Northern Parula—A common to very common spring and summer breeder almost throughout, but rare and local in South Florida and absent from the Keys. Migrates throughout, often commonly, beginning spring migration in mid-February. Winters regularly in small numbers in the southern half of the peninsula and the Keys.

Yellow Warbler—As a migrant occurs throughout, most commonly from late July through early September. Cuban Yellow Warbler (*Dendroica petechia gundlachi*) is a rather common resident (possibly with some withdrawal in winter) of mangrove forests of the extreme southwestern peninsula and Keys. The largely West Indian "Golden Warbler" complex (of which the Cuban Yellow Warbler is a race) was formerly considered a species separate from the Yellow Warbler and may be re-split in the future. The birds occur mostly away from human disturbance and are easily attracted to pishing and Eastern Screech-Owl calls. Search areas near the Card Sound Bridge toll booth, on Saddlebunch Key, and on Boca Chica Key. (The two races cannot be identified in the field except by breeding range and habitat.)

Yellow-throated Warbler—An uncommon to locally common resident of the Panhandle and northern half of the peninsula, although rare in winter in the western Panhandle. A rather common migrant and winter resident in the southern half of the peninsula and the Keys, beginning fall migration in mid-July and usually departing by March.

Pine Warbler—A common resident of pine forests throughout, except irregular in the Keys, when usually seen in winter.

Prairie Warbler—Represented in Florida by two races that have very different seasonal and distributional patterns. The nominate race is a rare to uncommon breeding resident in the Panhandle and North Florida, and an uncommon migrant throughout, beginning fall migration in mid-July. Uncommon in winter in the southern half of the peninsula and the Keys, rare or irregular farther north. The endemic Florida Prairie Warbler (*Dendroica discolor paludicola*) is resident in mangrove forests from Central Florida southward through the Keys. Its northern range limits have declined in the past decade due possibly to brood parasitism by Brown-headed Cowbirds. (Except by breeding range and habitat, the two races cannot be distinguished in the field.)

Prothonotary Warbler—An uncommon to common migrant throughout. Breeds rather commonly in swamps, bayheads, and riparian forests in the Panhandle and the northern half of the peninsula, less common south to Big Cypress National Preserve.

Swainson's Warbler—An elusive migrant throughout (much more common in spring), preferring moist, shady areas with abundant leaf litter. Breeds locally along the edges of swamps and in other wet forested areas in the Panhandle, rarely south to the Steinhatchee and Gainesville areas.

Louisiana Waterthrush—An uncommon migrant throughout, among the first migrants to move north in spring and south in fall. Breeds rarely to uncommonly in the Panhandle and irregularly in North Florida. Very rare in winter, usually in South Florida and the Keys.

Kentucky Warbler—A rare to uncommon migrant, restricted chiefly to the Gulf coast in spring but widespread in fall. Breeds uncommonly in moist forests in the Panhandle, with a few reports from the Big Bend region.

Hooded Warbler—An uncommon to occasionally abundant migrant throughout. Breeds rather commonly in the Panhandle and North Florida.

Yellow-breasted Chat—A rarely seen migrant throughout. Breeds fairly commonly in thickets and other brushy areas in the Panhandle, rarely south to Gainesville. Rare in winter in South Florida and the Keys, irregular elsewhere.

Bananaquit—An occasional visitor from the Bahamas to the southeast coast and Upper Keys, with about 30 accepted reports. Dates of accepted reports range from late December to mid-May, with most of them from January through March. All birds in Florida have represented the white-throated race *Coereba flaveola bahamensis.* The most recent report was in Spanish River Park in April 1994.

Stripe-headed Tanager—A rare to uncommon, irregular visitor from the Bahamas to the southeast coast and Keys. There are almost 40 published reports since the first one in 1957, occurring from September to June. Most birds seen in Florida have been males. Two races have strayed to the state: *Spindalis zena townsendi,* a greenish-backed race from the Little Bahama Bank (i.e., Grand Bahama and Great Abaco islands) and *S. z. zena,* a black-backed race from the Grand Bahama Bank (i.e., the remaining Bahama islands). Recent accepted reports have been in Spanish River Park (April 1994) and MacArthur State Recreation Area (August to September 1995). The largest number reported in Florida was 7 birds in West Palm Beach in spring 1973.

Summer Tanager—A fairly common spring and summer resident of oak hammocks, sandhills, and pine flatwoods south to about Lake Okeechobee, rare or absent farther south. Migrates uncommonly throughout. A few are found in winter, mostly in the southern half of the peninsula and Keys. Unlike Scarlet Tanagers, adult male Summer Tanagers retain their red plumage year round.

Painted Bunting—A common spring and summer resident of northeast coastal counties, less common south to Orlando and Merritt Island, where it occurs chiefly in abandoned citrus groves. There are a few isolated breeding reports from the Apalachicola area. Elsewhere, a regular migrant along the Atlantic coast, but rare or irregular inland and along the Gulf coast. Uncommon in winter (often at feeders) in the southern half of the peninsula, irregular farther north. Winters in Everglades National Park, Corkscrew Swamp Sanctuary, and Castellow Hammock Park, among many other sites.

Yellow-faced Grassquit (*Tiaris olivacea*)—An accidental visitor from the West Indies to the extreme southern mainland and Keys. There are only 2 verified records in the state: Homestead (July 1990) and Dry Tortugas National Park (April 1994). Not included in any North American field guide, the species is illustrated in Bond's *Birds of the West Indies* and photographed in Vriends (a male) and Downer and Sutton's *Birds of Jamaica* (both male and female). Grassquits are kinglet-sized finches common in shrubby habitats in the West Indies (Greater Antilles) and Central America. Yellow-faced Grassquits are grayish-olive overall, with black eyes, bill, and legs. Males have bright yellow eye-brows and throat, bordered by black. In females, these colors are muted.

Black-faced Grassquit—An occasional visitor from the West Indies to the southeast coast and Keys, with about 10 accepted reports. Recent reports have occurred in Dania, Broward County (December 1987 and April 1988); Homestead (March 1993); and Key West (May 1993).

Cuban Grassquit (*Tiaris canora*)—Exotic, native to Cuba and the Isle of Pines. All 9 Florida reports, including 1 breeding report, are believed to represent escaped cage birds, as the species is very popular with Cuban immigrants now living in South Florida. It is becoming rare in its native range, and Bill Smith considers it unlikely that any Florida report will be accepted as a natural vagrant. A bloody base to the bill of a male found at Miami International Airport in April 1995 was proof of its recent captivity. Photographed in Vriends (male and female) and illustrated in Peterson and *Birds of the West Indies*, but not in the National Geographic guide, the species is tiny, olive above, with a black breast and pale belly and undertail coverts. A large yellow crescent outlines the black face and upper breast. The female is similar but has a rusty face and entirely pale underparts.

Sparrows—Florida has only 4 regularly breeding sparrows, but about 15 additional species winter annually in the state. Most sparrows are typically found in open, weedy or grassy "sparrow fields." Some species prefer dry fields, others prefer wet areas, and still others may be found in either. Similarly, the height, thickness, and type of plant cover (grass, weeds, or shrubs) all affect the composition of sparrows inhabiting a field. Abandoned citrus groves in Central Florida, hurricane-killed orchards in the Homestead/Florida City area, and cleared areas overgrown with weedy vegetation throughout the state are all excellent habitats for wintering sparrows. Sparrows usually not found in dry fields are Salt-marsh Sharp-tailed, Nelson's Sharp-tailed, Seaside, and Swamp Sparrows, which are found variously in fresh, brackish, or salt marshes.

Eastern Towhee—A common to abundant resident nearly throughout, but only a rare winter resident in the Keys. The race that inhabits the extreme western Panhandle, *Pipilo erythrophthalmus canaster*, has red irides. *P. e. rileyi*, also resident in the western Panhandle, has orange irides. Elsewhere in Florida, *P. e. alleni* has white or pale yellow irides.

Bachman's Sparrow—A rather common but *inconspicuous* resident of the peninsula north of the Everglades. Occurs in open pinewoods, pine plantations, and dry prairies. Hard to locate except when males sing from perches, most commonly from March to July. In winter, responds well to recorded Bachman's Sparrows songs, usually by chipping excitedly.

Grasshopper Sparrow—A rare to fairly common winter resident of grassy fields, dry prairies, and overgrown areas throughout. The Florida Grasshopper Sparrow (*Ammodramus savannarum floridanus*) is a Federally Endangered race that inhabits dry prairies in south-central Florida. Apparently formerly widespread, it is now restricted to Highlands, Okeechobee, Osceola, and Polk counties. Delany and Cox estimated a statewide population of only about 120 pairs from 1980 to 1984, but the population probably numbers 300 or more pairs currently. Protected populations are located in Avon Park Air Force Range, Three Lakes Wildlife Management Area, and a few sites not included in this guide.

Henslow's Sparrow—Generally a rare winter resident of the Panhandle and peninsula south to about Lake Okeechobee, but fairly common in Apalachicola National Forest. Extremely secretive and probably overlooked. Prefers wet weedy areas such as pitcher plant bogs, dry prairies, drainage ditches, fields, and powerline rights-of-way. Occurs also in savannahs and open pinewoods with an abundance of wiregrass, as in Apalachicola National Forest and Ochlockonee River State Park.

Le Conte's Sparrow—A rare winter resident of the Panhandle and greater part of the peninsula, although probably irregular farther south. Prefers fields with low stubble or grasses. Like Henslow's Sparrow, it is extremely secretive and probably overlooked.

Nelson's Sharp-tailed Sparrow (*Ammodramus nelsoni*) and **Saltmarsh Sharp-tailed Sparrow** (*A. caudacutus*)—Uncommon to common winter residents of brackish and salt marshes south to about Tampa Bay on the Gulf coast and Merritt Island on the Atlantic coast. Generally rare farther south although they may be uncommon around Cape Sable in Everglades National Park. Now possibly absent from the Atlantic coast south of Fort Pierce.

Formerly considered a single species, the Sharp-tailed Sparrow, but split into two species by the AOU in 1995. The distribution of the two species in Florida is uncertain; even the published literature is contradictory. However, it is believed that Nelson's Sharp-tailed Sparrow is predominant on the Gulf coast, while Saltmarsh Sharp-tailed Sparrow should be more common along the Atlantic. Further study of the two species in Florida is certainly warranted. Sibley (1996) is a good reference and contains numerous color photographs, including some that illustrate that some sharp-tailed sparrows perhaps cannot be positively identified to species. Because the status and distribution of the two species in Florida is uncertain, this guide refers only to "Sharp-tailed Sparrows."

Seaside Sparrow—A rather common but local resident of marshes, represented by three (formerly four) distinct populations. Along the Gulf coast, occurs in salt and brackish marshes from Apalachicola to Port Richey, with two isolated populations near Pensacola and Choctawhatchee Bay, respectively. On the Atlantic coast, breeding populations occur south only to Jacksonville, although wintering birds may be found along the entire coastline. The Cape Sable Seaside Sparrow, once considered a separate species, occurs in fresh and brackish marshes wholly within Everglades National Park and Big Cypress National Preserve. A 1981 survey estimated a total population of about 6,000 birds, but the population has probably declined since then. Most easily found along Shark River Slough near the turn-off to Mahogany Hammock in Everglades National Park, especially from March to July, when males are singing. The Dusky Seaside Sparrow, once also considered a separate species, has been extinct since 1987. Occurring only in salt and brackish marshes of Brevard County, it had the most restricted range of any bird in North America, but alteration of its habitat for mosquito control, construction of highways through its core area, and other human-caused events caused its extinction.

Tawny-shouldered Blackbird (*Agelaius humeralis*)—An accidental visitor from Cuba to the Keys. There is only 1 verified record in North America: 2 birds collected at Key West 27 February 1936. Stevenson and Anderson do not accept two fairly recent reports: Marathon (25 May 1955) and Dry Tortugas National Park (18 May 1976). The male is nearly identical to a male Red-winged Blackbird but has tawny (i.e., tan) rather than red lesser wing-coverts. This field mark is difficult to see conclusively except under ideal conditions, and variation in the plumage of some Red-wings adds to the difficulty of identification. Female Tawny-shouldered Blackbirds resemble males, but their wingpatches are less conspicuous.

Shiny Cowbird—An expanding West Indian species first noted in Florida in 1985. By 1990 Will Post et al. reported its range as being along the entire Florida coastline, with reports as far away as Maine, Oklahoma, and Texas. Its present distribution in Florida is limited mainly to coastal areas. It was originally thought to be moving rapidly into the state, and would likely impact many breeding species, including those with extremely restricted breeding ranges (e.g., Black-whiskered Vireo, Florida Prairie Warbler, Cuban Yellow Warbler, Cape Sable Seaside Sparrow, and Florida Grasshopper Sparrow). However, there is only one breeding report to date (a fledgling fed by a Red-winged Blackbird in Homestead in 1991), and numbers moving through South Florida seem to have peaked in the early 1990s (although numbers were up in spring 1995). Usually found in spring at Flamingo, Key West, and Dry Tortugas National Park and in winter at Briggs Nature Center near Naples. Outside these few areas, its occurrence is unpredictable but should not be considered surprising.

This species is not included in the National Geographic guide or any other North American field guide. It is illustrated in Bond's *Birds of the West Indies* only as a black-and-white sketch, but is well-photographed in a 1987 *American Birds* article by Bill Smith and Sandy Sprunt. Identifying male Shiny Cowbirds is relatively easy, but birds in female plumage must be identified with great care. Shiny Cowbirds are similar in size to Brown-headed Cowbirds, but Shiny Cowbirds have a somewhat sleeker profile, with longer, thinner bills. This field mark may not be obvious except under ideal viewing conditions. Adult male Shiny Cowbirds are black overall with extensive purplish iridescence, especially on the upperparts and breast; they are unmistakable. (Curiously, when observed from below, such as on a wire, male Shiny Cowbirds resemble male Purple Martins.) Shiny Cowbirds in female plumage can best be distinguished by bill shape.

Boat-tailed Grackle—Generally a common to abundant resident of the peninsula. Rare to uncommon in the Panhandle, especially the western part and inland, and only casual in the Keys. Virtually impossible to miss in the peninsula.

Orchard Oriole—A common spring and summer resident of the Panhandle, uncommon in the peninsula south to about Gainesville, rarely to Orlando. In spring, migrates across the Gulf and is seldom seen inland or on the Atlantic coast. It is very rare throughout as an early fall migrant. A few have been found in winter, including recently at Belle Glade Marina.

Spot-breasted Oriole—Exotic, native to southern Mexico and northern Central America. First noted in Miami in the late 1940s, it had extended its range north along the Atlantic coast to Cocoa Beach by the 1970s. The population declined rapidly in numbers and range by the early 1980s and is now limited to a few suburban areas of the southeast coast, especially the Fort Lauderdale and Miami areas.

Bullock's Oriole—A generally rare but regular migrant and winter resident throughout, apparently most common in the western Panhandle. Birds in female plumage are reported far more frequently than are adult males. Bullock's and Baltimore Orioles often flock together in winter; search oriole flocks carefully. Often visits bird feeders in winter.

House Finch—An established exotic, native to western North America and Central America. A population that originated from a few birds released in New York in the early 1940s now occupies most of the eastern United States. It was first reported in Florida in Fort Lauderdale in 1980, but that one may have been a locally escaped cagebird. Many birds wintered in Pensacola and Tallahassee in 1987-1988 and bred at the latter site in 1989. As of early 1996, House Finch is a rare to uncommon, *local* resident of suburban areas in the Panhandle and northern peninsula south to Cedar Key and Gainesville, with a few reports in South Florida. Numbers and range continue to increase in the Panhandle (especially around Pensacola and Tallahassee), and southward into the peninsula, but expansion has not been rapid.

EXOTIC BIRDS OF FLORIDA

The following list includes 173 species of birds thought to consist entirely of individuals that were accidentally or intentionally released into Florida. The 61 species that have reportedly bred in the wild are marked with an asterisk (*), and those 10 considered by the AOU and ABA to be established are marked with an **E**.

Spotted Nothura (*Nothura maculosa*)
White Spoonbill (*Platalea leucorodia*)
Woolly-necked Stork (*Ciconia episcopus*)
White Stork (*Ciconia ciconia*)
Black-necked Stork (*Ephippiorhynchus asiaticus*)
Chilean Flamingo (*Phoenicopterus chilensis*)
White-faced Whistling-Duck (*Dendrocygna viduata*)
West Indian Whistling-Duck (*Dendrocygna arborea*)
     also a likely vagrant
Whooper Swan (*Cygnus cygnus*)
*****Mute Swan** (*Cygnus olor*)
Coscoroba Swan (*Coscoroba coscoroba*)
*****Black Swan** (*Cygnus atratus*)
*****Bean Goose** (*Anser fabalis*)
*****Greylag Goose** (*Anser anser*)
Bar-headed Goose (*Anser indica*)
*****Swan Goose** (*Anser cygnoides*)
*****Egyptian Goose** (*Alopochen aegypticus*)
Orinoco Goose (*Neochen jubatus*)
Ruddy Shelduck (*Tadorna ferruginea*)
Common Shelduck (*Tadorna tadorna*)
*****Muscovy Duck** (*Cairina moschata*)
Ringed Teal (*Callonetta leucophrys*)
*****Mandarin Duck** (*Aix galericulata*)
Hottentot Teal (*Anas puctata*)
Spot-billed Duck (*Anas poecilorhynchos*)
Rosy-billed Pochard (*Netta peposaca*)

King Vulture (*Sarcoramphus papa*)
"Griffon-type Old World vulture"(*Gyps* sp.)
Crane Hawk (*Geranospiza caerulescens*)
*Great Black-Hawk (*Buteogallus urubitinga*)
Harris's Hawk (*Parabuteo unicinctus*)
*Black Francolin (*Francolinus francolinus*)
Ruffed Grouse (*Bonasa umbellus*)
Chukar (*Alectoris chukar*)
*Red Junglefowl (*Gallus gallus*)
*Ring-necked Pheasant (*Phasianus colchicus*)
*Common Peafowl (*Pavo cristatus*)
Helmeted Guineafowl (*Numida meleagris*)
*Gray-necked Wood-Rail (*Aramides cajanea*)
*Sarus Crane (*Grus antigone*)
Gray Crowned Crane (*Balearica regulorum*)
Southern Lapwing (*Vanellus chilensis*)
*Rock Dove (*Columba livia*) E
*Eurasian Collared-Dove (*Streptopelia decaocto*) E
*Ringed Turtle-Dove (*Streptopelia "risoria"*)
Spotted Dove (*Streptopelia chinensis*)
*Diamond Dove (*Geopelia cuneata*)
*Inca Dove (*Columbina inca*)
*Red Lory (*Eos bornea*)
Ornate Lorikeet (*Trichoglossus ornatus*)
Rainbow Lorikeet (*Trichoglossus haematodus*)
Scaly-breasted Lorikeet (*Trichoglossus chlorolepidotus*)
Chattering Lory (*Lorius garrulus*)
Galah (*Eolophus roseicapillus*)
*Greater Sulphur-crested Cockatoo (*Cacatua galerita*)
Salmon-crested Cockatoo (*Cacatua moluccensis*)
White Cockatoo (*Cacatua alba*)
Tanimbar Cockatoo (*Cacatua goffini*)
Cockatiel (*Nymphicus hollandicus*)
Eclectus Parrot (*Eclectus roratus*)
Gray Parrot (*Psittacus erithacus*)
*Senegal Parrot (*Poicephalus senegalus*)
*Rueppell's Parrot (*Poicephalus rueppellii*)
Peach-faced Lovebird (*Agapornis roseicollis*)
Fischer's Lovebird (*Agapornis fischeri*)
Masked Lovebird (*Agapornis personata*)
Red-rumped Parrot (*Psephotus haemantonotus*)

*Budgerigar (*Melopsittacus undulatus*) **E**
Alexandrine Parakeet (*Psittacula eupatria*)
*Rose-ringed Parakeet (*Psittacula krameri*)
Plum-headed Parakeet (*Psittacula cyanocephala*)
Blossom-headed Parakeet (*Psittacula roseata*)
Maroon-bellied Parakeet (*Pyrrhura frontalis*)
Green-cheeked Parakeet (*Pyrrhura molinae*)
*Monk Parakeet (*Myiopsitta monachus*) **E**
*Black-hooded Parakeet (*Nandayus nenday*)
*Blue-crowned Parakeet (*Aratinga acuticauda*)
Green Parakeet (*Aratinga holochlora*)
*Red-masked Parakeet (*Aratinga erythrogenys*)
Scarlet-fronted Parakeet (*Aratinga wagleri*)
*Mitred Parakeet (*Aratinga mitrata*)
Crimson-fronted Parakeet (*Aratinga finschi*)
White-eyed Parakeet (*Aratinga leucopthalmus*)
Hispaniolan Parakeet (*Aratinga chloroptera*)
*Dusky-headed Parakeet (*Aratinga weddellii*)
*Orange-fronted Parakeet (*Aratinga canicularis*)
*Brown-throated Parakeet (*Aratinga pertinax*)
Peach-fronted Parakeet (*Aratinga aurea*)
Hyacinth Macaw (*Anodorhynchus hyacinthinus*)
*Chestnut-fronted Macaw (*Ara severa*)
Military Macaw (*Ara militaris*)
Scarlet Macaw (*Ara macao*)
*Blue-and-yellow Macaw (*Ara ararauna*)
Yellow-collared Macaw (*Ara auricollis*)
Red-shouldered Macaw (*Ara nobilis*)
Maroon-fronted Parrot (*Rhyncopsitta terrisi*)
Burrowing Parrot (*Cyanoliseus patagonus*)
*Canary-winged ("White-winged") Parakeet (*Brotogeris versicolurus*)
    E
Yellow-chevroned Parakeet (*Brotogeris chiriri*)
Orange-chinned Parakeet (*Brotogeris jugularis*)
Tui Parakeet (*Brotogeris sanctithomae*)
Black-headed Parrot (*Pionites melanocephala*)
White-crowned Parrot (*Pionus senilis*)
*White-fronted Parrot (*Amazona albifrons*)
*Hispaniolan Parrot (*Amazona ventralis*)
Red-spectacled Parrot (*Amazona pretrei*)
*Red-crowned Parrot (*Amazona viridigenalis*)

Lilac-crowned Parrot (*Amazona finschi*)
*Red-lored Parrot (*Amazona autumnalis*)
Mealy Parrot (*Amazona farinosa*)
Festive Parrot (*Amazona festiva*)
Yellow-shouldered Parrot (*Amazona barbadensis*)
*Turquoise-fronted Parrot (*Amazona aestiva*)
*Orange-winged Parrot (*Amazona amazonica*)
*Yellow-headed Parrot (*Amazona oratrix*)
Yellow-naped Parrot (*Amazona auropiliata*)
*Yellow-crowned Parrot (*Amazona ochrocephala*)
Schalow's Turaco (*Turaco schalowi*)
Violet Turaco (*Musophaga violacea*)
Spectacled Owl (*Pulsatrix perspicillata*)
Snowy Owl (*Nyctea scandiaca*) also an unverified straggler
Wreathed Hornbill (*Aceros undulatus*)
Silvery-cheeked Hornbill (*Ceratogymna brevis*)
Abyssinian Ground-Hornbill (*Bucorvus abyssinicus*)
Citron-throated Toucan (*Ramphastos citrolaemus*)
Keel-billed Toucan (*Ramphastos sulfuratus*)
Toco Toucan (*Ramphastos toco*)
Great Kiskadee (*Pitangus sulphuratus*) possibly also a vagrant from
    the western U.S. or West Indies.
Banded Pitta (*Pitta guajana*)
Green Jay (*Cyanocorax yncas*)
Azure Jay (*Cyanocorax caeruleus*)
Black-billed Magpie (*Pica pica*)
Common Raven (*Corvus corax*)
Blue-mantled Fairy-Bluebird (*Irena puella*)
*Red-whiskered Bulbul (*Pycnonotus jocosus*) E
Common Nightingale (*Luscinia megarhynchos*)
Greater Necklaced Laughing-Thrush (*Garrulax pectoralis*)
Red-billed Leiothrix (*Leiothrix lutea*)
*European Starling (*Gracula religiosa*) E
*Common Myna (*Acridotheres tristis*)
*Jungle Myna (*Acridotheres fuscus*)
*Crested Myna (*Acridotheres cristatellus*)
*Hill Myna (*Gracula religiosa*)
*Blue-gray Tanager (*Thraupis episcopus*)
*Red-crested Cardinal (*Paroaria coronata*)
*Red-capped Cardinal (*Paroaria gularis*)
*Cuban Grassquit (*Tiaris canorus*)

Saffron Finch (*Sicalis flaveola*)
Troupial (*Icterus icterus*)
*****Spot-breasted Oriole** (*Icterus pectoralis*) **E**
Montezuma Oropendola (*Psarocolius montezuma*)
Vitelline Masked Weaver (*Ploceus velatus*)
*****House Finch** (*Carpodacus mexicanus*) **E**
European Goldfinch (*Carduelis carduelis*)
European Greenfinch (*Carduelis chloris*)
Yellow-fronted Canary (*Serinus mozambicus*)
*****House Sparrow** (*Passer domesticus*) **E**
Golden Sparrow (*Passer luteus*)
Red Bishop (*Euplectes orix*)
Orange Bishop (*Euplectes franciscanus*)
Yellow-crowned Bishop (*Euplectes afer*)
Red-collared Widowbird (*Euplectus ardens*)
Red-cheeked Cordonbleu (*Uraeginthus bengalus*)
Orange-cheeked Waxbill (*Estrilda melpoda*)
Red Avadavat (*Amandava amandava*)
Zebra Finch (*Amandava subflava*)
Madagascar Mannikin (*Lonchura nana*)
African Silverbill (*Lonchura cantans*)
*****Nutmeg Mannikin** (*Lonchura punctulata*)
*****Chestnut Mannikin** (*Lonchura malacca*)
White-headed Mannikin (*Lonchura maja*)
*****Java Sparrow** (*Padda oryzivora*)
Pin-tailed Whydah (*Vidua macroura*)

FLORIDA BIRDS

The following bar-graphs are designed to help the reader in learning the seasonal and regional status of birds in Florida. All verified species (natives and established exotics) are included, except those now considered extinct or extirpated (*see* Robertson and Woolfenden). Also included are 4 unverified but frequently reported species (Red-necked Grebe, Rough-legged Hawk, Cuban Emerald, and Tropical Kingbird), two species of uncertain origin (Band-tailed Gull and European Turtle-Dove), and exotics that appear to be becoming established (e.g., Black-hooded Parakeet and Common Myna). A few other exotics are also included (e.g., Chestnut-fronted Macaw and Hill Myna). Neither the unverified birds nor the marginal exotics has a check-box before the species name in the bar-graphs.

The bar-graphs are based primarily on the actual abundance of a species rather than its "visibility." Therefore, small, less conspicuous species may require more effort to locate than large, conspicuous ones. Most landbirds are easiest to find in spring and summer, when males are singing from exposed perches; these same species may be difficult to locate at other seasons, especially in winter. **Note also that the graphs refer to the likelihood of *finding* a bird, which does not necessarily mean *seeing* it**. Some species (rails, owls, nightjars) are heard much more frequently than they are seen.

The six abundance codes used in the graphs follow:

Very common to abundant: ▬▬▬▬▬▬▬▬▬▬▬▬
species virtually certain to be found, often in numbers. Although one can never rule out the possibility of missing a very common species, most of these birds will be seen easily and usually with little effort (e.g., Great Egret, Red-bellied Woodpecker, and Northern Cardinal).

Fairly common to common: ▬▬▬▬▬▬▬▬▬▬
species that probably will be found, often with little effort (e.g., Mottled Duck, Bald Eagle, and Yellow-throated Warbler). Other equally common species may require a special effort to locate. These include birds that are very locally distributed (e.g., Piping

318

Plover, Red-cockaded Woodpecker, and Florida Scrub-Jay), inconspicuous (e.g., Bachman's Sparrow), nocturnal (e.g., Eastern Screech-Owl), or occur in habitats difficult to reach (e.g., Seaside Sparrow).

Uncommon:

species that occur regularly in small numbers and may be seen on perhaps 25 to 50% or more of the trips per season. Many of these species will be found, although often requiring a special search, but others will be missed (e.g., American Bittern, Western Kingbird, and Vesper Sparrow).

Rare but regular:

species that occur regularly in very small numbers and are found only a few times per season. Some of these species will be found, but usually require a special effort to locate, and many will be missed (e.g., Pacific Loon, White-tailed Kite, and Wilson's Warbler).

Occasional:

species with 10 or more accepted reports this century, but whose occurrence in the state is irregular and unpredictable (e.g., Manx Shearwater, Fork-tailed Flycatcher, and Evening Grosbeak), or whose occurrence in the state was more frequent in the past than at present (e.g., Bewick's Wren).

Accidental or casual:

species acceptably reported fewer than 10 times this century (e.g., Yellow-nosed Albatross, Scaly-naped Pigeon, and Golden-cheeked Warbler).

Obviously, you may find some "rare" species more easily than is shown here, while other species may be harder to find. Some other points to keep in mind are:

- The graphs were compiled by active, experienced Florida birders knowledgeable about the birds, habitats, and seasons. Beginning birders and out-of-state visitors may find it more difficult to locate some of these species.
- The five regional and twelve monthly columns attempt to "average" many distributional variables present over a large area. The bars represent the range of species occurrence and (except for rarities) make no attempt to list all outlying regional and seasonal reports.

- For many species, only verified occurrences are used (i.e., questionable sightings are excluded).
- Some species are followed by dittoes and a second or third line. This is done when seasonal occurrence or abundance varies considerably among regions of the state. For example, Short-tailed Hawks are rare summer visitors in the Panhandle and northern Florida, rare to uncommon residents in the southern mainland, and uncommon migrants and winter residents in the Keys.
- Other species have dittoes and a second line because they have clearly identifiable races with differing distributions.
- The Panhandle column is divided into two sections denoting the eastern and western sections, because of well-defined differences in the distribution of many species between Pensacola and Tallahassee (about 200 miles distant). Except for a few species with well-defined range-limits, none of the other four regions is similarly divided. The Keys column denotes only the mainline keys (Key Largo to Key West), so Dry Tortugas National Park is not represented in the graphs.
- The Status column may contain one of four letters, each denoting a different category:

    B breeds regularly in at least part of the state. (Irregular breeders are not marked.)
    E exotic. These species are all residents; therefore, all breed in the state. Nearly all of these species are restricted to areas of human development, and most have extremely limited ranges.
    M migrant, wholly or in large part. Distribution of these species may vary greatly from day to day, depending on local weather conditions.
    R documentation of these species is required by the Florida Ornithological Society Records Committee.

- A great deal of subjectivity is included in these bar-graphs; most Florida birders would have slightly different interpretations of how these graphs should look. Florida is a large and very diverse state. Birds inland in central Florida can differ substantially in distribution from those on the coast, and even some Atlantic coast birds have different patterns of occurrence from those along the Gulf coast. Furthermore, even the most comprehensive publications on Florida birds do not specify the **weekly** abundance of all species throughout the state. *Use these graphs only as a visual guide to determine your chances of encountering a particular species.*

- Note those species marked "Unverified in Florida" or "Unverified in winter." These are birds reported in the state (frequently on Christmas Bird Counts for the latter), but for which verifiable documentation is lacking. Should you observe any of these species, notify others immediately and especially photograph or videotape the bird if possible. Using Robertson and Woolfenden's system, sight-only reports cannot admit a species to the state list (even if it is only seasonally rare), so verifying the report is essential. Verified species for which the Florida Ornithological Society Records Committee requires written details are marked in the following bar-graphs with an "R" (for "Report"). (All unverified species also must be documented, but few of these species are included in the bar-graphs). For more information or to submit a report, contact P. William Smith, FOSRC Secretary, P.O. Box 901341, Homestead, FL 33090.

- In early 1998 Cornell Laboratory of Ornithology's Library of Natural Sounds is expected to release an audio guide to 112 characteristic Florida birds. A star— ★ — in the following bar-graph section indicates which species and identifiable forms will be featured in *Bird Songs of Florida*. Contact ABA Sales for further information about ordering this new CD/cassette.

✓		Panhandle	North Florida	Central Florida	South Florida	Keys	Status	January	February	March	April	May	June	July	August	September	October	November	December
☐	**Red-throated Loon** Coastal					x x													
☐	**Pacific Loon** Coastal	x	x	x	x	x x x x													
☐	**Common Loon** Mainly coastal, but local inland																		
☐	**Least Grebe** 				x	x	R			xxxxxxxxx							xxxx	xx	
☐	**Pied-billed Grebe** " "	★					B B												
☐	**Horned Grebe** Mainly coastal, but local inland																		
	Red-necked Grebe Unverified in Florida																		
☐	**Eared Grebe** Mainly coastal, but local inland																		
☐	**Western Grebe** Coastal	x x	x	x		R				xxxx	x						xxx	xx	
☐	**Yellow-nosed Albatross** Offshore	x		x	x	x	R	x				x		xx					
☐	**Black-capped Petrel** Offshore in Atlantic				x	x	R												
☐	**Cory's Shearwater** Offshore																		
☐	**Greater Shearwater** Offshore																		
☐	**Sooty Shearwater** Offshore																		
☐	**Manx Shearwater** Offshore						R												
☐	**Audubon's Shearwater** Offshore																		
☐	**Wilson's Storm-Petrel** Offshore																		
☐	**Leach's Storm-Petrel** Offshore																		
☐	**Band-rumped Storm-Petrel** Offshore						R												

✓	Species	Panhandle	North Florida	Central Florida	South Florida	Keys	Status	January	February	March	April	May	June	July	August	September	October	November	December
☐	White-tailed Tropicbird Mainly at Dry Tortugas																		
☐	Red-billed Tropicbird Offshore		x	x	x		R						x		x	x x			
☐	Masked Booby Offshore; breeds at Dry Tortugas						B												
☐	Brown Booby Offshore in Atlantic																		
☐	Red-footed Booby Mainly at Dry Tortugas	x		x		x	R					x x x x x x x x x x x x x x x x x				x	x		
☐	Northern Gannet Offshore																		
☐	American White Pelican " "																		
☐	Brown Pelican Mainly coastal, but local inland						B												
☐	Great Cormorant Coastal																		
☑	Double-crested Cormorant						B												
☑	Anhinga 3/ₒₒ " "						B B												
☐	Magnificent Frigatebird Coastal; breeds at Dry Tortugas						B												
☐	American Bittern																		
☐	Least Bittern ★ " "						B B												
☑	Great Blue Heron						B												
	Great White Heron						B												
☐	Great Egret						B												
☑	Snowy Egret						B												
☑	Little Blue Heron						B												
☐	Tricolored Heron						B												
☐	Reddish Egret Breeds coastally, but disperses inland						B												

✓	Panhandle	North Florida	Central Florida	South Florida	Keys	Status	January	February	March	April	May	June	July	August	September	October	November	December
☑ Cattle Egret						B												
" "						B												
☐ Green Heron						B												
" "						B												
☐ Black-crowned Night-Heron						B												
Generally more common inland																		
☐ Yellow-crowned Night-Heron						B												
" "						B												
☑ White Ibis						B												
" "						B												
☐ Scarlet Ibis						R												
☐ Glossy Ibis						B												
☐ White-faced Ibis	x	x	x	x		R			xxxx		xxxx							
☐ Roseate Spoonbill																		
" "						B												
Breeds coastally, but disperses inland																		
☐ Wood Stork ★						B												
☐ Greater Flamingo	x x	x x	x x	x=	x x													
Mainly Everglades National Park																		
☐ Fulvous Whistling-Duck																		
" "						B												
Local																		
☐ Black-bellied Whistling-Duck	x					B												
Expanding from Sarasota County																		
☐ Tundra Swan																		
☐ Greater White-fronted Goose																		
☐ Snow Goose																		
☐ Ross's Goose	x	x				R		x									x	x
☐ Brant																		
Coastal																		
☐ Canada Goose (wild)																		
" " (feral)						E												
Muscovy Duck						E												
☐ Wood Duck						B												

✓	Panhandle	North Florida	Central Florida	South Florida	Keys	Status	January	February	March	April	May	June	July	August	September	October	November	December
☐ Green-winged Teal																		
☐ American Black Duck																		
☐ Mottled Duck ★						B												
☐ Mallard (wild)																		
" " (feral)						E												
☐ White-cheeked Pintail						R												
☐ Northern Pintail																		
☐ Blue-winged Teal																		
Rare and irregular breeder																		
" "																		
Rare and irregular breeder																		
☐ Cinnamon Teal																		
☐ Northern Shoveler																		
☐ Gadwall																		
☐ Eurasian Wigeon																		
☐ American Wigeon																		
☐ Canvasback																		
☐ Redhead																		
☐ Ring-necked Duck																		
Irregular breeder																		
☐ Greater Scaup																		
Coastal																		
☐ Lesser Scaup																		
☐ Common Eider																		
Coastal																		
☐ King Eider	x x		x	x	x	R	xxxxxxxxxxxxxxxxxxxxxx											xxx
Coastal																		
☐ Harlequin Duck																		
Coastal																		
☐ Oldsquaw																		
Mostly Panhandle and Atlantic coasts																		
☐ Black Scoter																		
Mostly Panhandle and Atlantic coasts																		
☐ Surf Scoter																		
Mostly Panhandle and Atlantic coasts																		

✓	Panhandle	North Florida	Central Florida	South Florida	Keys	Status	January	February	March	April	May	June	July	August	September	October	November	December
☐ White-winged Scoter Mostly Panhandle and Atlantic coasts													x					
☐ Common Goldeneye Coastal																		
☐ Bufflehead Mainly coastal, but local inland													x					
☐ Hooded Merganser Irregular breeder																		
☐ Common Merganser		x	x	x	x	R				xx	x	x	x					
☐ Red-breasted Merganser Mainly coastal, but local inland																		
☐ Ruddy Duck Locally common																		
☐ Masked Duck						R												
☑ Black Vulture						B												
☑ Turkey Vulture						B												
☐ Osprey " "	★					B B												
☐ Swallow-tailed Kite	★					B												
☐ White-tailed Kite Local	★					B												
☐ Snail Kite	★					B												
☐ Mississippi Kite						B												
☐ Bald Eagle	★					B												
☐ Northern Harrier																		
☐ Sharp-shinned Hawk																		
☐ Cooper's Hawk " "						B												
☐ Northern Goshawk	x	x	x		x	R										xx	xx	
☐ Red-shouldered Hawk	★					B												

✓	Panhandle	North Florida	Central Florida	South Florida	Keys	Status	January	February	March	April	May	June	July	August	September	October	November	December
☐ Broad-winged Hawk						B												
" "																		
May be common in the Keys in fall																		
☐ Short-tailed Hawk ★						B												
" "						B												
" "																		
☐ Swainson's Hawk																		
☑ Red-tailed Hawk 3/60						B												
" "																		
☐ Ferruginous Hawk	x	x				R	xxxxxxxxxxx									x		x
Rough-legged Hawk	x x	x x		x x														
Unverified in Florida																		
☐ Golden Eagle																		
☐ Crested Caracara ★						B												
☑ American Kestrel 3/60						B												
" "																		
☐ Merlin																		
Much more common coastally																		
☐ Peregrine Falcon																		
Much more common coastally																		
☐ Wild Turkey						B												
☐ Northern Bobwhite ★						B												
☐ Yellow Rail																		
☐ Black Rail ★						B												
" "						B												
☐ Clapper Rail ★						B												
☐ King Rail ★						B												
☐ Virginia Rail							xxxxxxxxxxxxxxxxxxxx											
☐ Sora																		
☐ Purple Gallinule ★						B												
" "																		
Local in winter																		
☐ Common Moorhen ★						B												

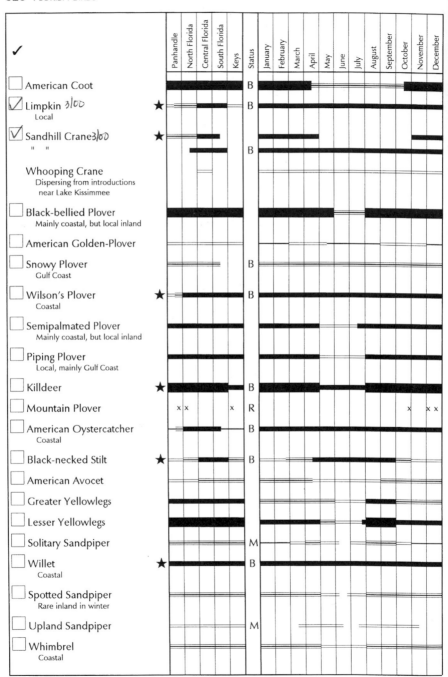

✓			Panhandle	North Florida	Central Florida	South Florida	Keys	Status	January	February	March	April	May	June	July	August	September	October	November	December
☐	American Coot							B												
☑	Limpkin 3/00 — Local	★						B												
☑	Sandhill Crane 3/00 — " "	★						B												
	Whooping Crane — Dispersing from introductions near Lake Kissimmee																			
☐	Black-bellied Plover — Mainly coastal, but local inland																			
☐	American Golden-Plover																			
☐	Snowy Plover — Gulf Coast							B												
☐	Wilson's Plover — Coastal	★						B												
☐	Semipalmated Plover — Mainly coastal, but local inland																			
☐	Piping Plover — Local, mainly Gulf Coast																			
☐	Killdeer	★						B												
☐	Mountain Plover		x	x		x		R											x	x x
☐	American Oystercatcher — Coastal							B												
☐	Black-necked Stilt	★						B												
☐	American Avocet																			
☐	Greater Yellowlegs																			
☐	Lesser Yellowlegs																			
☐	Solitary Sandpiper							M												
☐	Willet — Coastal	★						B												
☐	Spotted Sandpiper — Rare inland in winter																			
☐	Upland Sandpiper							M												
☐	Whimbrel — Coastal																			

✓	Panhandle	North Florida	Central Florida	South Florida	Keys	Status	January	February	March	April	May	June	July	August	September	October	November	December
☐ Long-billed Curlew Gulf Coast																		
☐ Black-tailed Godwit Coastal		x		x		R		xxxxxxxx xx										
☐ Hudsonian Godwit																		
☐ Bar-tailed Godwit	x		x x			R	xxxxxxxxxxxxxxxx								xxxxxxxxxxxxxxx			
☐ Marbled Godwit Mainly coastal, but local inland					x x													
☐ Ruddy Turnstone Mainly coastal, but local inland																		
☐ Surfbird Coastal	x			x		R	x		xxx									
☐ Red Knot Coastal; local in winter																		
☐ Sanderling Coastal																		
☐ Semipalmated Sandpiper Winters in extreme S Florida						M												
☐ Western Sandpiper Rare in winter in W Panhandle																		
☐ Least Sandpiper																		
☐ White-rumped Sandpiper Unverified in winter						M												
☐ Baird's Sandpiper						M												
☐ Pectoral Sandpiper						M												
☐ Sharp-tailed Sandpiper		x		x		R								x x				
☐ Purple Sandpiper Mainly Atlantic coast																		
☐ Dunlin																		
☐ Curlew Sandpiper	x					R												
☐ Stilt Sandpiper Locally abundant inland in fall " "																		
☐ Buff-breasted Sandpiper																		
☐ Ruff	x x						xxxxxxxxxxxxxxxxx											xx

✓	Panhandle	North Florida	Central Florida	South Florida	Keys	Status	January	February	March	April	May	June	July	August	September	October	November	December
☐ Short-billed Dowitcher ★ Mainly coastal, but local inland; rare in winter in W Panhandle																		
☐ Long-billed Dowitcher ★ Restricted to fresh water																		
☐ Common Snipe																		
☐ American Woodcock Casual breeder in C and S Florida						B												
☐ Wilson's Phalarope Unverified in winter																		
☐ Red-necked Phalarope Most common in Atlantic																		
☐ Red Phalarope Most common in Atlantic																		
☐ Pomarine Jaeger Most common in Atlantic																		
☐ Parasitic Jaeger Most common in Atlantic																		
☐ Long-tailed Jaeger Offshore						R												
☐ South Polar Skua			x			R						x						
☐ Laughing Gull ★ Mainly coastal, but local inland						B												
☐ Franklin's Gull																		
☐ Little Gull Mainly Atlantic coast						R												
☐ Black-headed Gull						R								xx				
☐ Bonaparte's Gull												xx		xx	x			
Band-tailed Gull Coastal, origin uncertain	x			x		R	xxxxxxxxx				x			x				xxxxxxx
☑ Ring-billed Gull																		
☑ Herring Gull Mainly coastal, but local inland																		
☐ Thayer's Gull Coastal	x		x	x		R	x x		xx		x						x	x
☐ Iceland Gull Coastal	x	x	x		x	R	xxxxxxxxxxxxxxx											xxxxxxx

✓	Panhandle	North Florida	Central Florida	South Florida	Keys	Status	January	February	March	April	May	June	July	August	September	October	November	December
☐ Lesser Black-backed Gull Coastal																		
☐ Glaucous Gull Coastal														x				
☐ Great Black-backed Gull Mainly Atlantic coast																		
☐ Black-legged Kittiwake Offshore in Atlantic																		
☐ Sabine's Gull Coastal																		
☐ Gull-billed Tern Rare in winter in extreme S Florida						B												
☐ Caspian Tern Absent from Panhandle in winter						B												
☐ Royal Tern ★ Mainly coastal, but local inland						B												
☐ Sandwich Tern ★ Coastal; rare in Panhandle in winter						B												
☐ Roseate Tern Mostly Lower Keys						B												
☐ Common Tern Coastal; casual breeder																		
☐ Arctic Tern Offshore						M												
☐ Forster's Tern																		
☐ Least Tern Mainly coastal, but local inland						B												
☐ Bridled Tern Offshore; very rare breeder in the Keys																		
☐ Sooty Tern ★ Offshore; breeds at Dry Tortugas						B												
☐ Black Tern																		
☐ Brown Noddy ★ Offshore; breeds at Dry Tortugas						B												
☐ Black Noddy ★ Dry Tortugas only																		
☐ Black Skimmer ★ Mainly coastal, but local inland						B												

✓

Name	★	Panhandle	North Florida	Central Florida	South Florida	Keys	Status	Jan	Feb	Mar	Apr	May	Jun	Jul	Aug	Sep	Oct	Nov	Dec
Dovekie Offshore in Atlantic								x											
Thick-billed Murre				x	x		R											x	x x
Razorbill Offshore in Atlantic			x	x	x	x	R	xxxxxxxxxxxxxxxxxxxx										xxxxxxxx	
Long-billed Murrelet			x		x		R					xx						x	x
Atlantic Puffin					x		R												x
Rock Dove		████████████████████					E	██											
Scaly-naped Pigeon						x	R					x					x		
White-crowned Pigeon	★				███████		B				████████████████								
Band-tailed Pigeon		x		x		x	R									x			xx
Ringed Turtle-Dove Mainly St. Petersburg				██			E												
European Turtle-Dove Origin uncertain						x	R				x								
Eurasian Collared-Dove	★			████			E												
White-winged Dove Gulf Coast	★						E												
" "				████			E												
Zenaida Dove					x	x	R	xxxxxxxxx					x			x		x	xx
Mourning Dove		████████████████████					B	██											
Common Ground-Dove	★	████████████████████					B	██											
Key West Quail-Dove						—	R												
Ruddy Quail-Dove						x x	R		x	x	x								xx
Budgerigar Central Gulf coast region				████			E												
Monk Parakeet Suburban areas				███████			E	██											
Black-hooded Parakeet Suburban areas							E												
White-winged Parakeet Southeast coast suburban areas							E												
Yellow-chevroned Parakeet Greater Miami							E												

✓	Panhandle	North Florida	Central Florida	South Florida	Keys	Status	January	February	March	April	May	June	July	August	September	October	November	December
Blue-crowned Parakeet Suburban areas						E												
Mitred Parakeet Suburban areas						E												
Red-masked Parakeet Suburban areas						E												
Chestnut-fronted Macaw Greater Miami						E												
Orange-winged Parakeet Greater Miami						E												
Rose-ringed Parakeet Suburban areas						E												
Red-crowned Parrot Southeast coast suburban areas						E												
☐ Black-billed Cuckoo						M												
☐ Yellow-billed Cuckoo	★					B												
☐ Mangrove Cuckoo	★	x				B												
☐ Smooth-billed Ani	★					B												
☐ Groove-billed Ani																		
☐ Barn Owl " "	★					B												
☐ Flammulated Owl				x		R										x		
☐ Eastern Screech-Owl	★					B												
☐ Great Horned Owl	★					B												
☐ Burrowing Owl	★					B												
☐ Barred Owl	★					B												
☐ Long-eared Owl			x x		x	R		x x								x		x
☐ Short-eared Owl " " West Indian race																		
☐ Northern Saw-whet Owl Northeast Florida		x				R	x								x x		xx	
☐ Lesser Nighthawk																		
☐ Common Nighthawk Unverified in winter	★					B												

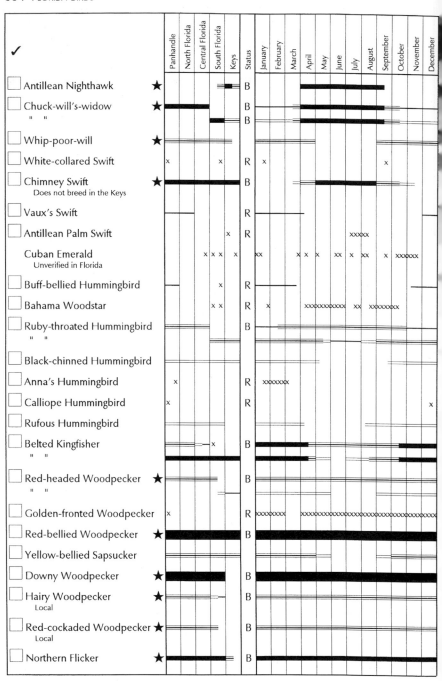

✓	Panhandle	North Florida	Central Florida	South Florida	Keys	Status	January	February	March	April	May	June	July	August	September	October	November	December
☐ Antillean Nighthawk ★					▬	B												
☐ Chuck-will's-widow ★						B												
" "						B												
☐ Whip-poor-will ★																		
☐ White-collared Swift	x			x		R	x							x				
☐ Chimney Swift ★						B												
Does not breed in the Keys																		
☐ Vaux's Swift						R												
☐ Antillean Palm Swift					x	R								xxxxx				
Cuban Emerald		x	x x		x	R	xx		x	x	x		xx	x	xx	x	x	xxxxxx
Unverified in Florida																		
☐ Buff-bellied Hummingbird				x		R												
☐ Bahama Woodstar				x	x	R	x			xxxxxxxxxxxx		xx		xxxxxxxxx				
☐ Ruby-throated Hummingbird						B												
" "																		
☐ Black-chinned Hummingbird																		
☐ Anna's Hummingbird		x				R	xxxxxxx											
☐ Calliope Hummingbird		x				R												x
☐ Rufous Hummingbird																		
☐ Belted Kingfisher					x	B												
" "																		
☐ Red-headed Woodpecker ★						B												
" "																		
☐ Golden-fronted Woodpecker	x					R	xxxxxxxx		xxxxxxxxxxxxxxxxxxxxxxxxxxxxxxxxxxxxxxxxxxx									
☐ Red-bellied Woodpecker ★						B												
☐ Yellow-bellied Sapsucker																		
☐ Downy Woodpecker ★						B												
☐ Hairy Woodpecker ★						B												
Local																		
☐ Red-cockaded Woodpecker ★						B												
Local																		
☐ Northern Flicker ★						B												

✓	Panhandle	North Florida	Central Florida	South Florida	Keys	Status	January	February	March	April	May	June	July	August	September	October	November	December
Pileated Woodpecker ★	▬	▬	▬	▬	=	B	▬	▬	▬	▬	▬	▬	▬	▬	▬	▬	▬	▬
Olive-sided Flycatcher						M												
Western Wood-Pewee Identification of silent birds impossible			x			R						x						
Eastern Wood-Pewee " "	▬					B / M												
Cuban Pewee				x		R		xx	x									
Yellow-bellied Flycatcher Identification of silent birds difficult						MR	xxxxxxxxxxxx										xxxxxxxx	
Acadian Flycatcher ★ " " Identification of silent birds difficult	▬					B / M												
Alder Flycatcher Identification of silent birds impossible						MR												
Willow Flycatcher Identification of silent birds impossible						MR												
Least Flycatcher Identification of silent birds difficult						M												
Black Phoebe				x	x x	R				x						xx		x
Eastern Phoebe ★ Two Panhandle breeding reports	▬						▬	▬								▬	▬	
Say's Phoebe	x	x x	x x				xx								x xx		xxxxxxx	
Vermilion Flycatcher																		
Ash-throated Flycatcher		x	x x	x x														
Great Crested Flycatcher ★ Rare to uncommon in winter in the southern peninsula and the Keys	▬					B				▬	▬	▬	▬	▬				
Brown-crested Flycatcher ★	x x		x x	— x														
La Sagra's Flycatcher Southeast coast				—														
Variegated Flycatcher Dry Tortugas						R			x									
Tropical Kingbird Unverified in Florida																		
Couch's Kingbird					x	R	xxxxx											

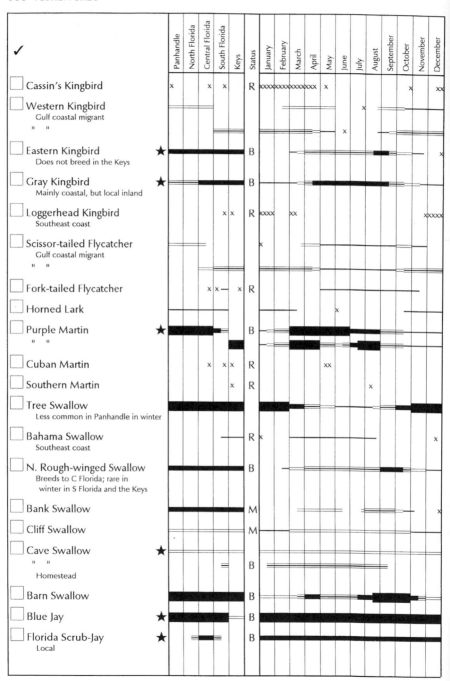

✓	Panhandle	North Florida	Central Florida	South Florida	Keys	Status	January	February	March	April	May	June	July	August	September	October	November	December
☐ Cassin's Kingbird	x		x	x		R	xxxxxxxxxxxxxxxx				x						x	xx
☐ Western Kingbird — Gulf coastal migrant													x					
☐ Eastern Kingbird — Does not breed in the Keys	★					B												x
☐ Gray Kingbird — Mainly coastal, but local inland	★					B												
☐ Loggerhead Kingbird — Southeast coast				x	x	R	xxxx	xx										xxxxx
☐ Scissor-tailed Flycatcher — Gulf coastal migrant							x											
☐ Fork-tailed Flycatcher		x	x —	x		R												
☐ Horned Lark											x							
☐ Purple Martin	★					B												
☐ Cuban Martin		x	x	x		R					xx							
☐ Southern Martin				x		R								x				
☐ Tree Swallow — Less common in Panhandle in winter																		
☐ Bahama Swallow — Southeast coast						R	x											x
☐ N. Rough-winged Swallow — Breeds to C Florida; rare in winter in S Florida and the Keys						B												
☐ Bank Swallow						M												x
☐ Cliff Swallow						M												
☐ Cave Swallow — Homestead	★					B												
☐ Barn Swallow						B												
☐ Blue Jay	★					B												
☐ Florida Scrub-Jay — Local	★					B												

✓	Panhandle	North Florida	Central Florida	South Florida	Keys	Status	January	February	March	April	May	June	July	August	September	October	November	December
American Crow ★	■	■	■	■	=	B												
Fish Crow ★	■	■	■	■	—	B												
Carolina Chickadee ★	■	■	—			B												
Tufted Titmouse ★	■	■	—			B												
Red-breasted Nuthatch (Irruptive)	=	=	—		x													
White-breasted Nuthatch	—	—	—			B												
Brown-headed Nuthatch ★	■	■	=			B												
Brown Creeper	=	=	—		x													
Red-whiskered Bulbul (Kendall) ★				■		E												
Rock Wren	x					R	xxxxxx											xxxxx
Carolina Wren ★	■	■	■	=		B												
Bewick's Wren	—	x	—			R												
House Wren	■	■	=															
Winter Wren	=	=																
Sedge Wren	=	=	—															
Marsh Wren (Coastal only) " " ★	■	■	—			B												
Golden-crowned Kinglet	=	=	—															
Ruby-crowned Kinglet	■	■	—									x						
Blue-gray Gnatcatcher ★ (Does not breed in the Keys and is rare in winter in N Florida)	■	■	■	■		B												
Northern Wheatear	x x			x		R									x	x xx		
Eastern Bluebird ★	■	■	—			B												
Veery	=	=	—			M												
Gray-cheeked Thrush (Some reports may refer to Bicknell's Thrush)	=	=	—			M												
Bicknell's Thrush (Status in Florida poorly known)						MR												

✓		Panhandle	North Florida	Central Florida	South Florida	Keys	Status	January	February	March	April	May	June	July	August	September	October	November	December
☐	Swainson's Thrush						M												
☐	Hermit Thrush																		
☐	Wood Thrush						B												
	" "						M												
☐	American Robin						B												
	" "																		
☐	Varied Thrush	x			x		R	xxx									x	x	
☐	Gray Catbird						B												
	" "																		
☐	Northern Mockingbird	★					B												
☐	Bahama Mockingbird Southeast coast																		
☐	Sage Thrasher	x	x				R	xxx		x	xxxxxx								
☐	Brown Thrasher	★					B												
☐	Curve-billed Thrasher	x x					R					x	xx						
☐	American Pipit														xx				
☐	Sprague's Pipit						R												
☐	Cedar Waxwing Irruptive																		
☐	Loggerhead Shrike	★					B												
☐	European Starling						E												
	Hill Myna Southeast coast suburban areas						E												
	Common Myna Suburban areas						E												
☐	White-eyed Vireo	★					B												
☐	Thick-billed Vireo Southeast coast						R												
☐	Bell's Vireo						R												
	" "						R												
☐	Solitary Vireo																		

✓	Panhandle	North Florida	Central Florida	South Florida	Keys	Status	January	February	March	April	May	June	July	August	September	October	November	December
Yellow-throated Vireo ★						B												
Most winter reports questionable																		
" "						M												
Warbling Vireo						MR												
Philadelphia Vireo						M												
Red-eyed Vireo ★						B												
Does not breed in the Keys																		
Yellow-green Vireo	x		x	x		R					xxxxxxxx							
Black-whiskered Vireo ★						B												
Does not occur on the Atlantic Coast N of Merritt Island																		
Blue-winged Warbler						M												
Unverified in winter																		
Golden-winged Warbler						M												
Tennessee Warbler						M												
Orange-crowned Warbler																		
Nashville Warbler						M												
Northern Parula ★						B												
" "						B												
" "																		
Yellow Warbler						M												
" " Cuban race ★						B												
Chestnut-sided Warbler						M												
Magnolia Warbler						M												
Unverified in winter																		
Cape May Warbler						M									x			
" "						M												
Black-throated Blue Warbler																		
Yellow-rumped Warbler																		
" " Myrtle race													x	x				
" " Audubon's race	x		x	x	x x	M	x			xxxx								x
Black-throated Gray Warbler																		
Townsend's Warbler			x			R	xxxxxxxxxxxx								x			xxx
Black-throated Green Warbler						M												
Unverified in winter																		

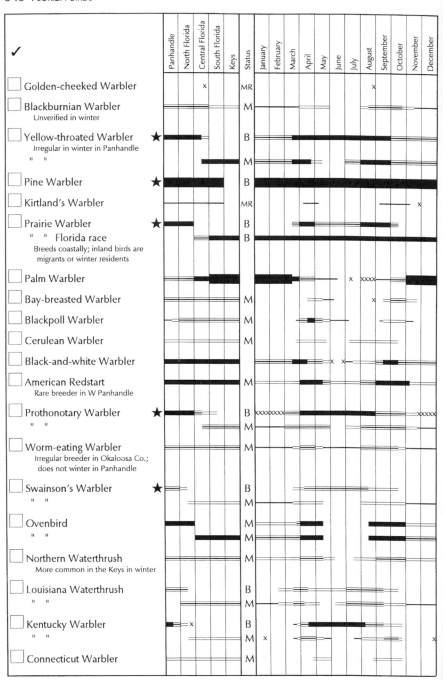

✔	Panhandle	North Florida	Central Florida	South Florida	Keys	Status	January	February	March	April	May	June	July	August	September	October	November	December
☐ Golden-cheeked Warbler			x			MR								x				
☐ Blackburnian Warbler Unverified in winter						M												
☐ Yellow-throated Warbler ★ Irregular in winter in Panhandle						B												
" "						M												
☐ Pine Warbler ★						B												
☐ Kirtland's Warbler						MR										x		
☐ Prairie Warbler ★						B												
" " Florida race Breeds coastally; inland birds are migrants or winter residents						B												
☐ Palm Warbler														x xxxx				
☐ Bay-breasted Warbler						M								x				
☐ Blackpoll Warbler						M												
☐ Cerulean Warbler						M												
☐ Black-and-white Warbler						M						x x						
☐ American Redstart Rare breeder in W Panhandle						M												
☐ Prothonotary Warbler ★						B	xxxxxxxxx											xxxxx
" "						M												
☐ Worm-eating Warbler Irregular breeder in Okaloosa Co.; does not winter in Panhandle						M												
☐ Swainson's Warbler ★						B												
" "						M												
☐ Ovenbird						M												
" "						M												
☐ Northern Waterthrush More common in the Keys in winter						M												
☐ Louisiana Waterthrush						B												
" "						M												
☐ Kentucky Warbler				x		B												
" "						M	x											x
☐ Connecticut Warbler						M												

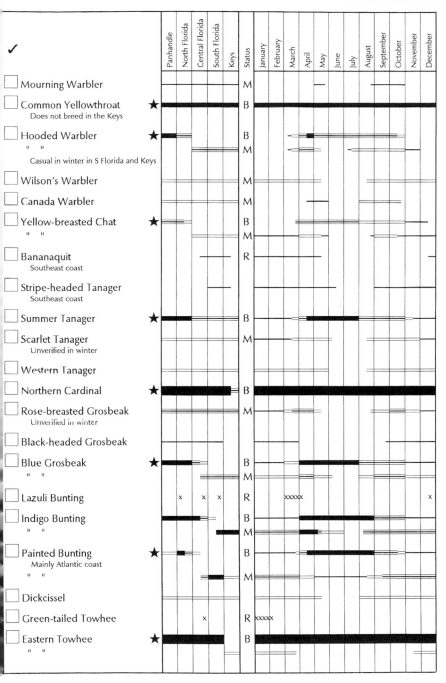

✓	Panhandle	North Florida	Central Florida	South Florida	Keys	Status	January	February	March	April	May	June	July	August	September	October	November	December
☐ Mourning Warbler						M												
☐ Common Yellowthroat ★ Does not breed in the Keys						B												
☐ Hooded Warbler ★						B												
" "						M												
Casual in winter in S Florida and Keys																		
☐ Wilson's Warbler						M												
☐ Canada Warbler						M												
☐ Yellow-breasted Chat ★						B												
" "						M												
☐ Bananaquit Southeast coast						R												
☐ Stripe-headed Tanager Southeast coast																		
☐ Summer Tanager ★						B												
☐ Scarlet Tanager Unverified in winter						M												
☐ Western Tanager																		
☐ Northern Cardinal ★						B												
☐ Rose-breasted Grosbeak Unverified in winter						M												
☐ Black-headed Grosbeak																		
☐ Blue Grosbeak ★						B												
" "						M												
☐ Lazuli Bunting	x	x	x			R	xxxxx											x
☐ Indigo Bunting						B												
" "						M												
☐ Painted Bunting ★ Mainly Atlantic coast						B												
" "						M												
☐ Dickcissel																		
☐ Green-tailed Towhee			x			R	xxxxx											
☐ Eastern Towhee ★						B												
" "																		

✓	Panhandle	North Florida	Central Florida	South Florida	Keys	Status	January	February	March	April	May	June	July	August	September	October	November	December
Spotted Towhee	x																	x
Yellow-faced Grassquit				x	x	R			x				xx					
Black-faced Grassquit				x	x	R		xxxxxxxxx		x						x		xx
Bachman's Sparrow ★						B												
Chipping Sparrow																		
Irregular breeder in the Panhandle																		
" "																		
Clay-colored Sparrow																		
Field Sparrow						B												
" "																		
Vesper Sparrow																		
Lark Sparrow																		
Black-throated Sparrow	x					R	xx											
Lark Bunting	x x		x		x	R	xxxxxxxx	xxxx						xxxxx				
Savannah Sparrow																		
" " Ipswich race / Atlantic coast																		
Grasshopper Sparrow																		
" " Florida race ★ / Very local, Endangered						B												
Henslow's Sparrow																		
Le Conte's Sparrow																		
Saltmarsh Sharp-tailed Sparrow / Mainly Atlantic coast																		
Nelson's Sharp-tailed Sparrow / Coastal																		
Seaside Sparrow ★ / Coastal						B												
" " Cape Sable race ★ / Everglades National Park						B												
Fox Sparrow																		
Song Sparrow											x		x					
Lincoln's Sparrow																		
Swamp Sparrow																		

✓	Species		Panhandle	North Florida	Central Florida	South Florida	Keys	Status	January	February	March	April	May	June	July	August	September	October	November	December
☐	White-throated Sparrow						x x							xxxxxxxxxx						
☐	Golden-crowned Sparrow						x	R						x						
☐	White-crowned Sparrow												x							
☐	Harris's Sparrow		x	x x		x		x	R	xxxxxxxxxxxxxxxxx										xxxxx
☐	Dark-eyed Junco																			
	" " Slate-colored race																			
	" " Oregon race		x		x	x									x						x
☐	Lapland Longspur								R											
☐	Chestnut-collared Longspur		x						R	xxx										xx
☐	Snow Bunting																			
	Mainly Atlantic coast																			
☐	Bobolink								M											
	Unverified in winter																			
☐	Red-winged Blackbird	★							B											
☐	Tawny-shouldered Blackbird						x		R	x										
☐	Eastern Meadowlark	★							B											
☐	Western Meadowlark								R											
☐	Yellow-headed Blackbird																			
☐	Rusty Blackbird																			
☐	Brewer's Blackbird						x x													
☐	Boat-tailed Grackle	★							B											
☐	Common Grackle	★							B											
	" "								B											
☐	Shiny Cowbird	★																		
	Mainly coastal, but local inland																			
☐	Bronzed Cowbird						x									x	xx			
☐	Brown-headed Cowbird	★							B											
☐	Orchard Oriole	★							B	x x										
	" "								M											
☐	Spot-breasted Oriole								E											
	Southeast coast suburban areas																			
☐	Baltimore Oriole																			

✓		Panhandle	North Florida	Central Florida	South Florida	Keys	Status	January	February	March	April	May	June	July	August	September	October	November	December
☐	Bullock's Oriole																		
☐	Purple Finch		x	x	x	x													
☐	House Finch						E												
	Local in Panhandle and North Florida; range expanding into peninsula																		
☐	Red Crossbill	x	x				R	xxxx											xxxx
☐	Pine Siskin													xx					
☐	American Goldfinch																		
☐	Evening Grosbeak																		
☐	House Sparrow						E												

OTHER FAUNAL LISTS FOR FLORIDA

U nlike the case with Florida's birds, there are no current, complete, and definitive lists for the state's dragonflies, butterflies, reptiles, amphibians, and mammals. Therefore, the lists that follow were compiled from a variety of sources that were often contradictory, especially concerning taxonomic sequence and English names. Fritz Davis and Buck and Linda Cooper are thanked for compiling the invertebrate lists, as is Walter Meshaka for updating the "herp" lists.

DRAGONFLIES OF FLORIDA
86 species

Gray Petaltail (*Tachopteryx thoreyi*)
Common Green Darner (*Anax junius*)
Comet Darner (*Anax longipes*)
Fawn Darner (*Boyeria vinosa*)
Blue-faced Darner (*Coryphaeschna adnexa*)
Regal Darner (*Coryphaeschna ingens*)
Mangrove Darner (*Coryphaeschna viriditas*)
Swamp Darner (*Epiaeschna heros*)
Taper-tailed Darner (*Gomphaeschna antilope*)
Harlequin Darner (*Gomphaeschna furcillata*)
Twilight Darner (*Gynacantha nervosa*)
Cyrano Darner (*Nasiaeschna pentacantha*)
Phantom Darner (*Triacanthagyna trifida*)
Two-striped Forceptail (*Aphylla williamsoni*)
Gray-green Clubtail (*Arigomphus pallidus*)
Southeastern Spinyleg (*Dromogomphus armatus*)
Black-shouldered Spinyleg (*Dromogomphus spinosus*)
Blackwater Clubtail (*Gomphus dilatatus*)
Clearlake Clubtail (*Gomphus australis*)
Sandhill Clubtail (*Gomphus cavillaris*)
Cypress Clubtail (*Gomphus minutus*)
Dragonhunter (*Hagenius brevistylus*)
Tawny Sanddragon (*Progomphus alachuensis*)
Common Sanddragon (*Progomphus obscurus*)
Shining Clubtail (*Stylurus ivae*)
Russet-tipped Clubtail (*Stylurus plagiatus*)

Twin-spotted Spiketail (*Cordulegaster maculata*)
Arrowhead Spiketail (*Cordulegaster obliqua*)
Say's Spiketail (*Cordulegaster sayi*)
Maidencane Cruiser (*Didymops floridensis*)
Stream Cruiser (*Didymops transversa*)
Georgia River Cruiser (*Macromia georgina*)
Royal River Cruiser (*Macromia taeniolata*)
Stripe-winged Baskettail (*Epitheca costalis*)
Common Baskettail (*Epitheca cynosura*)
Prince Baskettail (*Epitheca princeps*)
Sepia Baskettail (*Epitheca sepia*)
Florida Baskettail (*Epitheca stella*)
Pale-sided Shadowfly (*Neurocordulia alabamensis*)
Umber Shadowfly (*Neurocordulia obsoleta*)
Cinnamon Shadowfly (*Neurocordulia virginiensis*)
Fine-lined Emerald (*Somatochlora filosa*)
Mocha Emerald (*Somatochlora linearis*)
Red Pennant (*Brachymesia furcata*)
Four-spotted Pennant (*Brachymesia gravida*]
Amanda's Pennant (*Celithemis amanda*)
Red-veined Pennant (*Celithemis bertha*)
Calico Pennant (*Celithemis elisa*)
Halloween Pennant (*Celithemis eponina*)
Banded Pennant (*Celithemis fasciata*)
Faded Pennant (*Celithemis ornata*)
Double-ringed Pennant (*Celithemis verna*)
Scarlet Skimmer (*Crocothemis servilia*)
Black Pondhawk (*Erythemis plebeja*)
Eastern Pondhawk (*Erythemis simplicicollis*)
Great Pondhawk (*Erythemis vesiculosa*)
Seaside Dragonlet (*Erythrodiplax berenice*)
Blue Dragonlet (*Erythrodiplax connata*)
Band-winged Dragonlet (*Erythrodiplax umbrata*)
Metallic Pennant (*Idiatrophe cubensis*)
Golden-winged Skimmer (*Libellula auripennis*)
Bar-winged Skimmer (*Libellula axilena*)
Corporal Skimmer (*Libellula exusta*)
Slaty Skimmer (*Libellula incesta*)
Purple Skimmer (*Libellula jesseana*)
Common Whitetail (*Libellula lydia*)
Needham's Skimmer (*Libellula needhami*)
Painted Skimmer (*Libellula semifasciata*)
Great Blue Skimmer (*Libellula vibrans*)
Marl Pennant (*Macrodiplax balteata*)
Greater Hyacinth Glider (*Miathyria marcella*)
Speckled Skimmer (*Micrathyria aequalis*)
Three-striped Skimmer (*Micrathyria didyama*)
Roseate Skimmer (*Orthemis ferruginea*)
Blue Dasher (*Pachydiplax longipennis*)
Wandering Glider (*Pantala flavescens*)
Spot-winged Glider (*Pantala hymenaea*)
Eastern Amberwing (*Perithemis tenera*)

Blue-faced Meadowfly (*Sympetrum ambiguum*)
Variegated Meadowfly (*Sympetrum corruptum*)
Garnet Glider (*Tauriphila australis*)
Vermilion Glider (*Tramea abdominalis*)
Violet-masked Glider (*Tramea carolina*)
Antillean Glider (*Tramea insularis*)
Black-mantled Glider (*Tramea lacerata*)
Red-mantled Glider (*Tramea onusta*)

BUTTERFLIES OF FLORIDA
176 species

Taxonomy follows North America Butterfly Association checklist

Pipevine Swallowtail (*Battus philenor*)
Polydamus Swallowtail (*Battus polydamus*)
Zebra Swallowtail (*Eurytides marcellus*)
Black Swallowtail (*Papilio polyxenes*)
Giant Swallowtail (*Papilio cresphontes*)
Schaus's Swallowtail (*Papilio aristodemus*) Endangered
Bahamian Swallowtail (*Papilio andraemon*)
Eastern Tiger Swallowtail (*Papilio glaucus*)
Spicebush Swallowtail (*Papilio troilus*)
Palamedes Swallowtail (*Papilio palamedes*)
Florida White (*Appias drusilla*)
Checkered White (*Pontia protodice*)
Cabbage White (*Pieris rapae*)
Great Southern White (*Ascia monuste*)
Falcate Orangetip (*Anthocharis midea*)
Clouded Sulphur (*Colias philodice*)
Orange Sulphur (*Colias eurytheme*)
Southern Dogface (*Colias cesonia*)
Yellow Angled-Sulphur (*Anteos maerula*)
Cloudless Sulphur (*Phoebis sennae*)
Orange-barred Sulphur (*Phoebis philea*)
Large Orange Sulphur (*Phoebis agarithe*)
Statira Sulphur (*Phoebis statira*)
Orbed Sulphur (*Aphrissa orbis*)
Lyside Sulphur (*Kricogonia lyside*)
Barred Yellow (*Eurema daira*)
Boisduval's Yellow (*Eurema boisduvaliana*)
Little Yellow (*Eurema lisa*)
Mimosa Yellow (*Eurema nise*)
Dina Yellow (*Eurema dina*)
Sleepy Orange (*Eurema nicippe*)
Dainty Sulphur (*Nathalis iole*)
Harvester (*Feniseca tarquinius*)
Atala (*Eumaeus atala*)
Great Purple Hairstreak (*Atlides halesus*)
Amethyst Hairstreak (*Chorostrymon maesites*) Threatened

Silver-banded Hairstreak (*Chlorostrymon simaethis*)
Coral Hairstreak (*Satyrium titus*)
Banded Hairstreak (*Satyrium calanus*)
King's Hairstreak (*Satyrium kingi*)
Striped Hairstreak (*Satyrium liparops*)
Southern Hairstreak (*Satyrium favonius*)
Henry's Elfin (*Callophrys henrici*)
Eastern Pine Elfin (*Incisalia niphon*)
Juniper Hairstreak (*Callophrys gryneus*)
Hessel's Hairstreak (*Callophrys hesseli*)
White M Hairstreak (*Parrhasius m-album*)
Martial Scrub-Hairstreak (*Strymon martialis*)
Bartram's Scrub-Hairstreak (*Strymon acis*)
Mallow Scrub-Hairstreak (*Strymon columella*)
Disguised Scrub-Hairstreak (*Strymon limenia*)
Ruddy Hairstreak (*Electrostrymon sangala*)
Fulvous Hairstreak (*Electrostrymon angelia*)
Muted Hairstreak (*Electrostrymon canus*)
Red-banded Hairstreak (*Calycopis cecrops*)
Gray Hairstreak (*Ministrymon azia*)
Eastern Pygmy Blue (*Brephidium isophthalma*)
Cassius Blue (*Leptotes cassius*)
Miami Blue (*Hemiargus thomasi*)
Ceraunus Blue (*Hemiargus ceraunus*)
Eastern Tailed-Blue (*Everes comyntas*)
Spring Azure (*Celastrina ladon*)
Little Metalmark (*Calephelis virginiensis*)
American Snout (*Libytheana carinenta*)
Gulf Fritillary (*Agraulis vanillae*)
Julia (*Dryas iulia*)
Zebra (*Heliconius charitonius*)
Variegated Fritillary (*Euptoieta claudia*)
Silvery Checkerspot (*Chlosyne nycteis*)
Texan Crescent (*Phyciodes texana*)
Cuban Crescent (*Phyciodes frisia*)
Phaon Crescent (*Phyciodes phaon*)
Pearl Crescent (*Phyciodes tharos*)
Question Mark (*Polygonia interrogationis*)
Eastern Comma (*Polygonia comma*)
Mourning Cloak (*Nymphalis antiopa*)
American Lady (*Vanessa virginiensis*)
Painted Lady (*Vanessa cardui*)
Red Admiral (*Vanessa atalanta*)
Common Buckeye (*Junonia coenia*)
Mangrove Buckeye (*Junonia evarete*)
Tropical Buckeye (*Junonia genoveva*)
Cuban Peacock (*Anartia chrysopelea*)
White Peacock (*Anartia jatrophae*)
Malachite (*Siproeta stelenes*)
Red-spotted Purple (*Limenitis arthemis*)
Viceroy (*Limenitis archippus*)
Dingy Purplewing (*Eunica monima*)

Florida Purplewing (*Eunica tatila*)
Pale Croaker (*Hamadryas amphichloe*)
Many-banded Daggerwing (*Marpesia chiron*)
Ruddy Daggerwing (*Marpesia petreus*)
Antillean Daggerwing (*Marpesia eleuchea*)
Florida Leafwing (*Anaea troglodyta*)
Goatweed Leafwing (*Anaea andria*)
Hackberry Emperor (*Asterocampa celtis*)
Tawny Emperor (*Asterocampa clyton*)
Southern Pearly-Eye (*Enodia portlandia*)
Appalachian Brown (*Satyrodes appalachia*)
Gemmed Satyr (*Cyllopsis gemma*)
Carolina Satyr (*Hermeuptychia sosybius*)
Georgia Satyr (*Neonympha areolata*)
Little Wood-Satyr (*Megisto cymela*)
Viola's Wood-Satyr (*Megisto viola*)
Common Wood-Nymph (*Cercyonis pegala*)
Monarch (*Danaus plexippus*)
Queen (*Danaus gilippus*)
Soldier (*Danaus eresimus*)
Mangrove Skipper (*Phocides pigmalion*)
Zestos Skipper (*Epargyreus zestos*)
Silver-spotted Skipper (*Epargyreus clarus*)
Hammock Skipper (*Polygonus leo*)
Long-tailed Skipper (*Urbanus proteus*)
Dorantes Longtail (*Urbanus dorantes*)
Golden-banded Skipper (*Autochton cellus*)
Hoary Edge (*Achalarus lyciades*)
Southern Cloudywing (*Thorybes bathyllus*)
Northern Cloudywing (*Thorybes pylades*)
Confused Cloudywing (*Thorybes confusis*)
Hayhurst's Scallopwing (*Staphlyus hayhurstii*)
Variegated Skipper (*Gorgythion begga*)
Florida Duskywing (*Ephyriades brunneus*)
Sleepy Duskywing (*Erynnis brizo*)
Juvenal's Duskywing (*Erynnis juvenalis*)
Horace's Duskywing (*Erynnis horatius*)
Zarucco Duskywing (*Erynnis zarucco*)
Funereal Duskywing (*Erynnis funeralis*)
Wild Indigo Duskywing (*Erynnis baptisiae*)
Common Checkered-Skipper (*Pyrgus communis*)
Tropical Checkered-Skipper (*Pyrgus oileus*)
Common Sootywing (*Pholisora catullus*)
Swarthy Skipper (*Nastra lherminier*)
Neamathla Skipper (*Nastra neamathla*)
Three-spotted Skipper (*Cymaenes tripunctus*)
Clouded Skipper (*Lerema accius*)
Least Skipper (*Ancyloxpha numitor*)
Southern Skipperling (*Copaeodes minima*)
Fiery Skipper (*Hylephila phyleus*)
Dotted Skipper (*Hesperia attalus*)
Meske's Skipper (*Hesperia meskei*) Threatened

Baracoa Skipper (*Polites baracoa*)
Tawny-edged Skipper (*Polites themistocles*)
Crossline Skipper (*Polites origenes*)
Whirlabout (*Polites vibex*)
Southern Broken-Dash (*Wallengrenia otho*)
Northern Broken-Dash (*Wallengrenia egeremet*)
Little Glassywing (*Pompeius verna*)
Sachem (*Atalopedes campestris*)
Arogos Skipper (*Atrytone arogos*)
Delaware Skipper (*Atrytone logan*)
Byssus Skipper (*Problema byssus*)
Zabulon Skipper (*Poanes zabulon*)
Aaron's Skipper (*Poanes aaroni*)
Yehl Skipper (*Poanes yehl*)
Broad-winged Skipper (*Poanes viator*)
Palmetto Skipper (*Euphyes arpa*)
Palatka Skipper (*Euphyes pilatka*)
Dion Skipper (*Euphyes dion*)
Duke's Skipper (*Euphyes dukesi*)
Berry's Skipper (*Euphyes berryi*)
Dun Skipper (*Euphyes vestris*)
Monk Skipper (*Asbolis capucinus*)
Dusted Skipper (*Atrytonopsis hianna*)
Pepper-and-Salt Skipper (*Amblyscirtes hegon*)
Lace-winged Roadside-Skipper (*Amblyscirtes aesculapius*)
Common Roadside-Skipper (*Amblyscirtes vialis*)
Dusky Roadside-Skipper (*Amblyscirtes alternata*)
Eufala Skipper (*Lerodea eufala*)
Twin-spot Skipper (*Oligoria maculata*)
Brazilian Skipper (*Calpodes ethlius*)
Salt-Marsh Skipper (*Panoquina panoquin*)
Obscure Skipper (*Panoquina panoquinoides*)
Ocola Skipper (*Panoquina ocola*)
Violet-banded Skipper (*Nyctelius nyctelius*)
Yucca Giant-Skipper (*Megathymus yuccae*)
Cofaqui Giant-Skipper (*Megathymus cofaqui*)

AMPHIBIANS OF FLORIDA
56 species

Salamanders

Gulf Coast Waterdog (*Necturus alabamensis*)—Streams in the Panhandle.
Two-toed Amphiuma (*Amphiuma means*)—Wetlands throughout.
One-toed Amphiuma (*Amphiuma pholeter*)—Muck beds in streams in the Panhandle and along the Gulf coast to Hernando County.
Greater Siren (*Siren lacertina*)—Wetlands throughout.
Lesser Siren (*Siren intermedia*)—Wetlands throughout.

Dwarf Siren (*Pseudobranchus striatus*)—Hyacinth-covered waters throughout the mainland.

Mole Salamander (*Ambystoma talpoideum*)—Moist woodlands in the Panhandle south to central Florida.

Marbled Salamander (*Ambystoma opacum*)—Hammocks in the Panhandle and North Florida.

Flatwoods Salamander (*Ambystoma cingulatum*)—Pinewoods in the Panhandle and North Florida.

Tiger Salamander (*Ambystoma tigrinum*)—Moist woodlands in the Panhandle south to the central peninsula.

Spotted Newt (*Notophthalmus viridescens*)—Quiet waters throughout the mainland.

Striped Newt (*Notophthalmus perstriatus*)—Quiet waters south to the central peninsula.

Northern Dusky Salamander (*Desmognathus fuscus*)—Streams in the Panhandle and a few sites in central Florida.

Southern Dusky Salamander (*Desmognathus auriculatus*)—Swamps south to central Florida.

Seal Salamander (*Desmognathus monticola*)—Only in Canoe Creek (Escambia County).

Slimy Salamander (*Plethodon glutinosus*)—Moist woodlands south to central Florida.

Four-toed Salamander (*Hemidactylium scutatum*)—Bogs and other wetlands of two regions in the Panhandle.

Many-lined Salamander (*Stereochilus marginatus*)—Bayhead swamps in the Okefenokee Swamp region.

Mud Salamander (*Pseudotriton montanus*)—Shallow streams in the Panhandle south to central Florida.

Red Salamander (*Pseudotriton ruber*)—Small streams in the Panhandle.

Two-lined Salamander (*Eurycea bislineata*)—Small streams in the Panhandle and the northwestern peninsula.

Long-tailed Salamander (*Eurycea longicauda*)—Moist woodlands in the Panhandle.

Dwarf Salamander (*Eurycea quadridigitata*)—Swamps south to central Florida.

Georgia Blind Salamander (*Haideotriton wallacei*)—About 15 caves near Marianna.

Toads and Frogs

Eastern Spadefoot Toad (*Scaphiopus holbrooki*)—Sandy woodlands throughout.

Southern Toad (*Bufo terrestris*)—Most habitats throughout.

Woodhouse's Toad (*Bufo woodhousei*)—Wetlands in the Panhandle.

Oak Toad (*Bufo quercicus*)—Pinewoods and oak hammocks throughout.

Giant Toad (*Bufo marinus*)—Exotic, native to Tropical America. Human-modified habitats from central Florida southward.

Greenhouse Frog (*Eleutherodactylus planirostris*)—Exotic, native to the West Indies. Wet woodlands throughout.

Puerto Rican Coqui (*Eleutherodactylus coqui*)—Exotic, native to Puerto Rico. Miami area.

Southern Cricket Frog (*Acris gryllus*)—Wetlands throughout.

Northern Cricket Frog (*Acris crepitans*)—Swamps in the Panhandle.

Spring Peeper (*Hyla crucifer*)—Moist woodlands south to central Florida.

Pine Barrens Treefrog (*Hyla andersonii*)—Swamps in the western Panhandle.

Green Treefrog (*Hyla cinerea*)—Wetlands throughout.

Barking Treefrog (*Hyla gratiosa*)—Woodlands throughout, except absent from the extreme south.

Pine Woods Treefrog (*Hyla femoralis*)—Pinewoods and cypress swamps throughout, except absent from the extreme south.

Squirrel Treefrog (*Hyla squirella*)—Moist woodlands throughout.

Gray Treefrog (*Hyla chrysoscelis*)—Woodlands in the Panhandle and North Florida.

Bird-voiced Treefrog (*Hyla avivoca*)—Swamps in the Panhandle.

Cuban Treefrog (*Osteopilus septentrionalis*)—Exotic, native to Cuba. Woodlands and human-modified habitats from central Florida southward.

Upland Chorus Frog (*Pseudacris triseriata*)—Moist woodlands in the upper Apalachicola River.

Southern Chorus Frog (*Pseudacris nigrita*)—Wet prairies and pinewoods throughout, except absent from the extreme south.

Ornate Chorus Frog (*Pseudacris ornata*)—Ponds south to central Florida.

Little Grass Frog (*Pseudacris ocularis*)—Brushy wetlands throughout.

Eastern Narrowmouth Toad (*Gastrophyne carolinensis*)—Wetlands throughout.

Bullfrog (*Rana catesbeiana*)—Permanent waters south to central Florida.

River Frog (*Rana heckscheri*)—Permanent waters south to the central peninsula.

Pig Frog (*Rana grylio*)—Permanent waters throughout.

Carpenter Frog (*Rana virgatipes*)—Okefenokee Swamp region of Baker and Columbia counties.

Bronze Frog (*Rana clamitans*)—Wetlands in the Panhandle and North Florida.

Southern Leopard Frog (*Rana utricularia*)—Wetlands throughout.

Pickerel Frog (*Rana palustris*)—One old and possibly erroneous record from Pensacola.

Gopher Frog (*Rana capito*)—Threatened. Gopher Tortoise burrows south to South Florida.

Florida Bog Frog (*Rana okaloosae*)—An endemic species discovered in 1982. All 23 known localities are in small streams of the Yellow and East Bay rivers in Okaloosa, Santa Rosa, and Walton counties. All but three localities are within Eglin Air Force Base.

REPTILES OF FLORIDA
112 species

Crocodilians

American Crocodile (*Crocodylus acutus*)—Endangered, with the Florida population numbering about 500 individuals, of which only about 30 are breeding females. In the United States, limited to extreme southern Florida, in mangrove systems from Cape Sable to southern Biscayne Bay, south to northern Key Largo. Non-breeding animals may be seen north to about Naples, and on the Lower Keys. Compared to American Alligators, American Crocodiles are pale greenish in color, with a narrow snout. The fourth tooth of the lower jaw is visible "bulldog fashion" when the mouth is closed.

American Alligator (*Alligator mississippiensis*)—Widespread in freshwater habitats throughout, but rare in salt water.

Brown (or **Spectacled**) **Caiman** (*Caiman crocodilus*)—Exotic, native to Central and South America. Rare in freshwater canals in the Miami area.

Turtles

Common Snapping Turtle (*Chelydra serpentina*)—Wetlands throughout.

Alligator Snapping Turtle (*Macroclemys temminckii*)—Slow-moving waters in the Panhandle and the northwestern peninsula.

Common Musk Turtle (aka **Stinkpot**) (*Sternotherus odoratus*)—Wetlands throughout.

Loggerhead Musk Turtle (*Sternotherus minor*)—Streams, lakes, and ponds south to the central peninsula.

Mud Turtle (*Kinosternon subrubrum*)—Shallow waters throughout.

Striped Mud Turtle (*Kinosternon bauri*)—Wetlands throughout, except absent from the western Panhandle.

Spotted Turtle (*Clemmys guttata*) Wetlands in the northern and central peninsula.

Box Turtle (*Terrapene carolina*)—Wooded areas throughout.

Diamondback Terrapin (*Melaclemys terrapin*)—Salt marshes and mangrove forests along both coasts.

Barbour's Map Turtle (*Graptemys barbouri*)—Chipola and Apalachicola rivers in the Panhandle.

Alabama Map Turtle (*Graptemys pulchra*)—Escambia and Yellow rivers in the western Panhandle.

Red-eared Slider (*Trachemys scripta*)—Wetlands in the Panhandle and northern Florida; introduced in Dade County and on Big Pine Key.

River Cooter (*Pseudemys concinna*)—Gulf coast streams and estuaries south to Tampa Bay.

Peninsula Cooter (*Pseudemys floridana*)—Wetlands throughout, except absent from the extreme south.

Florida Redbelly Turtle (*Pseudemys nelsoni*)—Endemic to wetlands in the peninsula.

Alabama Redbelly Turtle (*Pseudemys alabamensis*)—Panhandle coast.

Chicken Turtle (*Deirochelys reticularia*)—Wetlands throughout.

Gopher Tortoise (*Gopherus polyphemus*)—Threatened. Well-drained areas throughout the mainland, except restricted to coastal areas south of Lake Okeechobee.

Green Turtle (*Chelonia mydas*)—Endangered, with only about 375 adult females in Florida. Oceanic; nests along virtually the entire Atlantic coast, but most numerous from Melbourne to Jupiter. Archie Carr National Wildlife Refuge in Brevard and Indian River counties is currently being established to prevent the extirpation of Florida's nesting sea turtles.

Hawksbill Turtle (*Eretmochelys imbricata*)—Endangered; only 1-2 nests are found in Florida annually, along the central and southern Atlantic coast. A Caribbean species restricted in the U.S. to Florida.

Loggerhead Turtle (*Caretta caretta*)—Threatened. Oceanic; nests in Florida along sandy Gulf coast beaches, Dry Tortugas National Park, and most of the Atlantic coast. Nesting densities from Melbourne to Jupiter can exceed 200 nests per linear mile (a nest every 25 feet!), one of the densest nesting concentrations in the world.

Atlantic Ridley Turtle (*Lepidochelys kempii*)—Endangered; does not normally nest in Florida. Adults are restricted to the Gulf of Mexico from Everglades National Park (Cape Sable) to the Yucatan Peninsula; a few turtles have also been found in Florida along the Atlantic coast.

Leatherback Turtle (*Dermochelys coriacea*)—Oceanic; nests in Florida very rarely, predominately along the central Atlantic coast.

Smooth Softshell (*Apalone muticus*)—In Florida, restricted to extreme northwest Escambia County in the western Panhandle.

Spiny Softshell (*Apalone spiniferus*)—Streams in the Panhandle.

Florida Softshell (*Apalone ferox*)—Quiet waters throughout the mainland; introduced on Big Pine Key.

Lizards

Tropical House Gecko (*Hemidactylus mabouia*)—Exotic, native to the Old World. Southern third of the peninsula.

Fox Gecko (*Hemidactylus frenatus*)—Exotic, native to the Old World. Southern third of the peninsula.

Mediterranean Gecko (*Hemidactylus turcicus*)—Exotic, native to the Old World. Central Florida southward, with scattered populations farther north.

Indo-Pacific Gecko (*Hemidactylus garnoti*)—Exotic, native to the Old World. Central Florida southward, with scattered populations farther north.

Ashy Gecko (*Sphaerodactylus elegans*)—Exotic, native to Cuba. Lower Keys.

Florida Reef Gecko (*Sphaerodactylus notatus*)—Wooded areas in extreme southern Florida.

Ocellated Gecko (*Sphaerodactylus argus*)—Exotic, native to the West Indies. Key West.

Yellow-headed Gecko (*Gonatodes albogularis*)—Exotic, native to Central America. Key West and South Miami.

Tokay Gecko (*Gekko gekko*)—Exotic, native to Indonesia. Scattered populations throughout.

Green Anole (*Anolis carolinensis*)—Woodlands throughout.

Brown Anole (*Anolis sagrei*)—Exotic, native to the West Indies. Spreading throughout.

Jamaican Giant Anole (*Anolis garmani*)—Exotic, native to Jamaica. Miami area.

Crested Anole (*Anolis cristatellus*)—Exotic, native to Puerto Rico. Miami area.

Large-headed Anole (*Anolis cybotes*)—Exotic, native to the West Indies. Fort Lauderdale and Miami.

Bark Anole (*Anolis distichus*)—Exotic, native to the Bahamas. Southeast coast and Keys.

Knight Anole (*Anolis equestris*)—Exotic, native to Cuba. Fort Lauderdale and Miami.

Brown Basilisk (*Basiliscus vittatus*)—Exotic, native to Tropical America. Canals in the Miami area.

Green Iguana (*Iguana iguana*)—Exotic, native to Tropical America. Miami southward.

Spiny-tailed Iguana (*Ctenosaura pectinata*)—Exotic, native to Tropical America. Miami.

Eastern Fence Lizard (*Sceloporus undulatus*)—Brushlands and pine flatwoods south to central Florida.

Florida Scrub Lizard (*Sceloporus woodi*)—Threatened. Endemic to coastal and interior ridge systems in the southern half of the peninsula.

Texas Horned Lizard (*Phrynosoma cornutum*)—Exotic, native to the western United States. Pensacola area.

Curly-tailed Lizard (*Leiocephalus carinatus*)—Exotic, native to the West Indies. Southeast coast.

Six-lined Racerunner (*Cnemidophorus sexlineatus*)—Well-drained soils throughout.

Tropical Racerunner (*Cnemidophorus lemniscatus*)—Exotic, native to Tropical America. Miami.

Ground Lizard (*Ameiva ameiva*)—Exotic, native to Tropical America. Miami.

Rainbow Whiptail (*Cnemidophorus lemniscatus*)—Exotic, native to Tropical America. Miami area.

Ground Skink (*Scincella lateralis*)—Woodlands throughout.

Northern Five-lined Skink (*Eumeces fasciatus*)—Woodlands in the Panhandle and northern half of the peninsula.

Broad-headed Skink (*Eumeces laticeps*)—Woodlands in the Panhandle and northern half of the peninsula.

Southeastern Five-lined Skink (*Eumeces inexpectatus*)—Woodlands throughout.

Coal Skink (*Eumeces anthracinus*)—Moist woodlands in the central Panhandle.

Mole Skink (*Eumeces egregius*)—Well-drained soils throughout.

Sand Skink (*Neoseps reynoldsi*)—Threatened. Endemic to ridge systems in interior central Florida.

Eastern Glass Lizard (*Ophisaurus ventralis*)—Moist woodlands and meadows throughout.

Slender Glass Lizard (*Ophisaurus attenuatus*)—Grassy areas throughout.

Island Glass Lizard (*Ophisaurus compressus*)—Well-drained uplands in the eastern Panhandle and peninsula.

Mimic Glass Lizard (*Ophisaurus mimicus*)—Pinewoods in the Panhandle and extreme northeast Florida.

Worm Lizard (*Rhineura floridana*)—Endemic. Sandy areas in the peninsula south to Lake Okeechobee.

Snakes

Brahminy Blind Snake (*Ramphotyphlops braminus*)—Exotic, native to the Old World. Scattered populations from central Florida southward.

Green Water Snake (*Nerodia floridana*)—Marshes and swamps throughout.

Brown Water Snake (*Nerodia taxispilota*)—Streams and rivers throughout.

Water Snake (*Nerodia fasciata*)—Shallow waters throughout.

Salt-Marsh Snake (*Nerodia clarkii*)—Brackish and salt marshes throughout.

Black Swamp Snake (*Seminatrix pygaea*)—Hyacinth-covered waters throughout.

Brown Snake (*Storeria dekayi*)—Wetlands throughout.

Red-bellied Snake (*Storeria occipitomaculata*)—Woodlands south to central Florida.

Red-bellied Water Snake (*Nerodia erythrogaster*)—Wetlands in the Panhandle and North Florida.

Midland Water Snake (*Nerodia sipedon*)—Escambia, Yellow, and Choctawhatchee rivers in Escambia County in the western Panhandle.

Queen Snake (*Regina septemvittata*)—Streams in the Panhandle.

Glossy Water Snake (*Regina rigida*)—Swamps in the Panhandle south to central Florida.

Striped Crayfish Snake (*Regina alleni*)—Vegetated ponds in the extreme eastern Panhandle and peninsula.

Garter Snake (*Thamnophis sirtalis*)—Wetland edges throughout.

Ribbon Snake (*Thamnophis sauritus*)—Wetland edges throughout.

Smooth Earth Snake (*Virginia valeriae*)—Deciduous forests in the Panhandle and North Florida, with scattered populations farther south.

Rough Earth Snake (*Virginia striatula*)—Dry uplands south to central Florida.

Eastern Hognose Snake (*Heterodon platyrhinos*)—Sandy areas throughout.

Southern Hognose Snake (*Heterodon simus*)—Sandy areas south to the central peninsula.
Ringneck Snake (*Diadophis punctatus*)—Moist woodlands throughout.
Pinewoods Snake (*Rhadinaea flavilata*)—Moist woodlands south to South Florida.
Eastern Mud Snake (*Farancia abacura*)—Swamps throughout.
Rainbow Snake (*Farancia erytrogramma*)—Moist areas south to central Florida.
Black Racer (*Coluber constrictor*)—Open habitats throughout.
Eastern Coachwhip (*Masticophis flagellum*)—Uplands throughout.
Rough Green Snake (*Opheodrys aestivus*)—Woodlands throughout.
Indigo Snake (*Drymarchon corais*)—Varied habitats throughout.
Corn Snake (*Elaphe guttata*)—Woodlands throughout.
Rat Snake (*Elaphe obsoleta*)—Varied habitats throughout.
Pine Snake (*Pituophis melanoleucus*)—Well-drained soils throughout the mainland, except absent from area south of Lake Okeechobee.
Common Kingsnake (*Lampropeltis getulus*)—Woodlands throughout.
Scarlet Kingsnake (*Lampropeltis triangulum*)—Woodlands throughout.
Mole Snake (*Lampropeltis calligaster*)—Fallow lands in the Panhandle, and scattered sites in the central peninsula.
Scarlet Snake (*Cemophora coccinea*)—Sandy areas throughout.
Short-tailed Snake (*Stilosoma extenuatum*)—Threatened. Endemic to sandhills in the northern half of the peninsula.
Crowned Snake (*Tantilla relicta*)—Dry uplands throughout.
Rim-Rock Crowned Snake (*Tantilla oolitica*)—Threatened. Endemic to woodlands in coastal Dade County and the Upper Keys.
Southeastern Crowned Snake (*Tantilla coronata*)—Upland habitats in the Panhandle.
Coral Snake (*Micrurus fulvius*)—Woodlands throughout.
Copperhead (*Agkistrodon contortrix*)—Swamps in the Upper Apalachicola River.
Cottonmouth (or **Water Moccasin**) (*Agkistrodon piscivorus*)—Wetlands throughout.
Dusky Pygmy Rattlesnake (*Sistrurus miliarius*)—Wet prairies and moist woodlands throughout.
Timber Rattlesnake (*Crotalus horridus*)—Wet woodlands in central North Florida.
Eastern Diamondback Rattlesnake (*Crotalus adamanteus*)—Pinewoods and savannahs throughout.

MAMMALS OF FLORIDA
106 species

Marsupials

Opossum (*Didelphis virginiana*)—Woodlands throughout.

Insectivores

Southeastern Shrew (*Sorex longirostris*)—Moist woodlands in the northern half of the peninsula.
Short-tailed Shrew (*Blarina carolinensis*)—Various habitats throughout.
Least Shrew (*Cryptotis parva*)—Marshes and prairies throughout
Eastern Mole (*Scalopus aquaticus*)—Sandy areas throughout.

Bats

Cuban House Bat *(Molossus molussus)*—Three colonies found in 1995 in the Middle and Lower Keys.

Jamaican Fruit-eating Bat *(Artibeus jamaicensis)*—One colony located in 1995 in the Keys.

Little Brown Bat *(Myotis lucifugus)*—Caves and buildings in the Panhandle and North Florida.

Gray Bat *(Myotis grisescens)*—Endangered. Mostly in caves near Marianna.

Keen's Bat *(Myotis keenii)*—One report from Marianna.

Southeastern Brown Bat *(Myotis austroriparius)*—Caves in the Panhandle and North Florida.

Indiana Bat *(Myotis sodalis)*—Endangered. One record in Florida Caverns State Park in 1955.

Silver-haired Bat *(Lasionycteris noctivagans)*—Trees in the Panhandle.

Eastern Pipistrelle *(Pipistrellus subflavus)*—Caves south to central Florida.

Rafinesque's Big-eared Bat *(Plecotus rafinesquii)*—Trees south to central Florida.

Big Brown Bat *(Eptesicus fuscus)*—Caves south to central Florida

Hoary Bat *(Lasiurus cinereus)*—Trees south to central Florida.

Red Bat *(Lasiurus borealis)*—Trees in the Panhandle and North Florida.

Seminole Bat *(Lasiurus seminolus)*—Trees south to Lake Okeechobee.

Yellow Bat *(Lasiurus intermedius)*—Trees throughout.

Evening Bat *(Nycticeius humeralis)*—Buildings and tree cavities throughout.

Brazilian Free-tailed Bat *(Tadarida brasiliensis)*—Caves, trees, and buildings throughout the mainland.

Mastiff Bat *(Eumops glaucinus)*—Buildings near Miami.

Primates

Rhesus Monkey *(Macaca mulatta)*—Exotic, native to India. A feral population lives in Silver Springs; the monkeys were released at this site, which was where the Tarzan television show was filmed!

Vervet Monkey *(Cercopithecus aethiops)*—Exotic, native to Africa. Released into Dania (Broward County) in the 1950s and 1970s.

Man *(Homo sapiens)*—Cosmopolitan.

Edentates

Nine-banded Armadillo *(Dasypus novemcinctus)*—Exotic; native to the southwestern U.S. and tropical America. Sandy woodlands throughout the mainland.

Lagomorphs

Eastern Cottontail *(Sylvilagus floridanus)*—Woodlands throughout the mainland.

Marsh Rabbit *(Sylvilagus palustris)*—Marshes throughout.

Black-tailed Jackrabbit *(Lepus californicus)*—Exotic, native to the western United States. Miami International Airport (at least formerly).

Rodents

Eastern Chipmunk (*Tamias striatus*)—Yellow River in the western Panhandle.
Gray Squirrel (*Scuirus carolinensis*)—Woodlands throughout.
Fox Squirrel (*Scuirus niger*)—Woodlands throughout the mainland.
Red-bellied Squirrel (*Scuirus aureogaster*)—Exotic, native to Mexico. Elliot Key and nearby keys near Miami.
Southern Flying Squirrel (*Glaucomys volans*)—Woodlands throughout.
Southeastern Pocket Gopher (*Geomys pinetis*)—Sandy areas south to central Florida.
Beaver (*Castor canadensis*)—Streams in the Panhandle.
Eastern Woodrat (*Neotoma floridana*)—Thickets south to central Florida. An endemic race is restricted to Key Largo.
Hispid Cotton Rat (*Sigmodon hispidus*)—Moist woodlands and marshes throughout.
Eastern Harvest Mouse (*Reithrodontomys humulis*)—Fields and marshes south to Lake Okeechobee.
Marsh Rice Rat (*Oryzomys palustris*)—Marshes throughout.
Florida Mouse (*Podomys floridanus*)—Threatened. Endemic to well-drained soils in central Florida.
Oldfield (or **Beach**) **Mouse** (*Peromyscus polionotus*)—Sandy areas south to central Florida.
Cotton Mouse (*Peromyscus gossypinus*)—Thickets throughout.
Golden Mouse (*Ochrotomys nuttalli*)—Thickets south to central Florida.
Pine Vole (*Microtus pinetorum*)—Pinewoods in the Panhandle and North Florida.
Meadow Vole (*Microtus pennsylvanicus*)—State-endangered. Salt marshes in Levy County.
Round-tailed Muskrat (*Neofiber alleni*)—Marshes in the peninsula.
House Mouse (*Mus musculus*)—Exotic, native to the Old World; now cosmopolitan. Human-modified habitats throughout.
Black (or **Roof**) **Rat** (*Rattus rattus*)—Exotic, native to the Old World; now cosmopolitan. Human-modified habitats throughout.
Norway Rat (*Rattus norvegicus*)—Exotic, native to the Old World; now cosmopolitan. Human-modified habitats throughout.
Nutria (*Myocastor coypus*)—Exotic, native to South America; widely introduced into the U.S. Marshes in several areas in the Panhandle and peninsula.

Carnivores

Black Bear (*Ursus americanus*)—Threatened. Scattered forests throughout the mainland.
Raccoon (*Procyon lotor*)—Woodlands throughout.
Mink (*Mustela vison*)—Woodlands throughout the mainland; near water.
Long-tailed Weasel (*Mustela frenata*)—Varied habitats south to central Florida.
Striped Skunk (*Mephitis mephitis*)—Open woodlands and prairies throughout.
Spotted Skunk (*Spilogale putorius*)—Open woodlands and prairies throughout the mainland.
River Otter (*Lutra canadensis*)—Streams and lakes throughout the mainland.
Gray Fox (*Urocyon cinereoargenteus*)—Open woodlands throughout the mainland.
Red Fox (*Vulpes vulpes*)—Exotic, native to Holarctic. Scattered areas throughout the mainland.

Coyote (*Canis latrans*)—Woodlands south to South Florida. Range continues to increase.

Red Wolf (*Canis rufus*)—Extirpated; formerly occurred throughout. St. Vincent Island National Wildlife Refuge in the eastern Panhandle currently serves as an island propagation site for wolves being reintroduced into North Carolina and Tennessee.

Bobcat (*Lynx rufus*)—Woodlands throughout.

Florida Panther (*Felis concolor coryi*)—Endangered. Formerly found throughout Florida and the Southeast, numbers of this race of the Mountain Lion have declined severely due to hunting pressure (now illegal) and habitat destruction. The current state population is believed to be 30-50 animals largely if not entirely restricted to the southern third of the peninsula south and west of Lake Okeechobee. Sightings elsewhere may represent other races that escaped or were released. The Florida Panther's survival remains uncertain despite intense efforts to preserve it.

Jaguarundi (*Felis yagouaroundi*)—Presumed exotic, native to the southwestern U.S. south to South America.

Cetaceans

Harbor Seal (*Phoca vitulina*)—1 record from Daytona Beach.

West Indian Monk Seal (*Monachus tropicalus*)—Extinct, last reported in Haiti in 1981. In Florida, formerly occurred from the Tampa Bay region south through the Keys and along the entire Atlantic coast.

Hooded Seal (*Cystophora cristata*)—2 records: Brevard County in 1917 and Fort Lauderdale in 1984.

Rough-toothed Dolphin (*Steno bredanensis*)—Oceanic.

Long-snouted Spinner Dolphin (*Stenella longirostris*)—Oceanic.

Short-snouted Spinner Dolphin (*Stenella clymene*)—Oceanic.

Striped Dolphin (*Stenella coeruleoalba*)—Oceanic.

Atlantic Spotted (or **Cuvier's**) **Dolphin** (*Stenella frontalis*)—Oceanic.

Spotted Dolphin (*Stenella plagiodon*)—Oceanic.

Pantropical Spotted Dolphin (*Stenella attenuata*)—Oceanic.

Saddle-backed Dolphin (*Delphinus delphis*)—Oceanic.

Fraser's Dolphin (*Lagenodelphis hosei*)—Oceanic.

Atlantic Bottle-nosed Dolphin (*Tursiops truncatus*)—Oceanic, common off both coasts.

False Killer Whale (*Pseudorca crassidens*)—Oceanic.

Killer Whale (*Orcinus orca*)—Oceanic.

Pygmy Killer Whale (*Feresa attenuata*)—Oceanic.

Risso's Dolphin (or **Grampus**) (*Grampus griseus*)—Oceanic.

Short-finned Pilot Whale (*Globicephala macrorhynchus*)—Oceanic.

Harbor Porpoise (*Phocoena phocoena*)—Oceanic.

Pygmy Sperm Whale (*Kogia breviceps*)—Oceanic.

Dwarf Sperm Whale (*Kogia simus*)—Oceanic.

Sperm Whale (*Physeter macrocephalus*)—Endangered. Oceanic.

Goose-beaked Whale (*Ziphius cavirostris*)—Oceanic.

Dense-beaked Whale (*Mesoplodon densirostris*)—Oceanic.

Antillean Beaked Whale (*Mesoplodon europaeus*)—Oceanic.

True's Beaked Whale (*Mesplodon mirus*)—Oceanic.

Fin Whale (*Balaenoptera physalus*)—Endangered. Oceanic.

Minke Whale (*Balaenoptera acutorostrata*)—Oceanic.
Sei Whale (*Balaenoptera borealis*)—Endangered. Oceanic.
Bryde's Whale (*Balaenoptera edeni*)—Oceanic.
Humpback Whale (*Megaptera novaeangliae*)—Endangered. Oceanic.
Right Whale (*Eubalaena glacialis*)—Endangered. Oceanic.

Sirenians

West Indian Manatee (*Trichecus manatus*)—Endangered. A rare to locally common resident of inland waterways and coastal estuaries and bays, evenly distributed on both coasts. During winter, this large, interesting, aquatic relative of the elephant moves into warmer waters of coastal streams, inland springs, and, recently, power-plant outlet canals. A census in February 1995 recorded 1,822 individuals in Florida and coastal Georgia, the third highest count ever (1,856 manatees were counted in January 1992). Unfortunately, 192 deaths were documented in 1994, with 70 of these deaths attributed to human causes, mostly collisions with power boats (*Resource Management Notes*). During the winter of 1995-1996, over 265 manatees were killed by an apparent epidemic, but subsequent surveys in January 1997 counted over 2,200 alive.

Artiodactyls

Wild Boar (Wild Pig or **Feral Hog)** (*Sus scrofa*)—Exotic, widely domesticated, native to Europe. Now occurs as a pest throughout the Panhandle and peninsula.
White-tailed Deer (*Odocoileus virginianus*)—Woodlands throughout.
"Key Deer" (*O. v. clavium*)—Endangered. Endemic, restricted to Big Pine Key and surrounding keys. The total population numbers 300-350 animals.
Sambar Deer (*Cervus unicolor*)—Exotic, native to India, Ceylon, the East Indies, and Philippines. Introduced onto St. Vincent Island in Franklin County in 1908.
Axis Deer (*Cervus axis*)—Exotic, native to Ceylon and India. Accidentally introduced into Volusia County in the 1930s.
Elk (*Cervus elaphus*)—Exotic, native to northern and western North America. Introduced into Highlands County in the late 1960s.
American Bison (*Bison bison*)—Extirpated, formerly found south to central Florida. Rare or absent from Florida until the late 1600s, when herds were observed commonly; bison possibly moved into the state due to deforestation. Apparently eliminated through hunting by the late 1700s. In 1975, 10 animals from Oklahoma were released into Paynes Prairie State Preserve outside Gainesville. The herd grew to 35 individuals, but then contracted brucellosis from a neighboring cattle ranch. By 1989, the population had been reduced to 6 bison.

LITERATURE CITED

Adams, Frank H. 1996. First bat colonies in the Keys. *Florida Wildlife* 50:2-5.

American Birding Association. 1994. *Birdfinding in Forty National Forests and Grasslands.* Colorado Springs, CO.

American Ornithologists' Union. 1983. *Check-list of North American Birds,* 6th edition. Allen Press. Lawrence, KS.

American Ornithologists' Union. 1995 (1996). Fortieth supplement to the American Ornithologists' Union *Check-list of North American Birds. Auk* 112:819-830.

Ashton, Ray E., Jr., and Patricia Sawyer Ashton. 1981. Handbook of Reptiles and Amphibians of Florida. Part 1: Snakes. Windward Publishing, Inc. Miami, FL.

Ashton, Ray E., Jr., and Patricia Sawyer Ashton. 1985. Handbook of Reptiles and Amphibians of Florida. Part 2: Lizards, Turtles, and Crocodilians. Windward Publishing, Inc. Miami, FL.

Ashton, Ray E., Jr., and Patricia Sawyer Ashton. 1988. Handbook of Reptiles and Amphibians of Florida. Part 3: Amphibians. Windward Publishing, Inc. Miami, FL.

Bancroft, G. Thomas. 1992. A closer look: White-crowned Pigeon. *Birding* 24:20-24.

Bent, Arthur Cleveland. 1948. *Life Histories of North American Nuthatches, Wrens, Thrashers, and Their Allies.* United States Government Printing Office. Washington D.C. (Reprinted in 1964 by Dover Publications, Inc., New York, NY.)

Bond, James. 1985. *Birds of the West Indies.* Fifth edition, reprinted in 1990. Collins. London, UK.

Bowman, Margaret Coon. 1995. Sighting of Masked Duck ducklings in Florida. *Florida Field Naturalist* 23:35.

Brown, Larry N. 1987. A checklist of Florida's mammals. Nongame Wildlife Program. Florida Game and Fresh Water Fish Commission. Tallahassee, FL.

Buhrman, Charles B. 1982. The Florida that birders need. *Birding* 14:136-139.

Cerulean, Susan, and Ann Morrow. 1993. *Florida Wildlife Viewing Guide.* Falcon Press. Helena and Billings, MT.

Cox, Jeffrey A. 1987. *Status and Distribution of the Florida Scrub Jay.* Special Publication No. 3. Florida Ornithological Society. Gainesville, FL.

Cox, James, Randy Kautz, Maureen McLaughlin, and Terry Gilbert. 1994. *Closing the Gaps in Florida's Wildlife Habitat Conservation System.* Florida Game and Fresh Water Fish Commission. Tallahassee, FL.

Cummins, Kenneth W., and Clifford N. Dahm. 1995. Introduction: Restoring the Kissimmee. *Restoration Ecology* 3:147-148.

Delany, Michael F., and Jeffrey A. Cox. 1986. Florida Grasshopper Sparrow breeding distribution and abundance in 1984. *Florida Field Naturalist* 14:100-104.

Deyrup, Mark, and Richard Franz. 1994. *Rare and Endangered Biota of Florida, Volume 4, Invertebrates.* University Press of Florida. Gainesville, FL.

Downer, Audrey, and Robert Sutton. 1990. *Birds of Jamaica.* Cambridge University Press. New York, NY.

Duncan, Robert A. 1991. *The Birds of Escambia, Santa Rosa, and Okaloosa counties, Florida.* Second printing. Published by the author. Gulf Breeze, FL.

Duncan, Robert A. 1994. *Bird Migration, Weather, and Fallout, Including the Migrant Traps of Alabama and Northwest Florida.* Published by the author. Gulf Breeze, FL.

Dunkle, Sydney. 1989. *Dragonflies of the Florida Peninsula, Bermuda, and the Bahamas.* Scientific Publishers. Gainesville, FL.

Evans, William R. 1994. Nocturnal flight call of Bicknell's Thrush. *Wilson Bulletin* 106:55-61.

Feduccia, Alan. 1980. *The Age of Birds.* Harvard University Press. Cambridge, MA.

Fernald, Edward A., and Donald J. Patton, editors. 1984. *Water Resources Atlas of Florida.* Florida State University. Tallahassee, FL.

Fitzpatrick, John W., Bill Pranty, and Brad Stith. 1994. Florida Scrub Jay statewide map, 1992-1993. Final report to United States

Fish and Wildlife Service, Cooperative Agreement No.
14-16-0004-91-950. Jacksonville, FL.

FOS 1990-1996. Florida Ornithological Society Field Observations
Committee seasonal bird reports. Compiled by Jim Cox
(1990-1992) and Bill Pranty (1992-1996). *Florida Field Naturalist.*

Forshaw, Joseph M. 1989. *Parrots of the World.* Third edition.
Lansdowne Editions. Willoughby, Australia.

Gerberg, Eugene J., and Ross H. Arnet Jr. 1989. *Florida Butterflies.*
Natural Science Publications. Baltimore, MD.

Gleasner, Diana, and Bill Gleasner. 1993. *Florida: Off The Beaten
Path.* Globe Pequot Press. Old Saybrook, CT.

Grow, Gerald. 1993. *Florida Parks: A Guide to Camping in Nature.*
Fifth Edition. Longleaf Publications. Tallahassee, FL.

Greenlaw, Jon S. 1993. Behavioral and morphological diversification
of Sharp-tailed Sparrows (*Ammodramus caudacutus*). *Auk*
110:286-303.

Haney, J. Christopher. 1985. Band-rumped Storm-Petrel occurrences
in relation to upwelling off the coast of the southeastern United
States. *Wilson Bulletin* 97:543-547.

Hardy, J. W., George B. Reynard, and Ben B. Coffey. 1989. *Voices of
the New World Pigeons and Doves.* ARA Records, Gainesville, FL.

Haug, Elizabeth, Brian A. Millsap, and Mark S. Martell. 1993.
Burrowing Owl (*Speotyto cunicularia*). *In* The Birds of North
America, No. 61 (Alan Poole and Frank Gill, editors). The
Academy of Natural Sciences, Philadelphia, PA; The American
Ornithologists' Union, Washington, DC.

Heindel, Matt T. 1996. Field Identification of the Solitary Vireo
Complex. *Birding* 28:458-471.

Hernando Audubon Society, Inc. 1995. *Birding Sites in Hernando
County.* Brooksville, FL.

Howell, Arthur H. 1932. *Florida Bird Life.* Coward and McCann.
New York, NY.

Humphrey, Steven R., editor. 1992. *Rare and Endangered Biota of
Florida, Volume 1: Mammals.* University Press of Florida.
Gainesville, FL.

Hyler, William R. 1995. Vervet Monkeys in the mangrove ecosystems
of southwest Florida: preliminary census and ecological data.
Florida Scientist 58:38-43.

Jewell, Susan D. 1993. *Exploring Wild South Florida: A Guide to Finding the Natural Areas and Wildlife of the Everglades and Florida Keys.* Pineapple Press. Sarasota, FL.

Jewell, Susan D. 1995. *Exploring Wild Central Florida: A Guide to Finding the Natural Areas and Wildlife of the Central Peninsula.* Pineapple Press. Sarasota, FL.

Johnson, Fred A., Frank Montalbano III, James D. Truitt, and Diane R. Eggeman. 1991. Distribution, abundance, and habitat use by Mottled Ducks in Florida. *Journal of Wildlife Management* 55:476-482.

Kale, Herbert W., II. 1978. *Rare and Endangered Biota of Florida, Volume 2: Birds.* University Presses of Florida. Gainesville, FL.

Kale, Herbert W., II, and David S. Maehr. 1990. *Florida's Birds: A Handbook and Reference.* Pineapple Press. Sarasota, FL.

Kale, Herbert W., II, Bill Pranty, Bradley M. Stith, and C. Wesley Biggs (editors). 1992. The Atlas of the Breeding Birds of Florida. Final report. Nongame Wildlife Program. Florida Game and Fresh Water Fish Commission. Tallahassee, FL.

Kaufman, Kenn. 1984. Identification of two potential Florida vagrants. *Birding* 16:112-113.

Kaufman, Kenn. 1990. *A Field Guide to Advanced Birding.* Houghton Mifflin Company. Boston, MA.

Klinkenberg, Marty, and Elizabeth Leach. 1993. *The Green Guide to Florida.* Country Roads Press. Castine, ME.

Lane, James A. 1981. *A Birder's Guide to Florida.* L & P Press. Denver, CO. Reprinted in 1984 and 1989 with revisions by Harold R. Holt.

Lantz, Peggy Sias, and Wendy A. Hale. 1994. *The Young Naturalist's Guide to Florida.* Pineapple Press. Sarasota, FL.

Layne, James N. 1993. History of an introduction of Elk in Florida. *Florida Field Naturalist* 21:77-80.

Layne, James N. 1995. Audubon's Crested Caracara in Florida. Pages 82-83 in *Our Living Resources: A Report to the Nation on the Distribution, Abundance, and Health of U.S. Plants, Animals, and Ecosystems* (Edward T. LaRoe, Gaye S. Farris, Catherine E. Puckett, Peter D. Doran, and Michael J. Mac, editors). National Biological Survey. Washington, DC.

Levin, Ted. 1995. Wanderer in search of escargot. *Living Bird* 14:22-28.

MacLaren, Ian. 1995. Field identification and taxonomy of Bicknell's Thrush. *Birding* 27:358-366.

Marth, Del, and Marty Marth. 1995. *1995 Florida Almanac.* Suwannee River Press. Branford, FL.

McKinley, Daniel. 1985. *The Carolina Parakeet in Florida.* Special Publication No. 2. Florida Ornithological Society. Gainesville, FL.

Millsap, Brian A. 1987. Summer concentration of American Swallow-tailed Kites at Lake Okeechobee, Florida, with comments on post-breeding movements. *Florida Field Naturalist* 15:85-92.

Moler, Paul E., editor. 1992. *Rare and Endangered Biota of Florida, Volume 3: Amphibians and Reptiles.* University Press of Florida. Gainesville, FL.

Moorman, Thomas E., and Paul N. Gray. 1994. Mottled Duck (*Anas fulvigula*). *In* The Birds of North America, No. 81 (Alan Poole and Frank Gill, editors). The Academy of Natural Sciences, Philadelphia, PA; The American Ornithologists' Union, Washington, D.C.

Myers, Ronald L., and John J. Ewel. 1990. *Ecosystems of Florida.* University of Central Florida Press. Orlando, FL.

National Audubon Society. 1993. *Birding in the Florida Keys.* National Audubon Research Department. Tavernier, FL.

North American Butterfly Association. 1995. *Checklist and English Names of North American Butterflies.* Morristown, N.J.

Office of Environmental Services. 1995. *1995 Conservation and Recreation Lands (CARL) Annual Report.* Division of State Lands. Florida Department of Environmental Protection. Tallahassee, FL.

Ogden, John C. 1994. A comparison of wading-bird nesting colony dynamics (1931-1946 and 1974-1989) as an indication of ecosystem conditions in the southern Everglades. Pages 533-570 in *Everglades: The Ecosystem and Its Restoration.* (Steven M. Davis and John C. Ogden, editors). St. Lucie Press. Delray Beach, FL.

Opler, Paul A., and Vichai Malikul. 1992. *A Field Guide to Eastern Butterflies.* Houghton Mifflin Company. Boston, MA.

Ouellet, Henri. 1993. Bicknell's Thrush: taxonomic status and distribution. *Wilson Bulletin* 105:542-572.

Paulson, Dennis. 1994. An early Tropical Kingbird report from Florida, based on calls. *Florida Field Naturalist* 22:14.

Perry, John, and Jane Greverus Perry. 1992. *The Sierra Club Guide to the Natural Areas of Florida.* Sierra Club Books. San Francisco, CA.

Post, William. 1992. First Florida specimens of the Shiny Cowbird. *Florida Field Naturalist* 20:1718.

Pritchard, Peter C. H., and Herbert W. Kale II. 1994. *Saving What's Left.* Florida Audubon Society. Casselberry, FL.

Reynard, George B., Orlando H. Garrido, and Robert L. Sutton. 1993. Taxonomic revision of the Greater Antillean Pewee. *Wilson Bulletin* 105:217-227.

Rising, James D., and John C. Avise. 1993. Applications of genealogical concordance principles to the taxonomy and evolutionary history of the Sharp-tailed Sparrow (*Ammodramus caudacutus*). *Auk* 110:844-856.

Robertson, Jr., William B., and C. Wesley Biggs. 1983. A West Indian *Myiarchus* in Biscayne National Park, Florida. *American Birds* 37:802-804.

Robertson, Jr., William B., and Glen E. Woolfenden. 1992. *Florida Bird Species: An Annotated List.* Special Publication No. 6. Florida Ornithological Society. Gainesville, FL.

Rodgers, James A., Jr., Herbert W. Kale II, and Henry T. Smith. 1996. *Rare and Endangered Biota of Florida, Volume 5: Birds.* University Press of Florida. Gainesville, FL.

Rowan, Rex, and Mike Manetz. 1995. *A Birdwatcher's Guide to Alachua County, Florida.* Published by the authors. Gainesville, FL.

Rumbold, Darren G., and Mary Beth Mahalik. 1994. Snail Kite use of a drought-related habitat and communal roost in West Palm Beach, Florida: 1987-1991. *Florida Field Naturalist* 22:29-38.

Runde, Douglas E., Peter D. Southall, Julie A. Hovis, Rick Sullivan, and Rochelle B. Renken. 1990. Recent records and survey methods for the Black Rail in Florida. *Florida Field Naturalist* 18:33-35.

Sarasota Audubon Society. 1994. *Birding Hotspots in Manatee and Sarasota counties.* Sarasota, FL.

Scott, Shirley L., editor. 1987. *Field Guide to the Birds of North America.* Second edition. National Geographic Society. Washington, D.C.

Sibley, Charles G., and Burt L. Monroe. 1990. *Distribution and Taxonomy of Birds of the World.* Yale University Press. New Haven, CT.

Sibley, David. 1996. Field Identification of the Sharp-tailed Sparrow Complex. *Birding* 28:196-208.

Smith, P. William. 1996. More Thoughts on Bicknell's Thrush. *Birding* 28:275-276.

Smith, P. William. 1987. The Eurasian Collared-Dove arrives in the Americas. *American Birds* 41:1370-1379.

Smith, P. William, and Alexander Sprunt IV. 1987. The Shiny Cowbird reaches the United States. *American Birds* 41:370-371.

Smith, P. William, and Duncan Stuart Evered. 1992. Photo Note—La Sagra's Flycatcher. *Birding* 24:294-297.

Smith, P. William, Duncan Stuart Evered, Lyla R. Messick, and Mary C. Wheeler. 1990. First verifiable records of the Thick-billed Vireo from the United States. *American Birds* 44:372-376.

Smith, P. William, William B. Robertson Jr., and Henry M. Stevenson. 1988. West Indian Cave Swallows nesting in Florida, with comments on the taxonomy of *Hirundo fulva. Florida Field Naturalist* 16:86-90.

Smith, P. William, and Susan A. Smith. 1989. A Zenaida Dove in Florida, with comments on the species and its appearance here. *Florida Field Naturalist* 17(3):67-69.

Smith, P. William, and Susan A. Smith. 1990. The identification and status of the Bahama Swallow in Florida. *Birding* 22:264-271.

Smith, P. William, and Susan A. Smith. 1993. An exotic dilemma for birders: the Canary-winged Parakeet. *Birding* 25:426-430.

Stevenson, Henry M. 1976. *Vertebrates of Florida.* University Presses of Florida. Gainesville, FL.

Stevenson, Henry M., and Bruce H. Anderson. 1994. *The Birdlife of Florida.* University Press of Florida. Gainesville, FL.

Stiling, Peter D. 1989. *Florida's Butterflies and Other Insects.* Pineapple Press. Sarasota, FL.

Strong, Allan M., and G. Thomas Bancroft. 1994. Postfledging dispersal of White-crowned Pigeons: Implications for conservation of deciduous seasonal forests in the Florida Keys. *Conservation Biology* 8:770-779.

Sykes, Paul W., Jr. 1980. Decline and disappearance of the Dusky Seaside Sparrow from Merritt Island, Florida. *American Birds* 34:728-737.

Sykes, Paul W., Jr. 1994. A closer look: Snail Kite. *Birding* 26:118-122.

Toops, Connie, and Willard E. Dilley. 1986. *Birds of South Florida.* River Road Press. Conway, AR.

Vriends, Matthew M. 1984. *Simon and Schuster's Guide to Pet Birds.* Simon and Schuster Inc. New York, NY.

Wamer, Noel. 1991. *Black Rails in Florida: How and where.* Published by the author. Tallahassee, FL.

Wanless, Harold R., Randall W. Parkinson, and Lenore P. Tedesco. 1994. Sea level control on stability of Everglades wetlands. Pages 199-223 in *Everglades: The Ecosystem and Its Restoration* (Steven M. Davis and John C. Ogden, editors). St. Lucie Press. Delray Beach, FL.

White, Tony. 1986. Collared Dove: the next new North American species? *Birding* 18:150-152.

Wood, Don A., compiler. 1994. Official Lists of Endangered and Potentially Endangered Flora and Fauna in Florida. Florida Game and Fresh Water Fish Commission. Tallahassee, FL.

Wood, Don A., and Anne Shapiro Wenner. 1983. *Status of the Red-cockaded Woodpecker in Florida: 1983 update.* Pages 89-91 in *Red-cockaded Woodpecker Symposium II Proceedings* (Don A. Wood, editor). Florida Game and Fresh Water Fish Commission. Tallahassee, FL.

Wood, Merrill. 1979. *Birds of Pennsylvania.* Pennsylvania State University. University Park, PA.

Woolfenden, Glen E., William B. Robertson, Jr., and Bill Pranty. 1996. Comparing the species lists in two recent books on Florida birds. *Florida Field Naturalist* 24:10-14.

American Birding Association

ABA is the organization of North American birders, and its mission is to bring all the excitement, challenge, and wonder of birds and birding to you. As an ABA member you will get the information you need to increase your birding skills so that you can make the most of your time in the field.

ABA supports the interests of birders of all ages and experiences, and promotes birding publications, projects, and partnerships. It focuses on bird identification and birdfinding skills and the development and dissemination of information on bird conservation. ABA also champions ethical birding practices.

Each year members receive six issues of ABA's award-winning magazine *Birding* and twelve issues of *Winging It*, a monthly newsletter. ABA conducts regular conferences and biennial conventions in the continent's best birding locations, publishes a yearly *Membership Directory and Yellow Pages*, compiles an annual *Directory of Volunteer Opportunities for Birders*, and offers discount prices for many bird books, optical gear, and other birding equipment through ABA Sales. The organization's *ABA/Lane Birdfinding Guide Series* sets the standard for accuracy and excellence in its field.

ABA is engaged in bird conservation through such institutions and activities as Partners in Flight and the American Bird Conservancy's Policy Council. ABA also actively promotes the economic and environmental values of birding.

ABA encourages birding among young people by sponsoring birding camp scholorships and "ABA/Leica Young Birder of the Year" competition, and by publishing *A Bird's-Eye View*, a newsletter by and for its younger members.

In cooperation with the National Audubon Society, ABA also publishes *Field Notes*, a quarterly which reviews all improtant bird sightings and significant population trends for the US, Canada, and the West Indies.

In short, ABA works to ensure that birds and birding have the healthy future that they deserve. In the words of the late Roger Tory Peterson, the American Birding Association is "the best value in the birding community." The American Birding Association gives active birders what they want. Consider joining today. You will find a membership form on the other side of this page.

American Birding Association Membership Services
PO Box 6599
Colorado Springs, CO 80934
telephone 800/850-2473 or 719/578-1614 - fax 719/578-1480
e-mail: member@aba.org
web site: http://www.americanbirding.org

AMERICAN BIRDING ASSOCIATION
Membership Application

All memberships include six issues of *Birding* magazine, monthly issues of *Winging It*, ABA's newsletter, and full rights of participation in all ABA activities.

Membership Classes and Dues:

❏ Individual - US $36.00 / yr   ❏ Student - Canada** $27.00 / yr
❏ Individual - Canada * $45.00 / yr   ❏ Family - US $43.00 / yr
❏ Individual - Int'l $45.00 / yr   ❏ Family - Canada* $52.00 / yr
❏ Student - US** $18.00 / yr   ❏ Family - Int'l $52.00 / yr
                                           ❏ Hooded Merganser $136.00 / yr

* Canadian dues include GST, which is paid to the Canadian government
*All membership dues include $27 for **Birding** magazine and $9 for **Winging It** newsletter.*
** **Students** - Write your date of birth, name and location of school, and expected date of graduation on the bottom of this form. This information is **required** to receive Student rates.

Application Type

❏ New Membership   ❏ Renewal   ❏ Gift

Please call 800/850-2473 or 719/578-1614 for information about how you may subscribe to Field Notes.

Member Information

Name _____

Address _____

_____

Phone _____

Payment Information

❏ Check or Money Order enclosed (US funds only)
❏ Charge to VISA / MasterCard (circle one)

    Account Number _____

    Exp Date _____

    Signature _____

Send this completed form with payment to: **ABA Membership**
                                         PO Box 6599
                                         Colorado Springs, CO 80934

FL 12/97

NOMENCLATURE CHANGES

The bird names used in this book basically follow those of the American Ornithologists' Union (AOU) and the American Birding Association (ABA). Below are also some names which differ from those used in older field guides, or which have yet to appear in even the most recent field guides.

Names Used in this Book	*Derivation or Former Name*
Swallow-tailed Kite	American Swallow-tailed Kite
Black-headed Gull	Common Black-headed Gull
Long-billed Murrelet	*split from* Marbled Murrelet
Yellow-chevroned Parakeet	*split from* Canary-winged Parakeet
White-winged Parakeet	*split from* Canary-winged Parakeet
Cuban Pewee	*split from* Greater Antillean Pewee
Florida Scrub-Jay	*split from* Scrub Jay
Bicknell's Thrush	*split from* Gray-cheeked Thrush
American Pipit	Water Pipit
Blue-headed Vireo	*split from* Solitary Vireo
Eastern Towhee	*split from* Rufous-sided Towhee
Spotted Towhee	*split from* Rufous-sided Towhee
Saltmarsh Sharp-tailed Sparrow	*split from* Sharp-tailed Sparrow
Nelson's Sharp-tailed Sparrow	*split from* Sharp-tailed Sparrow
Baltimore Oriole	*split from* Northern Oriole
Bullock's Oriole	*split from* Northern Oriole

INDEX

Sarus 314
Whooping 155, 157, 281, 328
Crawfordville 76
Creeper
Brown 44, 48, 67, 337
Crescent Beach 109
Crestview 49
Crews Lake County Park (Spring Hill) 116
Crocodile Lake National Wildlife Refuge 246
Crossbill
Red 344
Crow
American 13-14, 16, 23, 302, 337
Fish 13-14, 16, 23, 301, 337
Crystal River 113-114
Cuckoo
Black-billed 333
Mangrove 19, 34, 60, 111, 125, 133, 136,
189, 193, 197, 225, 238, 240, 243, 247,
249, 251, 253, 256-257, 259, 293, 333
Yellow-billed 13-14, 16-17, 263, 333
Curlew
Long-billed 57, 106, 124, 192, 195, 282-283,
329

D

Dania 215
Davie 217
Deer Flies 30
Deer Point Lake (Panama City) 57
Destin 51
Dickcissel 341
Disney Wilderness Preserve 154
Dog Island (Carrabelle) 64
Dove
Diamond 314
Inca 314
Mourning 13-14, 23, 26, 243, 332
Rock 23-26, 228, 314, 332
Spotted 314

White-winged 29, 59, 75, 165, 229, 236,
279, 289, 332
Zenaida 243, 289, 332
Dovekie 332
Dowitcher
Long-billed 22, 133, 165, 205, 282, 284, 330
Short-billed 20-21, 282, 284, 330
Dr. Julian D. Bruce St. George Island State Park
61
Dry Tortugas National Park 243, 260
Duck
American Black 44, 274, 325
Harlequin 55, 58, 325
Mandarin 313
Masked 150, 243, 256, 276, 326
Mottled 22, 81, 111, 125, 127, 131, 139,
147, 150-151, 154, 169, 173, 183, 202,
205, 212, 217, 232, 238, 276, 325
Muscovy 22, 25, 127, 275, 313, 324
Ring-necked 22, 127, 143, 228, 274, 325
Ruddy 21, 131, 133, 143, 149, 180, 274, 326
Spot-billed 313
Wood 16, 22, 143, 145, 324
Dunedin 124-125
Dunedin Hammock City Park 125
Dunlin 20-21, 329

E

E. G. Simmons Regional Park (Ruskin) 135
Eagle
Bald 16, 19, 22, 26, 28-29, 44, 59-60, 67,
71, 93, 95-96, 98, 113, 123, 129, 138, 144,
148-152, 154-155, 157-158, 160, 165, 177,
189, 197, 207, 231, 240, 251, 253, 278, 326
Golden 29, 44, 327
East Key (Dry Tortugas National Park) 263
East Lake Tohopekaliga 154
Easterlin Park (Oakland Park) 215
Eastpoint 60, 62
Eco Pond (Everglades National Park) 240
Edward Ball Wakulla Springs State Park 76
Eglin Air Force Base 53
Egret
Cattle 23, 108, 261, 271, 324
Great 7, 16, 20, 22, 108, 270, 323
Reddish 20, 57, 65, 101, 109, 111, 118,
123-124, 131, 135-136, 182, 193, 195,
197-198, 224, 240, 243, 246, 248-250,
256, 259-260, 271, 323
Snowy 6-7, 16, 20, 22, 108, 152, 270, 323
Eider
Common 180, 325
King 325
Elaenia
Caribbean 47
Emerald
Cuban 296, 318, 334
Everglades City 200
Everglades National Park 232-238, 240-241
Everglades National Park (Chekika section) 229

Goldeneye
Common 44, 60-61, 73, 78, 113, 274, 326
Goldfinch
American 14-15, 17, 344
European 317
Goose
Bar-headed 313
Bean 313
Canada 45, 72, 274, 324
Egyptian 313
Greater White-fronted 59, 324
Greylag 313
Orinoco 313
Ross's 70, 324
Snow 44, 78, 127, 274, 324
Swan 313
Goshawk
Northern 326
Grackle
Boat-tailed 20, 22, 44, 59-60, 311, 343
Common 13-14, 16, 22, 343
Grassquit
Black-faced 243, 259, 308, 342
Cuban 308, 316
Yellow-faced 243, 261, 308, 342
Grassy Key 250
Grayton Beach State Recreation Area 53
Great White Heron National Wildlife Refuge
257
Grebe
Eared 51, 55, 59, 267, 322
Horned 21, 322
Least 243, 256, 267, 322
Pied-billed 21-22, 322
Red-necked 318, 322
Western 78, 322
Greenfinch
European 317
Greenshank
Common 6
Greynolds Park (North Miami Beach) 220

Grosbeak
Black-headed 341
Blue 17, 27, 49, 57, 93, 99, 111, 204, 341
Evening 344
Rose-breasted 17, 27, 341
Ground-Dove
Common 13-14, 23, 290, 332
Ground-Hornbill
Abyssinian 316
Grouse
Ruffed 314
Guana River State Park 105
Guana River Wildlife Management Area 105
Guineafowl
Helmeted 314
Gulf Breeze 47
Gulf Islands National Seashore 47-48
Gull
Band-tailed 285, 318, 330
Black-headed 285, 330
Bonaparte's 29, 109, 118, 124, 133, 210, 285, 330
Franklin's 29, 70, 215, 285, 330
Glaucous 101, 215, 285, 331
Great Black-backed 20-21, 101, 106, 174, 178, 215, 285, 331
Herring 6, 20-21, 285, 330
Iceland 101, 285, 330
Laughing 20-22, 60, 65, 285, 330
Lesser Black-backed 101, 131, 215, 231, 285, 331
Little 285, 330
Ring-billed 20-22, 285, 330
Sabine's 175, 268, 285, 331
Thayer's 215, 285, 330
Gumbo Limbo Nature Center (Boca Raton) 213
Gumbo Limbo Trail (Everglades National Park)
237

H

Hagens Cove (Steinhatchee) 83
Hal Scott Regional Preserve and Park (Orlando)
150
Hanna County Park (Mayport area) 103
Harbor Palms Nature Park (Tampa) 122
Harney Pond Canal Recreation Area (Lake Okeechobee) 173
Harrier
Northern 20, 22-23, 253, 326
Harry Harris County Park (Key Largo) 249
Hawk
Broad-winged 13-14, 17, 29, 45, 47, 58, 62, 65, 68, 71, 81, 127, 215, 243, 253, 256, 278, 327
Cooper's 16, 71, 111, 224, 251, 253, 263, 278, 326
Crane 314
Ferruginous 327
Harris's 314

King
  Burger 233
Kingbird
  Cassin's 212, 232, 300, 336
  Couch's 204, 299, 335
  Eastern 14, 17, 23, 27, 160, 165, 168, 189, 336
  Gray 19-20, 44, 48, 59, 61, 73-74, 83, 103, 106, 109, 111, 113, 124, 133, 136, 193-194, 217, 221, 226-227, 243, 248, 257, 300, 336
  Loggerhead 243, 249, 261, 300, 336
  Tropical 299, 318, 335
  Western 29, 57, 60, 75, 165, 232, 238, 250, 259, 300, 336
Kingfisher
  Belted 17, 20, 22, 334
Kinglet
  Golden-crowned 44, 50, 65, 67, 337
  Ruby-crowned 14-15, 17, 27, 337
Kingsley Plantation (Jacksonville) 99
Kiskadee
  Great 316
Kissimmee 152, 154, 156
Kite
  Mississippi 13-14, 17, 29, 45, 47, 49, 51, 57, 62, 65, 67-68, 70, 77, 81, 91, 93, 96, 277, 326
  Snail 111, 150, 152, 154-155, 173, 183, 185, 200, 202, 210, 212, 218-219, 277, 326
  Swallow-tailed 11, 14, 16, 23, 27, 29, 44, 51, 62, 65, 67, 77, 91, 98, 111, 113, 119, 147, 150, 158-161, 170, 202, 204, 229, 231, 237-238, 240, 245, 249, 276, 326
  White-tailed 165, 170, 229, 277, 326
Kittiwake
  Black-legged 55, 175, 268, 285, 331
Knot
  Red 21, 65, 73, 124, 192, 195, 282, 284, 329

L

Lake Adair (Orlando) 143
Lake Alice (Gainesville) 95
Lake Edna (Grassy Key) 250
Lake Estelle (Orlando) 143
Lake George (Ocala National Forest) 98
Lake Kissimmee 281
Lake Kissimmee State Park 158
Lake Maggiore (St. Petersburg) 129
Lake Okeechobee 170-171, 204
Lake Placid 165-166
Lake Region Audubon Society 157
Lake Sybelia (Orlando) 145
Lake Tohopekaliga 152
Lake Wales 158
Lake Wales Ridge 166
Lake Wales Ridge Ecosystem Preserve 166
Lake Wales Ridge National Wildlife Refuge 166
Lake Wales Ridge State Forest 159
Lakeland 157
Lakes County Park (Fort Myers) 190
Lanark Reef 64-65
Lapwing
  Southern 314
Largo 125
Lark
  Horned 55, 70, 336
Laughing-Thrush
  Greater Necklaced 316
Leiothrix
  Red-billed 316
Lettuce Lake Regional Park (Tampa) 133
Lighthouse Park (Anastasia Island) 108
Lighthouse Park (Sanibel Island) 194
Lighthouse Point Park (New Smyrna Beach) 174
Limpkin 16, 22, 77, 84, 95, 98, 111, 113-114, 117, 122-123, 127, 134, 139, 143, 145, 148-150, 154-155, 157-158, 164, 169, 173, 183, 199, 202-204, 210, 212, 218, 232, 238, 280, 328
Little Duck Key 255
Little Hamaka City Park (Key West) 259
Little Talbot Island State Park 101
Little-Big Econ State Forest 149
Loggerhead Key (Dry Tortugas National Park) 263-264
Long Key 250
Long Key (Dry Tortugas National Park) 263
Long Key State Recreation Area 249
Longboat Key 136
Longspur
  Chestnut-collared 343
  Lapland 99, 343
Loon
  Common 21, 322
  Pacific 85, 267, 322
  Red-throated 55, 73, 115, 267, 322
Lori Wilson Park (Cocoa Beach) 180
Lorikeet
  Ornate 314

Ponce de Leon City (Punta Gorda) 189
Robert K. Rees County (New Port Richey) 118
Saddle Creek County (Lakeland) 157
Safety Harbor City 123
Sandhill Crane (Port St. Lucie) 185
Sawgrass Lake County (St. Petersburg) 127
Shoreline (Gulf Breeze) 47
Smyrna Dunes (New Smyrna Beach) 175
Sombrero Beach County (Marathon) 250
Southport (Lake Tohopekaliga) 152
Spanish River (Boca Raton) 213
Sunset Beach (Tarpon Springs) 122
Tigertail Beach County (Marco Island) 198
Topeekeegee Yugnee ("T.Y.") (Hollywood) 217
Treasure Shores County (Vero Beach) 183
Tree Tops County (Davie) 217
Trimble County (Zellwood) 148
Upper Tampa Bay Regional 122-123
Wilderness (Tampa) 134
Parrot
Black-headed 315
Blue-fronted 221, 227
Burrowing 315
Eclectus 314
Festive 316
Gray 314
Hispaniolan 315
Lilac-crowned 227, 316
Maroon-fronted 315
Mealy 316
Orange-winged 187, 221, 227, 316
Red-crowned 187, 217, 221, 293, 315, 333
Red-lored 316
Red-rumped 314
Red-spectacled 315
Rueppell's 314
Senegal 314
Turquoise-fronted 316
White-crowned 315

White-fronted 227, 315
Yellow-crowned 316
Yellow-headed 221, 316
Yellow-naped 316
Yellow-shouldered 316
Parula
Northern 14, 17, 27, 305, 339
Paynes Prairie State Preserve 93, 95
Peafowl
Common 314
Pelican
American White 55, 58, 85, 113, 131, 147, 149-150, 152, 180, 193, 240, 269, 323
Brown 19-20, 65, 269, 323
Pensacola 47-48
Perry 83
Petrel
Black-capped 71, 268, 322
Pewee
Cuban 213, 298, 335
Greater Antillean 298
Hispaniolan 298
Jamaican 298
Phalarope
Red 21, 175, 268, 282, 284, 330
Red-necked 21, 175, 268, 282, 284, 330
Wilson's 22, 147, 205, 282, 284, 330
Pheasant
Ring-necked 24, 314
Philippe County Park (Safety Harbor) 123
Phipps/Overstreet Park (Tallahassee) 70
Phoebe
Black 335
Eastern 14-15, 23, 335
Say's 335
phosphate-mining district 157
Pigeon
Band-tailed 332
Passenger 4
Scaly-naped 243, 289, 332
White-crowned 16, 19, 225-227, 238, 240, 243, 247-248, 255, 257, 259, 287, 332
Pine Island County Park (Weeki Wachee) 115
Pinhook Swamp 91
Pintail
Northern 22, 131, 179, 274, 325
White-cheeked 139, 179, 228, 240, 276, 325
Pipit
American 22-23, 60, 151, 338
Sprague's 44, 59-60, 304, 338
Pitta
Banded 316
Plantation Key 289
Playalinda Beach 178-179
Plover
Black-bellied 20-21, 148, 328
Mountain 282, 328
Piping 55, 65, 73-74, 106, 109, 111, 117, 124-125, 130, 137, 174, 182, 195, 198, 224-225, 255, 282-283, 328
Semipalmated 20-21, 328

Abbreviated Table of Contents

Abbreviated Table of Contents